KEY WORKS
TO THE FAUNA AND FLORA
OF THE BRITISH ISLES
AND NORTHWESTERN EUROPE

THE SYSTEMATICS ASSOCIATION
SPECIAL VOLUME No. 9

KEY WORKS
TO THE FAUNA AND FLORA OF THE BRITISH ISLES AND NORTHWESTERN EUROPE

Edited by

G. J. KERRICH
Formerly, Commonwealth Institute of Entomology, London

D. L. HAWKSWORTH
Commonwealth Mycological Institute, Kew, Surrey

R. W. SIMS
British Museum (Natural History), London

1978

Published for the
SYSTEMATICS ASSOCIATION
by
ACADEMIC PRESS
LONDON · NEW YORK · SAN FRANCISCO

ACADEMIC PRESS INC. (LONDON) LTD.
24/28 Oval Road,
London NW1

United States Edition published by
ACADEMIC PRESS INC.
111 Fifth Avenue
New York, New York 10003

Copyright © 1978 by
THE SYSTEMATICS ASSOCATION

All Rights Reserved

No part of this book may be reproduced in any form by photostat, microfilm, or any other means, without written permission from the publishers

Library of Congress Catalog Card Number: 77-85105
ISBN: 0-12-405550-8

TYPESET IN GREAT BRITAIN BY KELMSCOTT PRESS LIMITED
PRINTED BY J. W. ARROWSMITHS LTD, BRISTOL

Preface

The primary purpose of this work is to provide references to scientific books and papers which can be used to identify living organisms to be found in the British Isles, surrounding seas and, to a lesser extent, other parts of northwest Europe. Studies on fossils are cited only where they include living forms also.

This book is a development of one previously published by the Systematics Association, the "Bibliography of Key Works for the identification of the British Fauna and Flora", which ran to three editions. The first, published in 1942 under the editorship of Dr John Smart, was of 500 copies and was exhausted within ten years. The second edition, for which Dr Smart was joined by Sir George Taylor for the botanical part, was of 1000 copies published in 1953, and was not much longer in print. For the third, the editorship was placed in the hands of a team of three, Dr G. J. Kerrich for the insects and other mainly non-marine "Arthropod" groups and to act as senior editor, Dr N. Tebble for the other animals, and Mr R. D. Meikle for the "botanical" part; this edition of 1500 paperback and 300 hardback copies was published in 1967.

By 1974 it had become apparent that a replacement work would be required, and Council decided that this commitment of the Association should still be maintained. Dr Kerrich was willing to act in a similar capacity again: his former co-editors not being available, he was joined by Mr R. W. Sims for all animal groups other than the Chelicerata and the Uniramia and Dr D. L. Hawksworth for all botanical groups, fungi, bacteria and viruses.

As was the practice for the previous volumes, the coeditors each selected a team of collaborators for individual groups. It was largely at the instigation of some marine biologists concerned, whose organisms are not limited by land boundaries, that the decision was reached to extend the geographical area covered. The area decided on by the Council of the Association was the British Isles, Iceland, the Scandinavian countries, the Benelux countries, the Federal German Republic, and France north of 49°. It was felt that this would increase the usefulness of the volume to biologists located within the enlarged area. Moreover a British biologist, having before him a species not previously recognized as British, would by having literature from the nearer continental countries drawn to his attention, be more likely to achieve a correct identification, and less tempted to "force" his specimen into a species already included in a specifically British publication. However, works on the species of individual countries have been included only where considered to be of special relevance to the geographical area as a whole or the British Isles in particular.

This book incorporates the ideas of the three editions of its predecessor but reflects the progress in different directions made in the intervening years. A great deal of additional systematic work has been published: for some groups this has greatly increased the number of items cited, though in others more comprehensive publications have become available and the number cited has been reduced. The extension of the geographical area has, inevitably, increased the number of citations needed in others. The language in which the work cited is written is normally indicated only when it is other than English, French or German. Brief comments are again appended in appropriate cases.

Two major innovations in classification, which accord with modern thinking, are accepted here. Following the work of Dr Sidnie Manton, the Arthropoda are now divided into three separate phyla indicating their different evolutionary lines: the Chelicerata (mostly Arachnida), the Crustacea and the Uniramia (mostly myriapods and insects). These newly recognized phyla are arranged in a sequence beginning with the Annelida so, for convenience, other worm-like groups of uncertain affinities are listed before the coelomate segmented worms. Secondly within the last few years the fungi have come to be widely accepted as a kingdom of living organisms distinct from those of animals and plants: the lichens (i.e. fungi whose method of nutrition is by symbiosis with an aiga) are naturally included with them.

In the preparation of this book, thought has been given to the advisory work of the librarian. Thus, a number of general guides to the fauna and flora have been included, as also the faunal lists of marine biological laboratories. Comprehensive works should be available in the main national and municipal libraries or on loan through them, and many are quoted in the catalogues of the most prominent scientific booksellers. The shorter works, mostly published in journals, may be found in the libraries of the larger natural history societies, the more specialized societies, and the larger universities and municipal museums. A photostat service is available at the Science Museum Library, South Kensington, London SW7. Xerox copies of most listed items can be provided through the services of the British Library Lending Division, Boston Spa, Yorkshire.

Journal title abbreviations are cited, so far as has been found possible, in accordance with the fourth edition of the "World List of Scientific Periodicals" (Butterworths, London, 1964; 3 vols.) and the "List of Serial Publications in the British Museum (Natural History) Library" (2nd edn., 1975; 3 vols).

Many persons have generously contributed to the preparation of this book. The Zoological Editor wishes especially to thank Dr Sidnie Manton for her advice on the classification and arrangement of the 'Arthropoda' also Dr C. R. Curds (Protozoa, free-living), Dr K. M. G. Adams (Protozoa, parasitic), Mr S. Prudhoe and Mr C. G. Hussey (Mesozoa, Platyhelminthes, Nemertinea, Aschelminthes, Acanthocephala, Priapulida), Miss S. M. K. Stone (Porifera), Dr P. F. S. Cornelius (Coelenterata, Ctenophora), Miss P. L. Cook (Entoprocta, Bryozoa), Dr A. C. Pierrot-Bults (Chaetognatha), Dr E. C. Southward (Pogonophora), Dr P. E. Gibbs (Sipuncula, Echiura), Dr J. D. George (Polychaeta), Mr E. G. Easton (Oligochaeta, Hirudinea), Dr G. A. Boxshall, Dr R. W. Ingle, Dr R. J. Lincoln, Dr A. J. Southward (Crustacea), Dr P. B. Mordan, Mr J. F. Peake, Dr J. D. Taylor (Mollusca), Mr E. F. Owen (Brachiopoda), Miss A. M. Clark (Phoronidea, Echinodermata, Hemichordata, Tunicata, Cephalochordata), Mr A. C. Wheeler (Pisces), Dr E. N. Arnold (Amphibia, Reptilia), the late Mr K. Williamson (Aves) and Dr G. B. Corbet (Mammalia).

In the construction of the list of general works of Insecta, the Entomological Editor has benefited from the advice of Professors C. H. Lindroth, O. W. Richards and G. C. Varley. Lists of references in individual sections have been made, in conjunction with the Entomological Editor, by the following: Mr P. N. Lawrence (Collembola etc.), Dr D. R. Ragge (Orthoptera), Mr P. H. Ward (Plecophora, Ephemeroptera, Odonata), Mr C. Moreby (Pscoptera, Phthiraptera), Dr L. A. Mound (Thysanoptera), Dr W. A. Knight (Hemiptera-Heteroptera and Auchenorrhyncha), Dr V. F. Eastop (Hemiptera-Sternorrhyncha), Mr P. C. Barnard (Neuroptera, Trichoptera), Dr J. D. Bradley (Lepidoptera), Mr K. T. Thompson (Coleoptera), Mr G. R. Else (Hymenoptera-Aculeata), Mr K. G. V. Smith (Diptera), Dr F. G. A. M. Smit (Siphonaptera) and Mr D. Macfarlane (Myriapoda, Tardigrada, Chelicerata).

The Botanical Editor wishes to thank many advisers and contributors, particularly Mr R. Ross (freshwater Algae), Mr J. H. Price (marine Algae), Dr A. J. E. Smith (Bryophyta), Mr D. H. Kent (Pteridophyta, Spermatophyta), Dr I. K. Fergusson and Dr G. C. S. Clarke (pollen identification), Mr B. Ing (Myxomycota), Dr D. A. Reid and Dr D. N. Pegler (Hymenomycetes), Professor P. H. A. Sneath and Dr J. Bradbury (Bacteria) and Professor P. Wildy (animal viruses).

G.J.K.   D.L.H.   R.W.S.

Contents

	Page
Preface ..	v
Nomenclature ..	1
Source books and abstracting services	2
General works ..	2
ANIMALIA ..	5
PROTOZOA ..	5
FREE-LIVING	6
Saracomastigophora	6
Ciliophora	9
PARASITIC ..	11
Sarcomastigophora	12
Ciliophora	13
Sporozoa	14
Cnidospora	17
MESOZOA ..	18
PORIFERA (=PARAZOA)	18
COELENTERATA (=CNIDARIA)	20
Hydrozoa	20
Scyphozoa	22
Anthozoa	23
CTENOPHORA	24
PLATYHELMINTHES	24
Turbellaria	24
Monogenea	25
Cestoda ..	27
NEMERTINEA	28
ASCHELMINTHES	28
Rotifera	29
Gastrotricha	29
Echinodera	30
Nematoda	30
Nematomorpha ..	33
ACANTHOCEPHALA	33
PRIAPULIDA	34
ENTOPROCTA (=KAMPTOZOA)	34
CHAETOGNATHA	34

POGONOPHORA	35
SIPUNCULA	35
ECHIURA	36
ANNELIDA	36
Polychaeta	36
Oligochaeta	37
Hirudinea	37
CHELICERATA (=ARACHNIDA)	38
Scorpiones	38
Araneae	38
Pseudoscorpiones	39
Opiliones	40
Acari	40
Pycnogonida	49
Pentastomida	49
CRUSTACEA	50
Branchiopoda	50
Ostracoda	50
Mystacocarida	51
Copepoda	51
Cirripedia	52
Malacostraca	53
UNIRAMIA	57
MYRIAPODA	57
Diplopoda	57
Chilopoda	57
Symphyla	57
Pauropoda	57
HEXAPODA (=INSECTA)	58
Thysanura and Diplura	60
Protura	60
Collembola	60
Pterygota	60
Orthoptera and Dermaptera	60
Isoptera	61
Plectoptera	61
Ephemeroptera	62
Odonata	62
Thysanoptera	62
Psocoptera	63
Phthiraptera	63
Hemiptera	63
Neuroptera, Megaloptera, Mecoptera	65
Trichoptera	66
Lepidoptera	67

Coleoptera	71
Strepsiptera	83
Hymenoptera	83
Diptera	91
Siphonaptera	109
TARDIGRADA	110
MOLLUSCA	111
MARINE	112
Gastropda	112
Bivalia	113
Polyplacophora	113
Aplacophora	113
Scaphopoda	114
Cephalopoda	114
NON-MARINE	114
Gastropoda	114
Bivalvia	115
BRACHIOPODA	115
BRYOZOA (=ECTOPROCTA)	116
PHORONIDEA	118
ECHINODERMATA	118
HEMICHORDATA	118
CHORDATA	119
Tunicata	119
Cephalochordata	119
Vertebrata	120
Pisces	120
Amphibia and Reptilia	121
Aves	121
Mammalia	124
FUNGI	125
MYXOMYCOTA	128
EUMYCOTA	130
Mastigomycotina and Zygomycotina	130
Ascomycotina	132
Basidomycotina	137
Deuteromycotina	150
LICHENES	151
PLANTAE	159
ALGAE	159
BRYOPHYTA	163
PTERIDOPHYTA	169

SPERMATOPHYTA	169
General	169
Lists	171
Foreign books	171
Monographs of special groups	172
Trees and shrubs	172
Water plants	173
Sedges and grasses (Cyperaceae and Gramineae)	173
Orchids (Orchidaceae)	174
Distribution	174
Bibliography	174
History	175
Glossary	175
Anatomy and morphology	175
Pollen identification	176
PROKARYOTES	177
BACTERIA	177
VIRUSES	178

GENERAL

NOMENCLATURE

General

See also Davis & Heywood (1963) on p.170 and Hawksworth (1974) on p.126.

JEFFREY, C. (1977). "Biological Nomenclature". viii + 72 pp., 2nd edn. E. Arnold, London.
An introduction to the various codes of nomenclature whose production was sponsored by the Systematics Association.

Bacteria

INTERNATIONAL CODE OF NOMENCLATURE OF BACTERIA. BACTERIOLOGICAL CODE. 1976 REVISION (S. P. Lapage *et al.*, eds). 1976. xxxv + 180 pp. American Society for Microbiology, Washington, D.C.

Cultivated Plants

INTERNATIONAL CODE OF NOMENCLATURE OF CULTIVATED PLANTS (J. S. L. Gilmour *et al.*, eds). 1969. *Regnum Vegetabile* **64,** 32 pp. International Bureau for Plant Taxonomy and Nomenclature, Utrecht.

Fungi, Lichens, Algae, Bryophyta, Pteridophyta and Spermatophyta
(Excluding cultivated plants)

INTERNATIONAL CODE OF BOTANICAL NOMENCLATURE ADOPTED BY THE ELEVENTH INTERNATIONAL BOTANICAL CONGRESS, SEATTLE, AUGUST 1969 (F. A. Stafleu *et al.*, eds). 1972. *Regnum Vegetabile* **82,** 426 pp. International Association for Plant Taxonomy, Utrecht.

Viruses

WILDY, P. (1971). "Classification and Nomenclature of Viruses". Monographs in Virology no. 5. 81 pp. Karger, Basel.

Zoology

INTERNATIONAL CODE OF ZOOLOGICAL NOMENCLATURE. 1964. 2nd edn. xvii + 176 pp. International Trust for Zoological Nomenclature, London.

AMENDMENTS TO THE CODE OF ZOOLOGICAL NOMENCLATURE ADOPTED SINCE 1963. 1976. 25 pp. International Trust for Zoological Nomenclature, London.

SOURCE BOOKS AND ABSTRACTING SERVICES

A general account of biological abstracting and indexing services is provided by Edwards, P. I. 1971. List of abstracting and indexing services in pure and applied biology. *Biol. J. Linn. Soc.* **3**: 277–286.

The Commonwealth Agricultural Bureaux (Farnham House, Farnham Royal, Slough SL2 JBN) provides a wide range of abstracting journals dealing with most aspects of agriculture, horticulture, forestry and veterinary science.

See also pp. 125–126 for Fungi and pp. 174–175 for Spermatophyta; indices of new taxa are omitted here.

Zoological Record. 1864 on. Zoological Society of London, London.
  References for each year gathered together by groups and arranged by titles under authors' names, with subject and systematic index; titles only (not abstracts).

Biological Abstracts. 1926 on. Biological Abstracts, Philadelphia.
  Published every two weeks with an annual author and subject index; abstracts.

Bulletin signalétique. 1940 on. Centre de Documentation du C.N.R.S., Paris.
  Part 14 deals with Fungi, 16 with animals, and 17 with vegetable biology and physiology; published monthly; abstracts.

Current Bibliography for aquatic sciences and fisheries. 1958 on. F.A.O., Rome.
  Published at least twice-yearly; abstracts.

Excerpta Botanica. 1959 on. G. Fischer, Stuttgart.
  Sect. A (Taxonomy and chorology) published at roughly monthly intervals; abstracts; covers all plant and fungal groups.

Fortschritte der Botanik. 1931 on. Springer, Heidelberg & New York.
  An annual series of review articles with extensive bibliographies; a particular plant or fungal group appearing every other year.

Natural History Book Reviews. 1976 on. Richmond Publishing, Richmond, Surrey.
  Thrice-yearly; reviews arranged under broad subject heads and articles concerned with introducing the literature on particular topics.

GENERAL WORKS

BROHMER, P. 1974. "Fauna von Deutschland. Ein Bestimmungsbuch unserer heimischen Tierwelt". 12th edn. viii + 580 pp., 1836 figs., 10 pls. Quelle & Meyer, Heidelberg.

DELAMARE DEBOUTTEVILLE, C. 1960. Biologie des eaux souterraines, littorales et continentales. *Vie Milieu* Suppl. **9**, 740 pp., 254 figs. and pls.
  Especially useful as an introduction to interstitial animals.

GRAF, J. 1958. "Animal Life in Europe. The Naturalist's Reference Book". English edition (P. & M. Michael). 595 pp., Warne, London & New York.
  Diagnoses of the main animal groups and many well-known species; no keys; very lavishly illustrated (many plates in colour).

HAWKSWORTH, D. L., ed. 1974. "The Changing Flora and Fauna of Britain". xiii + 461 pp. Academic Press, London and New York.
  Includes contributions dealing with better known groups of plants and animals in the British Isles.

LEVER, C. 1977. "The Naturalised Animals of the British Isles". 600 pp. Hutchinson, London.
  A comprehensive well illustrated account, with maps dealing with birds, mammals, fish, etc.

MARINE

For fungi see also p.127, for lichens p.152 and for algae p.160.

BARRETT, J. H. & YONGE, C. M. 1958. "Collins Pocket Guide to the Sea Shore". 272 pp., 40 pls (20 in colour), over 200 figs. Collins, London.

A very well illustrated and useful book which approaches identification more from the ecological than the systematic point of view. All marine groups are covered except Protozoa, Mesozoa and mammals.

CAMPBELL, A. C. 1976. "The Hamlyn Guide to the Seashore and Shallow Seas of Britain and Europe". 320 pp., 49 figs., 132 pls. Hamlyn, London.

An excellent paperback, beautifully illustrated with colour plates. Includes all main groups of plants and animals.

EALES, N. B. 1961. "The Littoral Fauna of Great Britain: A Handbook for Collectors". 3rd edn., 305 pp., 111 figs. Cambridge University Press, Cambridge.

A very useful book which covers species in most groups, with comprehensive introductions and keys to aid identification; some of the nomenclature is now in need of revision.

HAAS, W. & KNORR, F. 1966. "The Young Specialist looks at Marine Life". 31 pp. Burke, London.

NEWELL, G. E. & NEWELL, R.C. 1963. "Marine Plankton. A practical guide". 207 pp., 51 pls. Hutchinson Educational, London.

An introduction to the study of plant and animal marine plankton which also provides descriptions of the major groups and common species, with comprehensive plates of figures. Selected references are provided by groups which provide a good guide to further reading.

FICHES D'IDENTIFICATION DU ZOOPLANKTON. 1949 on. Conseil Permanent International pour l'Exploration de la Mer, Copenhagen.

A series of sheets each of which provides keys and diagrams for the identification of groups of zooplankton together with a literature list. As each sheet is recommended for its particular group below, its author, number and date are noted; these, together with the title given above, provide the complete reference to particular sheets.

RASMUSSEN, E. 1973. Systematics and ecology of the Isefjord marine fauna. *Opehlia* **11**: 1–507.

THORSEN, G. 1946. Reproduction and larval development of Danish marine bottom invertebrates, with special reference to the planktonic larvae in the Sound (Øresund). *Meddr Komm Danm. Fisk.-og Havunders, ser. Plankton,* **4**(1), 523 pp., 199 figs.

A fundamental work essential to all serious students of marine biology. Includes studies on all invertebrate groups (except Protozoa) with a very extensive bibliography.

FAUNA AND FLORA LISTS

These lists are valuable in that they indicate what you might expect to collect in the areas, utilise classification schemes covering a large number of animal groups, and often also include references to descriptions of the species treated and very comprehensive bibliographies.

BRUCE, J. R., COLMAN, J. S. & JONES, N. S., eds. 1963. "Marine Fauna of the Isle of Man". 307 pp. Liverpool University Press, Liverpool.

BOYDEN, C. R., CROTHERS, J. H., LITTLE, C. & METTAM, C. 1977. Invertebrate fauna of the Severn Estuary. *Fld Stud.* **4**: 477–554.

DAVIS, D. S. 1967. The marine fauna of the Blackwater estuary and adjacent waters, Essex. *Essex Nat.* **32**: 1–61.
MAGHRABY, H. M. & PERKINS, E. J. 1966. Additions to the marine fauna of Whitstable. *Ann. Mag. nat. Hist., ser.* 12, **9**: 481–496.
NEWELL, G. E. 1954. The marine fauna of Whitstable. *Ann. Mag. nat. Hist.,* ser. 12, **7**: 321–350, 1 map.
PLYMOUTH MARINE FAUNA. 1957. 3rd edn. 457 pp. Marine Biological Assocation of the United Kingdom, Plymouth.
THE MARINE FAUNA OF LUNDY. 1974 on. *Rep. Lundy Fld Soc.* **25** on.
  Each annual report contains accounts of the fauna (and fiora) as data become available.
INVENTAIRE DE LA FAUNA MARINE DE ROSCOFF. 1951 on. Station Biologique, Roscoff.
  Numerous volumes, each dealing with a major group of marine animals occurring on the coast of Brittany.
INVENTAIRE DE LA FLORE MARINE DE ROSCOFF. 1954 on. Station Biologique, Roscoff.
ADDITIONS A L'INVENTAIRE DE LA FLORE MARINE DE ROSCOFF. 1964 on. Station Biologique, Roscoff.

LAND AND FRESHWATER

For algae see also p.159, for vascular plants p.171, and for insects p.60.

CLEGG, J. 1974. "Freshwater Life". 288 pp. Warne, London.
  A very sound general introduction.
MACAN, T. T. 1959. "A Guide to Freshwater Invertebrate Animals". x + 118 pp. Longmans Green, London.
MACAN, T. T. & WORTHINGTON, E. B. 1974. "Life in Lakes and Rivers" 3rd edn. New Naturalist No. 15. 320 pp. Collins, London.
MELLANBY, H. 1963. "Animal Life in Freshwater. A Guide to British Freshwater Invertebrates". viii + 308 pp., 211 figs. 6th edn. Methuen, London.
MORTIMER, M. E. 1976. Looking at life in freshwater. *Natural History Book Reviews* **1**: 58–65.
  Introduction to books dealing with freshwater life and its ecology; identification manuals discussed by group.
PENNAK, R. W. 1953. "Freshwater Invertebrates of the United States". ix + 769 pp., illustrated. Ronald Press, New York.
WARD, M. B. & WHIPPPLE, G. E. 1969. "Freshwater Biology". 2nd edn. (revised W. T. Edmunson). 1248 pp. Wiley & Sons, New York.
GLUECK, H. 1905–24. "Biologische und morphologische Untersuchungen über Wasser-under Sumpfgewachse". 4 vols. Gustav Fischer, Jena.
SMITH, K. P. & WHITTAKER, J. B. 1967. "A Key to the major Groups of British free-living Terrestrial Invertebrates. 12 pp., 4 figs. Blackwell Scientific Publications, Oxford & Edinburgh.
DARLINGTON, A. 1968. "The Pocket Encyclopaedia of Plant Galls in Colour". 191 pp., text-illustr., 293 col. pls. Blandford Press, London.

ANIMALIA

ROTHSCHILD, LORD. 1961 (A later impression available). "A Classification of Living Animals". vii + 106 pp. Longmans, London.
 This is an outline classification of the Animal Kingdom down to class, order or sub-order, into which selected genera are grouped. No group definitions are given. Some alternative and common names are supplied. There is a group bibliography, an alphabetical list of references and an index to all group names employed in the text giving the major units into which the genera are placed.

PROTOZOA

The number of European species in this phylum is unknown

GENERAL

HONIGBERG, B. M., BALAMUTH, W., BOVÉE, E. C., CORLISS, J. O., GODJICS, M., HALL, R. P., KUDO, R. R., LEVINE, N. D., LOEBLICH, A. R. Jr., WEISER, J. & WENRICH, D. H. 1964. A revised classification of the phylum Protozoa. *J. Protozool.* **11**: 7–20.
 Classification to sub-order with taxonomic characters.
JAHN, T. L. & JAHN, F. L. 1949. "How to know the Protozoa". 234 pp. 394 figs. W. C. Brown, Dubuque, Iowa.
GRASSÉ, P. P., ed. 1952. "Traité de Zoologie". Vol. 1 (1), 1071 pp., 830 figs.; Vol. 1(2), 1160 pp., 833 figs. Masson & Cie, Paris.
 General text book, systematic description of Protozoa except ciliates.
MACKINNON, D. L. & HAWES, R. S. J. 1961. "An introduction to the Study of Protozoa". 506 pp., 180 figs. Oxford.
KUDO, R. R. 1966. "Protozoology". 5th edn. 1174 pp., 388 figs. Charles C. Thomas, Springfield, USA.
 A general text-book with keys to families and descriptions of many genera.
GRELL, K. G. 1973. "Protozoology". 554 pp., 443 figs. Springer Verlag, Berlin.
WENYON, C. M. 1926. "Protozoology. A manual for medical men, veterinarians and zoologists". 2 vols. 1563 pp., 565 figs. 20 col. pls. London.

JOHNSON, L. P. 1956. "Key to some common freshwater Protozoa". *Bios* **27**: 32 pp.
REICHENOW, E. 1949-52. "Dofleins Lehrbuch der Protozoen-Kunde". 2 vols. 6th edn. 776 pp., 762 figs. Jena.
WESTPHAL, A. 1969. 1. Stamm: Protozoa, Urtiere. In "Fauna von Deutschland. Ein Bestimmungsbuch unserer heimischen Tierwelt" (P. Brohmer, ed.), pp. 1–26, 140 figs. Quelle & Meyer, Heidelberg.
GITTLESON, S. M. & HOOVER, R. L. 1970. Protozoa of underground waters in caves. *Annls Spéléol.* **25**: 91–106, 5 figs.

FREE LIVING PROTOZOA
SARCOMASTIGOPHORA

Mastigophora

PASCHER, A. "Süsswasserflora Deutschlands, Oesterreichs und der Schweiz". Jena.
PASCHER, A. & LEMMERMANN, E. 1914. Flagellatae I. Pantosotomatinae, Protomastiginae, Distomatinae. 138 pp., 252 flgs.
PASCHER, A. & LEMMERMANN, E. 1913. Flagellatae II. Chrysomonadinae, Cryptomonadinae, Eugleninae, Chloromonadinae. 192 pp., 398 figs.
SCHILLING, A. J. 1913. Dinoflagellatae (Peridineae). 66 pp., 69 figs.
PASCHER, A. 1927. Volvocales = Phytomonadinae. Flagellatae IV = Chlorophyceae I. 506 pp., 451 figs.
KÜHN, A. 1921. "Morphologie der Tiere in Bildern. Teil I. Flagellaten". 106 pp., figs. Berlin.
Keys to families and genera.
BOURRELLY, P. 1970. "Les Algues d'eau douce. Initiation à la Systématique. III. Algues bleues et rouges. Les Eugleniens, Peridiniens at Cryptomonadines." Bourbée & Cie, Paris.
KOFOID, C. A. & SWEZY, O. 1921. The free-living unarmored Dinoflagellata. *Mem. Univ. Calif.* **5**: 1–562, 388 figs.
LEBOUR, M. V. 1925. "The Dinoflagellates of Northern Seas". vi + 250 pp. 53 figs, 35 pls. Plymouth.
SCHILLER, J. 1933-35. Dinoflagellatae. *Rabenh. Krypt.-Fl.* **10**(1), 599 pp.; **10**(2), 617 pp.
SKUJA, H. 1948. Taxonomie des Phytoplanktons einiger Seen in Uppland, Schweden. *Symb. biol. upsal.* **9**(3): 399pp., 39 figs.
SKUJA, H. 1956. Taxonomische und Biologische Studien über das Phytoplankton schwedischer Binnengewässer. *Nova Acta R. Soc. Scient. Upsal.* (IV) **16**, 404 pp., 63 pls.
DEFLANDRE, M. G. 1926-27. Monographie du genre *Trachelomonas* Ehr. *Rev. gén. Bot.* **38**: 358–380, 449–469, 518–528, 580–592, 646–658, 687–706; **39**: 26–51, 73–98. 8 figs, 15 pls., a graph.
WEST, G. S. & FRITSCH, F. E. 1927. "A Treatise on the British Freshwater Algae". xviii + 534 pp., 207 figs. Cambridge.
Keys to families and genera with note on the commoner British species of all but the exclusively holozoic classes.
CONRAD, W. 1935. Étude systématique du Genre *Lepocinclis* Perty. *Mém. Mus. r. Hist. nat. Belg. (2)* **1**: 1–84, 84 figs.
Key to species.
POCHMANN, A. 1942. Synopsis der Gattung *Phacus. Arch Protistenk.* **95**: 81–252, figs.
Key to species.

PRINGSHEIM, E. G. 1942. Contributions to our knowledge of saprophytic algae and flagellata. 111. *New Phytol.* **41**: 171–205, figs.
  Astasia key to species.
SMITH, G. M. 1944. A comparative study of the species of *Volvox*. *Trans. Am. microsc. Soc.* **63**: 265–310.
  Descriptions with keys to species.
CALAWAY, W. T. & LACKEY, J. B. 1962. "Waste Treatment Protozoa; Flagellata". Florida Engineering Ser. No. 3. Gainsville, Florida. 140 pp., 149 figs.
  Keys to species.
BOUCAD-CAMON, E. 1966. Les choanoflagellés des côtes de la Manche. 1 Systématique. *Bull. Soc. linn. Normandie* **7**: 191–209, 28 figs.
LEEDALE, G. F. 1967. "Euglenoid Flagellates". Prentice-Hall, Englewood Cliffs, N. J. 242 pp., 176 figs.
  Descriptions and keys to orders, genera, species.
ETTL, H. 1970. Die Gattung *Chloromonas* Gobi emend. Wille. *(Chlamydomonas und die nachstrerwandten Gattungen I)*. *Beih. Nova Hedwigia* **34**: 1–283, 223 figs, 25 pls.
GLEZER, Z. I. 1970. "Cryptogamic plants of the USSR". Vol. 7 "Silicoflagellatophycae". Israel Progm scient. Transl. Jerusalem no. 5698. 1–363 pp., 58 figs.
REINHARDT, P. 1972. "Coccolithen Kakige Plankton seit Jahrmillionen". 99 pp., 183 flgs. A. Ziemsen, Wittenburg Lutherstadt.

Sarcodina

JEPPS, M. W. 1956. "The Protozoa Sarcodina". vi + 183 pp. 80 figs. Oliver and Boyd, Edinburgh & London.
OLIVE, L. S. 1969. "The Mycetozoa: a revised classification". *Bot. Rev. Lond.* **36**: 59–89, 6 figs.
BOVEE, E. C. & JAHN, T. L. 1973. Taxonomy and phylogeny. In "The Biology of Amoeba" (K. W. Jeon, ed.), pp. 37–82. Academic Press, New York & London.
LEIDY, J. 1879. Fresh-water Rhizopods of North America. *U.S. Geol. Survey of Territories* (Washington) **12**: 324 pp. 48 pls.
PENARD, E. 1902. "Faune Rhizopodique du Bassin de Leman". 714 pp., figs. and pls. Geneva.
PENARD, E. 1904. "Les Héliozoaires d'Eau Douce". 341 pp., figs. Geneva.
  Descriptions and keys to orders, genera and species.
CASH, J., WAILES, C. H. & HOPKINSON, J. 1905–21. "The British Freshwater Rhizopoda and Heliozoa I–V". xiv + 674 pp. 176 figs, 74 pls., Ray Society London.
KÜHN, A. 1926. Rhizopoden. In "Morphologie der Tiere in Bildern". **2** (2): 107–272, 206 figs. Berlin.
SCHAEFFER, A. A. 1926. Taxonomy of the amebas, with descriptions of thirty-nine new marine and freshwater species. *Pap. Dep. mar. Biol. Carnegie Instn Wash.* **24**: 1–116, 35 figs, 12 pls.
DEFLANDRE, G. 1928. Le genre *Arcella* Ehrenberg. Morphologie-Biologie. Essai phylogénétique et systématique. *Arch. Protistenk.* **64**: 152–287, 403 figs.
DEFLANDRE, G. 1936. Étude monographique sur le genre *Nebela* Leidy (Rhizopoda-Testacea). *Annls Protist.* **5**: 201–286, x-xxvii, 161 figs., pls.
HOOGENRAAD, H. R. & DE GROOT, A. A. 1940. Zoetwaterrhizopoden en Heliozoën. *Fauna Ned.* **9**, 303 pp. (in Dutch)
GROSPITSCH, T. G. 1958. Beitraege zur Rhizopoden fauna Deutschlands. I Thekamoeben des Rhoen. *Hydrobiologia* **10**: 305–322.
BONNET, L. & THOMAS, R. 1960. "Faune terrestre et d'eau douce des Pyrénées-

Orientales". Fasc. 5. "Thécamoebiens du Sol." 103 pp., 182 figs. Hermann, Paris.
HEAL, O. W. 1961. The distribution of testate amoebae in some fens and bogs in northern England. *J. Linn. Soc., Zool.* **44:** 369–382.
DECLOITRE, L. 1965. Amoebida testacea (Rhizopoda). *Zoology Iceland* **2**(1): 1–58, 40 figs.
RAINER, H. 1968. Urtiere, Protoza Wurzelfüssler, Rhizopoda Sonnenterchen, Heliozoa. *Tierwelt Dtl.* **56:** 1–176. 86 figs.
BOVÉE, E. C. 1970. The lobose amebas. 1. A key to the suborder Conopodina Bovee and Jahn, 1966 and descriptions of thirteen new or little known *Mayorella* species. *Arch. Protistenk.* **112:** 178–227, 13 figs.
SINGH, B. N. & DAS, S. R. 1970. Studies on pathogenic and non-pathogenic small freeliving amoebae and the bearing of nuclear division on the classification of the order Amoebida. *Phil. Trans. R. Soc.* (B) **259:** 435–476, 12 pls.
GROSPIETSCH, T. G. 1972. "Einführung in die Kleinlebewelt. Wechseltierchen (Rhizopoden)". 80 pp., 73 figs. Franch'sche Verlagshandlung, W. Keller and Co., Stuttgart.
CORBET, S. A. 1973. An illustrated introduction to the Testate Rhizopods in *Sphagnum,* with special reference to the area around Malham Tarn, Yorkshire. *Fld Stud.* **3:** 801–838. 11 figs. 2 pls.
BRADY, H. B. 1884. Report on the Foraminifera dredged by H.M.S. Challenger during the years 1873-76. *Rep. scient. Results Voy. Challenger Zoology* **9** (in 2 vols.), 814 pp. 115 pls.
CUSHMAN, J. A. 1918–31. 1. The Foraminifera of the Atlantic Ocean. *Bull. U.S. natn. Mus.* **104** (1–8), 866 pp., 199 pls.
GLAESSNER, M. F. 1945. "Principles of Micropalaeontology". xvi + 296 pp. 64 figs, 14 pls., Tables. Melbourne and Oxford University Presses.
  Keys to families, subfamilies, genera, fossil (very many) and recent.
HERON-ALLEN, E. & EARLAND, A. 1908–11. On the recent and fossil Foraminifera of the shore-sands of Selsey Bill, Sussex. *Jl R. microsc. Soc.* **1908:** 529–543, 1 pl.; **1909:** 306–336, 422–446, 677–698, 6 pls.; **1910:** 401–426, 693–695, 6 pls.; **1911:** 298–343, 5 pls., 436–448.
HERON-ALLEN, E. & EARLAND, A. 1913. Foraminifera. Clare Island Survey, no. 64. *Proc. R. Ir. Acad.* **31:** 1–188, 13 pls.
  Contains a full list of references up to 1912.
HERON-ALLEN, E. & EARLAND, A. 1916. Foraminifera of the shore-sands and shallow-water zone of the South Coast of Cornwall. *Jl R. microsc. Soc.* **1916:** 29–55. 5 pls.
HERON-ALLEN, E. & EARLAND, A. 1916. The Foraminifera of the West of Scotland. *Trans. Linn. Soc. Lond., Zool.* **11:** 197–299, 5 pls.
HERON-ALLEN, E. & EARLAND, A. 1930. The Foraminifera of the Plymouth district. *Jl R. microsc. Soc.* **50:** 6–84. 3 pls.
NQRVANG, A. 1945. Foraminifera. *Zoology Iceland* **2**(2): 1–79, 14 figs.
HOGLUND, H. 1947. Foraminifera of the Gullmar Fjord and the Skaggerak. *Zool. Bidr. Uppsala* **26:** 1–328, 312 figs, 32 pls.
  Maps, tables, diagrams, figures and descriptions of many species likely to be found along British coasts.
BARKER, R. W. 1960. Taxonomic notes on the species figured by H. B. Brady in his Report on the Foraminifera dredged by H.M.S. Challenger during the years 1873–1876. Accompanied by a reproduction of Brady's Plates. *Am. Ass. Petrol. Geol. Publ.* **9:** 1–238, 115 pls.
GEORGE VANDERBILT FOUNDATION. 1961. "An Index to the Genera and Species of the Foraminifera, 1890–1950". 393 pp. Stanford University Press.
BE A. W. H. 1976. Foraminifera. Families Globigerinidae and Globorotaliidae. *Fich. Ident. Zooplancton* **108:** 2–3, figs.

LOEBLICH, A. R. Jr. & TAPPAN, H. 1964. "Treatise on Invertebrate Paleontology. Part C. Protista 2". Vol. 1, xxxi + 1–50, "Sarcodina. Chiefly Thecamoebians"; 2, 511–900, "Foraminiferida". The Geological Society of America and the University of Kansas Press.
POKORNY, V. 1963. "Principles of Zoological Micropalaeontology". Vol. 1. Translated from the German by K. A. Allen (J. W. Neale, ed.). 652 pp., 548 figs. Pergamon Press, Oxford.
MURRAY, J. W. 1965. On the Foraminiferida of the Plymouth region. *J. mar. Biol. Ass. U.K.* **45**: 481–505.
PHLEGER, F. B. 1960. "Ecology and Distribution of Recent Foraminifera". viii + 297 pp., 82 figs., 6 pls. Hopkins University, Baltimore.
ELLIS, B. F. & MESSINA, A. R. 1940 *et seq.* "Catalogue of Foraminifera". American Museum of Natural History, New York". 59 vols., Index and Bibliography.
This publication includes the original descriptions and figures of all new species of Foraminifera.
BRANDT, K. A. H., ed. 1901–1929. "Nordisches Plankton". Kiel and Leipzig. Containing:
BORGERT, A. 1901. Die nordishcen Tripyleen-Arten. **15**: 1–52, 56 figs.
POPOFSKY, A. 1905 & 1907. Die nordischen Acantharien. Teil I: Acanthometriden. Teil II: Acanthophracten. **16**: 53–90, 29 figs.
SCHRÖDER, O. 1929 & 1909. Die nordischen Supmellarian. Teil I: Unterlegion Sphaerocollida, **16**: 91–120, 22 figs. Teil II: Unterlegion Sphaerellaria, **17**: 1–66, 37 figs.
SCHRÖDER, O. 1914. Die nordischen Nassellarien. **17**: 67–146, 124 figs.
HENSEN, V. A. C., ed. 1904–1926. "Ergebn. der Plankton-Expedition der Humboldt-Stiftung". Vol. 3. Kiel and Leipzig. Containing:
DREYER, F. 1913. Die Polycystinen der Plankton-Expedition. (Lde): 1–104, 4 figs., 3 pls.
IMMERMAN, F. 1904. Die Tripyleen-Familie der Aulacanthiden. (Lh1): 1–92, 8 pls.
BORGERT, A. 1905. Die Tripyleen Radiolarien der Plankton-Expedition. Tuscaroridae. (Lh2): 93–113, 2 figs., 1 pl.
BORGERT, A. 1905. Atlanticellidae. (Lh3): 117–128, 1 pl.
BORGERT, A. 1906. Medusettidae. (Lh4): 133–192, 4 pls.
BORGERT, A. 1907. Concharidae. (Lh5): 195–232, 3 pls.
SCHMIDT, W. J. 1908. Castanellidae. (Lh6): 235–279, 4 pls.
BORGERT, A. 1909. Phaeodinidae, Caementellidae und Cannorrhaphidae. (Lh7): 283–316, 2 pls.
BORGERT, A. 1909. Circopordiae. (Lh8): 319–352, 3 pls.
BORGERT, A. 1909. Cannosphaeridae. (Lh9): 355–380, 2 pls.
BORGERT, A. 1910. Porospathidae und Cadiidae. (Lh10): 383–415, 2 pls.
BORGERT, A. 1911. Challengeridae. (Lh11): 419–536, 22 figs., 6 pls.
BORGERT, A. 1913. Atlanticellidae. II Teil. (Lh12): 539–610, 22 figs., 8 pls.
POPOFSKY, A. 1926. Die Tripyleen Radiolarien der Plankton-Expedition. Coelodendridae (einschliesslich Coelographidae Haeckel). (Lh 13): 1–101, 53 figs., 6 pls.

CILIOPHORA

CORLISS, J. O. 1961. "The Ciliated Protozoa: characterization, classification and guide to the literature". 310 pp., figs. Pergamon Press, Oxford, London, New York, Paris.

CORLISS, J. O. 1972. Current status of the International collection of ciliate type-specimens and guide lines for future contributors. *Trans. Am. microsc. Soc.* **91**: 221–235.

CORLISS, J. O. 1975. Taxonomic characterization of the supra-familial groups in a revision of recently proposed schemes of classification for the phylum Ciliophora. *Trans. Am. microsc. Soc.* **94**: 224–267, 51 figs.

SAND, R. 1899–1901. Étude monographique sue le groups des infusoires tentaculières. *Annls Soc. belge Microsc.* **24**: 57–189; **25**: 7–205; **26**: 14–119.

COLLIN, B. 1911. Étude monographique sur les Acinétiens. I: Recherches expérimentales sur l'étendue des variations et les facteurs tératogènes. *Arch. Zool. exp. gen.* (5) **8**: 421–497, 29 figs., 2 pls.

PENARD, E. 1921. "Études sur les Infusoires d'Eau Douce". 331 pp., 301 figs. Geneva.

LEPSI, I. 1927. "Die Infusorien des Süsswassers und Meeres". iv + 100 pp., figs., 14 pls. Berlin
    Keys to genera and species.

JÖRGENSEN, E. 1927. Tintinnidae. *Tierwelt N.- u. Ostsee* **2c**: 1–66, 33 figs.

SCHEWIAKOFF, V. T. 1927. Keys for the determination of the holotrichous ciliates. Translated from the Russian by Cecil A. Hoare. *Proc. zool. Soc. Lond.* **1927**: 399–418.

NOLAND, L. E. & FINLEY, H. 1931. Studies on the taxonomy of the genus *Vorticella. Trans. Am. microsc. Soc.* **50**: 81–123.

KAHL, A. 1930–1935. Urtiere oder Protozoa. I: Wimpertiere oder Ciliata (Infusoria). *Tierwelt Dtl.* **18, 21, 25, 30**: 886 pp., 3407 figs.
    Keys to genera and species. Descriptions and figures of all known species of non-parasitic ciliates, except marine Tintinnidae.

KAHL, A. 1934. Suctoria. *Tierwelt N.-u. Ostsee* **2c**: 184–226, 228 figs.

BULLINGTON, W. E. 1939. A study of spiraling in the ciliate *Frontonia* with a review of the genus and a description of two new species. *Arch. Protistenk.* **92**: 10–66.

McKIM, J. 1942. Renfrewshire records. *Trans. Paisley Nat. Soc.* **4**: 1–28.
    Ciliates of Renfrewshire.

TUFFRAU, M. 1960. Révision de genre *Euplotes,* fondée sur las comparaison des structures superficielles. *Hydrobiologia* **15**: 1–77.

TARTAR, V. 1961. "The Biology of Stentor". Pergamon Press, London.
    Keys to species in Ch 18, pp. 333–338, 1 fig.

FELINSKA, M. 1965. Marine ciliata from Plymouth: Pertricha, Vaginicolidae. *J. mar. biol. Ass. U.K.* **45**: 229–239, figs.

BOCK, K. J. 1967. Protozoa. Order: Oligotrichida. Families: Halteriidae, Strombiliidae. *Fich. Ident. Zooplancton* **110**: 2–4, figs.

CURDS, C. R. 1969. An illustrated key to the British Freshwater Ciliated Protozoa commonly found in activated sludge. *Wat. Pollut. Res. Tech. Pap.* No. **12**: 89 pp., 89 figs. HMSO, London.

MARSHALL, S. M. 1969. Order: Tintinnida. *Fich. Ident. Zooplancton* **117–127**: 70 pp., 263 figs.

RAABE, Z. 1971. Orde Thigmotrichida (Ciliatea–Holotricha) 4. Familia Thigmophryidae. *Acta Protozool.* **9**: 121–170, 11 figs.

STILLER, J. 1971. Szajkosorous caillosok-peritricha. *Fauna Hung.* **105**: 1–245, 148 figs. (in Hungarian).

BICK, H. 1972. "Ciliated Protozoa. An illustrated guide to the species used as biological indicators in freshwater biology". 198 pp., 94 figs. WHO, Geneva.

BORROR, A. C. 1972. Revision of the order Hypotrichida (Ciliophora, Protozoa). *J. Protozool.* **19**: 1–23.

BORROR, A. C. 1973. *Tracheloraphis haloetes* sp.n. (Ciliphora, Gymnostomatida):

Description and a key to species of the genus *Tracheloraphis*. *J. Protozool.* **20:** 554–558.
GIESE, A. C. 1973. *"Blepharisma*. The biology of light-sensitive protozoan". Stanford University Press. Includes keys to species. Ch 12, pp. 304–332, Classification, Distribution and Evolution.
CORLISS, J. O. 1973. History, taxonomy, ecology, and evolution of species of *Tetrahymena*. In "Biology of *Tetrahymena*", A. M. Elliott, ed.), 1–55, 46 figs. Dowden, Hutchinson & Ross, Stroudsburg, Penna.
VIVIER, E. 1974. Morphology, taxonomy and general biology of the genus *Paramecium*. In *"Paramecium*. A Current Survey" (W. J. Van Wagtendonk, ed.), pp. 1–89, 44 figs. Elsevier, Amsterdam, London & New York.
CURDS, C. R. 1975. A guide to the species of the genus *Euplotes* (Hypotrichida, Ciliatea). *Bull. Br. Mus. nat. Hist. (Zool.)* **28:** 1–61, 58 figs.

PARASITIC PROTOZOA

General

HOARE, C. A. 1949. "Handbook of Medical Protozoology: for medical men, parasitologists and zoologists". 334 pp. Baillière, Tindall & Cox, London.
LEVINE, N. D. 1972. "Protozoan Parasites of Domestic Animals and Man". 2nd edn. 406 pp. Burgess Publishing, Minneapolis, Minnesota.
DOBELL, C. & O'CONNOR, F. W. 1921. "The Intestinal Protozoa of Man". 209 pp. London.
BRUMPT, E. 1949. "Précis de Parasitologie". 6th edn., 1042 pp. Paris.
BAKER, J. R. 1969. "Parasitic Protozoa". 176 pp. Hutchinson, London.
ADAM, K. M. G., PAUL, J. & ZAMAN, V. 1971. "Medical and Veterinary Protozoology, an illustrated guide". 200 pp. Churchill Livingstone, Edinburgh & London.
FLYNN, R. J. 1973. "Parasites of Laboratory Animals. 884 pp. Iowa State University Press, Ames, Iowa.
COLES, A. C. Blood parasites found in mammals, birds and fishes in England. *Parasitology* **7:** 17–61.
NIESCHULZ, O. 1925. Die parasitischen Protozoen der Pflanzen. *Handb. pathogen. Protozoen* **3,** Lief. 11: 1799–1813.
STILES, C. W. & NOLAN, M. O. 1931. Key-catalogue of parasites reported for Chiroptera with their possible public health importance. *Natn. Inst. Hlth Bull.* **155:** 603–742.
STILES, C. W. & STANLEY, S. F. 1932. Key-catalogue of parasites reported for Insectivora with their possible public health importance. *Natn. Inst. Hlth Bull.* **159:** 791–911.
STILES, C. W. & BAKER, C. E. 1935. Key-catalogue of parasites reported for Carnivora with their possible public health importance. *Natn. Inst. Hlth Bull.* **163,** 913–1223.
SEMANS, F. M. 1943. Protozoan parasites of Orthoptera IV. Classified list of the protozoan parasites of Orthoptera of the world. *Ohio Sci.* **43:** 221–234, 271–276.
SPRAGUE, V. & COUCH, J. 1971. An annotated list of protozoan parasites, hyperparasites and commensals of decapod Crustacea. *J. Protozool.* **18:** 526–537.
NIE, D. 1950. Morphology and taxonomy of the intestinal protozoa of the guinea pig, *Cavia porcella. J. Morph.* **86:** 381–493.
RING, M. 1959. Studies on the parasitic protozoa of wild mice from Berkshire with a description of a new species of *Trichomonas. Proc. Zool. Soc. London* **132:** 381–401.

New parasitic Protozoa are recorded in *Annls Parasit. hum. comp.* (1923 on). The *Zoological Record* has given annual host-lists since 1929.

SARCOMASTIGOPHORA

Phytomastigophorea

CHATTON, E. 1920. Les péridiniens parasites. Morphologies, reproduction, éthologie. *Archs. Zool. exp. gen.* **59**: 475 pp.

REICHENOW, E. 1930. Parasitische Peridinea. *Tierwelt N.- u. Ostsee* **2d**: 85-100, 10 figs.

LEE, J. S. & ZUCKER, W. 1968. Algal flagellate symbiosis in the foraminifer *Archaias. J. Protozool.* **16**: 71-81.

MICHAJLOW, W. 1972. "Euglenoidina Parasitic in Copepoda". 224 pp. PWN-Polish, Scientific Publishers, Warsaw.

Zoomastigophorea

HOARE, C. A. 1972. "The Trypanosomes of Mammals". 749 pp. Blackwell, Oxford and Edinburgh.

REICHENOW, E. 1931. Parasitische Flagellata (ausschliesslich Peridinea). *Tierwelt N.- u. Ostsee* **2e**: 1-18, 10 figs.
   Fish hosts of trypanosomes.

HILTON, D. F. J. & MAHRT, J. L. 1972. Taxonomy of trypanosomes (Protozoa: Trypanosomatidae) of *Spermophilus* spp. (Rodentia: Sciuridae). *Parasitology* **65**: 403-425.

BARDSLEY, J. E. & HARMSEN, R. 1973. The Trypanosomes of Anura. *Adv. Parasitol.* **11**: 1-73.

VICKERMAN, K. 1976. The diverstiy of kinetoplastid fiagellates. In "Biology of Kinetoplastida" (W. H. R. Lumsden and D. A. Evans, eds.). Academic Press, New York & London.

WALLACE, F. G. 1966. The trypanosomatid parasites of insects and arachnids. *Expl. Parasit.* **18**: 124-193.

GARNHAM, P. C. 1971. The genus *Leishmania. Bull Wld. Hlth Org.* **44**: 477-489.

BRAY, R. S. 1974. *Leishmania. Ann. Rev. Microbiol* **28**: 189-217.

HONIGBERG, B. M. 1963. Evolutionary and systematic relationships in the flagellate order Trichomonadida Kirby. *J. Protozool.* **10**: 20-63.

WENRICH, D. H. 1944. Morphology of the intestinal trichomonad flagellates in man and of similar forms in monkeys, cats, dogs and rats. *J. Morph.* **74**: 189-211.

JENSEN, E. A. & HAMMOND, D. M. 1964. A morphological study of trichomonads and related flagellates from the bovine digestive tract. *J. Protozool.* **11**: 386-394.

KIRBY, H. & HONIGBERG, B. M. 1949. Flagellates of the caecum of ground squirrels. *Univ. Calif. Publs. Zool.* **53**: 315-366.

CLEVELAND, L. R., HALL, S. R., SANDERS, E. P. & COLLIER, J. 1934. The wood-feeding roach *Cryptocercus,* its protozoa and the symbiosis between protozoa and roach. *Mem. Am. Acad. Arts Sci.* **17**: 1-342.

KIRBY, H. 1932. Flagellates of the genus *Trichonympha. Univ. Calif. Publs Zool.* **37**: 349-476.

CROSS, J. B. 1946. The flagellate subfamily Oxymonadinae. *Univ. Calif. Publs Zool.* **53**: 67-162.

CAMP, R. R., MATTERN, C. F. T. & HONIGBERG, B. M. 1974. Study of *Dientamoeba fragilis* Jepps & Dobell. I. Electronmicroscopic observations of the binucleate stages. II. Taxonomic position and revision of the genus. *J. Protozool.* **21** 69-82.

Opalinata

METCALF, M. M. 1923. The opalinid ciliate infusorians. *Bull. U.S. natn. Mus.* **120**: 1-471.

METCALF, M. M. 1940. Further studies on the opalinid ciliate infusorians. *Proc. U.S. natn. Mus.* **87**: 465–634.

Sarcodina (Rhizopodea)

DOBELL, C. 1919. "The Amoebae living in Man". 155 pp. Bale, Sons & Daniellson, London.
HOARE, C. A. 1959. Amoebic infections in animals. *Vet. Revs. Annot.* **5**: 91–102.
NOBLE, G. A. & NOBLE, E. R. 1952. Entamoebae in farm animals. *J. Parasit.* **38**: 571–595.
POKORNY, K. S. 1967. *Labyrinthula. J. Protozool.* **14**: 697–708.
CHANG, S. L. 1971. Small, free-living amebas: cultivation, quantitation, identification, classification, pathogenesis and resistance. *Current Topics in Pathobiology* **1**: 205–254.
CULBERTSON, C. G. 1971. The pathogenicity of soil amebas. *A. Rev. Microbiol.* **25**: 231–254.
PAGE, F. C. 1974. A further study of taxonomic criteria for limax amoebae with descriptions of new species and a key to genera. *Arch. Protistenk.* **116**: 149–184.

CILIOPHORA

Ciliatea

CORLISS, J. O. 1961. See above p.9.
DOGIEL, V. A. 1927. Monographie der Familie Ophryoscolecidae. *Arch. Protistenk.* **59**: 1–288.
KOFOID, C. A. & MACLENNAN, R. F. 1931. Ciliates from *Bos indicus* Linn. I. The genus *Entodinium* Stein. *Univ. Calif. Publs. Zool.* **33**: 471–544.
KOFOID, C. A. & MACLENNAN, R. F. 1933. Ciliates from *Bos indicus* Linn. II. A revision of *Diplodinium* Scuberg. *Univ. Calif. Publs. Zool.* **37**: 53–152.
KOFOID, C. A. & MACLENNAN, R. F. 1935. Ciliates from *Bos indicus* Linn. III. *Epiplastron* gen. nov., *Epidinium* Crawley and *Ophryoscolex* Stein. *Univ. Calif. Publs. Zool.* **39**: 1–34.
HSIUNG, T. 1930. A monograph on the protozoa of the large intestine of the horse. *Iowa St. Coll. J. Sci.* **4**: 356–423.
STRELKOW, A. 1939. [Parasitic protozoa of the intestine of *Ungulata* belonging to the family Equidae.] *Uchen. Zap. pedegogich Inst. Gercena* **17**: 262 pp. [An English translation of this Russian monograph (pp. 11–133) is available in the library of the Department of Zoology, University of Edinburgh, Scotland.]
WOLSKA, M. 1971. Studies on the family Blepharocorythidae Hsiung. V. A review of genera and species. *Actaprotozool.* **9**: 23–40.
POWERS, P. B. A. 1933. Studies on ciliates from sea urchins. *Biol. Bull. mar. biol. Lab. Woods Hole* **65**: 106–121.
POWERS, P. B. A. 1935. Studies on ciliates of sea urchins. *Pap. Tortugas Lab.* **29**: 293–326.
BEERS, C. D. 1948. The ciliates of *Stronylocentrotus dröbachiensis:* incidence, distribution in the host and division. *Biol. Bull. mar. biol. Lab. Woods Hole* **94**: 99–112.
BERGER, J. & PROFANT, R. J. 1961. The entocommensal fauna of the pink sea urchin, *Allocentrotus fragilis. J. Parasit.* **47**: 417–418.
LYNN, D. H. & BERGER, J. 1972. Morphology, systematics and demic variation of *Plagiopyliella pacifica* Poljansky, 1951 (Ciliates: Philasterina), an entocommensal of strongylocentrotid echinoids. *Trans. Am. microsc. Soc.* **91**: 310–336.
LYNN, D. H. & BERGER, J. 1973. The Thyrophylacidae, a family of carnivorous philasterine ciliates entocommensal in strongylocentrotid echinoids. *Trans. Am. microsc. Soc.* **92**: 533–557.

KAHL, A. 1934. Ciliata entocommensalia et parasitica. *Tierwelt N.- u. Ostsee* **2c**: 184–226.
BHATIA, B. L. 1936. Fauna of British India. Protozoa: Ciliophora. 493 pp. London.
HEIDENREICH, E. 1935. Untersuchungen an parasitischen Ciliaten aus Anneliden. (Astomatida). *Arch. Protistenk.* **84**: 315–392.
FENCHAL, T. 1968. Ciliates from Scandinavian molluscs. *Ophelia* **2**: 71–174.
BURRESON, E. M. 1973. Symbiotic ciliates from solitary ascidians of the Pacific northwest with a description of *Parahypocoma rhamphisokarya* n. sp. *Trans. Am. microsc. Soc.* **92**: 517–522.
CHATTON, E. & LWOFF, A. 1934. Sur un infusoire parasite des poils secréteurs des crustacés Edriophtalmes et la famille nouvelle des Pilisuctoridae. *C.r. hebd. Séanc. Acad. Sci. Paris* **199**: 696–699, 1 fig.
CHATTON, E. & LWOFF, A. 1935. Les ciliés apostomes. Morphologie, cytologie, éthologie, évolution, systématique. *Archs. Zool. exp. gén.* **77**. 1–453, 217 figs., 21 pls.
CHATTON, E. & LWOFF, A. 1936. Les Pilisuctoridae Ch. et Lw., ciliés parasites des poils secréteurs des Crustacés Edriophthalmes. Polarité, orientation ed desmodexie chez les infusoires. *Bull. biol. Fr. Belg.* **70**: 86–144, 7 figs., 2 pls.
LOM, J. 1959. Beiträge zur Kenntnis der parasitischen Ciliaten aus Evertebraten IV. Neue Ciliaten aus der Familie Haptophryidae Cépède 1923, nebst einigen Bermerkungen zum heutigen Stand dieser Gruppe. *Arch. Protistenk.* **104**: 133–154.
CORLISS, J. A., de PUYTORAC, P. & LOM, J. 1965. Resolution of persistent taxonomic and nomenclatural problems involving ciliate protozoa assignable to the astome family Haptophryidae Cépède, 1923. *J. Protozool.* **12**: 265–273.
LOM, J. 1958. A contribution to the systematics and morphology of endoparasitic trichodinids from amphibians with a proposal of uniform specific characteristics (Urceolaridae). *J. Protozool.* **5**: 251–263.
RAABE, Z. 1963. Systematics of the family Urceolaridae Dujardin 1841. *Acta Protozool.* **1**: 121–138.
CHATTON, E. & LWOFF, A. 1949. Recherches sur les ciliés thigmotriches, I. *Archs. Zool. exp. gén.* **86**: 169–253.
CHATTON, E. & LWOFF, A. 1950. Recherches sur les ciliés thigmotriches II. *Archs. Zool. exp. gén.* **86**: 393–485.
RAABE, Z. 1967–1972. Ordo Thigmotricha (Ciliata-Holotricha) I–V. *Acta Protozool.* **5**: 1–36, **7**: 117–180, **8**: 385–463, **9**: 121–170, **10**: 115–184.

SPOROZOA

Telosporea

Gregarinia
SCHELLACK, C. 1912. Die Gregarinen. *Handb. pathogen. Protoz.* **1**(4): 487–515.
REICHENOW, E. 1921. Die Gregarinen (Nachtrag) *Handb. pathogen. Protoz.* **3**(8): 1278–1294.
WATSON, M. E. 1916. Studies on gregarines. *Illinois biol. Monogr.* **2**: 211–468.
KAMM, M. W. 1922. Studies on gregarines. II. *Illinois biol. Monogr.* **7**: 1–104.
BHATIA, B. L. 1930, Synopsis of genera and classification of haplocyte gregarines. *Parasitology* **22**: 156–167.
WEISER, J. 1955. A new classification of Schizogregarina. *J. Protozool.* **2**: 6–12.
THÉODRIDÈS, J. 1955. Les Eugrégarines du genre *Gregarina* parasites de coléoptères ténébrionides. *Annls. Parasit. hum. comp.* **30**: 5–21.
VAVRA, J. 1969. *Lankesteria barretti* n.sp. (Eugregarinida, Diplocystidae a parasite of the mosquito *Aedes triseriatus* and a review of the genus *Lankesteria* Mingazzini. *J. Protozool.* **16**: 546–570.

LEVINE, N. D. 1971. Taxonomy of the Archigregarinorida and Selenidiidae (Protozoa: Apicomplexa). *J. Protozool.* **18:** 704–717.
SCHRÉVEL, J. 1971. Observations biologiques et ultra-structurales sur les Selenidiidae et leur conséquences sur las systématique des grégarinomorphes. *J. Protozool.* **18:** 448–470.
SEGUN, A. O. 1971. Acephaline gregarines of earthworms — additions to the British records. *J. Protozool* **18:** 313–317.
SEGUN, A. O. 1972. Distribution of acephaline gregarines of British earthworms and their comparison with those of neighbouring European countries. *Parasitology* **65:** 47–53.

Coccidia
REICHENOW, E. 1912. Die Hämogregarinen. *Handb. pathogen. Protoz.* **2**(5): 602–632.
REICHENOW, E. 1921. Die Coccidien. *Handb. pathogen. Protoz.* **3**(8): 1136–1277.
LEVINE, N. D. & BECKER, E. R. 1933. A catalog and host-index of the species of the coccidian genus *Eimeria*. *Iowa St. Coll. J. Sci.* **8:** 402–405.
BECKER, E. R. 1934. Coccidia and coccidiosis of domesticated, game and laboratory animals and of man. *Iowa St. Coll. Monogr.* **1:** 147 pp.
BECKER, E. R. 1934. A check-list of the coccidia of the genus *Isospora*. *J. Parasit.* **20:** 195–196.
HOARE, C. A. 1957. Classification of Coccidia Eimeriidae in a periodic system of homologous genera. *Rev. brasil. Malar. Doenc. trop.* **8:** 197.
DAVIES, S. F. M., JOYNER, L. P. & KENDALL, S. B. 1963. "Coccidiosis". 264 pp. Oliver & Boyd, Edinburgh.
BECKER, E. R. 1956. Catalogue of Eimeriidae in genera occurring in vertebrates and not requiring intermediate hosts. *Iowa St. Coll. J. Sci.* **31:** 85.
PELLÉRDY, L. P. 1974. "Coccidia and Coccidiosis". 2nd edn. 959 pp. Akadémiai Kiadó, Budapest.
LEVINE, N. D. & IVENS, V. 1965. The coccidian parasites (Protozoa, Sporozoa) of rodents. *Illinois biol. Monogr.* **33:** 1–365, figs.
LEVINE, N. D. & IVENS, V. 1970. The coccidian parasites (Protozoa, Sporozoa) of ruminants. *Illinois biol. Monogr.* **44:** 278 pp.
LEVINE, N. D. & IVENS, V. 1972. Coccidia of Leporidae. *J. Protozool.* **19:** 572–581.
TODD, K. S. & HAMMOND, D. M. 1970. "Diseases of Wildlife". Iowa State University Press, Ames, Iowa.
  Coccidia of wild birds.
HAMMOND, D. M. & LONG, P., eds. 1973. "The Coccidia". 482 pp. University Park Press, Baltimore; Butterworths, London.
VETTERLING, J. M., JERVIS, H. R., MERRILL, t. g. 0 sprinz, H. 1971. *Cryptosporidium wrairi* sp.n. from the guinea pig *Cavia porcellus* with an emendation of the genus. *J. Protozool.* **18:** 243–247.
FRENKEL, J. K. 1974. Advances in the biology of Sporozoa. *Z. Parasitenk.* **45:** 125–162.
  Toxoplasma, Sarcocystis, Frenkelia.
MANDOUR, A. M. & KEYMER, I. F. 1970. Sarcocystis infection in African antelopes. *Ann. trop. Med. Parasit.* **64:** 513–523.
  Infestation also of deer in N. W. Europe.
KALINER, G. 1975. Observations on the histomorphology of sarcosporidian cysts of some East African game animals (Artiodactyla). *Z. Parasitenk.* **46:** 13–23.
ZAMAN, V. & COLLEY, F. C. 1975. Light and electron microscopic observations of the life cycle of *Sarcocystis orientalis* sp.n. in the rat *(Rattus norvegicus)* and the Malaysian python *(Python reticulatus)*. *Z. Parasitenk.* **47:** 169–185.

MARKUS, M. B., KILLICK-KENDRICK, R. & GARNHAM, P. C. C. 1974. The coccidial nature and life-cycle of *Sarcocystis*. *J. trop. Med. Hyg.* **77:** 248–259.
COATNEY, G. R. 1936. A check-list and host-list of the genus *Haemoproteus*. *J. Parasit.* **22:** 88–105.
COATNEY, G. R. & ROUDABUSH, R. L. 1936. A catalog and host-index of the genus *Plasmodium*. *J. Parasit.* **22:** 338–353.
COATNEY, G. R. 1937. A catalog and host-index of the genus *Leucocytozoon*. *J. Parasit.* **23:** 202–212.
MANWELL, R. D. 1938. The identification of the avian malarias. *Am. J. trop. Med.* **18:** 565–575.
GIOVANNOLA, A. 1939. I plasmodi aviara. *Riv. Parasitol.* **3:** 1–46.
HEWITT, R. 1940. "Bird Malaria". Monographic series No. 15, 228 pp. Baltimore.
HUFF, C. G., BOYD, G. H. & MANWELL, R. D. 1942. Report of the committee on terminology of strains of avian malaria. *J. Parasit.* **28:** 250–254.
GARNHAM, P. C. C. 1966. "Malaria Parasites and other Haemosporidia". 1114 pp. Blackwell, Oxford.
BAKER, J. R., BENNETT, G. F., CLARK, G. W. & LAIRD, M. 1972. Avian blood coccidians. *Adv. Parasitol.* **10:** 1–30.
BRAY, R. S. 1957. Studies on the exo-erythrocytic cycle of the genus *Plasmodium*. *Memoir Ser. Lond. Sch. Hyg. trop. Med.* **12,** 192 pp.
GARNHAM, P. C. C. 1967. Malaria of mammals excluding man. *Adv. Parasitol.* **5:** 139–204.
GARNHAM, P. C. C. 1973. Recent research on malaria in mammals excluding man. *Adv. Parasitol.* **11:** 603–630.
KILLICK-KENDRICK, R. 1974. Parasitic protozoa of the blood of rodents: a revision of *Plasmodium berghei*. *Parasitology* **69:** 225–237.
LEVINE, N. D. & CAMPBELL, G. R. 1971. A check-list of the genus *Haemoproteus* (Apicomplexa, Plasmodiidae). *J. Protozool.* **18:** 475–484.
HSU, C. K., CAMPBELL, G. R. & LEVINE, N. D. 1973. A check-list of the species of the genus *Leucocytozoon* (Apicomplexa, Plasmodiidae). *J. Protozool.* **20:** 195–203.
FALLIS, A. M. & DESSER, S. S. 1974. On species of *Leucocytozoon*. *Adv. Parasitol.* **12.** 1–67.
LANDAU, I. 1973. Diversité des mécanismes assurant la pérennité de l'infection chez les sporozoaires coccidiomorphes. *Mem. Mus. natn. Hist. nat., Paris* (A). **77:** 1–62.
LAINSON, R., LANDAU, I. & SHAW, J. J. 1971. On a new family of non-pigmented parasites in the blood of reptiles: Garniidae fam. nov. (Coccidiida, Haemosporidiidea). Some species of the new genus *Garnia*. *Int. J. Parasitol.* **1:** 241–250.

Piroplasmea

SERGENT, E., DONATIEN, A., PARROT, L. & LESTOQUARD, F. 1945. "Études sur les Piroplasmoses Bovines. 816 pp. Institut Pasteur d'Algérie.
NEITZ, W. O. 1956. Classification, transmission and biology of piroplasms of domestic animals. *Ann. N.Y. Acad. Sci.* **64:** 56–111.
JAKOWSKA, S. & NIGRELLI, R. F. 1956. *Babesioma* gen. nov. and other babesioids in erythrocytes of cold blooded vertebrates. *Ann. N.Y. Acad. Sci.* **64:** 112–127.
RIEK, R. F. 1968. Babesiosis. In "Infectious Blood Diseases of Man and Animals" 2, (D. WEINMAN and M. RISTIC, eds.), **2,** pp. 219–268. Academic Press, New York & London.
BARNETT, S. F. 1968. Theileriasis. In "Infectious Blood Diseases of Man and

Animals" (D. WEINMAN and M. RISTIC, eds.), **2**, pp. 269–328. Academic Press, New York, & London.
LEVINE, N. D. 1971. Taxonomy of the piroplasms. *Trans. Am. microsc. Soc.* **90**: 2–33.
NEITZ, W. O. 1957. Theileriosis, gonderioses and cytauxzoonoses. *Onderstepoort J. vet. Res.* **27**: 275.

CNIDOSPORA

Myxosporidea

KUDO, R. R. 1920. Studies on Myxosporidia. A synopsis of genera and species of Myxosporidia. *Illinois biol. Monogr.* **5**: 1–265.
KUDO, R. R. 1933. A taxonomic consideration of Myxosporidia. *Trans. Am. microsc. Soc.* **52**: 195–216.
KUDO, R. R. 1934. Studies on some protozoan parasites of fishes of Illinois (Myxosporidia). *Illinois biol. Monogr.* **13**: 1–44.
TRIPATHI, Y. R. 1949. Some new Myxosporidia from Plymouth with a proposed new classification of the order. *Parasitology* **39**: 110–118.
KABATA, Z. 1962. Five new species of Myxosporidia from marine fishes. *Parasitology* **52**: 177–186.
HOFFMAN, G. L., PUTZ, R. E. & DUNBAR, C. E. 1965. Studies on *Myxosoma cartilaginis* n.sp. of centrarchid fish and a synopsis of the *Myxosoma* of North American freshwater fishes. *J. Protozool.* **12**: 319–332.
MITCHELL, L. G. 1967. *Myxidium macrocheili* n.sp. (Cnidospora, Myxidiidae) from the largescale sucker *Catostomus macrocheilus* and a synopsis of the *Myxidium* of North American freshwater vertebrates. *J. Protozool.* **14**: 415–424.
JANISZWESKA, J. 1955. Actinomyxidia: morphology, ecology, history of investigations, systematics, development. *Actua parasit. pol.* **2**: 406–433, figs.
JANISZWESKA, J. 1957. Actinomyxidia. II. New systematics, sexual cycle, descriptions of new genera and species. *Zoologica Pol.* **8**: 3–34.
SPRAGUE, V. 1963. Revision of genus *Haplosporidium* and restoration of genus *Minchinia* (Haplosporidia, Haplosporidiidae). *J. Protozool.* **10**: 263–266.

Microsporidea

KUDO, R. R. 1924. A biologic and taxonomic study of the Microsporidia. *Illinois biol. Monogr.* **9**: 1–268.
JIROVEC, O. 1936. Zur Kenntnis von in Oligochäten parasitierenden Microsporidien aus der Familie Mrazekidae. *Arch. Protistenk.* **87**: 314–344.
JIROVEC, O. 1943. Revision der Simulienlarven parasitierenden Microsporidien. *Zool. Anz.* **142**: 173–179.
PUTZ, R. E., HOFFMAN, G. L. & DUNBAR, C. E. 1965. Two new species of *Plistophora* (Microsporidea) from North American fish with a synopsis of Microsporidea of freshwater and euryhaline fishes. *J. Protozool.* **12**: 228–236.
WEISER, J. 1961. Die Microsporidien als Parasiten des Insekten. *Monogrm angew. Ent.* **17**.
THOMSON, H. M. 1960. A list and brief description of Microsporidia infecting insects. *J. Insect. Path.* **2**: 346.
GASSOUMA, M. S. S. 1972. Microsporidian parasites of *Simulium ornatum* Mg in south England. *Parasitology* **65**: 27–45.
SPRAGUE, V. & VAVRA, J. "Biology and Systematics of the Microsporidia". In press. Academic Press; New York & London.

MESOZOA

This group is very little known in British waters; the following references have been used to identify 3 reported species

GENERAL

GRASSÉ, P.-P. & CAULLERY, N. 1961. Mesozoa. In "Traité de Zoologie: Anatomie, Systématique, Biologie". (P.-P. Grassé, ed.), 4(1): 693–729 figs.

DICYEMIDA

HYMAN, L. H. 1940. "The Invertebrates. I. Protozoa through Ctenophora". 235 pp., 68 figs. McGraw-Hill, New York.
For the species *Pseudicyema truncatum* Whitman, known from Plymouth, infesting the kidney of all adult *Sepia officinalis* examined.

ORTHONECTIDA

ATKINS, D. 1933. *Rhopalura granosa* sp.nov., an orthonectid parasite of a Lamellibranch, *Heteranomia squamula* L., with a note on its swimming behaviour. *J. mar. biol. Ass. U.K.* 19: 233–52.
NERESHEIMER, E. 1933. Mesozoa. *Tierwelt N.- u. Ostsee* 2h: 10 pp.
Rhopalura ophiocomae Giard, from Port Erin, Isle of Man.

PORIFERA

About 233 British species, of which 5 are fresh water

GENERAL

BOWERBANK, J. S. 1864–82. "A Monograph of the British Spongiadae". 4 vols. lxxxii + 1295 pp., 96 pls., Ray Society, London.
HANITSCH, R. 1894. Revision of the generic nomenclature and classification in Bowerbank's "British Spongiadae". *Proc. Trans. Lpool biol. Soc.* 8: 173–206.
BOROJEVIC, R., FRY. W. G., JONES. W. C., LÉVI. C., RASMONT. R., SARA. M. & VACELET. J. 1968(1967). Mise au point actuelle de la terminologie des éponges. *Bull. Mus. Natn. Hist. Nat. Paris.* (2) 39(6): 1224–1235.
A reassessment of the terminology for sponges.
BRIEN, P., LÉVI, C., SARA, M., TUZET, O. & VACELET, J. 1973. Spongiaires. Anatomie, Physiologie, Systématique, Ecologie. In "Traité de Zoologie" (P.-P. Grassé, ed.) 3(1), 716 pp., 484 figs., 2 col. pls. Masson & Cie, Paris.
FRY, W. G., ed. 1970. The biology of the Porifera. *Symp. zool. Soc. Lond.* 25, xxviii + 512 pp., text-figs.
HYMAN, L. H. 1940. Metazoa of the cellular grade of construction — Phylum Porifera, the Sponges. In "The Invertebrates: Protozoa through Ctenophora". Vol. 1. McGraw-Hill, New York & London.
Sponges pp. 284–364, text-figs.
MINCHIN, E. A. 1900. Sponges. Phylum Porifera. In "A Treatise on Zoology. Part II. The Porifera and Coelenterata" (E. R. Lankester, ed.). Adam & Charles Black, London.
Sponges, pp. 178, 97 figs.
VOSMAER, G. C. J. 1882–1886, published title, 1887. "Dr H. G. Bronn's Klassen

und Ordnungen der Spongien (Porifera) wissenschaftlich dargestellt in Wort und Bild". xii + 499 pp., 34 pls. Leipzig & Heidelberg.

FRESHWATER

PENNY, J. T. & RACEK, A. A. 1968. Comprehensive revision of a worldwide collection of freshwater sponges (Porifera: Spongillidae). *Bull. U.S. natn. Mus.* **272**: vi + 184 pp., 15 pls.

SIMON, L. 1967. Sponges. In "Limnofauna Europaea. Eine Zusammenstellung aller die europäischen Binnengewässer bewohnenden mehrzelligen Tierarten mit Angaben über ihre Verbreitung und Ökologie" (J. Illies, ed.). xv + 473 pp., text-figs. Gustav Fisher, Stuttgart.

STEPHENS, J. 1920. The Fresh-water sponges of Ireland. *Proc. R. Ir. Acad.* **35**: 205–254, 4 pls.

MARINE

ARNDT, W. 1935. Porifera. *Tierwelt N.-u. Ostsee* **3a**: 1–140, 239 figs.

BOROJEVIC, R., CABIOCH, L. & LÉVI, C. 1968. Spongiaires. In "Inventaire de la Faune Marine de Roscoff". 44 pp. Éditions de la Station Biologique, Roscoff.

BURTON, M. 1930. Additions to the sponge fauna at Plymouth. *J. mar. biol. Ass. U.K.* **16**: 489–507, 9 figs.

BURTON, M. 1935. Notes on British sponges with a description of a new genus and species. *Ann. Mag. nat. Hist.* (10) **15**: 651–653.

BURTON, M. 1947. The identity of *Halichondria albescens* Johnston and *Hymeniacidon albescens* Bowerbank. *Ann. Mag. nat. Hist.* (11) **14**: 252–256.

BURTON, M. 1947. Notes on the sponge *Haliclona indistincta* (Bowerbank). *Ann. Mag. nat. Hist.* (11) **14**: 369–372.

BURTON, M. 1948. The ecology and natural history of *Tethya aurantium* Pallas. *Ann. Mag. nat. Hist.* (12) **1**: 122–130.

BURTON, M. 1948. The synonymies of *Haliclona angulata* T&$\frac{1}{8}$(Bowerbank) and *H. arcoferus* Vosmaer. *Ann. Mag. nat. Hist.* (12) **1**: 273–284.

BURTON, M. 1950. The synonymy and distribution of *Myxilla fimbriata* (Bowerbank), with notes on other related species of sponges. *Ann. Mag. nat. Hist.* (12) **3**: 888–892.

BURTON, M. 1953. *Suberites domuncula* (Olivi); its synonymy, distribution, and ecology. *Bull. Br. Mus. nat. Hist., Zool.* 1(12): 353–378.

BURTON, M. 1956. The sponges of West Africa. *Atlantide Rep.* **4**: 111–147, 4 figs.

BURTON, M. 1959. Spongia. *Zoology Iceland.* **2** (3–4): 1–71, 1 fig.

BURTON, M. 1963. "A revision of the classification of the calcareous sponges. With a catalogue of the specimens in the British Museum (Natural History)". 693 pp., 375 figs. British Museum (Natural History), London.

LUNDBECK, W. 1902, 1905, 1910. Porifera. *Dan. Ingolf Exped.* 1902, Homorrhaphidae & Heterorrhaphidae, **6** (1): 1–108, 19 pls.; 1905, Desmacidonidae (pars), **6**(2): 1–219, 20 pls; 1910, Desmacidonidae (pars), **6**(3): 1–124, 11 pls.

STEPHENS, J. 1912. Marine Porifera. Clare Island Survey, Pt. 59. *Proc. R. Ir. Acad.*, **31**: 1–42, 1 pl.

STEPHENS, J. 1915. Sponges of the coasts of Ireland. I. The Triaxonida and part of the Tetraxonida. *Scient. Invest. Fish. Brch Ire.* (1914) **4**: 1–43, 5 pls.

STEPHENS, J. 1917. Sponges collected by the dredging expeditions of the Royal Irish Academy... *Proc. R. Ir. Acad.* **34B**(1): 1–16, 1 pl.

STEPHENS, J. 1921. Sponges of the coast of Ireland. II. The Tetraxonida (concluded). *Scient. Invest. Fish. Brch Ire.* (1920) **2**: 1–75, 6 pls.

TOPSENT, E. 1894–1900. Étude monographique des Spongaires de France. *Arch.*

Zool. exp. gen. (Paris), 1894, Tetractinellida (3) **2**: 259–400, 6 pls.; 1896 Carnosa (3)**3**: 493–590, 3 pls.; 1900, Monaxonida (Hadromerina). (3)**8**: 331, 8 pls.
TOPSENT, E. 1924. Révision des *Mycale* de l'Europe occidentale. *Annls. Inst. océanogr. Monaco* (NS) **1**(3): 77–118, 16 figs.

COELENTERATA (= CNIDARIA)

About 270 British species

GENERAL

KRAMP, P. L. 1935. Polypdyr (Coelenterata). I. Ferskvands-polypper og Goplepolypper. *Danm. Fauna* **41**: 1–207, 81 figs. (in Danish).
KRAMP, P. L. 1937. Polypdyr (Coelenterata). II. Gopler. *Danm. Fauna* **43**: 1–233: 90 figs. (in Danish).
CARLGREN, O. 1945. Polypdyr (Coelenterata). III. Koraldyr. *Danm. Fauna* **51**: 1–167, 75 figs. (in Danish).
HYMAN, L. 1940. "The Invertebrates: Protozoa through Ctenophora". 726 pp. McGraw Hill, New York & London.
LELOUP, E. 1952. Coelentérés. *Faune Belg.*; 283 pp., 160 figs.
HARDY, A. C. 1956. "The Open Sea. Its Natural History. Part one: The World of Plankton". 335 pp., 93 figs. 24 pls. Collins, London.

Illustrations of common planktonic forms likely to occur in British waters.

KRAMP, P. L. 1961. Synopsis of the medusae of the world. *J. mar. biol. Ass. U.K.* **40**: 1–469.

No illustrations; includes diagnoses of medusa stages of all species and higher taxa, excepting *Velella,* for which see Brinckmann-Voss, 1970. Includes the sessile Stauromedusae.

Eales (1961) and Barrett & Yonge (1958) see above p. 3 are useful for identifying intertidal species (the latter particularly for the intertidal hydroids). The *Fiches d'Identification* and Newell & Newell (1963) cover planktonic coelenterates whereas the *'Tierwelt der Nord- und Ostsee'* series deals with all coelenterates.

HYDROZOA

GENERAL

NAUMOV, D. V. 1969. Hydroids and hydromedusae of the U.S.S.R. *Fauna SSSR* **70**, 660 pp., 463 figs., 30 pls. Israel Program for Scientific Translations, No. 5108.

Some overlap with northern European fauna, providing descriptions of many British species.

"Hydras" (Hydridae and Actinulida)

EWER, R. F. 1948. A review of the Hydridae, and two new species from Natal. *Proc. Zool. Soc. Lond.* **118**: 226–244.
GRAYSON, R. F. 1971. The freshwater hydras of Europe. *Arch. Hydrobiol.* **68**: 436–449.

Synopsis of described *Hydra* species.

MAXWELL, T. 1972. The freshwater hydras of Europe. 2. Description of *Hydra graysoni* sp.nov. [From N.E. England). *Arch. Hydrobiol.* **69**: 547–556.
BALL, I. R. 1967. Notes on the morphology and taxonomy of three hydras from a rheocrene spring at Ashwell (Hertfordshire). *Naturalist, Hull* **1967**: 81–88.

GRAYSON, R. F. & HAYES, A. D. 1968. The British freshwater hydras. *Countryside* **20**: 539–546.
  Probably the best available identification guide to British freshwater hydras.
SWEDMARK, B. & TEISSIER, G. 1966. The Actinulida and their evolutionary significance. *Symp. zool. Soc. Lond.* **16**: 119–133. (Interstitial forms).
CLAUSEN, C. 1971. Interstitial Cnidaria: Present status of their systematics and ecology. *Smithson. Contr. Zool.* **76**: 1–8.
  Review. See also Delamare-Deboutteville, p.2 above (interstitial forms) and Clegg, J., p.4 above (coloured illustrations of *Hydra*).

Hydroids and Hydromedusae

HINCKS, T. 1868. "A History of the British Hydroid Zoophytes". 2 vols. lxviii + 338 pp., 67 pls + 45 woodcuts. J. van Voorst, London.
  Outdated but well illustrated.
ALLMAN, G. J. 1871–72. "A Monograph of the Gymnoblastic or Tubularian Hydroids". 2 vols., 450 pp., 23 pls. Ray Society, London.
BROCH, H. 1928. Hydrozoa. I. *Tierwelt N.- und Ostsee* **3b**: 1–100, 105 figs.
  Key to species.
VERWOORT, W. 1946. Hydrozoa (C I). A. Hydropolypen. *Fauna Ned.* **14**: 1–336, figs. (in Dutch).
HAMOND, R. 1957. Notes on the Hydrozoa of the Norfolk coast. *J. Linn. Soc. (Zool.)* **43**: 294–324, 26 figs, 1 pl.
  Notes on several species. See next reference also.
HAMOND, R. 1963. Further notes on the Hydrozoa of the Norfolk coast. *Ann. Mag. nat. Hist.* (13)**6**: 659–670.
KRAMP, P. L. 1959. The hydromedusae of the Atlantic Ocean and adjacent waters. *Dana Rep.* **46**: 1–283, 335 figs, 2 pls.
TOTTON, A. K. 1965. "A Synopsis of the Siphonophora". 230 pp., 153 figs., 40 pls. British Museum (Natural History), London.
  Descriptions and illustrations of all species.
REES, W. J. & ROWE, M. 1969. Hydroids of the Swedish west coast. *Acta R. Soc. scient. litt. gothoburg.* **3**: 1–24.
  Species list only.
BRINCKMANN-VOSS, A. 1970. Anthomedusae/Athecatae (Hydrozoa, Cnidaria) of the Mediterranean. Part I. Capitata. *Fauna Flora Golfo Napoli* **39**: 1–96, 106 text-figs., 11 pls. Includes several forms found further north, notably *Velella*.
RUSSELL, F. S. 1953. "The Medusae of the British Isles. Anthomedusae, Leptomedusae, Limnomedusae, Trachymedusae and Narcomedusae". 319 figs., 35 pls. Cambridge University Press.
  Medusa-producing forms only. Supplement in Russell, 1970 (see under Scyphozoa).
BOUILLON, J. 1971. Sur quelques hydroides de Roscoff. *(Dipurena simulana, Acauloides ammisatum, Stylactis claviformis, Thecodium brieni, Lafoeina vilaevelebiti, Helgicirrha schulzei). Cah. biol. mar.* **13**: 323–364.
  Detailed descriptions of these six species.
EDWARDS, C. 1972. The hydroids and the medusae *Podocoryne areolata, P. borealis* and *P. carnea. J. mar. biol. Ass. U.K.* **52**: 97–144.
EDWARDS, C. 1973. The hydroid *Trichydra pudica* and its medusa *Pochella polynema. J. mar. biol. Ass. U.K.* **53**: 87–92.
EDWARDS, C. 1973. The medusa *Modeeria rotunda* and its hydroid *Stegopoma fastigiatum,* with a review of *Stegopoma* and *Stegolaria. J. mar. biol. Ass. U.K.* **53**: 573–600.

EDWARDS, C. 1973. The medusa *Mitrocomella polydiademata* and its hydroid. *J. mar. biol. Ass. U.K.* **53**: 601–607.

EDWARDS, C. & HARVEY, S. M. 1975. The hydroids *Clava multicornis* and *Clava squamata*. *J. mar. biol. Ass. U.K.* **55**: 879–886.

Recognise *C. multicornis* only.

CORNELIUS, P. F. S. 1975. The hydroid species of *Obelia* (Coelenterata, Hydrozoa: Campanulariidae), with notes on the medusa stage. *Bull. Br. Mus. nat. Hist.* (Zool.) **28**: 249–293.

CORNELIUS, P. F. S. 1975. A revision of the species of Lafoeidae and Haleciidae (Coelenterata: Hydroida) recorded from Britain and nearby seas. *Bull. Br. Mus. nat. Hist.* (Zool.), **28**: 373–426.

CORNELIUS, P. F. S. 1978. A revision of the species of Sertulariidae (Coleneterata: Hydroida) recorded from Britain and nearby seas. *Bull. Br. Mus. nat. Hist.* (Zool.), **34**.

Barrett & Yonge (1958) is adequate for most intertidal Hydrozoa. See also Kramp (1935) and Leloup (1952); and Russell (1970, appendix) for literature between 1953 and 1970.

SCYPHOZOA

Scyphomedusae

RUSSELL, F. S. 1970. "The Medusae of the British Isles. II. Pelagic Scyphozoa, with a supplement to the first volume on Hydromedusae". 283 pp., 102 figs., 15 pls. Cambridge University Press.

Most useful work on British planktonic Scyphozoa. See also Hardy (1956) and Kramp (1961) (above, p. 20).

Stauromedusae

NAUMOV, D. V. 1961. Scyphomedusae of the seas of the U.S.S.R. *Fauna SSSR* **75**, 98 pp., text-figs. 1–72, pls. 1–111. (In Russian; translation of Stauromedusae chapter in library of Marine Biological Assocation, Plymouth).

For *Lucernaria quadricornis, Lucernariopsis campanulata, Haliclystus auricula* and *H. salpinx* (as *Octomanus monstrosus*).

BERRILL, N. J. 1962. The biology of three New England Stauromedusae, with a description of a new species. *Can. J. Zool.* **40**: 1249–1262.

For *Halyclistus salpinx:* the species occurs at Bergen, possibly also in Orkney and Shetland and perhaps on the mainland north coast of Scotland; and for *Lucernaria quadricornis*.

CLARK, H. J. 1878. Lucernariae and their allies. *Smithson. Contr. Knowl.* **2**(2): 1–30. (For *H. auricula).*

EALES, N. B. 1938. *Lucernaria discoides,* a new species from the Channel Islands. *J. mar. biol. Ass. U.K.* **23**: 167–170. For *Lucernariopsis campanulata* as *Lucernaria discoides.*

HAECKEL, E. 1881. Report on the deep-sea medusae dreged by H.M.S. Challenger during the years 1873–1876. *Rep. scient. Results Voy. Challenger, Zoology* **4**(12): cv + 154 pp.

For *Lucernaria bathyphila.*

JOHNSTON, G. 1838. "A History of the British Zoophytes". 341 pp. Lizars, Edinburgh (2nd edn., J. van Voorst, London, 1847, 2 vols.).

For *Craterolophus convolvulus* as *Lucernaria campanulata.*

SARS, M. 1846. "Fauna littoralis Norvegiae, oder Beschreibung und Abbildungen neuer oder wenig bekannten Seethiere, nebst Beobachtungen über die Organisation, Lebensweise u. Entwicklung derselben". Vol. 1. Christiania (Oslo).

Pp. 1-94 for *Depastrum cyathiforme* (as *Lucernaria cyathiformis*) and *L. quadricornis*.
See also Barrett & Yonge (1958) for four intertidal species; and Kramp (1961) for specific diagnoses (without illustrations).

ANTHOZOA

GENERAL

PAX, F. 1934, 1936. Anthozoa. *Tierwelt N.- und Ostsee* **3e**: 1-317, 211 figs.
CARLGREN, O. 1945. See above p. 20.

Octocorallia (= Alcyonaria)
There is no work covering all British representatives.

HERDMAN, W. A. 1895. Note upon the yellow variety of *Sarcodictyon catenata* Forbes, with remarks upon the genus and its species. *Proc. Trans. Lpool biol. Soc.* **9**: 163-168, 1 pl.
HICKSON, S. J. 1901. *Alcyonium. Lpool mar. biol. Cmte Mem.* **5**: 1-22, pls 1-2. (Also published in *Proc. Trans. Lpool. biol. Soc.* **15**: 92-113 + 3 pls.)
RENOUF, L. P. W. 1931. On a new species of alcyonarian, *Parerythropodium hibernicum. Acta zool., Stock* **12**: 205-223, 28 figs.

Zoantharia

Ceriantharia

LELOUP, E. 1952. See p. 20, for *Cerianthus lloydi*.
BRATTSTRÖM, H. 1957. *Branchiocerianthus norvegicus* n.sp. from the Hardanger Fjord, western Norway. *Univ. Bergen Arb.* **19**(6): 1-10.

Zoanthidea

HADDON, A. C. & SHACKLETON, A. M. 1891. A revision of the British species of Actiniae. Part II. The Zoantheae. *Scient. Trans. R. Dubl. Soc.* (2) **4**: 609-672, 3 pls.

Actiniaria

STEPHENSON, T. A. 1928, 1935. "British Sea Anemones" 2 vols. 574 pp., 33 pls. Ray Society, London.
MANUEL, R. L. 1975. A new sea-anemone from a brackish lagoon in Sussex, *Edwardsia ivelli* sp. nov. *J. nat. Hist.* **9**: 705-711.
WILLIAMS, R. B. 1975. A redescription of the brackish-water sea-anemone *Nematostella vectensis* Stephenson, with an appraisal of congeneric species. *J. nat. Hist.* **9**: 51-64.
   Barrett & Yonge (1958) and Campbell (1976), see p. 3, treat many intertidal species.

Scleractinia

BEST, M. 1969. Étude systématique et écologique des madréporaires de la région de Banyuls-sur-Mer (Pyrénées-Orientales). *Vie Milieu* (A) **20**: 293-325.
   Includes all species recorded from British waters except *Spherotrochus andrewianus*, for which see next entry.
ZIBROWIUS, H. 1976. "Les scléractinaires de la Mediterranée et de l'Atlantique nord-oriental". Institut Océanographique, Monaco.

CTENOPHORA

KRUMBACH, T. 1927. *Ctenophora. Tierwelt N.- und Ostsee* **3f:** 1–50, 27 figs.
LILEY, R. 1958. Ctenophora. *Fich. Ident. Zooplancton* **82:** 1–5, 5 figs.
See Cnidaria references: Kramp (1937), Hardy (1956) and Hyman (1940), the last includes most North Atlantic genera.

PLATYHELMINTHES

GENERAL

HYMAN, L. H. 1951. "The Invertebrates" Vol. 2. "Platyhelminthes and Rhynchocoela. The acoelomate Bilateria". viii + 550 pp., 208 figs. McGraw-Hill, New York, Toronto, London.
GRASSÉ, P.-P., ed. 1961. "Traité de Zoologie: Anatomie, Systématique, Biologie". Vol. 4(1). "Platyhelminthes", pp. 21–692 (addendum: pp 887–895). Masson & Cie, Paris.

TURBELLARIA

GENERAL   About 100 British species

GRAFF, L. von 1882. "Monographie der Turbellarien". Vol. 1. 441 pp., 20 pls. Leipzig.
SOUTHERN, R. 1936. Turbellaria of Ireland. *Proc. R. Ir. Acad.* **43B**(5): 43–72.

Rhabdocoelida

GENERAL

GAMBLE, F. W. 1893. Contributions to a knowledge of British marine Turbellaria. *Q. Jl microsc. Sci.* **34:** 433–528, 3 pls.
GRAFF, L. von 1905. Acoela. *Tierreich* **23,** 35 pp., 8 figs.
GRAFF, L. von 1913. Rhabdocoela. *Tierreich* **35,** 484 pp., 394 figs.
LUTHER, A. 1960. Die Turbellarian Ostfennoskandiens. I. Acoela, Catenulida. *Fauna fenn.* **7:** 1–155, 39 figs., 1 pl.
  Keys to genera and descriptions of species.
LUTHER, A. 1962. Die Turbellarien Ostfennoskandiens. III. Neorhabdocoela 1. Dalyellioida, Typhlopanoida: Brysophlebidae und Trigonostomidae. *Fauna fenn.* **12:** 1–69, 29 figs.
  Keys to genera and descriptions of species.
LUTHER, A. 1963. Die Turbellarien Ostfennoskandiens. IV. Neorhabdocoela 2. Typhloplanoida: Typhloplanidae, Solenopharyngidae und Carcharodopharyngidae. *Fauna fenn.* **16:** 1–163, 17 figs., 2 pls.
KARLING, T. G. 1962. Die Turbellarien Ostfennoskandiens. V. Neorhabdocoela 3. Kalyptorhynchia. *Fauna fenn.* **17:** 1–59, 126 figs.

FRESHWATER

GRAFF, L. von 1909. *Süsswasserfauna Dtl.* **19,** 94 pp., 120 figs.
STEINMANN, P. & BRESSLAU, E. 1913. "Die Strudelwürmer. Mongraphien einheimischer Tiere". Vol. 5. 380 pp., 156 figs., 2 pls. Klinkhardt, Leipzig.
YOUNG, J. O. 1970. British and Irish freshwater Microturbellaria: historical records, new records and a key for their identification. *Arch. Hydrobiol.* **67**(2): 210–241, 4 figs.

MARINE

BOADEN, P. J. S. 1963. The interstitial Turbellaria Kalyptorhynchia from some North Wales beaches. *Proc. zool. Soc., Lond.* **141**: 173–205, 41 figs.
BOADEN, P. J. S. 1963. The interstitial fauna of some North Wales beaches. *J. mar. biol. Ass. U.K.* **43**: 79–96, 1 fig.

Tricladida

LUTHER, A. 1961. Die Turbellarien Ostfennoskandiens. II. Tricladida. *Fauna fenn.* **2**: 1–42, 3 pls.

FRESHWATER

BALL, I. R. 1968. "The Freshwater Triclads of Wicken Fen". Guides to Wicken Fen No. 6. 4 pp. National Trust Wicken Fen Local Committee, Cambridge.
BALL, I. R., REYNOLDSON, T. B. & WARWICK, T. 1969. The taxonomy, habitat and distribution of the freshwater triclad *Planaria torva* (Platyhelminthes: Turbellaria) in Britain. *J. Zool., Lond.* **157**(1): 99–123, 9 figs.
REYNOLDSON, T. B. 1967. A key to the British species of freshwater triclads. *Scient. Publs. Freshwat. biol. Ass.* **23**, 28 pp., 7 figs.

MARINE

BÖHMIG, L. 1906. Tricladenstudien. I. Tricladida Maricola. *Z. wiss. Zool.* **81**: 344–504, 8 pls.
All species described up to 1906.
WILHELMI, J. 1909. Tricladen. *Fauna Flora Golf. Neapel* **32**, 405 pp., 16 pls. Friedländer, Berlin.
All species described up to 1909.
HARTOG, C. Den 1968. Marine triclads of the Plymouth area. *J. mar. biol. Ass. U.K.* **48**: 209–223, 2 figs.

TERRESTRIAL

PANTIN, C. F. A. 1950. Locomotion in British terrestrial nemertines and planarians: with a discussion on the identity of *Rhynchodemus bilineatus* (Mecznikow) in Britain, and on the name *Fasciola terrestris* O. F. Müller. *Proc. Linn. Soc., Lond.* **162**(1): 23–37, 4 figs, 2 pls.
PANTIN, C. F. A. 1953. On the name of the ground fluke *Fasciola terrestris* O. F. Müller, on *Othelosoma symondsi* Gray, and on the genus *Amblyplana* von Graff. *J. Linn. Soc. Lond.* (Zool.) **42** no. 285: 207–218, 1 fig., 3 pls.

Polycladida

LANG, A. 1884. Die Polycladen (Seeplanarien) des Golfes von Neapel . . . . . *Fauna Flora Golf. Neapel* **2**, 688 pp., 39 pls.
Descriptions of all species.
BOCK, S. 1913. Studien über Polycladen. *Zool. Bidr. Uppsala* **2**: 31–343. 8 pls.

MONOGENEA

GENERAL   Number of British species not known

BYCHOWSKY, B. E. 1961. "Monogenetic Trematodes. Their systematics and phylogeny". (Hargis, W. J., ed., translated by P. C. Oustinoff.) xx + 627 pp., 315 figs. American Institute of Biological Sciences, Washington.

HARGIS, W. J. et al. 1969. Bibliography of the monogenetic trematode literature of the world, 1758 to 1969. *Spec. Sci. Rep. Virginia Inst. mar. Sci.* **55**, v + 195 pp. Supplement I with errata. iv + 13 pp., 1970.

SPROSTON, N. G. 1947. A synopsis of the monogenetic Trematodes. *Trans. zool. Soc., Lond.* **25**(4): 185–600.

Diagnoses, keys to suborders, families, genera. Lists species with references to literature. World host-list, distribution. List British species, with hosts.

YAMAGUTI, S. 1963. "Systema helminthum. IV. Monogenea and Aspidocotylea". viii + 699 pp., 134 pls. Interscience Publishers, New York & London.

OF FRESHWATER FISHES

BYCHOWSKAYA-PAVLOVSKAYA, I. E., et al. 1962. "Key to Parasites of Freshwater Fish of the U.S.S.R." [Transl.] Akad. Nauk SSSR. Zool. Inst., Leningrad. English translation: Israel Program for Scientific Translations, Jerusalem, 1964, 919 pp., 1628 figs.

CHAPPELL, L. H. & OWEN, R. W. 1969. A reference list of parasite species recorded from freshwater fish from Great Britain and Ireland. *J. nat. Hist.* **3**: 197–216.

KENNEDY, C. R. 1974. A checklist of British and Irish freshwater fish parasites with notes on their distribution. *J. Fish. Biol.* **6**: 613–644.

MALMBERG, G. 1970. The excretory systems and the marginal hooks as a basis for the systematics of *Gyrodactylus* (Trematoda, Monogenea). *Ark. Zool.* **23**: 1–235, 40 figs., 8 pls.

OF OTHER BRITISH VERTEBRATES

DAWES, B. 1947. "The Trematoda of British Fishes". viii + 364 pp. Ray Society, London.

Key to families and higher groups, diagnoses. Short descriptions of many species. Host-list.

COX, F. E. G. 1971. Parasites of British amphibians. *J. biol. Educ.* **5**: 35–51.

Popular survey with keys.

Trematoda (Digenea and Aspidocotylea)

GENERAL   Number of British species not known

DAWES, B. 1946. "The Trematoda, with special reference to British and other European Forms". xvi + 644 pp., 81 figs. Cambridge University Press.

Diagnoses, key to suborders, families, genera. Short descriptions of many species.

SKRJABIN, K. I., ed. 1947–74. "Trematodes of Animals and Man. Essentials of Trematology". [Transl.] 25 vols. Akad. Nauk SSSR., Moscow.

Series of monographs on trematode classification. The Israel Program for Scientific Translations has published two in English, vols. 17 (1964) and 18 (1965).

SKRJABIN, K. I. et al. 1964. "Keys to the Trematodes of Animals and Man". (H. P. Arai, ed., translated by R. W. Dooley). xvi + 351 pp., 919 figs. University of Illinois Press, Urbana.

YAMAGUTI, S. 1971. "Synopsis of Digenetic Trematodes of Vertebrates". Vol. 1, 1074 pp. Vol. 2, 1796 pp. Keigaku Publishing, Tokyo.

OF EUROPEAN FRESHWATER FISHES

BYCHOWSKAYA-PAVLOVSKAYA, I. E., et al. 1962. See above.

CHAPPELL, L. H. & OWEN, R. W. 1969. See above.

DAWES, B. 1947. See above p. 26.
KENNEDY, C. R. 1974. See above p. 26.
LÜHE, M. 1909. Parasitische Plattwürmer. I. Trematoda. *Süsswasserfauna Dtl.* **17**, 217 pp., 188 figs.

OF EUROPEAN MARINE HOSTS

DAWES, B. 1947. See above p. 26.
DELYAMURE, S. L. 1955. "Helminthofauna of marine mammals. (Ecology and Phylogeny)" [Transl.] Akad. Nauk SSSR., Moscow. English translation by Israel Program for Scientific Translations, Jerusalem 1968. ix + 522 pp., 240 figs.
SPREHN, C. 1933. Trematoda. *Tierwelt N.- u. Ostsee* **4c**: 1–60, 20 figs.
   Diagnoses families. List of genera (with key), species.

OF AMPHIBIANS AND REPTILES

BAYLIS, H. A. 1951. The parasitic worms of British reptiles and amphibians. "British Amphibians and Reptiles", (M. Smith, ed.), pp. 267–273. Collins, London.
COX, F. E. G. 1971. See above p. 26.
   Popular survey with keys.
WALTON, A. C. 1964. Parasites of Amphibia. *Wildl. Dis.* **39–40**, 160 pp. [on microfiche].
   Complete host-list, parasite list and bibliography.
WALTON, A. C. 1966–67. Supplemental catalog of the parasites of amphibia. *Wildl. Dis.* **48** (1966), 58 pp. [on microfiche]. *Wildl. Dis.* **50** (1967), 38 pp. [on microfiche].

OF EUROPEAN BIRDS AND MAMMALS

DUBOIS, G. 1968–70. Synopsis des Striigeidae et des Diplostomatidae (Trematoda). *Mém. Soc. neuchât. Sci. nat.* **10**(1): 1–258, 270 figs; **10**(2): 259–727, 480 figs.
SPREHN, C. E. W. 1932. "Lehrbuch der Helminthologie". 998 pp., 374 figs. Berlin.

OF MAN AND DOMESTIC ANIMALS

BAYLIS, H. A. 1929. "A Manual of Helminthology, Medical and Veterinary". 303 pp., 200 figs. Baillière, Tindall & Cox, London.
NEVEU-LEMAIRE, M. 1936. "Traité d'Helminthologie Médicale et Vétérinaire". 1515 pp., 787 figs. Vigot Frères, Paris.

CESTODA

GENERAL   Number of British species not known

DOLLFUS, R. P. 1942. Études critiques sur les Tétrarhynches du Muséum de Paris. *Arch. Mus. natn. Hist. nat. Paris* **19**: 466 pp.
JOYEUX, C. & BAER, J. G. 1936. Cestodes. *Faune Fr.* **30**, 613 pp., 569 figs.
WARDLE, R. A. & McLEOD, S. A. 1952. "The Zoology of Tapeworms". xxiv + 780 pp., 419 figs. University of Minnesota Press, Minneapolis.
YAMAGUTI, S. 1959. "Systemahelminthum. II. The Cestodes of Vertebrates". viii + 860 pp., 7 pls. Interscience Publishers, New York & London.
   Key to genera and families and lists of species.

OF FRESHWATER HOSTS

BYCHOWSKAYA-PAVLOVSKAYA, I. E. *et al.* 1962. See above p. 26.
CHAPPEL, L. H. & OWEN, R. W. 1969. See above p. 26.
KENNEDY, C. R. 1974. See above p. 26.

OF MARINE HOSTS
SPREHN, C. E. W. 1934. Cestoidea. *Tierwelt N.- u. Ostsee* **26**(4c2), 30 pp., 21 figs.

OF BIRDS AND MAMMALS
FUHRMANN, O. 1932. Les Ténias des Oiseaux. *Mém. Univ. Neuchâtel* **8**, 383 pp., 147 figs.
MEGGITT, F. J. 1924. "The Cestodes of Mammals". 282 pp. Goldston, London.
SPREHN, C. E. W. 1932. See above p. 27.
BAYLIS, H. A. 1929, See above p. 27.

NEMERTINEA
About 30–40 British species

GENERAL
GIBSON, R. 1972. "Nemerteans". 224 pp., 33 figs., 2 pls. Hutchinson, London.
GONTCHAROFF, M. 1961. In "Traité de Zoologie, Anatomie, Systématique, Biologie" (P.-P. Grassé, ed.) **4**(1), pp. 783–886, 103 figs., 3 pls. Masson & Cie, Paris.

MARINE
McINTOSH, W. C. 1873–74. "Monographs of British Annelids, Pt. I". xviii + 244 pp., 23 pls. Ray Society, London.
BÜRGER, O. 1895. Nemertinen. *Fauna Flora Golf. Neapel* **22**, 743 pp., 31 pls. Friedländer, Berlin.
BÜRGER, O. 1904. Nemertini. *Tierreich* **20**, xv + 150 pp. Berlin.
BRINKMANN, A. 1917. Die pelagischen Nemertinen. *Bergens Mus. Skr.* (n.s.) **3**(1): 1–180, 29 figs., 16 pls.
COE, W. R. 1945. Plankton of the Bermuda Oceanographic Expeditions. XI. Bathypelagic Nemerteans of the Bermuda Area and other parts of the North and South Atlantic Oceans, with evidence as to their means of dispersal. *Zoologica* **30**: 145–168, 26 figs., 2 pls.
STEPHENSON, J. 1912. The Nemertines of Millport and its Vicinity. *Trans. R. Soc. Edinb.* **48**: 1–29, 1 pl.
Several species described.
SOUTHERN, R. 1913. Clare Island Survey. Part 55. Nemertinea. *Proc. R. Ir. Acad.* **31**: 1–20, 1 pl.
Check-list of Irish species.
FRIEDRICH, H. 1936. Nemertini. *Tierwelt N.- u. Ostsee* **4d**: 1–69, 18 figs.

TERRESTRIAL
PANTIN, C. F. A. 1969. The genus *Geonemertes*. *Bull. Br. Mus. nat. Hist.* (Zool.) **18**(9): 261–310, 28 figs., frontispiece.

ASCHELMINTHES
GENERAL
HYMAN, L. H. 1951. "The Invertebrates: The Pseudocoelomate Bilateria — Phylum Aschelminthes" **3**: 53–520, 183 figs. McGraw-Hill, New York, Toronto & London.

GRASSÉ, P.-P., ed. 1965. "Traité de Zoologie: Anatomie, Systématique, Biologie". Vol. 4 (2–3). "Nemathelminthes [Nématodes — Gordiacés], Rotifères — Gastrotriches. Kinorhynques. 1497 pp. Masson & Cie, Paris.

ROTIFERA

GENERAL AND FRESHWATER
About 500 British species

BARTOS, E. 1951. The Czechoslovak Rotatoria of the Order Bdelloidea. *Vestn. csl. zool. Spol.* **15**: 241–500, 66 figs. Keys to genera and species, in English.

DONNER, J. 1965. Ordnung Bdelloidea (Rotatorien, Rädertiere). *Bestimm. Büch. Bodenfauna Europ.* **6**, 297 pp., 203 figs.

HOLLOWDAY, E. D. 1945–50. Introduction to the study of the Rotifera. I–XVII. *Microscope* (London) **5**(10): 253–256; (11): 292–295; (12): 300–306; **6**(1): 3–9; (2): 31–34; (3): 78–82; (4): 98–100; (6): 160–164; (8): 205–211; (9): 237–244; (12): 309–311; **7**(1): 2–6; (3): 65–68; (7): 169–174; (8): 197–199; (11): 287–290; (12): 322–324.

GALLIFORD, A. L. 1961–63. How to begin the study of Rotifers. Parts 1–7. *Countryside (n.s.)* **19**(4): 150–156; (5): 188–194; (6): 246–250; (7): 291–294; (8): 334–339; (9): 382–388; (10): 424–430.
   Part 7 gives a review of the literature.

HUDSON, C. T. & GOSSE, P. H. 1886–89. "The Rotifera; or Wheel-Animalcules". 2 vols. & suppl. (text and plates). 144 + 64 pp., 34 pls.

HARRING, H. K. 1913. Synopsis of the Rotatoria. *Bull. U.S. natn. Mus.* **81**, 226 pp.

DONNER, J. 1966. "Rotifers". 80 pp., 88 figs., 5 pls. Warne, London.
   This edition is a translation from the German by H. G. S. Wright. Biology and systematics with a key to genera.

VOIGT, M. 1956–57. "Rotatoria — Die Rädertiere Mitteleuropas". 2 vols. 508 pp., 27 figs., 115 pls. Borntraeger, Berlin-Nikolassee.
   Keys to orders, families, genera, species with brief descriptions.

EDMONDSON, W. T. 1959. Rotatoria. In "Freshwater Biology" (M. B. Ward and G. E. Whipple,) 2nd edn. (W. T. Edmondson, ed.), pp. 420–494, 125 figs. John Wiley & Sons, New York. Keys to genera.

MARINE AND BRACKISH WATER
Number of British species not known

REMANE, A. 1929. Rotatoria. *Tierwelt N.- u. Ostsee* **7e**, 156 pp., 198 figs.

HOLLOWDAY, E. D. 1949. A preliminary report on the Plymouth marine and brackish-water Rotifera. *J. mar. biol. Ass. U.K.* **28**: 239–253, 2 figs.

BERZINS, B. 1960. "Zooplankton Sheets", *Fich. Ident. Zooplancton*.: **84**, Synchaetidae; **85**, Trichocercidae; **86** & **87**, Brachionidae; **88**, Asplanchnidae & Synchaetidae; **89**, Testudinellidae, Conochilidae & Collothecidae.
   Short descriptions, figures and literature.

THANE-FENCHEL, A. 1968. A simple key to the genera of marine and brackish-water Rotifers. *Ophelia* **5**: 299–311, 6 figs.

GASTROTRICHA

GENERAL
Number of British species not known

BRUNSON, R. B. 1950. An introduction to the taxonomy of the Gastrotricha, with a study of eighteen species from Michigan. *Trans. Am. microsc. Soc.* **69**: 325–352.

FRESHWATER
COLLIN, A. 1912. Gastrotricha. *Süsswasserfauna Dtl.* **14:** 240–265, 33 figs.
VOIGT, M. 1958. Gastrotricha Gastrotrichen. *Tierwelt Mitteleur.* 1(4a): 1–74, 12 pls.

MARINE
REMANE, A. 1927. Gastrotricha. *Tierwelt N.- u. Ostsee* **7d**, 56 pp., 62 figs.
BOADEN, P. J. S. 1963. Marine Gastrotricha from the interstitial fauna of some North Wales beaches. *Proc. zool. Soc., Lond.* **140:** 485–502, 8 figs.
  Key to marine genera.
FORNERIS, L. 1961. Beiträge zur Gastrotrichenfauna der Nord- u. Ostsee. *Kieler Meeresforsch.* **17:** 206–218, 4 pls.
  Descriptions of species, with check list and bibliography.
HONDT, J. L. d' 1974. Clés tabulaires de déterination des genres marins de Gastrotriches. *Bull. Soc. zool. Fr.* **99:** 645–665, 7 figs.
HONDT, J. L. d' 1971. Gastrotricha. *Oceanogr. mar. Biol. Ann. Rev.* **9:** 141–192, 18 figs.

ECHINODERA (KINORHYNCHA)   About 11 British species known

CHITWOOD, B. G. 1958. The classification of the phylum Kinorhyncha. *Proc. Int. Congr. Zool.* **15:** 941–943.
HIGGINS, R. P. 1969. Indian Ocean Kinorhyncha 2. Neocentrophyidae; a new Homalorhagid family. *Proc. biol. Soc. Wash.* **82:** 113–128, 5 figs.
  Includes a key to genera of adults of the Echinoderida.
ZELINKA, K. 1928. "Monograph der Echinodera". 396 pp., 73 figs., 27 pls. Leipzig.
McINTYRE, A. D. 1962. The class Kinorhyncha (Echinoderida) in British waters. *J. mar. biol. Ass. U.K.* **42:** 503–509, 2 figs.
KRISHNASWAMY, S. 1962. Occurrence of *Echinoderella* (Echinoderida) off Plymouth. *Ann. Mag. nat. Hist.* (13) **5:** 61–63, fig.

NEMATODA

GENERAL   Number of British species not known
BAYLIS, H. A. & DAUBNEY, R. 1926. "A Synopsis of the Families and Genera of Nematoda". 274 pp. British Museum (Natural History), London.

FREE-LIVING
General

SCHNEIDER, W. 1939. Freilebende und pflanzenparasitishe Nematoden. *Tierwelt Dtl.* **36**, 260 pp., 455 figs.
GERLACH, S. A. & RIEMANN, F. 1973–74. The Bremerhaven checklist of aquatic Nematodes. *Veröff. Inst. Meeresforsch., Bremerh.,* Suppl. 4(1&2), 736 pp.
  A catalogue of Nematoda, Adenophorea excluding the Dorylaimida. Includes all families, subfamilies, genera, species and subspecies, and quotations of every contribution to these taxa in the bibliography. The marine records are complete, but freshwater and soil species less so.

Freshwater and Soil

GOODEY, T. 1963. "Soil and Freshwater Nematodes". 2nd edn. (revised and rewritten by J. B. Goodey). 576 pp., 298 figs. Methuen, London.

MEYL, A. 1960. Freilebende Nematoden. *Tierwelt Mitteleur.* **1**(5a), 164 pp., 54 pls.
  Keys to genera of soil and freshwater nematodes, brief descriptions and figures of many species from Central Europe.
CHITWOOD, B. G. & ALLEN, M. W. 1959. Nemata. In "Freshwater Biology" (M. B. Ward and G. E. Whipple), 2nd edn. (W. R. Edmondson, ed.), pp. 368–401, 23 figs. John Wiley & Sons, New York.
JÄGERSKIOLD, L. A. 1909. Freilebende Süsswassernematoden. *Süsswasserfauna Dtl.* **15**, 46 pp., 65 figs.
MICOLETZKY, H. 1925. Die Freilebenden Süsswasser- und Moornematoden Dänmarks ... *K. Danske Vidensk. Selsk. Skr.* (8) **10**(2), 256 pp., 13 pls.

Marine
SOUTHERN, R. 1914. Nemathelmia, Kinorhyncha and Chaetognatha. (Clare Island Survey, Part 54) *Proc. R. Ir. Acad.* **31**, 80 pp., 12 pls.
HOPE, W. D. & MURPHY, D. G. 1972. A taxonomic hierarchy and checklist of the genera and higher taxa of marine Nematodes. *Smithson. Contr. Zool.* **137**: iii + 101 pp.
STEKHOVEN, J. H. S. Jr. 1935. Nematoda Errantia. *Tierwelt N.- u. Ostsee* **5b**, 173 pp., 277 figs.
STEKHOVEN, J. H. S. Jr. & ADAM, W. 1931. The free-living marine Nemas of the Belgian Coast. *Mém. Mus. r. hist. nat. Belg.* **49**, 58 pp., 10 pls.
CONINCK, L. A. P. de & STEKHOVEN, J. H. S. Jr. 1933. The free-living marine Nemas of the Belgian Coast II. *Mém. Mus. r. hist. nat. Belg.* **58**, 163 pp., 163 figs.
WIESER, W. 1953–59. Free-living Marine Nematodes. (Reports of the Lund University Chile Expedition 1948–49) I–IV. *Acta. Univ. lund.* (N.F.) **49**(6): 1–155; **50**(16): 1–148; **52**(13): 1–115; **55**(5): 1–111. Containing altogether 253 figs.
  Keys to genera of world (not all marine genera covered).
WIESER, W. 1951. Untersuchungen über die algen bewohnende Mikrofauna mariner Hartböden. I. Zur Oekologie und Systematik der Nematodenfauna von Plymouth. *Öst. zool. Z.* **3**: 425–480, 16 figs.
  15 new species described which occur around the British Isles.
GERLACH, S. A. 1951. Nematoden aus der Familie der Chromadoridae von den deutschen Küsten. *Kieler Meeresforsch.* **8**: 106–132, 13 pls.
GERLACH, S. A. 1951. Revision der Metachromadoracea einer Gruppe freilebende Nematoden. *Kieler Meeresforsch* **8**: 59–75, 5 pls.
COLES, J. W. 1965. A critical review of the marine Nematode genus *Euchromadora* de Man, 1886. *Bull. Br. Mus. nat. Hist.* (Zool.) **12**(5): 157–194, 34 figs.
  Includes descriptions of five species from British waters.
WARWICK, R. M. 1970. Fourteen new species of freeliving marine nematodes from the Exe Estuary. *Bull. Br. Mus. nat. Hist.* (Zool.) **19**(4): 137–177, 16 text-figs.
BOADEN, P. J. S. 1963. The interstitial fauna of some North Wales beaches. *J. mar. biol. Ass. U.K.* **43**: 79–96, 1 fig.

PARASITIC

Of Vertebrates
YAMAGUTI, S. 1961. "Systema Helminthum". Vol. 3. "The Nematodes of Vertebrates". 2 pts. 1261 pp., 909 figs. Interscience Publishers, New York.
YORKS, W. & MAPLESTONE, P. A. 1926. "The Nematode Parasites of Vertebrates". 536 pp., 307 figs. Churchill, London. Reprint 1962. Hafner Publishing, New York.
SPREHN, C. 1961 Parasitische Nematoden. *Tierwelt Mitteleur.* **1**(5b): 1–191, 11 pls.

Of Mammals and Birds

SPREHN, C. E. W. 1932. "Lehrbuch der Helminthologie. 998 pp., 374 figs. Berlin.
HALL, M. C. 1916. Nematode parasites of mammals of the orders Rodentia, Lagomorpha and Hyracoidea. *Proc. U.S. natn. Mus.* **50,** 258 pp., 290 figs.
CRAM, E. B. 1927. Bird parasites of the nematode sub-orders Strongylata, Ascaridata and Spirurata. *Bull. U.S. natn. Mus.* **140,** 465 pp., 444 figs.
MATTRICK, D. F. 1959. On the Nematode genus *Capillaria* in British birds. *Ann. Mag. nat. Hist.* (13) **2:** 64–84, 13 figs.
BAYLIS, H. A. 1929. See above p. 27.

Of Amphibia

WALTON, A. C. 1964. See above p. 27.
WALTON, A. C. 1966–67. See above p. 27.
COX, F. E. G. 1971. See above p. 26.

Of Freshwater Hosts

LINSTOW, O. von 1909. Parasitische Nematoden. *Süsswasserfauna Dtl.* **15:** 37 pp., 80 figs.
BYCHOWSKAYA-PAVLOVSKAYA, I. E. *et al.* 1962. See above p. 26.
CHAPPELL, L. H. & OWEN, R. W. 1969. See above p. 26.
KENNEDY, C. R. 1974. See above p. 26.

Of Insects and other Invertebrates

FILIPJEV, I. N. & SHUURMANS STEKHOVEN, J. H. S. 1941. "A Manual of Agricultural Helminthology". 878 pp., 460 figs. E. J. Brill, Leiden.
LEIBERSPERGER, E. 1960. Die Oxyuroidea der europäischen Arthropoden. *Parasit. SchrReihe* **11:** 1–150, 39 figs.
WACHEK, F. 1955. Die entoparasitischen Tylenchiden. *Parasit. SchrReihe* **3,** 119 pp., 60 figs.
RÜHM, W. 1956. Die Nematoden der Ipiden. *Parasit. SchrReihe* **6,** 437 pp., 145 figs.
MENGERT, H. 1953. Nematoden und Schnecken. *Z. Morph. Ökol. Tiere* **41**(4): 311–349, figs.
Van ZWALUWENBURG, R. H. 1928. The inter-relationships of insects and roundworms. *Bull. exp. Stn. Hawaiian Sugar Planters' Ass., Honolulu, entom. Ser.* **20:** 68 pp.

Of Marine Hosts

STEKHOVEN, J. H. S. 1935. Nematoda Parasitica. *Tierwelt N.- u. Ostsee* **5c,** 47 pp., 71 figs.
DELYAMURE, S. L. 1955. See above p. 27.

Of Plants

GOODEY, T. 1933. "Plant Parasitic Nematodes and the Diseases they cause". 306 pp., 136 figs. Methuen, London.
GOODEY, J. B., FRANKLIN, M. T. & HOOPER, D. J. 1965. "T. Goodey's The Nematode Parasites of Plants Catalogued under their Hosts". 3rd edn. iv + 214 pp. Commonwealth Agricultural Bureaux, Farnham Royal, Slough.
FILIPJEV, I. N. & SCHUURMANS STEKHOVEN, J. H. S. 1941. "A Manual of Agricultural Helminthology". 878 pp., 460 figs. E. J. Brill, Leiden.
THORNE, G. 1961. "Principles of Nematology". xiv + 553 pp., figs. McGraw-Hill, New York.

NEMATOMORPHA (Gordiacea)

GENERAL — Four British species

CAMERANO, L. 1897. Monografia dei Gordii. *Memorie R. Accad. Sci. Torino* **47**: 80 pp., 3 pls.
CAMERANO, L. 1915. Revisione dei Gordii. *Memorie R. Accad. Sci. Torino* (2) **46**: 66 pp.

FRESHWATER AND SOIL

BAYLIS, H. A. 1943. Notes on the distribution of Hairworms (Nematomorpha: Gordiidae) in the British Isles. *Proc. Zool. Soc. Lond.* (B) **113**: 193–197, 1 fig.
GOODEY, T. 1963. Hairworms (Nematomorpha: Gordiidae). In "Soil and Freshwater Nematodes", 2nd edn., (revised and rewritten by J. B. Goodey), pp. 522–524, 1 fig. Methuen, London.
RITCHIE, J. 1915. Scottish hairworms ... with a key for the discrimination of the species recorded from Britain. *Scott. Nat.* **1915**: 111–115, 136–142, 255–262.
MÜLLER, G. W. 1926. Über Gordiaceen. *Z. Morph. Ökol. Tiere* **7**: 134–219, figs, 1 pl.
HEINZE, K. 1937. Die Saitenwürmer (Gordioidea) Deutchslands ... *Z. Parasitenk.* **9**: 263–344, figs.
HEINZE, K. 1941. Saitenwürmer oder Gordioidea (Nematomorpha). *Tierwelt Dtl.* **39**: 1–78, 179 figs.

MARINE

STEKHOVEN, J. H. S. 1934. Nematomorpha. *Tierwelt N.- u. Ostsee* **6f**: 1–10, 6 figs.

ACANTHOCEPHALA

GENERAL — Number of British species not known

BAER, J. G. 1961. Embranchement des Acanthocéphales. In "Traité de Zoologie: Anatomie, Systématique, Biologie" (P.-P. Grassé, ed.), vol. 4(1), pp. 731–782, 70 figs. Masson & Cie, Paris.
MEYER, A. 1932–33. Acanthocephala. *Bronn's Kl. Ordn. Tierreichs* **4** (2), 2(1–2), 582 pp., figs, 1 pl. Leipzig.
MEYER, A. 1938. Acanthocephala. *Tierwelt Mitteleur.* 1(6): 1–40, 46 figs.
SPREHN, C. 1967. Nachtrag zu "Dr. Anton Meyer — Klasse: Acanthocephala, Akanthozephalen, Kratzer". *Tierwelt Mitteleur.* 1(6) Suppl.: 1–20.
GOLVAN, Y. J. 1969. Systematique des Acanthocephales (Acanthocephala Rudolphi, 1801). Première partie. L'ordre des Palaeacanthocephala Meyer 1931, premier fascicule la super-famille des Echinorhynchoidea (Cobbold 1876) Golvan et Houin 1963. *Mém. Mus. natn. Hist. nat. Paris (Zool).* **57**: 5–373, 260 figs.
PETROCHENKO, V. I. 1965. [Acanthocephala of domestic and wild animals.] English translation: Israel Program for Scientific Translations, Jerusalem 1971. Vol. I, iii + 465 pp., 182 figs. Vol. II. iv + 478 pp., 178 figs.
YAMAGUTI, S. 1963. "Systema Helminthum". Vol. 5. "Acanthocephala". 423 pp., 855 figs. Interscience Publishers, New York. Keys to orders, families and genera, etc.

FRESHWATER HOSTS

BYCHOWSKAYA-PAVLOVSKAYA, I. E. *et al.* 1962. See above p. 26
CHAPPELL, L. H. & OWEN, R. W. 1969. See above p. 26.
KENNEDY, C. R. 1974. See above p. 26.

AMPHIBIA

COX, F. E. G. 1971. See above p. 27.

MARINE MAMMALS

DELYAMURE, S. L. 1955. See above p. 27.

PRIAPULIDA

LAND, J. van der 1970. Systematics, zoogeography, and ecology of the Priapulida. *Zool. Verh. Leiden* **112**, 118 pp., 89 figs., 5 pls.
CUENOT, L. 1922. Sipunculiens, Echiuriens, Priapuliens. *Faune Fr.* **4**: 1–30, 14 figs.
STEPHEN, A. C. 1960. British Echiurids (Echiuroidea), Sipunculids (Sipunculoidea) and Priapulids (Priapuloidea) with keys and notes for the identification of the species. *Synopses Br. Fauna* (Ser. 1) **12**, 27 pp., 18 figs.

ENTOPROCTA (KAMPTOZOA)

EGGLESTON, D. 1965. The Loxosomatidae of the Isle of Man. *Proc. zool. Soc. Lond.* **145**(4): 529–547.
EMSCHERMANN, P. 1972. Cuticular pores and spines in the Pedicellinidae and Barentsidae (Entoporcta)... *Sarsia* **50**: 7–16.
PRENANT, M. & BOBIN, G. 1956. Bryozoaires (première partie), Entoproctes, Phylactolèmes, Ctenostomes. *Faune Fr.* **60**, 117 pp., 57 figs.
RYLAND, J. S. & AUSTIN, A. P. 1960. Three species of Kamptozoa new to Britain. *Proc. zool. Soc. Lond.* **133**(3): 423–433.
NIELSEN, C. 1964. Studies on Danish Entoprocta. *Ophelia* **1**(1): 1–76.
NIELSEN, C. 1971. Entoproct life-cycles and the entoproct/ectoproct relationship. *Ophelia* **9**: 209–341.

CHAETOGNATHA

About 18 species are known from the NE Atlantic

BURFIELD, S. T. 1927. Sagitta. *L.M.B.C. Mem. typ. Br. Mar. Pl. Anim.* **28**, 96 pp., 10 figs., 12 pls.
FRASER, J. H. 1952. The Chaetognatha and other zooplankton of the Scottish area and their value as biological indicators of hydrographical conditions. *Màr. Res.* **2**, 52 pp., 4 figs., 3 pls., 21 charts.
FRASER, J. H. 1957. Chaetognatha. (First Revision). *Fich. Ident. Zooplancton* **1**, 6 pp., 18 figs.
FURNESTIN, M. L. 1957. Chaetognathes et zooplancton du secteur atlantique marocain. *Revue Trav. Inst. Pêch. marit.* **21**(1–2): 1–356, 104 figs.
KUHL, W. 1938. Chaetognatha. *Bronn's Kl. Ordn. Tierreichs* **4**(4), 2(1), 220 pp., 165 figs.
PIERROT-BULTS, A. C. 1974. Taxonomy and distribution of certain members of the "*Sagitta serratodentata*-group" (Chaetognatha). *Bijdr. Dierk.* **44**(2): 215–234, 11 figs.

PIERROT-BULTS, A. C. 1975. Taxonomy and zoogeography of *Sagitta planctonis*. *Beaufortia* **23** (297): 27–51, 14 figs.
RITTER-ZAHONY, R. 1911. Revision der Chaetognathen. *Dt. Südpol. Exped.* **13** (Zool. 5, 1): 1–71, 51 figs.

POGONOPHORA

Ten species known from areas adjacent to the British Isles

IVANOV, A. V. 1963. "Pogonophora". 479 pp., 325 figs. Academic Press, London.
SOUTHWARD, E. C. & SOUTHWARD, A. J. 1958. On some Pogonophora from the northeast Atlantic, including two new species. *J. mar. biol. Ass. U.K.* **37**: 627–632, 3 figs.
SOUTHWARD, E. C. 1959. Two new species of Pogonophora from the northeast Atlantic. *J. mar. biol. Ass. U.K.* **38**: 439–444, 2 figs.
SOUTHWARD, E. C. 1963. On a new species of *Siboglinum* (Pogonophora), found on both sides of the north Atlantic. *J. mar. biol. Ass. U.K.* **43**: 513–517, 1 fig.
WEBB, M. 1964. A new bitentaculate pogonophoran from Hardanger-fjorden, Norway. *Sarsia* **15**: 49–55.
SOUTHWARD, E. C. 1971. Pogonophora of the northwest Atlantic: Nova Scotia to Florida. *Smithsonian Contr. Zool.* **88**, 29 pp.

SIPUNCULA

About 15 sipunculan species are known from north-western European seas

THÉEL, H. 1905. Northern and arctic invertebrates in the collection of the Swedish State Museum (Riksmuseum). 1. Sipunculids. *K. svenska VetenskAkad. Handl.* **39**(1): 1–130, pls. 1–15.
   Most of the British species are included in this work, the figures of which are classic.
SOUTHERN, R. 1913. Gephyrea of the coasts of Ireland. *Scient. Invest. Fish. Brch Ire.* **1912** (3); 1–46, pls 1–7.
   A review of Irish species with descriptions of deep water forms.
CUÉNOT, L. 1922. Sipunculiens, Échiuriens, Priapuliens. *Faune Fr.* **4**: 1–29, figs. 1–14.
   Most of the British species are described.
STEPHEN, A. C. 1960. See above p. 34.
STEPHEN, A. C. & EDMONDS, S. J. 1972. "The Phyla Sipuncula and Echiura". 528 pp., 60 figs. British Museum (Natural History), London.
   A monograph with descriptions of, and keys to, all known species, many of which are illustrated. Includes synonymies.
GIBBS, P. E. 1973. On the genus *Golfingia* (Sipuncula) in the Plymouth area with a description of a new species. *J. mar. biol. Ass. U.K.* **53**: 73–86, 9 figs.
   Description of *G. rimicola* from southwest England. Key to *Golfingia* species.
GIBBS, P. E. 1977. British Sipunculans. Keys and notes for the identification of the species. *Synopses Br. Fauna n.s.* **12**, 35 pp., 13 figs.

ECHIURA

Five species are known from north-western European seas

THÉEL, H. 1906. Northern and arctic invertebrates in the collection of the Swedish State Museum (Riksmuseum) II. Priapulids, echiurids, etc. *K. svenska VetenskAkad. Handl.* **40**(4): 1–28, pls. 1–2.

BOCK, S. 1942. On the structure and affinites of *'Thalassema' lankesteri* Herdman and the classification of the Group Echiuroidea. *Göteborgs K. Vetensk.-o. VitterhSamh. Handl.* (B2) **6**(6): 1–94, 11 figs., 6 pls.

See also Sipuncula references: Southern (1913), Cuénot (1922), Stephen (1960), Stephen & Edmonds (1972).

ANNELIDA

POLYCHAETA   About 600 European species of which *c.* 500 are British

CLARK, R. B. 1960. "The Fauna of the Clyde Sea area. Polychaeta with keys to the British genera". 71 pp. Scottish Marine Biological Association, Millport.

Keys to families and genera with a list of British species.

DAY, J. H. 1967. "A monograph on the Polychaeta of Southern Africa". Part I. "Errantia". Part 2. "Sedentaria". 878 pp. British Museum (Natural History), London.

Many British species are included with useful biological and ecological notes.

ELWES, E. V. 1908. Notes on the littoral Polychaeta of Torquay. *J. mar. biol. Ass. U.K.* **8**: 197–206.

Key to the species of syllid found in the English Channel.

FAUVEL, P. 1923. Polychètes errantes. *Faune Fr.* **5**: 1–488, 181 figs.

FAUVEL, P. 1927. Polychètes sédentaires. Addenda aux errantes, archiannélides myzostomaires. *Faune Fr.* **16**: 1–494, 152 figs.

These two volumes are still the most useful books for the identification of British polychaetes.

FAUCHALD, K. 1963. Nephtyidae (Polychaeta) from Norwegian waters. *Sarsia* **13**: 1–32, 9 figs.

FAUCHALD, K. 1977. The polychaete worms, definitions and keys to the orders, families and genera. *Nat. Hist. Mus. Los Ang. Cty. Sci. Ser.* **28**, 190 pp.

GIDHOLM, L. 1966. A revision of Autolytinae (Syllidae, Polychaeta) with special reference to Scandinavian species, and with notes on external and internal morphology, reproduction and ecology. *Ark. Zool.* (2) **19**: 157–213, 31 figs.

HARTMAN, O. 1959. Catalogue of the polychaetous annelids of the world. Parts 1 and 2. *Occ. Pap. Allan Hancock Fdn* **23**: 1–628.

HARTMAN, O. 1965. Catalogue of the polychaetous annelids of the world. Supplement 1960–1965 and index. *Occ. Pap. Allan Hancock Fdn* **23** (Suppl.): 1–197.

The only comprehensive list of polychaete species available. Very useful as a synonymic index and for references to original species descriptions.

HARTMANN-SCHRÖDER, G. 1971. Annelida, Borstenwürmer, Polychaeta. *Tierwelt Dtl* **58**: 1–594, 191 figs.

The most recently available comprehensive work on the polychaetes of northern Europe. In addition to keys there are useful biological notes and drawings.

KNIGHT-JONES, P. and KNIGHT-JONES, E. W. 1977. Taxonomy and ecology of British Spirorbidae (Polychaeta). *J. mar. biol. Ass. U.K.* **57**: 453–499.

PEARSON, T. H. 1969. *Scionella lornensis* sp.n., a new terebellid (Polychaeta: Annelida) from the west coast of Scotland, with notes on the genus *Scionella* Moore, and a key to the genera of the Terebellidae recorded from european waters. *J. nat. Hist.* **3**: 509–516, 3 figs.

HOLTHE, T. 1975. "A simple key to the northern European species of terebellomorph Polychaeta." 32 pp. Scandinavian University Books, Oslo. Includes the families Pectinariidae, Ampharetidae, Trichobranchidae and Terebellidae.

OLIGOCHAETA   About 400 European species of which *c.* 150 are British

AQUATIC

BRINKHURST, R. O. & JAMIESON, B. G. M. 1971. "Aquatic Oligochaeta of the World". 860 pp., many figs., 4 pl. Oliver & Boyd, Edinburgh.

BRINKHURST, R. O. 1971. A guide for the identification of British aquatic Oligochaeta. *Scient. Publs Freshwat. biol. Ass.* **22**: 1–55, 15 figs., 1 pl.

SPERBER, C. 1952. A guide for the determination of European Naididae. *Zool. Bidr. Uppsala* **29**: 45–78, 28 figs., 3 pls.

For Enchytraeidae see Terrestrial section.

TERRESTRIAL

GERARD, B. M. 1964. Lumbricidae (Annelida). *Synopses Br. Fauna* **6**, 36 pp., 12 figs.

STØP-BOWITZ, C. 1969. A contribution to our knowledge of the systematics and zoogeography of Norwegian Earthworms (Annelida Oligochaeta: Lumbricidae). *Nytt Mag. Zool.* **17**: 169–280, 65 figs.

BOUCHÉ, M. B. 1972. Lombriciens de France, Ecologie et Systematique. *Annls Zool. Ecol. anim.* **72-2**, 671 pp., 100 figs.

The classification and nomenclature differ from those of earlier workers.

NIELSON, C. O. & CHRISTENSEN, B. 1959. The Enchytraeidae. Critical revision and taxonomy of European species. *Natura jutl.* **8–9**, 160 pp., 177 figs.

TYNEN, M. J. 1966. A new species of *Lumbricillus* with a revised checklist of British Enchytraeidae (Oligochaeta). *J. mar. biol. Ass. U.K.* **46**: 89–95, 1 fig.

TYNEN, M. J. & NURMINEN, M. 1969. A key to the European littoral Enchytraeidae (Oligochaeta). *Ann. Zool. Fenn.* **6**: 150–155, 4 figs.

HIRUDINEA   About 70 European species (*c.* 50 marine and *c.* 20 freshwater or terrestrial habitats) of which some 40 occur in the British area (26 marine and 14 freshwater).

GENERAL

MANN, K. H. 1962. "Leeches (Hirudinea). Their structure, physiology, ecology and embryology". 201 pp., 112 figs., 1 pl. Pergamon Press, London.

MARINE

SOOS, A. 1965. Identification key to the leech (Hirudinoidea) genera of the world, with a catalogue of species. I. Family: Piscicolidae. *Acta zool. hung.* **11**: 417–463.

SRIVASTAVA, L. P. 1966. Three new leeches (Piscicolidae) from marine shores fishes (Cottidae) in British waters. *J. Zool., Lond.* **150:** 297–318, 18 figs.

FRESHWATER AND TERRESTRIAL

MANN, K. H. 1964. A key to the British freshwater leeches with notes on their ecology. *Scient. Publs Freshwat. biol. Ass.* **14,** 50 pp., 48 figs., 14 maps. 1 pl.

BENNIKE, S. A. B. 1943. Contributions to the ecology and biology of the Danish freshwater leeches (Hirudinea). *Folia limnol. scand.* **2,** 109 pp., 29 figs., 16 tabs.

AUTRUMN, H. 1958. Hirudinea. *Tierwelt Mitteleur.* 1(7b): 1–30, 56 figs.

SOOS, A. 1966. Identification key to the leech (Hirudinoidea) genera of the world, with a catalogue of the species. III. Family: Erpobdellidae. *Acta zool. hung.* **12:** 371–407.

SOOS, A. 1969. Identification key to the leech (Hirudinoidea) genera of the world, with a catalogue of the species. VI. Family: Glossiphoniidae. *Acta zool. hung.* **15:** 397–454.

SOOS, A. 1963. Identification key to the species of the genus *Dina* R. Blanchard, 1892 (emend. Mann, 1952) (Hirudinea: Erpobdellidae). *Acta biol. Szeged.* **9:** 253–261.

SOOS, A. 1966. On the genus *Glossiphonia* Johnson, 1816, with a key and catalogue to the species (Hirudinoidea: Glossiphoniidae). *Annls hist.-nat. Mus. natn. hung.* **58:** 271–279.

SOOS, A. 1967. On the genus *Batracbdella* Viguier, 1879, with a key and catalogue to the species (Hirudinoidea: Glossiphoniidae). *Annls Hist.-nat. Mus. natn. hung.* **59:** 243–257, 43 figs.

SOOS, A. 1968. Identification key to the species of the genus *Erpobdella* de Blainville, 1818 (Hirudinoidea: Erpobdellidae). *Annls Hist.-nat. Mus. natn. hung.* **60:** 141–145.

CHELICERATA (ARACHNIDA)

SCORPIONES   One British species

WANLESS, F. R. (1977). On the occurrence of the scorpion *Euscorpius flavicaudis* (DeGeer) at Sheerness Port, Isle of Sheppey, Kent. *Bull. Br. arachnol. Soc.* **4:** 74–76, 2 pls.

ARANEAE (spiders)   British species about 616

BLACKWALL, J. 1861–64. "The Spiders of Great Britain and Ireland". 2 vols. 384 pp., 29 pls. Ray Society, London.

BONNET, P. 1945–61. "Bibliographia Araneorum". Vol. 1 (1945), 832 pp., 28 pls. Vol. 2 (1955–1959), 5508 pp. Vol. 3 (1961), 591 pp. Privately printed, Toulouse.

BRISTOWE, W. S. 1939–41. "The Comity of Spiders". Vol.(1939), pp. x + 228, 15 figs. 19 pls. Vol. **2** (1941), pp. xiv + 229–560, 81 figs, 3 pls. Ray Society, London.

BRISTOWE, W. S. 1971. "The World of Spiders". Revised edn. xvi + 304 pp., 116 figs, 32 pls. Collins, London.

CRAWFORD, R. & LOCKET, G. H. 1976. The occurrence of *Tegenaria gigantea* Chamberlin & Ivie in North America and western Europe. *Bull. Br. arachnol. Soc.* **3:** 199.

DAHL, M. 1926, 1931 and 1937. Spinnentiere oder Arachnoidea: I, Springspinnen (Salticidae); VI, 24 Familie, Agelenidae; VIII, 19 Familie, Hahniidae, 20 Familie, Argyronetidae. *Tierwelt Dtl.* **3:** 1–55, 159 figs; **23,** 1–136, 218 figs; **33:** 100–118, 38 figs.

DAHL, F. & DAHL, M. 1927. Spinnentiere oder Arachnoidea II: Lycosidae s.lat. (Wolfspinnen im weiteren Sinne). *Tierwelt Dtl.* **5**: 1–80, 192 figs.
HOLM, A. 1947. Egentliga spindlar. Araneae. Fam. 8–10, Oxyopidae, Lycosidae och Pisauridae. In "Svensk Spindelfauna", Vol. 3, pp. 1–48, 20 figs. 10 pls. Entomologiska Föreningen, Stockholm (in Swedish).
LOCKET, G. H. 1975. The identity of Blackwall's *Tegenaria saeva* (Araneae, Agelenidae). *Bull. Br. arachnol. Soc.* **3**: 85–90, 19 figs.
LOCKET, G. H. & MILLIDGE, A. F. 1951–53. "British Spiders", Vol. 1, (1951), pp. ix + 310, 142 figs, 1 pl.; Vol. 2 (1953), pp. vii + 449, 254 figs. Ray Society, London.
LOCKET, G. H., MILLIDGE, A. F. & MERRETT, P. 1974. "British Spiders". Vol. 3 ix + 315 pp, 75 figs, 612 maps. Ray Society, London.
MERRETT, P. & SNAZELL, R. G. 1975. New and rare British spiders. *Bull. Br. arachnol. Soc.* **3**: 106–112, 16 figs.
MILLIDGE, A. F. 1975. Re-examination of the erigonine spiders *"Micrargus herbigradus"* and *"Pocadicnemis pumila"* (Araneae: Linyphiidae). *Bull. Br. arachnol. Soc.* **3**: 145–155, 46 figs.
REIMOSER, E. 1937. Spinnentiere oder Arachnoidea. VIII, 16 Familie, Gnaphosidae oder Plattbauchspinnen; 17 Familie, Anyphaenidae oder Zartspinnen; 18 Familie, Clubionidae oder Röhrenspinnen. *Tierwelt Dtl.* **33**: 1–99, 104 figs.
ROEWER, C. F. 1942–54. "Katalog der Araneae von 1758 bis 1940". Vol. 1 (1942), pp. viii + 1040. Vol. 2 (1954), 1751 pp. Bremen, Brussels.
SIMON, E. 1874–1937, "Les Arachnides de France". Vol. I (1874), 350 pp., 3 pls. Vol. 2 (1875), 358 pp., 4 pls. Vol. 3 (1876), 360 pp., 4 pls. Vol. 4 (1878), 334 pp., 5 pls. Vol. 5 (1881), 885 pp., 1 pl. Vol. 6 (1914–37), 1298 pp., 2028 figs.
TULLGREN, A. 1944. Egentliga spindlar. Araneae. Fam. 1–4. Salticidae, Thomisidae, Philodromidae och Eusparrassidae. In "Svensk Spindelfauna", Vol. 3, pp. 1–138, 48 figs, 18 pls. Entomologiska Föreningen, Stockholm (in Swedish).
TULLGREN, A. 1946. Egentliga spindlar. Araneae. Fam. 5–7. Clubionidae, Zoridae och Gnaphosidae. In "Svensk Spindelfauna", Vol. 3, pp. 1–141, 39 figs, 10 pls. Entomologiska Föreningen, Stockholm (in Swedish).
WIEHLE, H. 1931–63. Spinnentiere oder Arachnoidea. VI, 27 Familie, Araneidae; VIII, 26 Familie, Theridiidae oder Haubennetzspinnen (Kugelspinnen); IX, Orthognatha-Cribellatae-Haplogynae-Entelegynae (Pholcidae, Zodariidae, Oxyopidae, Mimetidae, Nesticidae); 28 Familie Linyphiidae Baldachinspinnen; XI, Micryphantidae-Zwergspinnen; XII, Tetragnathidae-Streckspinnen und Dickkiefer. *Tierwelt Dtl.* **23**: 47–136, 218 figs; **33**: 119–222, 286 figs; **42**: 1–150, 305 figs; **44**: viii + 1–337, 551 figs; **47**: xi + 1–620, 1147 figs; **49**: viii + 1–76, 124 figs.

PSEUDOSCORPIONES (= CHELONETHIDA)   British species about 27

BEIER, M. 1963. Ordnung Pseudoscorpionidea (Afterscorpione). *Bestimm. Büch. Bodenfauna Europ* **1**, 313 pp., 300 figs.
CHAMBERLIN, J. C. 1931. The arachnid order Chelonethida. *Stanf. Univ. Publs, Biol. Sciences* **7**(1), 284 pp., 71 figs.
 Detailed account of morphology. Systematic review with keys to families, genera and some species. Extensive bibliography.
EVANS, G. O. & BROWNING, E. B. 1954. Pseudoscorpiones. *Synopses Br. Fauna* **10**, 23 pp., 24 figs.
GABBUTT, P. D. 1966. A new species of pseudoscorpion from Britain. *J. Zool. Lond.* **150**: 165–181, 5 figs.
 Keys European species of *Chthonius (Ephippiochthonius)*.

GABBUTT, P. D. 1969. A key to all stages of the British species of the family Neobisiidae (Pseudoscorpiones: Diplosphyronida). *J. nat. Hist.* **3:** 183–195, 13 figs.

KEW, H. W. 1911 and 1916. A synopsis of the false-scorpions of Britain and Ireland. *Proc. R. Ir. Acad.* **29B:** 38–64, 3 pls; **33B:** 71–85, 3 figs.

The classic work on British pseudoscorpions.

LEGG, G. 1975. The genitalia and associated glands of five British species belonging to the family Chthoniidae (Pseudoscorpiones: Arachnida). *J. Zool., Lond.* **177:** 99–121, 15 figs.

LEGG, G. 1975. The genitalia and associated glands of five British species belonging to the family Neobisiidae (Pseudoscorpiones: Arachnida). *J. Zool., Lond.* **177:** 123–151, 21 figs.

Both above papers include keys to species based on genitalia.

VACHON, M. 1957. Remarques sur les Chernetidae (Pseudoscorpiones) de la faune britannique. *Ann. Mag. nat. Hist.* (12) **10:** 389–394, 9 figs.

Keys genera: illustrates spermathecal types in Chernetidae.

OPILIONES (= PHALANGIDA)   British species 22

MARTENS, J. (in press) Spinnentiere, Arachnida — Weberknechte, Opiliones. *Tierwelt Dtl.* **64,** xx pp., 815 figs, 38 maps.

SANKEY, J. H. P. & SAVORY, T. H. 1974. British harvestmen. *Synopses Br. Fauna* (N.S.) **4,** 76 pp., 27 figs, 7 maps.

SPOEK, G. L. 1964. Spinachtigen-Arachnida III De Hooiwagens (Opilionida) van Nederland. *Wet. Meded. K. ned. natuurh. Veren.* **4,** 28 pp., 13 figs. (in Dutch).

TODD, V. 1948. Key to the determination of the British harvestmen (Arachnida, opiliones). *Entomologist's mon. Mag.* **84:** 109–113, 11 figs.

ACARI
GENERAL WORKS

ACAROLOGIA. Paris. 1959 on. A scientific journal devoted to acarology.

BAKER, E. W. & WHARTON, G. W. 1952. "An Introduction to Acarology". 465 pp., 377 figs, 1 pl. Macmillan, New York.

BREGETOVA, N. G. *et al.* 1955. [Mites of the rodent fauna of the USSR.] *Opred. Faune SSSR* **59,** 459 pp., 984 figs. (In Russian).

EVANS, G. O., SHEALS, J. G. & MACFARLANE, D. 1961. "The Terrestrial Acari of the British Isles. An introduction to their morphology, biology and classification". Vol. 1. "Introduction and Biology". 219 pp., 216 figs. British Museum (Natural History), London.

HALBERT, J. N. 1915. Clare Island Survey, part 39 ii. Acarinida ii. Terrestrial and marine Acarina. *Proc. R. Ir. Acad.* **31**(39): 45–136, 5 pls.

HALBERT, J. N. 1920. The Acarina of the seashore. *Proc. R. Ir. Acad.* **35B:** 106–152, 3 pls.

HUGHES, A. M. 1976. The mites of stored food and houses. *Tech. Bull. Ministr. Agric. Fish Fd.* **9,** 400 pp., 437 figs.

KRANTZ, G. W. 1970. "A Manual of Acarology". xi + 335 pp., 35 figs. 144 pls. O.S.U. Book Stores, Cornvallis.

JEPPSON, L. R., KEIFER, H. H. & BAKER, E. W. 1975. "Mites Injurious to Economic Plants". xxiv + 614 pp., 138 figs, 74 pls. University of California Press, Berkeley.

TREAT, A. E. 1975. "Mites of Moths and Butterflies". 362 pp., 150 figs. Comstock Publishing Associates, Ithaca, New York.

TURK, F. A. 1953. A synonymic catalogue of British Acari. *Ann. Mag. nat. Hist.* (12) **6**: 1–26, 88–99.
VITZTHUM, H. Graf 1940–43. Acarina. *Bronn's Kl. Ordn. Tierreichs* **5**(4), 5, xi + 1011 pp., 522 figs.
ZUMPT, F. *et al.* The arthropod parasites of vertebrates in Africa south of the Sahara 1. *Publ. S. Afr. Inst. med. Res.* **9**(1), ix + 457 pp., 247 figs. South African Institute for Medical Research, Johannesburg.

Metastigmata or Ixodoidea (ticks)

ARTHUR, D. R. 1960. "Ticks, a monograph of the Ixodoidea. Part V. On the genera *Dermacentor, Anocentor, Cosmiomma, Boophilus* & *Margaropus*". xviii + 251 pp., 510 figs, 4 pls. Cambridge University Press, Cambridge.
ARTHUR, D. R. 1963. "British Ticks". ix + 213 pp., 362 figs. Butterworth, London.
DOSS, M. A. *et al.* 1974. "Index Catalogue of Medical and Veterinary Zoology". Special Publication Vol. 3. "Ticks and Tickborne Diseases. I. Genera and Species of Ticks". Part I, 429 pp., part 2, 593 pp., part 3, 329 pp. II. "Hosts". Parts 1–3, 1268 pp. U.S. Department of Agriculture, Washington.
HOOGSTRAAL, H. 1970 on "Bibliography of ticks and tickborne diseases from Homer (about 800 B.C.) to 31 December 1969". Vol. 1 (1970), 499 pp. Vol. 2 (1970), 495 pp. Vol. 3 (1971), 435 pp. Vol. 4 (1972), 355 pp. Vol. 5 (1) (1974), 492 pp. U.S. Naval Medical Research Unit 3, Cairo.
NUTTALL, G. H. F., WARBURTON, C., COOPER, W. F. & ROBINSON, L. E. 1908–15. "Ticks, a Monograph of the Ixodoidea". Vol. 1 (1) "Argasidae", (2) *"Ixodes"* (3) *"Haemaphysalis"*. 550 pp., 449 figs, 13 pls. Cambridge University Press.

Mesostigmata

ATHIAS-HENRIOT, C. 1960. Phytoseiidae et Aceosejidae (Acarina, Gamasina) d'Algérie IV Genre *Typhlodromus* Scheuten 1857. *Bull. Soc. Hist. nat. Afr. N.* **51**: 62–107, 41 figs.
  Keys species of *Typhlodromus*.
ATHAIS-HENRIOT, C. 1966. Contribution à l'étude des *Amblyseius* paléarctiques (Acariens actinotriches, Phytoseiidae). *Bull. scient. Bourgogne* **24**: 181–230, 133 figs, 1 pl.
  Reviews all palaearctic species.
ATHIAS-HENRIOT, C. 1967–1968. Observations sur les *Pergamasus* 1–5. *Acarologia* **9**: 669–761, 334 figs, 3 pls; **9**: 762–800, 152 figs, 3 pls; **10**: 181–190, 1 fig. *Bull. scient. Bourgogne* **25**: 175–228, 162 figs.
  Keys species.
BERNHARD, F. 1963. Die Familie Ascaidae (Oudemans, 1905) Bernhard nov. comb. In "Beiträge zur Systematik und Ökologie mitteleuropäischer Acarina", (H. J. Stammer, ed.), Vol. 2 (Mesostigmata 1), Abschnitt III, 33–177, 90 figs. Geest & Portig, Leipzig.
BHATTACHARYYA, S. K. 1963. A revision of the British mites of the genus *Pergamasus* Berlese s.lat. (Acari: Mesostigmata). *Bull. Br. Mus. nat. Hist.* (Zool.) **11**: 1–112, 313 figs, 8 pls.
BLASZAK, C. 1974. "Zerconidae (Acari, Mesostigmata) Polski". [Monografie Fauny Polski 3.] 315 pp., 173 figs. Polish Academy of Science, Warsaw (in Polish, figure captions and keys in English).
  Keys genera and species.
BREGETOVA, N. G. 1956. [Gamasid mites (Gamasoidea)]. *Opred. Faune SSSR* **61**: 1–246, 562 figs (in Russian).
CHANT, D. A. 1958. Immature and adult stages of some British Phytoseiidae Berl., 1916 (Acarina). *J. Linn. Soc., Zool.* **43**: 599–643, 26 figs.

CHANT, D. A. 1959. Phytoseiid mites (Acarina: Phytoseiidae). Part I. Bionomics of seven species in southeastern England. Part II. A taxonomic review of the family Phytoseiidae with descriptions of 38 new species. *Can. Ent. Suppl.* **12**: 1–166, 306 figs.

EVANS, G. O. 1955. A revision of the family Epicriidae (Acarina-Mesostigmata). *Bull. Br. Mus. nat. Hist.* (Zool.) **3**: 169–200, 41 figs, 2 pls.

EVANS, G. O. 1955. British mites of the genus *Veigaia* Oudemans (Mesostigmata — Veigaiaidae). *Proc. zool. Soc. Lond.* **125**: 569–586, 21 figs.

EVANS, G. O. 1957. An introduction to the British Mesostigmata (Acarina) with keys to families and genera. *J. Linn. Soc. Zool.* **43**: 203–259, 92 figs.

EVANS, G. O. 1958. A revision of the British Aceosejinae (Acarina: Mesostigmata). *Proc. zool. Soc. Lond.* **131**: 177–229, 73 figs.

EVANS, G. O. & BROWNING, E. 1956. British mites of the sub-family Macrochelinae Trägårdh (Gamasina-Macrochelidae). *Bull. Br. Mus. nat. Hist.* (Zool.) **4**: 1–55, 85 figs, 4 pls.

EVANS, G. I. & HYATT, K. H. 1956. British mites of the genus *Pachylaelaps* Berlese (Gamasina-Pachylaelaptidae). *Ent. mon. Mag.* **92**: 118–129, 35 figs.

EVANS, G. O. & HYATT, K. H. 1960. A revision of the Platyseiinae (Mesostigmata: Aceosejidae) based on material in the collection of the British Museum (Natural History). *Bull. Br. Mus. nat. Hist.* (Zool.) **6**: 25–101, 204 figs.

EVANS, G. O. & TILL, W. M. 1965–66. Studies on the British Dermanyssidae. Part 1, external morphology. *Bull. Br. Mus. nat. Hist.* (Zool.) **13**: 247–294, 21 figs. Part II, classification. *Bull. Br. Mus. nat. Hist.* (Zool.) **14**: 107–370, 101 figs.

FAIN, A. 1962–66. Les acariens parasites nasicoles des oiseaux de Belgique. I–V. *Bull. Annls Soc. r. ent. belg.* **98**: 252–270, 16 figs; **99**: 168–181, 20 figs; **99**: 471–485, 24 figs; **100**: 55–61, 14 figs; **102**: 117–122, 8 figs.
Contain many descriptions of Rhinonyssidae.

GILYAROV, M. S. & BREGETOVA, N. G. 1977. [Key to soil-inhabiting mites] Mesostigmata. 718 pp., 538 figs. Nauka, Leningrad (in Russian).

HIRSCHMANN, W. 1957–76. Gangsystematik der Parasitiformes. Teile 1–232. In "Acarologie, Schriftenreihe für vergleichende Milbenkunde", Folge 1–12, 14–22. Hirschmann, Fürth-i-Bayern.
A most important series of well illustrated generic revisions.

HOLZMANN, C. 1969. Die Familie der Parasitidae Oudemans 1901. Acarologie. In "Acarologie, Schriftenreihe für vergleichende Milbenkunde", Folge 13, 55 pp., 23 pls. Hirschmann, Fürth-i-Bayern.

HYATT, K. H. 1956. British mites of the genera *Halolaelaps* Berlese and *Saprolaelaps* Leitner (Gamasina: Rhodacaridae). *Ent. Gaz.* **7**: 7–26, 55 figs.

HYATT, K. H. 1956. British mites of the genus *Pachyseius* Berlese, 1910 (Gamasina: Neoparasitidae). *Ann. Mag. nat. Hist.* (12) **9**: 1–6, 10 figs.

KARG, W. 1971. Acari (Acarina), Milben, Unterordnung Anactinochaeta (Parasitiformes). Die freilebenden Gamasina (Gamasides), Raubmilben. *Tierwelt Dtl.* **59**: 1–475, 516 figs.

KRAUSS, W. 1970. Die europäischen Arten der Gattungen *Macrocheles* Latreille 1829 u. *Geholaspis* Berlese 1918. In Acarologie. "Schriftenreihe für vergleichende Milbenkunde", Folge 14 pp. 2–43, 16 pls. Hirschmann-Verlag, Fürth i Bayern.

LINDQUIST, E. E. & EVANS, G. O. 1965. Taxonomic concepts in the Ascidae with a modified setal nomenclature for the idiosoma of the Gamasina. *Mem. ent. Soc. Can.* **47**: 1–64, 70 figs.
Key to genera.

MICHERDZINSKI, W. 1969. "Die Familie Parasitidae Oudemans" 1901. 690 pp., 452 figs. Pánstwowe Wydawnictwo Naukowe, Cracow.

RUDNICK, A. 1960. A revision of the mites of the family Spinturnicidae (Acarina). *Univ. Calif. Publs Ent.* **17**: 157–284, 31 pls.
SAMŠIŇÁK, K. & DUSBÁBEK, F. 1971. Podřád Čmelíkovci — Mesostigmata. *Klíč Zvířeny ČSSR* **4**: 313–352, 175 figs. (in Czech).
Keys families and genera.
SELLNICK, M. 1958. Die Familie Zerconidae Berlese. *Acta zool. hung.* **3**: 313–368, 58 figs.
Keys genera and species.
STRANDTMANN, R. W. & WHARTON, G. W. 1958. Manual of mesostigmatid mites parasitic on vertebrates. *Contr. Inst. Acarol Univ. Md* **4**, xi + 330 pp., 69 pls.
Keys families and genera and lists species. Host list and excellent bibliography.
WESTERBOER, I. 1963. Die Familie Podocinidae Berlese 1916. In "Beiträge zur Systematik und Ökologie mitteleuropäischer Acarina" (H. J. Stammer, ed.), 2 (Mesostigmata 1), Abschnitt IV: 179–450, 778–804, 177 figs. Geest & Portig, Leipzig.
Keys genera and species. Immature stages and both sexes described and figured.
WESTERBOER, I. & BERNHARD, F. 1963. Die Familie Phytoseiidae Berlese 1916. In "Beiträge zur Systematik und Okologie mitteleuropaischer Acarina" (H. J. Stammer, ed.) 2, Abschnitt V: 451–777, 231 figs. (pp. 778–804: references and index for Vol. 2).
Keys genera and species. Immature stages and both sexes described and figured.

Astigmata

ATYEO, W. T. & BRAASCH, N. L. 1966. The feather mite genus *Proctophyllodes (Sarcoptiformes: Proctophyllodidae). Bull. Univ. Nebraska St. Mus.* **5**: 1–354, 313 figs.
Keys species.
ČERNY, V. & SAMSINÁK, K. 1971. Nadkohorta Acaridiae. *Klíč Zvířeny ČSSR* **4**: 496–529, 106 figs. (in Czech).
Keys to families and genera.
DUBININ, V. B. 1953. [Feather mites (Analgesoidea). Part II, Epidermoptidae and Freyanidae; part III, Pterolichidae.] *Faune SSSR,* Arachnida **6**(6): 1–411, 167 figs; **6**(7): 1–813, 398 figs. (in Russian).
FAIN, A. 1965. A review of the family Epidermoptidae Trouessart parasitic on the skin of birds (Acarina: Sarcoptiformes). *Verh. K. vlaam. Acad. Wet.,* Klasse der Wetenschappen, **27**(84): (pt. 1) 1–176; (pt. 2) 1–144, 185 figs.
FAIN, A. 1967. Les hypopes parasites des tissus cellulaires des oiseaux (Hypodectidae: Sarcoptiformes). *Bull. Inst. r. Sci. nat. Belg.* **43**(4): 1–139, 150 figs.
FAIN, A. 1967. Le genre *Dermatophagoides* Bogdanov 1864, son importance dans les allergies respiratoires et cutanées chez l'homme (Psoroptidae: Sarcoptiformes). *Acarologia* **9**: 179–225, 48 figs.
Key to species of *Dermatophagoides.*
FAIN, A. 1968. Étude de la variabilité de *Sarcoptes scabiei* avec une revision des Sarcoptidae. *Acta zool. path. antverp.* **47**: 1–196, 209 figs.
FAIN, A. 1969. Les deutonymphes hypopiales vivant en association phoretique sur les mammifères (Acarina: Sarcoptiformes). *Bull. Inst. r. Sci. nat. Belg.* **45**(33): 1–262, 367 figs.
FAIN, A. 1969. Morphologie et cycle evolutif des Glycyphagidae commensaux de la taupe *Talpa europaea* (Sarcoptiformes). *Acarologia* **11**: 750–795, 44 figs.
FAIN, A. 1975. Acariens récoltés par le Dr J. Trave sur îles subantarctiques. I. Familles Saproglyphidae et Hyadesidae (Astigmates). *Acarologia* **16**: 684–708, 51 figs.
Keys species of *Hyadesia.*

FAIN, A. & ELSEN, P. 1967. Les acariens de la famille Knemidokoptidae producteurs de gale chex les oiseaux. *Acta zool. path. antverp.* **45:** 1–142, 74 figs.

FAIN, A., MUNTING, A. J. & LUKOSCHUS, F. 1970. Les Myocoptidae parasites des rongeurs en Hollande et en Belgique (Acarina: Sarcoptiformes). *Ibidem* **50:** 67–172, 80 figs.

GRIFFITHS, D. A. 1970. A further systematic study of the genus *Acarus* L., 1758 (Acaridae, Acarina), with a key to species. *Bull. Br. Mus. nat. Hist.* (Zool.) **19:** 83–118, 40 figs, 4 pls.

GILYAROV, M. S. & KRIVOLUTSKII, D. A. 1975. [Key to soil-inhabiting mites] Sarcoptiformes. 491 pp., 1196 figs. Nauka, Leningrad (in Russian).

JOHNSTON, D. E. & BRUCE, W. A. 1965. *Tyrophagus neiswanderi,* a new acarid mite of agricultural importance. *Res. Bull. Ohio agric. exp. Stn* **977,** 17 pp., 4 figs.
Key to species of *Tyrophagus.*

MICHAEL, A. D. 1901–03. "British Tyroglypidae". Vol. 1, xv + 291 pp., 19 pls. Vol. 2, xi + 183 pp., 20 pls. Ray Society, London.

SCHEUCHER, R. 1957. Systematik und Ökologie der deutschen Anoetinen. In Beiträge zur Systematik und Ökologie mitteleuropäischer Acarina (H. J. Stammer, ed.). Vol. 1. pp. 233–384, 79 figs. Geest & Portig, Leipzig.

TÜRK, E. & TÜRK, F. 1957. Sytematik und Ökologie der Tyroglyphiden Mitteleuropas. In "Beiträge zue Systematik und Ökologie mitteleuropäischer Acarina" (H. J. Stammer, ed.), Vol. 1, pp. 1–231, 182 figs.

ZACHVATKIN, A. A. 1941. [Tyroglyphoidea (Acari).] *Faune SSSR,* Arachnoidea **6**(1): 475 pp., 705 figs. (in Russian). Also available in English translation published by American Insitute of Biological Sciences.

Cryptostigmata (Oribatei)

BALOGH, J. 1972. "The Oribatid Genera of the World". 188 pp., 16 figs, 71 pls. Akadémiai Kiàdó, Budapest.
Keys genera. Setal diagnoses.

EVANS, G. O. 1952. British mites of the genus *Brachychthonius* Berl. 1910. *Ann. Mag. nat. Hist.* (12) **5:** 227–239, 8 figs.

GILYAROV, M. S. & KRIVOLUTSKII, D. A. 1975. See above.

GRANDJEAN, F. 1948. Sur les *Hydrozetes* (Acariens) de l'Europe occidentale. *Bull. Mus. Hist. nat. Paris* (2) **20:** 328–335, 3 figs.

HAMMEN, L. van der 1952. The Oribatei (Acari) of the Netherlands. *Zool. Verh., Leiden* **17:** 1–139, 12 figs.

HAMMEN, L. van der 1959. Berlese's primitive oribatid mites. *Zool. Verh., Leiden* **40:** 1–93.
Key to families of 'lower' Cryptostigmata.

KARPPINEN, E. 1971. Studies on the Oribatei (Acari) of Norway. *Suom. hyönt. Aikak.* **37:** 30–53, 14 maps.

KNÜLLE, W. 1957. Morphologische und entwicklungsgeschichtliche Untersuchungen zum phylogenetischen System der Acari: Acariformes Zach. 1, Oribatei, Malaconothridae. *Mitt. zool. Mus. Berl.* **33:** 97–213, 41 figs.
Keys to genera and species. Comprehensive bibliography.

MICHAEL, A. D. 1884–88. "British Oribatidae". 2 vols. 657 pp., 54 pls. Ray Society, London.
Notes on life histories, habits, etc. Still useful but nomenclature out of date.

SELLNICK, M. & FORSSLUND, K.-H. 1953. Die Gattung *Carabodes* C. K. Koch in der schwedischen Bodenfauna (Acar. Oribat.). *Ark Zool.* (2) **4:** 367–390, 13 figs.

SELLNICK, M. & FORSSLUND, K.-H. 1955. Die Camisiidae Schwedens (Acar. Oribat.). *Ark. Zool.* (2) **8:** 473–530, 47 figs.

SENICZAK, S. 1975. Revision of the family Oppiidae Grandjean 1953 (Acarina, Oribatei). *Acarologia* **17:** 331–345, 4 figs.
SELLNICK, M. 1929, 1960. Formenkreis: Hornmilben, Oribatei. *Tierwelt Mitteleur* **3** (4), 9, 42 pp., 91 figs; pp. 45–134, 2 pls. (Ergänzung).
  Keys to genera and species.
STRENZKE, K. 1951. Bestimmungstabelle der holsteinischen *Suctobelba*-Arten. *Arch. Hydrobiol.* **45:** 340–348.
STRENZKE, K. 1951. Die norddeutschen Arten der Oribatiden-Gattung *Suctobelba*. *Zool. Anz.* **147:** 147–166, 20 figs.
TUXEN, S. L. 1952. Die Jugendstadien der nordischen Camisiiden (Acar. Orib.) und etwas über die Systematik der Erwachsenen I. *Ent. Meddr.* **26:** 392–403, 6 pls.
  Keys genera and species of immature Camissiidae.
WILLMANN, C. 1931. Moosmilben oder Oribatiden (Cryptostigmata). *Tierwelt Dtl.* **22:** 79–200, 364 figs.
  Keys to genera and species. Descriptions. Nomenclature now substantially out of date.

Prostigmata (including Endeostigmata, Heterostigmata and Hydrachnellae)

GENERAL

CUNLIFFE, F. 1955. A proposed classification of the trombidiform mites (Acarina). *Proc. ent. Soc. Wash.* **57:** 209–218.
  Keys families.
DANIEL, M. 1971. Podřád Sametkovci — Trombidiformes. *Klíč Zvířeny ČSSR* **4:** 357–422, 194 figs. (in Czech).
  A modern comprehensive key to families and genera.
THOR, S. 1931. Acarina. Bdellidae, Nicoletiellidae, Cryptognathidae. *Tierreich* **56:** 1–84, 93 figs.
THOR, S. & WILLMANN, C. 1941. Acarina Prostigmata 6–11. Eupodidae, Penthalodidae, Penthaleidae, Rhagidiidae, Pachygnathidae, Cunaxidae. *Tierreich* **71a:** 1–186, 252 figs.

Anystoidea

OUDEMANS, A. C. 1935. Neues über Anystidae (Acari). *Arch. Naturgesch.* (N.F.) **5:** 364–446, 28 pls.

Bdelloidea (Cunaxoidea)

ATYEO, W. T. & TUXEN, S. L. 1962. The Icelandic Bdellidae (Acarina). *J. Kans. ent. Soc.* **35:** 281–298, 29 figs.
BAKER, E. W. & HOFFMAN, H. G. 1948. Acaros de la familia Cunaxidae. *An. Esc. nac. Cienc. Biol. Méx.* **5:** 229–273, 100 figs. (in Spanish).
  Keys to genera and species.
THOR, S. 1931. See above.
THOR, S. & WILLMANN, C. 1941. See above.

Cheyletoidea

BAKER, E. W. 1949. A review of the mites of the family Cheyletidae in the United States National Museum. *Proc. U.S. natn. Mus.* **99:** 267–320, 17 pls.
FAIN, A., 1975. Observations sur les Myobiidae parasites des rongeurs. Évolution parallèle hôtes-parasites (Acariens: Trombidiformes). *Acarologia* **16:** 441–475, 17 figs.
  Keys to genera and species. Host lists.
KETHLEY, J. B. 1970. A revision of the family Syringophilidae (Prostigmata: Acarina). *Contr. Am. ent. Inst.* **5**(6): 1–76, 38 figs.

DUBININ, V. B. 1957. [New classification of the mites of the super-families Cheyletoidea W. Dub. and Demodicoidea W. Dub.] *Mag. Parasit.* **17**: 71–136, 51 figs. (in Russian).

LUKOSCHUS, F., FAIN, A. & BEAUJEAN, M. M. J. 1967. Beschreibung neuer *Psorergates*-Arten (Psorergatidae: Trombidiformes). *Tidschr. Ent.* **110**: 133–181, 84 figs.
  Key to species.

SUMMERS, F. M. & PRICE, D. W. 1970. Review of the mite family Cheyletidae. *Univ. Calif. Publs Ent.* **6**: 1–153, 59 figs.
  Keys to genera and species.

VOLGIN, V. I. 1969. [Mites of the family Cheyletidae of the world fauna.] *Opred. Faune SSSR* **101**: 1–431. 536 figs. (in Russian).
  Keys to genera and species.

Demodicoidea

HIRST, S. 1919. "Studies on Acari I. The genus *Demodex* Owen." 44 pp., 4 figs, 13 pls. British Museum (Natural History), London.

Endeostigmata (Pachygnathoidea)

GRANDJEAN, F. 1939–43. Quelques genres d'acariens appartenant au groupe des Endeostigmata. *Ann. Sci. nat.* (11) **2**: 1–122, 25 figs; **4**: 81–135; **5**: 137–195, 18 figs.

THOR, S. & WILLMANN, C. 1941. See above.

Eriophyoidea

BUHR, H. 1964–65. See below p.59.
  Keys species on each plant genus according to gall type.

FARKAS, H. 1965. Familie Eriophyidae. Gallmilben. *Tierwelt Mitteleur.* **3** (3) (Neubearb.): 1–155, 115 figs.

NALEPA, A. 1910. Eriophyiden-Gallenmilben. II Teil. Systematik der Gallmilben. Beschreibung der Gallmilben Deutschlands. *Zoologica, Stuttg.* **24**: 205–293, 6 pls.
  Descriptions and illustr.

JEPPSON, L. R. *et al.* 1975. See above: Acari general.
  Keys to genera. Latest generic concepts and nomenclature. Useful taxonomic and bibliographic references.

von SCHLECHTENDAL, D. H. R. 1916. Eriophyidocecidien, die durch Gallmilben verursachten Pflanzengallen. *Zoologica, Stuttg.* **24**: 295–498, 34 figs, 24 pls.
  Excellent illustrations of galls, many in colour.

Erythraeoidea

OUDEMANS, A. C. 1912. Die bisjetzt bekannten Larven von Trombidiidae und Erythraeidae. *Zool. Jahrb.*, Suppl. **14**: 1–230, 271 figs.

SCHWEIZER, J. 1951. Die Landmilben des schweizerischen Nationalparkes. II Trombidiformes Reuter 1909. *Ergebn. wiss. Unters. schweiz. Nat.-Parks* (N.F.) **3**: 119–164, 71 figs.
  Keys to species. Excellent illustrations.

SOUTHCOTT, R. V. 1961. Studies on the systematics and biology of the Erythraeoidea (Acarina), with a critical revision of the genera and subfamilies. *Aust. J. Zool.* **9**: 367–610, 25 figs, 1 pl.

Eupodoidea

STRANDMANN, R. W. 1971. The eupodoid mites of Alaska (Acarina, Prostigmata). *Pacif. Insects* **13**: 75–118, 15 figs.
  Keys genera and known species.

THOR, S. & WILLMANN, C. 1941. See above.

Hydracarina (Hydrachnellae, Halacaridae, Limnochalacaridae)

ANDRÉ, M. 1946. Halacariens marins. *Faune Fr.* **46**: 152 pp., 83 figs.
ANGELIER, E. 1965. Les Porohalacaridae de la faune française. *Annls Limnologie* **1**: 213–220, 8 figs.
BESSELING, A. J. 1964. De nederlandse Watermijten (Hydrachnellae Latreille 1802). *Monographieen ned. ent. Vereen* **1**, 199 pp., 333 figs. (in Dutch).
  Keys genera and species.
COOK, D. R. 1974. Water mite genera and subgenera.02Mem. Am. ent. Inst. **21**, vii + 860 pp., 1942 figs.
  Illustrated keys and diagnoses for families, sub-families and genera.
GLEDHILL, T. & VIETS, K. O. 1976. A synonymic and bibliographic check-list of the freshwater mites (Hydrachnellae and Limnohalacaridae, Acari) recorded from Great Britain and Ireland. *Occ. Publs freshwat. biol. Ass.* **1**, 59 pp.
GREEN, J. 1960. A check-list of British marine Halacaridae (Acari) with notes on two species of the subfamily Rhombognathinae. *J. mar. biol. Ass. U.K.* **39**: 63–69, 4 figs.
HALBERT, J. N. 1911–15, Clare Island Survey, part 39. Acarinida: I, Hydracarina; II, Terrestrial and marine Acarina. *Proc. R. Ir. Acad.* **31**(39): 1–44, 45–136.
LUNDBLAD, O. 1927, 1962 and 1968. Hydracarinen Schwedens I–III. *Zool. Bidr. Uppsala* **11**: 185–540, 5 pls; *Ark. Zool.* **14**: 1–635, 534 figs; **21**: 1–633, 15 figs, 7 pls.
NEWELL, I. M. 1947. A systematic and ecological study of the Halacaridae of eastern North America. *Bull. Bingham oceanogr. Coll.* **10**(3): 1–232, 331 figs.
  Keys families, genera and species many of which occur in N.W. Europe.
PRASAD, V. & COOK, D. R. 1972. The taxonomy of water mite larvae. *Mem. Am. ent. Inst.* **18**, ii + 326 pp., 126 figs.
  Illustrated keys and diagnoses for families and genera.
SOAR, C. D. & WILLIAMSON, W. 1925, 1927, and 1929. "The British Hydracarina". Vol. 1, x + 216 pp., 20 pls. Vol. 2, viii + 215 pp., 20 pls. Vol. 3, viii + 184 pp., 20 pls. Ray Society, London.
VIETS, K. 1928, 1960. Abteilung: Wassermilben, Hydracarina. *Tierwelt Mitteleur.* 3(4), 8, 57 pp., 135 figs; (with Viets, K. O.) pp. 1–44, 6 pls. (Ergänzung).
  Keys families, genera and species.
VIETS, K. 1936 Spinnentiere oder Arachnoidea VII: Wassermilben oder Hydracarina (Hydrachnellae und Halacaridae). *Tierwelt Dtl* **31–32**, x + 574 pp, 652 figs.
VIETS, K. 1955–56. "Die Milben des Süsswassers und des Meeres. Hydrachnellae und Halacaridae (Acari)". Teil 1, "Bibliographie", 476 pp.; Teil 2, "Katalog und Nomenclator", 870 pp., 140 figs. Gustav Fischer, Jena.

Raphignathoidea

ATYEO, W. T. *et al.* 1961. The genus *Raphignathus* Dugès (Acarina, Raphignathidae) in the United States with notes on the Old World species. *Acarologia* **3**: 14–20, 7 figs.
GONZALEZ-RODRIGUEZ, R. H. 1965. A taxonomic study of the genera *Mediolata, Zetzellia* and *Agistemus* (Acarina: Stigmaeidae). *Univ. Calif. Publs Ent.* **41**: 1–64, 116 figs.
  Key to genera of Stigmaeidae.
SUMMERS, F. M. 1960. *Eupalopsis* and eupalopsellid mites (Acarina: Stigmaeidae, Eupalopsellidae). *Florida Ent* **43**: 119–138, 22 figs.

SUMMERS, F. M. & SCHLINGER, F. I. 1955. Mites of the family Caligonellidae (Acarina). *Hilgardia* **23**: 539–561, 9 pls.
SUMMERS, F. M. & PRICE, D. W. 1961. New and redescribed species of *Ledermuelleria* from North America (Acarina: Stigmaeidae). *Hilgardia* **31**: 369–381, 6 pls.
SUMMERS, F. M. 1962. The genus *Stigmaeus* (Acarina: Stigmaeidae). *Hilgardia* **33**: 491–537, 55 figs.

Tarsonemina (= Heterostigmata)

BEER, R. E. 1954. A revision of the Tarsonemidae of the western hemisphere (Order Acarina). *Kans. Univ. Sci. Bull.* **36**: 1091–1387, 25 pls.
BEER, R. E. & NUCIFORA, A. 1965. Revisione dei generi della famiglia Tarsonemidae (Acarina). *Boll. Zool. agric. Bachic.* (2) **7**: 19–43, 77 figs. (in Italian).
CROSS, E. A. 1965. The generic relationships of the family Pyemotidae (Acarina: Trombidiformes). *Kans. Univ. Sci. Bull.* **45**: 29–275, 100 figs.
  Keys genera and species lists.
CROSS, E. A. & MOSER, J. C. 1975. A new dimorphic species of *Pyemotes* and a key to previously described forms (Acarina: Tarsonemoidea). *Ann. ent. Soc. Amer.* **68**: 723–732, 19 figs.
KARAFIAT, H. 1959. Systematik und Ökologie der Scutacariden. In "Beiträge zur Systematik und Ökologie mitteleuropäischer Acarina" (H. J. Stammer, ed.), Vol. 1(2), pp. 627–712, 42 figs. Geest & Portig, Leipzig.
  Keys genera and species.
KRCZAL, H. 1959. Systematik und Ökologie der Pyemotiden. In "Beiträge zur Systematik und Ökologie mitteleuropäischen Acarina" (H. J. Stammer, ed.), Vol. 1(2), pp. 385–625, 85 figs. Geest & Portig, Leipzig.
  Keys genera and species.
MAHUNKA, S. 1965. Identification keys for the species of the family Scutacaridae (Acari: Tarsonemini). *Acta zool. Bpest.* **11**: 353–401, 29 figs.
MAHUNKA, S. 1969. Beiträge zur Tarsonemini-Fauna Ungarns, VI. (Acari, Trombidiformes). *Opusc. zool. Bpest* **9**: 363–372, 13 figs.
  Key to species of *Siteroptes*.
MAHUNKA, S. 1970. Considerations on the systematics of the Tarsonemina and the description of new European taxa (Acari: Trombidiformes). *Acta zool. hung.* **16**: 137–174, 23 figs.
  Keys to families and to genera of Pyemotoidea and Pygmephoroidea.
MAHUNKA, S. & RACK, G. 1975. Bibliographica Tarsonemidologica (1971–74). *Folia ent. hung.* (N.S.) **28**: 117–126.
RACK, G. 1975. Phoretisch auf Kleinsaugern gefundene Arten der Gattung *Pygmephorus* (Acarina, Pygmephoridae). *Mitt. Hamburg zool. Mus. Inst.* **72**: 157–176, 26 figs.
  Key species of *Pygmephorus s. str.*
SCHAARSCHMIDT, L. 1959. Systematik und Ökologie der Tarsonemiden. In "Beiträge zur Systematik und Ökologie mitteleuropäischen Acarina" (H. J. Stammer, ed.), Vol. 1(2), pp. 713–823, 55 figs. Geest & Portig, Leipzig.

Tetranychoidea

JEPPSON, L. R. *et al.* 1975. See above p. 40.
  Descriptions, illustrations, life histories.
PRITCHARD, A. E. & BAKER, E. W. 1955. A revision of the spider mite family Tetranychidae. *Mem. Pacif. Coast ent. Soc.* **2**: 472 pp., 391 figs., 1 pl.
PRITCHARD, A. E. & BAKER, E. W. 1958. The false spider mites (Acarina: Tenuipalpidae). *Univ. Calif. Publs Ent.* **14**: 175–275, 51 figs.

Trombidioidea

BERLESE, A. 1912. Trombidiidae. Prospetto dei generi e delle specie finora noti. *Redia* **8**: 1–291, 137 figs., 1 pl. (in Italian).
FEIDER, F. 1955. Acarina, Trombidoidea. *Fauna Rep. pop. Romina* **5**(1): 1–190, 110 figs. (in Rumanian).
OUDEMANS, A. C. 1912. See above p. 46.
SCHWEIZER, J. 1951. See above p. 46.
THOR, S. & WILLMANN, C. 1947. Acarina. Trombidiidae. *Tierreich* **71b**: 187–541, 347 figs.

Tydeoidea

BAKER, E. W. 1965. A review of the genera of the family Tydeidae (Acarina). In "Advances in Acarology" (J. A. Naegele, ed.), Vol. 2. pp. 95–133, 13 pls. Comstock, Ithaca, N.Y.
BAKER, E. W. 1968. The genus *Lorryia. Ann. ent. Soc. Am.* **61**: 986–1008, 55 figs.
BAKER, E. W. 1970. The genus *Tydeus:* subgenera and species groups with descriptions of new species. (Acarina: Tydeidae). *Ann. ent. Soc. Am.* **63**: 163–177, 53 figs.
FAIN, A. 1965. Les Ereynetidae de la collection Berlese à Florence; designation d'une espèce type pour le genre *Ereynetes* Berlese. *Redia* **49**: 87–111, 5 figs.
    Descriptions, illustrations, list of known species of *Ereynetes*.
FAIN, A. 1970. Notes sur les speleognathines parasites nasicoles des mammifères (Ereynetidae: Trombidiformes). *Acarologia* **12**: 509–521, 21 figs.
    Key to species, host list.
FAIN, A. 1971. Clé et liste des espèces du genre *Boydaia* Wormersley (Ereynetidae: Trombidiformes). *Acarologia* **13**: 98–112.
THOR, S. 1933. Acarina. Tydeidae, Ereynetidae. *Terreich* **60**: 1–84, 102 figs.
WOOD, T. G. 1965, New and redescribed species of Tydeidae (Acari) from moorland soils in Britain. *Acarologia* **7**: 663–672, 5 figs.

PYCNOGONIDA (sea spiders) British species about 21

BOUVIER, E.-L. 1923. Pycnogonides. *Faune Fr.* **7**: 1–71, 61 figs.
GILTAY, L. 1928. Note sur les Pycnogonides de la Belgique. *Bull. Annls Soc. r. ent. Belg.* **68**: 193–229, 13 figs.
GILTAY, L. 1929. Quelques pycnogonides des environs de Banyuls (France). *Bull. Annls Soc. r. ent. Belg.* **69**: 172–176, 2 figs.
GILTAY, L. 1934. Remarques sur le genre *Ammothea* Leach, et description d'une espèce nouvelle de la Mer d'Irlande. *Bull. Mus. r. Hist. nat. Belg.* **10**(18): 1–6, 3 figs.
HEDGPETH, J. W. 1948. The Pycnogonida of the western North Atlantic and the Caribbean. *Proc. U.S. natn. Mus.* **97**: 157–342, 339 figs., 3 charts.
KING, P. E. 1974. British sea spiders. *Synopses Br. Fauna* (N.S.) **5**, 68 pp., 28 figs., 5 maps.
SARS, G. O. 1891, Pycnogonida. *Norske Norhavs-Exped.* **20**: 1–163, 15 pls, 1 map.
SCHLOTTKE, E. 1932. Die Pantopoden der deutschen Küsten. *Wiss. Meeresunters.* **18**: 1–10, 8 figs.
STOCK, J. H. 1952. Revision of the European representatives of the genus *Callipallene* Flynn, 1929. *Beaufortia* **13**: 1–15, 27 figs.

PENTASTOMIDA British species 3 or 4

FAIN, A. 1973. Pentastomids. In "Parasites of Laboratory Animals" (R. J. Flynn, ed.), pp. 493–503. Iowa State University Press, Iowa.

HEYMONS, R. 1935. Pentastomida. *Bronn's Kl. Ordn. Tierreichs* **5** (4), 1, vi + 268 pp., 148 figs.
NICOLI, R.-M. 1963. Phylogénèse at systématique. Le phylum des Pentastomida. *Annls Parasit. hum. comp.* **38**: 483–516.
SAMBON, L. W. 1922. A synopsis of the family Linguatulidae. *J. trop. Med. Hyg.* **25**: 188–206, 391–428, 47 figs.
SHEALS, J. G. 1973. Pentastomida (Tongue worms). In "Insects and other Arthropods of Medical Importance" (K. G. V. Smith, ed.), pp. 479–481, 1 fig. British Museum (Natural History), London.

CRUSTACEA

BRANCHIOPODA

Anostraca

DADAY DE DEES, E. 1910. Monographie systematique des phyllopodes Anostraces. *Ann. sci. nat. Zool. Paris* (9) **11**: 91–489.

Notostraca

LONGHURST, A. R. 1955. A review of the Notostraca. *Bull. Br. Mus. nat. Hist.* (Zool.) **3**: 1–57.

Cladocera

LILLJEBORG, W. 1900. Cladocera Sueciae. *Nova Acta R. Soc. Scient. upsal.* (3) **19**: 1–700.
JOHNSON, D. S. 1952. The British species of the genus *Daphnia* (Crustacea, Cladocera). *Proc. zool. Soc. Lond.* **122**: 435–462.
SCOURFIELD, D. J. & HARDING, J. P. 1958. A key to the British species of freshwater Cladocera with notes on their ecology. *Scient. Publs Freshwat. biol. Ass.* **5**: 1–55.
DELLA CROCE, N. 1974. Cladocera. *Fich. Ident. Zooplancton* **143**, 4 pp., 8 figs.

OSTRACODA

SARS, G. O. 1922–28, "Ostracoda. An account of the Crustacea of Norway with short descriptions and figures of all the species". Vol. 9, 277 pp., many pls. Bergen Museum.
BRADY, G. S. & NORMAN, A. M. 1889. A monograph of the marine and freshwater Ostracoda of the North Atlantic and of North-western Europe. Section 1, Podocopa. *Scient. Trans. R. Dubl. Soc.* (2) **4**: 63–270.
BRADY, G. S. & NORMAN, A. M. 1896. A monograph of the marine and freshwater Ostracoda of the North Atlantic and of North-western Europe. Sections 2–4, Myodocopa, Cladocopa and Platycopa. *Scient. Trans. R. Dubl. Soc.* (2) **5**: 621–746.
MÜLLER, G. W. 1894. Die Ostracoden des Golfes von Neapel und der angrenzenden Meeres Abschnitte. *Fauna Flora Golfo Napoli* **21**: 1–404.
KLIE, W. 1938. Ostracoda Muschelkrebse. *Tierwelt Dtl.* **34** (3): 1–230.
ELOFSON, O. 1941. Zur Kenntnis der mariner Ostracoden Schwedens mit besonderer Berücksichtigung des Skageraks. *Zool. Bidr. Uppsala* **19**: 215–534, 52 figs., 42 maps. English translation 1969, Israel Program for scientific translations, No. 5113.

NEALE, J. W. 1970. The marine flora and fauna of the Isles of Scilly. Crustacea: Ostracoda. *J. nat. Hist.* **4**: 399–411.

MYSTACOCARIDA

DELAMARE-DEBOUTTEVILLE, C. 1953. Revision des mystacocarides du genre *Derocheilocaris. Vie Milieu* **4**: 321–380.

COPEPODA

GENERAL

SARS, G. O. 1901–21. "Copepoda. An Account of the Crustacea of Norway". Vol. 4 (1901–03), xiii + 171 pp., pls. Vol. 5 (1903–11) xiv + 499 pp., pls. Vol. 6 (1913–18), ix + 225 pp. pls. Vol. 7 (1919–21), 121 pp., pls. Vol. 8 (1921), 91 pp., pls. Bergen Museum.
KIEFER, F. 1929. Crustacea Copepoda 2. Cyclopoida Gnathostoma. *Tierreich* **53**: 1–102.
WILSON, C. B. 1932. Keys to the Suborders and genera of Copepoda. *Bull. U.S. natn. Mus.* **158** (Appendix B): 538–623.
LANG, K. 1948. "Monographie der Harpacticiden". 2 vols, 1683 pp., 610 figs, 378 maps. Stockholm.

MARINE

PEARSON, J. 1905–06. A list of Marine Copepoda of Ireland. 1. Littoral Forms and Fish Parasites. 2. Pelagic Species. *Scient. Invest. Fish Brch. Ire.* **3** (1904) & **6** (1905), 30 pp.
ROSE, O. 1933. Copepodes pelagiques. *Faune Fr.* **26**: 1–374, 456 figs.
PERKINS, E. J. 1956. *Microarthridion fallax,* a species of Harpacticid copepod new to science from Whitstable, Kent. *Ann. Mag. nat. Hist.* (12) **9**: 108–111, 1 fig.
PERKINS, E. J. 1956. The Harpacticoid genus *Tetanopala* Brady, with a description of *Tetanopsis smithii* sp. nov. and *T. medius* sp. nov. *Ann. Mag. nat. Hist.* (12) **9**: 497–504, 3 figs.
KRISHNASWAMY, S. 1959. A new species of copepod from the Eddystone shell gravel. *J. mar. biol. Ass. U.K.* **38**: 553–546.
HARDING, J. P. 1956. *Laophonte foxi,* a new species of harpacticid copepod crustacean found living in mud. *Ann. Mag. nat. Hist.* (12) **9**: 669–672, 14 figs.
ROE, K. M. 1958. The littoral harpacticids of the Dalkay (Co. Dublin) area, with descriptions of six new species. *Proc. R. Ir. Acad.* **59B**: 221–225, 150 figs.
ROE, K. M. 1959. Some Harpacticids from Lough Ine, with descriptions of two new species. *Proc. R. Ir. Acad.* **60B**: 277–289, 44 figs.
WELLS, J. B. J. 1961. Intersititial Copepods from the Isles of Scilly. *Crustaceana* **2**: 262–274, 4 figs.
WELLS, J. B. J. 1966. Two new genera of harpacticoid copepods of the family Ectinosomidae. *Revta Biol. Lisb.* **5** (1964–65): 30–35, 22 figs, 1 tab.
HAMOND, R. 1968. Some marine copepods (Nisophrioida, Cyclopoida, and Notodelphyoida) from Norfolk, Great Britain. *Crustaceana* (Suppl.) **1**: 37–60, 5 figs., tabs.
HAMOND, R. 1968. *Pseudonychocamptus carthyi* nov. sp. (Harpacticoida) from Hunstanton, Norfolk. *Crustaceana* (suppl. **1**): 172–176, figs.
GEDDES, D. C. 1968. A new species of *Diagoniceps* (Copepoda Harpacticoidea) and two previously undescribed male harpacticoids from the Isle of Anglesey. *J. nat. Hist.* **2**: 439–448, figs., tabs.

WELLS, J. B. J. 1968. New and rare Copepoda Harpacticoida from the Isles of Scilly. *J. nat. Hist.* **2:** 397–424, figs.

FRESHWATER

GURNEY, R. 1931–33. "British Freshwater Copepoda". Vol. 1, lii + 238 pp, figs. Vol. 2, ix + 336 pp., figs. Vol. 3, xxix + 384 pp., figs. Ray Society, London.
LINDBERG, K. 1953. La sous-famille des Cyclopininae Kiefer. *Ark Zool.* **4:** 311–325, 1 fig.
HARDING, J. P. & SMITH, W. A. 1960. A key to the British freshwater cyclopid and calanoid copepods. *Scient. Publs Freshwat. biol. Ass.* **18:** 1–54, 16 figs.
DUSSART, B. 1967. "Les Copepodes des Eaux continentales d'Europe occidentale. I. Calanoides et Harpacticoïdes". 500 pp., text-illust. N. Boubee, Paris.
DUSSART, B. 1969. "Les Copepodes des Eaux continentales d'Europe occidentale. II. Cyclopoides et Biologie". 292 pp., figs, tabs. N. Boubee, Paris.

ASSOCIATED AND PARASITIC

GIESBRECHT, W. 1899. Die Asterocheriden. *Fauna Flora Golfo Napoli:* **25:** 1–217.
OORDE DE LINT, G. M. van & SCHUURMANS STEKHOVEN, J. H. 1936. Copepoda Parasitica. *Tierwelt N.- u. Ostsee* **10** (c): 73–198, 192 figs.
GOODING, R. U. 1957. On some Copepoda from Plymouth, mainly associated with invertebrates, including three new species *J. mar. biol. Ass. U.K.* **36:** 195–221, 6 figs.
GREEN, J. 1958. Copepoda parasitic on British amphipoda (Crustacea), with a description of a new species of *Sphaeronella*. *Proc. zool. Soc. Lond.* **131:** 301–313, 26 figs.
GOTTO, R. V. 1960. A key to the ascidicolous copepods of British water with distributional notes. *Ann. Mag. nat. Hist.* (13) **3:** 211–229, 30 figs.
HUMES, A. G. & STOCK, J. H. 1973. A revision of the family Lichomolgidae Kossmann, 1877, cyclopoid copepods mainly associated with marine invertebrates. *Smithsonian Contr. Zool.* **127,** i–v + 1–368, 190 figs.
SCHIRL, K. 1973. Cyclopoida Siphonostoma (Crustacea) von Banyuls (Frankreich, Pyrenees Orientales) mit besonderer Berücksichtigung des Gast-Wirtverhältnisses. *Bijdr. Dierk.* **43**(1): 64–92, 12 figs.
KABATA, Z. 1978. "Parasitic Copepoda of British Fishes". Ray Society, London.

CIRRIPEDIA

DARWIN, C. 1851–54. "Cirripedia". 2 vols. 1100 pp., figs. Ray Society, London.
GRUVEL, A. 1905. "Monographie des Cirrhipedes ou Thécostracés". 472 pp., figs. Masson, Paris.
NAGABHUSHANAM, A. K. 1958. *Sacculina gonoplaxae* Ganivet 1911, a Rhizocephalan parasite new to British waters. *Nature, Lond.* **181:** 57–58.
BASSINDALE, R. 1958. The local barnacles. *Proc. Bristol nat. Soc.* **29:** 382–392, figs.
KISCH, B. S. 1959. *Balanus tulipiformis* Ellis on the Atlantic coast of France. *Nature, Lond.* **183:** 341.
HARDING, J. P. 1962. Darwin's type specimens of varieties of *Balanus amphitrite*. *Bull. Br. Mus. nat. Hist.* (Zool.) **9:** 273–296, figs, pls.
SOUTHWARD, A. H. & CRISP, D. J. 1963. "Barnacles of European Waters. Catalogue of main marine fouling organisms found on ships coming into European

waters". [Introduced by D. L. Ray.] 46 pp., figs. Organisation for Economic Co-operation and Development, Paris.

NEWMAN, W. A. & ROSS, A. 1976. A revision of the balanomorph barnacles; including a catalog of the species. *Mem. S. Diego Soc. nat. Hist.* **9**, 108 pp., 17 figs.

SOUTHWARD, A. J. 1976. On the taxonomic status and distribution of *Chthamalus stellatus* (Crustacea, Cirripedia) in the north-east Atlantic region; with a key to the common intertidal barnacles of Britain. *J. Mar. biol. Ass. U.K.* **56** (4): 1007–1028, 6 figs., 2 pls.

STUBBINGS, H. G. 1975. *Balanus balanoides*. *L.M.B.C. Mem. typ. Br. mar. Pl. Anim.* **37**: 1–174, 190 figs.

MALACOSTRACA

GENERAL

GLEDHILL, T., SUTCLIFFE, D. W. & WILLIAMS, W. D. 1976. A revised key to the British species of Crustacea: Malacostraca occurring in fresh water with notes on their ecology and distribution. *Scient. Publs Freshwat. biol. Ass.* **32**: 1–72, 48 figs.

Bathynellacea

SPOONER, G. M. 1961. *Bathynella* and other interstitial Crustacea in Southern England. *Nature, Lond.* **190**: 104–105.

MAITLAND, P. S. 1962. *Bathynella natans*, new to Scotland. *Glasg. Nat.* **18**: 175–176.

GLEDHILL, T. & DRIVER, D. B. 1962. *Bathynella natans* Vejdovsky (Crustacea: Syncarida) and its occurrence in Yorkshire. *Naturalist, Hull* **1964**: 104–106, 1 fig.

Mysidacea

TATTERSALL, W. M. & TATTERSALL, O. S. 1951. "The British Mysidacea" viii + 460 pp., 118 figs. Ray Society, London.

Cumacea

SARS, G. O. 1900. "Cumacea. An account of the Crustacea of Norway". Vol. 3, 115 pp., 72 pls. Bergen Museum.

CALMAN, W. T. 1905. The marine fauna of the west coast of Ireland. Cumacea. *Scient. Invest. Fish. Brch. Ire.* **1**: 1–52, 5 pls.

JONES, N. S. 1958. *Fich. Ident. Zooplancton* **71–76**: 46 pp., 248 figs.

JONES, N. S. 1976. British Cumacea. *Synopsis Br. Fauna* (N.S.) **7**, 66 pp. 20 figs.

Isopoda and Tanaidacea

MARINE AND FRESHWATER

SARS, G. O. 1899. "Isopoda. An account of the Crustacea of Norway". Vol. 2. 270 pp., 104 pls. Bergen Museum.

HOLTHUIS, l. b. 1956. Isopoda en Tansidacea (KV). *Fauna Ned.* **16**: 1–280, 89 figs. (in Dutch.)

PIKE, R. B. 1953. The Bopyrid parasites of the Anomura from British and Irish waters. *J. Linn. Soc. (Zool.)* **42**: 219–237, 1 fig., 5 pls.

NAYLOR, E. 1957. *Fich. Ident. Zooplancton* **77** (Isopoda, Valvifera, Asellota); **78** (Isopoda, Flabellifera): 8pp., 32 figs.

HANSEN, H. J. 1905. Revision of the european marine forms of the Cirolanidae, a subfamily of Crustacea Isopoda. *J. Linn. Soc. (Zool.)* **29**: 337–373, pls 33–35.

MONOD, T. 1926. Les Gnathiidae; essai mongraphique. *Mém. Soc. Sci. nat. Phys. Maroc.* **13**: 1–668, 277 figs, 1 pl.

OMER-COOPER, J. & RAWSON, J. H. 1934. Notes on British Sphaeromatidae. (Crustacea Isopoda). *Rep. Dove mar. Lab.* **2**(3): 22–58, 6 pls.

NAYLOR, E. 1955. The comparative external morphology and revised taxonomy of the British species of *Idotea*. *J. mar. biol. Ass. U.K.* **34**: 467–493, 11 figs.

LANG, K. 1958. *Leptognathia paramanca* n.sp. *Ark. Zool.* **11**: 431–434.

SPOONER, G. M. 1959. The occurrence of *Microcharon* in the Plymouth offshore bottom fauna, with description of new species. *J. mar. biol. Ass. U.K.* **38**: 57–63, 2 figs.

CARTON, Y. 1961. Étude des représentants du genre *Munna* Kröyer sur les Côtes françaises de la Manche. *Bull. Soc. linn. Normandie* **10** (2): 222–242, 8 pls.

NAYLOR, E., SLINN, D. J. & SPOONER, G. M. 1961. Observations on the British species of *Jaera* (Isopoda: Asellota). *J. mar. biol. Ass. U.K.* **41**: 817–828, 4 figs.

GREVE, L. 1965. A new epicaridean from western Norway, parasite on Tanaidacea. *Sarsia* **20**: 15–19, 6 figs.

GREVE, L. 1966. Tanaidacea from Trondheimsfjorden. *K. norske Vidensk. Selsk. Forh.* **38**: 140–143.

JONES, D. A. & NAYLOR, E. 1967. The distribution of *Eurydice* (Crustacea: Isopoda) in British waters, including *E. affinis* new to Britain. *J. mar. biol. Ass. U.K.* **47**: 373–382, figs, tab.

HOLDICH, D. M. 1968. A systematic revision of the genus *Dynamene* (Crustacea: Isopoda) with a description of three new species. *Pubbl. Staz. Zool. Napoli* **36**: 401–426, figs.

GREVE, L. 1968. Tanaidacea from Hardangerfjorden, western Norway. *Sarsia* **36**: 77–84, 3 figs.

GREVE, L. 1972. Some new records of Tanaidacea from Norway. *Sarsia* **48**: 33–38, 1 fig.

NAYLOR, E. 1972. British marine Isopods. *Synopsis Br. Fauna* (n.s.) **3**: 1–86, 24 figs., 1 tab.

CHAPPIUS, P. A. 1949. Les Asellides d'Europe et Pays Limitrophes. *Archs Zool. exp. gén.* Notes et Revue **86**: 78–94, figs.

MOON, H. P. 1953. A re-examination of certain records for the genus *Asellus* (Isopoda) in the British Isles. *Proc. zool. Soc. Lond.* **123**: 411–417.

PIKE, R. B. 1961. Observations on Epicaridea obtained from hermit-crabs in British waters, with notes on the longevity of the host-species. *Ann. Mag. nat. Hist.* (13) **4**: 225–240, 7 figs.

TERRESTRIAL

VANDEL, A. 1960–62. Isopodes terrestres. *Faune Fr.* **64**: 1–416, 205 figs; **66**: 417–931, 409 figs.

SUTTON, S. L. 1972. "Woodlice". 144 pp., 37 figs., 8 pls. Ginn, London.
Check-list and keys to all British species.

Amphipoda

SARS, G. O. 1890–95. "Amphipoda. An account of the Crustacea of Norway". Vol. I. 711 pp., 248 pls. Bergen Museum.

NORMAN, A. M. 1900. British Amphipoda; Tribe Hyperiidae, Families Orchestiidae, Lysianassidae, Pontoporeidae, Ampeliscidae, Stegocephalidae, Oediceridae. *Ann. Mag. nat. Hist.* (7) **5**: 126–144, 326–346; **6**: 32–51.

CHEVREUX, E. & FAGE, L. 1925. Amphipodes. *Faune Fr.* **9**: 1–488, 438 figs.

SCHELLENBERG, A. 1932. Bemerkungen über subterrane Amphipoden Grossbritanniens. *Zool. Anz.* **99**: 49–58, 3 figs.
STEPHENSEN, K. 1935–1942. The Amphipoda of N. Norway and Spitsbergen with adjacent waters. *Tromsø Mus. Skr.* **3**(1): 1–140, 19 figs, 2 maps; **3**(2): 141–278; **3**(3): 279–362; **3**(4): 363–526, figs.
CRAWFORD, G. I. 1937. A review of the Amphipod genus *Corophium* with notes on the British species. *J. mar. biol. Ass. U.K.* **21**: 589–630, 4 figs.
WATKIN, E. E. 1938. A revision of the Amphipod genus *Bathyporeia* Lindström. *J. mar. biol. Ass. U.K.* **23**: 211–236, 6 figs.
SEXTON, E. W. & SPOONER, G. M. 1940. An account of *Marinogammarus* (Schellenberg), gen. nov. (Amphipoda) with a description of a new species *M. pirloti*. *J. mar. biol. Ass. U.K.* **24**: 633–682, 11 figs, 1 pl.
SEXTON, E. W. 1942. The relation of *Gammarus zaddachi* Sexton to some other species of *Gammarus* occurring in estuarine and marine waters. *J. mar. biol. Ass. U.K.* **25**: 575–606, 1 fig., 3 pls.
SCHELLENBERG, A. 1942. Krebstiere oder Crustacea. IV: Flohkrebse oder Amphipoda. *Tierwelt Dtl.* **40**(4): 1–252, 204 figs.
HARRISON, R. J. 1944. Caprellidae (Amphipoda, Crustacea). *Synopsis Br. Fauna* **2**: 1–27, figs.
REID, D. M. 1944. Gammaridae (Amphipoda) with keys to the families of British Gammaridea. *Synopsis Br. Fauna* **3**: 1–33, figs.
SEGERSTRÅLE, S. G. 1947. New observations on the distribution and morphology of the amphipod, *Gammarus zaddachi* Sexton, with notes on related species. *J. mar. biol. Ass. U.K.* **27**: 219–244, figs.
REID, D. M. 1947. Talitridae (Crustacea Amphipoda). *Synopsis Br. Fauna* **7**: 1–25, figs.
SPOONER, G. M. 1951. On *Gammarus zaddachi oceanicus* Segerstråle. *J. mar. biol. Ass. U.K.* **30**: 129–148, 3 figs.
SEGERSTRÅLE, S. G. 1959. Synopsis of date on the crustaceans, *Gammarus locusta*, *Gammarus oceanicus*, *Pontoporeia affinis* and *Corophium volutator* (Amphipoda Gammaridea). *Societas Scientiarum Fennica* **10**(5): 3–23, 5 figs.
    Includes key of *Gammarus* species occurring in coastal waters of northern Europe.
SPOONER, G. M. 1960. The occurrence of *Ingolfiella* in the Eddystone shell gravel, with description of a new species. *J. mar. biol. Ass. U.K.* **39**: 319–329, 5 figs.
INGLE, R. W. 1963. *Corophium multisetosum* Stock, a crustacean amphipod new to Great Britain, with notes on the distribution of *C. volutator* (Pallas) and *C. arenarium* Crawford. *Ann. Mag. nat. Hist.* (13) **6**: 449–460, 3 figs.
DAHL, E. 1964. The Amphipod genus *Acidostoma*. *Zool. Meded.* **39**: 48–58, 18 figs.
GLENNIE, E. A. 1967. The distribution of the hypogean Amphipoda in Britain. *Trans. Cave Res. Grp Gt Br.* **9**(3): 132–136, figs.
STOCK, J. H. 1967. A revision of the european species of the *Gammarus locusta*-group (Crustacea: Amphipoda). *Zool. Verh. Leiden* **90**: 1–56, figs.
MYERS, A. A. 1968. A revision of the amphipod genus *Microdeutopus* Costa (Gammaridea: Aoridae). *Bull. Br. Mus. nat. Hist.* (Zool.) **17** (4): 93–148, 22 figs, 1 pl.
BARNARD, J. L. 1969. The families and genera of marine Gammaridean Amphipoda. *Bull. U.S. natn. Mus.* **271**: 1–535, 173 figs.
LINCOLN, R. J. & HURLEY, D. E. 1974. *Scutocyamus parvus*, a new genus and species of whale-louse (Amphipoda: Cyamidae) ectoparasitic on the North Atlantic white-beaked dolphin. *Bull. Br. Mus. nat Hist.* (Zool.) **26**: 59–64, 2 figs, 1 pl.
LINCOLN, R. J. (in prep.) "Marine Amphipoda of the British Isles: Gammaridea". British Museum (Natural History).
    With check-list, keys and figures to all British families, genera and species.

Decapoda

KEMP, S. 1910. The Decapoda Natantia of the coasts of Ireland. *Scient. Invest. Fish. Brch Ire.* **1:** 1–190, 23 pls.

SELBIE, C. M. 1914. The Decapoda Reptantia of the coasts of Ireland. Pt. 1. Palinura, Astacura and Anomura (except Paguridea). *Scient. Invest. Fish. Brch Ire.* **1:** 1–116, 15 pls.

SELBIE, C. M. 1921. The Decapoda Reptantia of the coasts of Ireland. Pt. 2. Paguridea. *Scient. Invest. Fish. Brch Ire.* **1:** 1–68, 9 pls.

PALMER, R. 1927. A revision of the genus *"Portunus"* (A. Milne Edwards, Bell, etc.) *J. mar. biol. Ass. U.K.* **14:** 877–908, 9 figs.

LEBOUR, M. V. 1928. The larval stages of the Plymouth Brachyura. *Proc. zool. Soc. Lond.* **1928**(2): 473–560, 5 figs, 16 pls.

BULL, H. O. 1937. Notes on the British species of the genus *Galathea* Fab. *Rep. Dove mar. Lab.* **4:** 38–52, 6 pls.

GURNEY, H. O. 1939. "Bibliography of the larvae of decapod Crustacea". i–vi + 1–123 pp. Ray Society, London.

BOUVIER, E. L. 1940. Decapodes Marcheurs. *Faune Fr.* **37:** 1–404, 222 figs, pls I–XIV.

GURNEY, R. 1942. "Larvae of Decapod Crustacea". viii + 306 pp., 122 figs. Ray Society, London.

LEBOUR, M. V. 1943. The larvae of the genus *Porcellana* (Crustacea Decapoda) and related forms. *J. mar. biol. Ass. U.K.* **25:** 721–737, 12 figs.

LEBOUR, M. V. 1944. The larval stages of *Portumnus* (Crustacea Brachyura) with notes on some other genera. *J. mar. biol. Ass. U.K.* **26:** 7–15, 5 figs.

HOLTHUIS, L. B. Decapoda (K IX) A. Natantia, Macrura Reptantia, Anomura en Stomatopoda (K X). *Fauna Ned.* **15:** 1–166, figs.

DRACH, P. & FOREST, J. 1953. Description et répartition des *Xantho* des mers d'Europe. *Archs Zool. exp. gén.* **90:** 1–36, 24 figs.

NOUVEL, H. 1953. Un *Hippolyte* (Crust. Decap. Nat.) méconnu, nouveau pour les côtes de France et commensal de la comatule, *Antedon bifida*. *Archs Zool. exp. gén.* **90:** 71–86, 41 figs.

HOLTHUIS, L. B. 1954. The names of the european species of the genus *Xantho* Leach, 1814 (Crustacea Decapoda Brachyura). *Proc. K. Akad. Wet.* **57C:** 103–107.

GORDON, I. & INGLE, R. W. 1956. On a pelagic Penaeid prawn, *Funchalia woodwardi* Johnson, new to the British Fauna. *J. mar. biol. Ass. U.K.* **35:** 475–481, 1 fig.

NAYLOR, E. 1957. *Brachynotus sexdentatus* (Risso), a Grapsoid crab new to Britain. *Ann. Mag. nat. Hist.* (12) **10:** 521–523, 1 fig.

NOUVEL, H. & HOLTHUIS, L. B. 1957. Les Processidae (Crustacea Decapoda Natantia) des eaux europeénnes. *Zool. Verh. Leiden* **32:** 1–53, 220 figs.

MACDONALD, J. M., PIKE, R. B. & WILLIAMSON, D. I. 1957. Larvae of the British species of *Diogenes, Pagurus, Anapagurus* and *Lithodes* (Crustacea, Decapoda). *Proc. zool. Soc. Lond.* **128:** 209–257, 11 figs.

MACDONALD, R. 1958. The Crustacea, Decapoda of Belfast Loch. *Ann. Mag. nat. Hist.* (12) **10:** 656–660.

PIKE, R. B. & WILLIAMSON, D. L. 1958. Crustacea Decapoda: Larvae XI. Paguridea, Coenobitidea, Dromiidea and Homolidea. (Revised 1959) *Fich. Ident. Zooplancton* **81:** 1–9, 66 figs.

SOLLAUD, E. 1959. Sur deux espèces de crevettes nouvelles pour la faune marine des côtes de Bretagne: *Periclimenes amethysteus* (Risso) et *Hippolyte leptocerus* (Heller) (Decapoda Natantia). *Bull. Lab. marit. Dinard* **44:** 4–6.

ELOFSSON, R. 1959. A new decapod larva referred to *Calocarides coronatus* (Trybon). *Univ. Bergen Arb.* **7:** 1–10, 20 figs.
ALMAÇA, C. 1959. Sobre a variabilidade e a posiçao sistematica do *Xantho incisus* Leach (= *X. floridus* (Montagu)) da zona intercotidal do litoral Português. 1. Populaçoes do Sul do Cabo da Roca. *Rev. Fac. Cienc. Lisboa* **2C:** 233–252, 1 fig. (in Portuguese).
HARTNOLL, R. G. 1961. A re-examination of the spider crab *Eurynome* Leach from British waters. *Crustaceana* **2:** 171–182, 7 figs.
CARLISLE, D. B. & TREGENZA, N. 1961. A hermit crab new to Britain. *Nature, Lond.* **190:** 931.
HARTNOLL, R. G. 1963. The biology of Manx spider crabs. *Proc. zool. Soc. Lond.* **141:** 423–496, 30 figs.
FOREST, J. & ZARIQUIEY ALVAREZ 1964. Le genre *Macropodia* Leach en Mediterranée. I. *Bull. Mus. nat. Hist. Paris* (2) **36:** 222–234, 16 figs.
ALLEN, J. A. 1967. "The Fauna of the Clyde Sea area. Crustacea: Euphausiacea and Decapoda, with an illustrated key to the British species". 116 pp., illust. Scottish Marine Biological Association, Millport.
CHRISTIANSEN, M. E. 1969. Marine invertebrates of Scandinavia 2. Crustacea Decapoda Brachyura. *Mar. Invert. Scand.* **2:** 1–143, figs., maps.
SMALDON, G. 1975. *Hippolyte longirostris* (Czerniavsky, 1868) (Caridea, Hippolytidae) off the Cornish Coast. *Crustaceana* (3) **29:** 314–315.
INGLE, R. W. 1978. "A Guide to the Identification of British Crabs (Decapoda Brachyura)". 150 pp. British Museum (Natural History), London.

UNIRAMIA

MYRIAPODA

DIPLOPODA   British species about 51

BLOWER, J. G. 1958. British Millipedes (Diplopoda). *Synopses Br. Fauna* **11,** 74 pp., 85 figs., 1 pl.
BLOWER, J. G. 1972. The distribution of British millipedes as known at the end of 1969. *Bull. Br. Myriapod Gr.* **1:** 9–38.
BRÖLEMANN, H. W. 1935. Myriapodes Diplopodes (Chilognathes I). *Faune Fr.* **29,** 369 pp., 748 figs.
  Orders Nematophora and Colobognatha only.
SCHUBART, O. 1934. Tausenfüssler oder Myriapoda I: Diplopoda. *Tierwelt Dtl.* **28,** vii + 318 pp., 480 figs.

CHILOPODA   British species about 47

BRÖLEMANN, H. W. 1930. "Éléments d'une faune des Myriapodes de France. Chilopodes." xx + 450 pp., 481 figs. Imprimerie Toulousaine, Toulouse.
EASON, E. H. 1964. "Centipedes of the British Isles". x + 294 pp., 495 figs., 5 pls. Warne, London.

SYMPHYLA AND PAUROPODA   British species about 14 + 22

EDWARDS, C. A. 1959. A revision of the British Symphyla. *Proc. zool. Soc. Lond.* **132:** 403–439, 13 figs. (compound).

REMY, P. A. 1956. Quelques stations de Symphyles et de Pauropodes dans les Îles Britanniques. *Ann. Mag. nat. Hist.* (12) **9**: 287–288.
SCHELLER, U. 1962. Some Symphyla and Pauropoda from south-western Germany. *Mitt. bad. Landesver. Naturk. N.F.* **8**: 261–265, 1 fig.
SCHELLER, U. 1974. Pauropoda from arable soil in Great Britain. *Symp. zool. Soc. Lond.* **32**: 405–410, 1 fig.
REMY, P. A. 1961. Sur la microfaune du sol de Grande-Bretagne. *Ann. Mag. nat. Hist.* (13) **4**: 149–154, 3 figs.
SCHELLER, U. 1976. The Pauropoda and Symphyla of the Geneva Museum II. A review of the Swiss Pauropoda and Symphyla of the Geneva Museum II. A review of the Swiss Pauropoda (Myriapoda). *Revue suisse Zool.* **83**: 3–37, 25 figs.

Keys to and illustrations of 26 species, most of which are likely to occur throughout NW Europe.

HEXAPODA (= INSECTA)

INSECTA GENERALLY

IMMS, A. D. 1977. "A General Text-book of Entomology". 11th edn. (revised by O. W. Richards and R. G. Davies) xxx + xxx pp., many figs. Methuen, London.

This is **the** British general textbook. Gives keys to the more important families of insects.

GRASSÉ, P.-P., ed. 1949–51. "Traité de Zoologie". Vols. 9 and 10 (1–2). Masson & Cie, Paris.
KÜKENTHAL, W. 1968 on. "Handbuch der Zoologie". Vol. 4(2). "Insecta". Revised edn. (M. Beier, ed.). W. de Gruyter, Berlin.

Parts by various authors.

TULLGREN, A. & WAHLGREN, E. 1920–22. "Svenska Insekter". 812 pp., 642 figs., 9 col. pls. Nordstedt & Söner, Stockholm.

Keys to families, genera, notes on species (in Swedish). Out of print.

BEI-BIENKO, G. Y. 1964. [Keys to the Insects of the European USSR **1.** Apterygota, Palaeoptera, Hemimetabola]. Israel Program for Scientific Translations, 1214 pp., Jerusalem 1967.

Other parts cited below under different orders: it is likely that yet other parts will be translated.

BRUES, C. T., MELANDER, A. L. & CARPENTER, F. M. 1954. "Classification of Insects (revised)". v + 917 pp., many illustrations. Boston, Mass.

Keys to families and some subfamilies, including fossils.

MACKERRAS, I. M., ed. 1970. "The Insects of Australia." 1029 pp., many illustrations, partly in colour. "Supplement" 1974, viii + 146 pp., illustrated. Melbourne.
CHAPMAN, R. F. 1969. "The Insects: Structure and Function". xii + 819 pp., illustrated. London.
CHINNERY, M. 1973. "A Field Guide to the Insects of Britain and N. Europe". 352 pp., many line drawings, 60 pls. Collins, London.

Keys to families or superfamilies, and fine coloured pictures of hundreds of our commoner insects.

BORROR, D. J. & WHITE, R. E. 1970. "Field Guide to the insects of America north of Mexico". 404 pp., many illustrations (Pocket size). Boston, Mass.
GRAF, J. see above p. 2.
BROHMER, P. see above p. 2.
WIGGLESWORTH, V. B. 1964. "The life of Insects". xii + 360 pp., 36 pls. Weidenfeld & Nicholson, London.

A book on insect life-processes.

IMMS, A. D. 1971. "Insect Natural History". 3rd edn. (G. C. Varley and B. M. Hobby, eds.) xviii + 317 pp., illustrated. Collins, London.
KLOET, G. S. & HINCKS, W. D. 1945. "A Check List of British Insects". 483 pp., Stockport. Partly revised in the Royal Entomological Society Handbooks.
ROYAL ENTOMOLOGICAL SOCIETY OF LONDON. 1949 on. "Handbooks for the Identification of British Insects". 12 vols., none complete.
SMART, J. 1973. "Instructions for Collectors". Revised B. H. Cogan & K. G. V. Smith). vi + 169 pp., illustrated. British Museum (Natural History), London.
LINDROTH, C. H. 1974. "Handledning för Insektsamlare". 67 pp., well illustrated. Entomological Society of Stockholm.
  Instructions for collecting, rearing, mounting (in Swedish), guide to literature.
GAEDIKE, R. 1976. Bibliographie der Bestimmungstabellen Europäischer Insekten (1964–1973). *Beitr. Ent.* **26**: 49–166.
  Cites publications listing works published in earlier years.

SPECIAL ASPECTS

SMITH, K. G. V., Ed. 1973. "Insects and other Arthropods of Medical Importance". 561 pp., 217 figs., 12 pls. British Museum (Natural History), London.
ZUMPT, F. 1968. Human- und veterinärmedizinische Entomologie. 9, 49 pp., 54 figs., In "Handbuch der Zoologie" (W. Kükenthal, ed.). W. de Gruyter, Berlin.
BUSVINE, J. R. 1966. "Insects and Hygiene". 2nd edn. xi + 467 pp. Methuen, London.
EDWARDS, C. A. & HEATH, G. W. 1964. "The Principles of Agricultural Entomology". xiv + 418 pp., 36 pls. Chapman & Hall, London.
  Includes slugs and some other non-insect groups.
MASSEE, A. M. 1946. "The Pests of Fruits and Hops". 2nd edn. (revised). 284 pp. + 26 pls. Crosby Lockwood, London.
CHRYSTAL, R. N. 1937. "Insects of the British Woodlands". xiii + 338 pp., 33 pls. Warne, London & New York.
NÜSSLIN, O. & RHUMBLER, L. 1927. "Forstinsektenkunde". 4th edn. xvi + 625 pp., 480 figs. Parey, Berlin.
TRÄGARDH, I. 1939. "Sveriges Skogsinsekter". 2nd edn. 509 pp., 570 illustrations. Geber, Stockholm (in Swedish).
CHU, H. F. 1949. "How to Know the Immature Insects". 234 pp., 631 figs. W. C. Brown, Dubuque, Iowa.
KEVAN, D. K. McE. 1955. A practical key to the orders and suborders of soil and litter inhabiting animals. In "Soil Zoology", (D. K. McE. Kevan, ed.), pp. 452–488. Butterworth, London.
GILYAROV, M. S., ed. 1964. [Determination of the larvae of insects found in the soil]. 919 pp., 567 figs. Akad. Nauk SSSR, Moscow (in Russian).
  Coleoptera pp. 45–573, Diptera pp. 605–806, Lepidoptera pp. 809–882.
CLAUSEN, C. P. 1940. "Entomophagous Insects". x + 688 pp., 257 figs. McGraw Hill, New York & London. Reprinted 1972, Hafner, New York.
  A survey of habits of predatory and parasitic insects.
ASKEW, R. R. 1971. "Parasitic Insects". xvii + 316 pp., 124 figs. Heinemann, London.
SWANTON, E. W. 1912. "British Plant-Galls: a classified textbook of cecidology". xv + 287 pp., illustrated (partly in colour). Methuen, London.
BUHR, H. 1964–65, "Bestimmungstabellen der Gallen an Pflanzen Mittel- und Nordeuropas". 2 vols. xvi + 1572 pp., 25 pls. Gustav Fischer, Jena.
  See also Eady & Quinlan p. 88 (below).
HERING, E. M. 1951. "Biology of the Leaf Miners". iv + 420 pp. W. Junk, The Hague. Translation by K. A. Spencer.

HERING, E. M. 1957. "Bestimmungstabellen der Blattminen von Europa". Vol. 1–2, 1185 pp. Vol. 3–221 pp. W. Junk, The Hague.

MACAN, T. T. 1959. See above p. 4.

REGIONAL

GRIMSHAW, P. H. 1939. Classified index of entomological contributions to the Scottish Naturalist from its commencement in 1871 to the end of 1938. *Scott. Nat.* **1939:** 105–120, 137–188.

BEIRNE, B. P. Unpublished. "A Bibliography of Irish Entomology". Copies deposited in the libraries of the Royal Entomological Society of London and the Royal Irish Academy and National Museum of Ireland; see *Entomologist's Gaz.* **7:** 177–178.

RICHARDS, O. W. 1964. The entomological fauna of southern England with special reference to the country round London. *Trans. Soc. Br. Ent.* **16**(1): 1–48.

HOBBY, B. M. 1933–35. A bibliography of entomological notes and papers contained in the serial publications issued by local scientific societies in the British Isles. *Trans. ent. Soc. S. Eng.* **8:** 117–139; *Trans. Soc. Br. Ent.* **1:** 85–102; **2:** 167–233.

Regional faunal lists have been published by a number of local societies, notably the Lancashire & Cheshire Fauna Committee and the Yorkshire Naturalists' Union, while others appear in the "Victoria Histories of the Counties of England".

Numerous notes and short papers recording species new to Britain or data additional to that contained in the latest standard work have been published in the *Entomologist,* the *Entomologist's Gazette,* the *Entomologist's Monthly Magazine,* and the *Entomolgist's Record and Journal of Variation.*

THYSANURA AND DIPLURA   British species 22

DELANY, M. J. 1954. Thysanura and Diplura. *Handbk Ident. Br. Insects* **1**(2): 1–7, 15 figs.

PROTURA   British species 12 approx.

TUXEN, S. L. 1964. "The Protura. A revision of the species of the world with keys for determination". 360 pp., 567 figs. Hermann, Paris.

NOSEK, J. 1973. "The European Protura, their taxonomy, ecology and distribution with keys for determination". 345 pp., 111 figs. Museum d'Histoire Naturelle, Geneva.

COLLEMBOLA   British species about 300

GISIN, H. 1960. "Collembolenfauna Europas". 360 pp., 554 figs. Museum d'Histoire Naturelle, Geneva.

PTERYGOTA

Orthoptera and Dermaptera
British species 42 and 6

RICHARDS, O. W. & WALOFF, N. 1954. Studies on the biology and population dynamics of British grasshoppers. *Anti-locust Bull.* **17,** 182 pp., 67 figs.

Keys to nymphs of British Acrididae in every instar.

HINCKS, W. D. 1956. Dermaptera and Orthoptera. *Handbk Ident. Br. Insects* **1** (5, revised). 24 pp., 74 figs.

RAGGE, D. R. 1965. "Grasshoppers, crickets and cockroaches of the British Isles". (With companion gramohone record of the songs.) xii + 299 pp., 130 figs., 22 pls. Warne, London and New York.
   Keys to adults. Life histories, habits, songs, distributions maps. Colour plates of every species.
PRINCIS, K. 1965. Ordnung Blattariae (Schaben). *Bestimm. Büch. Bodenfauna Europ.* **3,** 50 pp., 56 figs.
   Keys, in German, to adults of all European cockroaches.
HARZ, K. 1969. "Die Orthopteren Europas I". 749 pp., 2360 figs. Junk, The Hague.
   Keys, in German and English, to adults of all European Ensifera (bush-crickets and crickets).
OSCHMANN, M. 1969. Bestimmungstabellen für die Larven mitteldeutscher Orthopteren. *Dt. ent. Z.* (N.F.): **16:** 227–291, 2 figs.
   Keys to nymphs of selected German Orthoptera and Dermaptera in every instar.
BROUGHTON, W. B. 1972. The grasshopper and the taxonomer. III. Keys to the species. *J. biol. Educ.* **6:** 385–395, 25 figs.
   Keys to adults of British Saltatoria (grasshoppers, crickets and bush-crickets) based on both songs and structure.
BROWN, V. K. 1973. A key to the nymphal instars of the British species of *Ectobius* Stephens (Dictyoptera: Blattidae). *Entomologist* **106:** 202–209, 4 figs.
HAES, E. C. M. 1973. "Crickets and grasshoppers of the British Isles". 15 pp., 3 pls. British Naturalists' Association.
   Introductory account, well suited to beginners.
RAGGE, D. R. 1973. The British Orthoptera: a supplement. *Entomologist's Gaz.* **24:** 227–245.
   Supplement to Ragge (1965), above.
MARSHALL, J. A. 1974. The British Orthoptera since 1800. In "The Changing Flora and Fauna of Britain" (D. L. Hawksworth, ed.). pp. 307–322. Academic Press, London and New York.
   An account of recent trends in the British Orthoptera fauna.
SKELTON, M. J. 1974. "Orthoptera, Dictyoptera and Odonata. Preliminary distribution maps". Biological Records Centre.
   Preliminary results of the Biolgial Records Centre's Distribution Maps Scheme.
HARZ, K. 1975. "Die Orthopteren Europas II". 939 pp., 3519 figs. Junk. The Hague.
   Keys, in German and English, to adults of all European Caelifera (grasshoppers and ground-hoppers).
PITKIN, L. M. 1976. A comparative study of the stridulatory files of the British Gomphocerinae (Orthoptera: Acrididae). *J. nat. Hist.* **10:** 17–28, 27 figs.
BRINDLE, A. 1977. British earwigs (Dermaptera). *Entomologist's Gaz.* **28:** in press, 11 figs.
   Key to adults.

Isoptera (Termites)

Not native of the faunal area. The timber-infesting species. *Reticulitermes flavipes* (Kollar), described from Vienna whence it has been eradicated, but native of Eastern U.S.A. and N. Mexico, successfully infested a centrally heated system of buildings in Hamburg in 1937.

Certain dry-wood termites, popularly called "white ants", have been kept as pets in the U.K., more in the past than at the present time.

Plecoptera
British species 35

HYNES, H. B. N. 1967. A key to the adults and nymphs of the British stoneflies

(Plecoptera), with notes on their ecology and distribution. 2nd revised edn. *Scient. Publs Freshwat. biol. Ass.* **17**: 1–91, 47 figs. + maps. See also *Trans. R. ent. Soc. Lond.* **91**: 549–557, *Proc. R. ent. Soc. Lond. A* **38**: 12–14 and 70–76.

KIMMINS. D. E. 1950. Plecoptera. *Handbk Ident. Br. Insects* **1**(6): 1–18, 49 figs.

MACPHEE, F.M. & HYNES, H. B.N. 1970. The maxillae of the British species of *Isoperla* (Plecoptera: Perlodidae). *Proc. R. ent. Soc. Lond. A (7–9): 123–124. 1 fig.*

BAUMANN, R. W. 1975. A revision of the stonefly family Nemouridae (Plecoptera): a study of the world fauna at the generic level. *Smithsonian Contr. Zool.* **211**: 1–74, 186 figs.

ILLIES, J. 1963. 7. Ordnung: Steinfliegen, Uferfliegen, Plecoptera. Neubearbeitung. *Tierwelt Mitteleuropas* **4** (2, 5): 1–19, 15 pls.

BRINCK, P. 1952. Bäcksländor. Plecoptera. *Svensk Insektfauna* **15**: 1–126, 76 figs. (in Swedish).

Ephemeroptera
British species 46

EATON, A. E. 1871. Monograph on the Ephemeridae. *Trans. ent. Soc. Lond.* **1871**: 1–164, 6 pls.

EATON, A. E. 1883–88. A revisional monograph of recent Ephemeridae. *Trans. Linn. Soc. Lond.* (2) **3**: 1–352, 65 pls.

KIMMINS, D. E. 1950. Ephemeroptera. *Handbk Ident. Br. Insects* **1**(9): 1–17, 55 figs.

MACAN, T. T. 1961. A key to the nymphs of the British species of Ephemeroptera. *Scient. Publs Freshwat. biol. Ass.* **20**: 1–63, figs. and distribution maps.

KIMMINS, D. E. 1972. A revised key to the adults of the British species of Ephemeroptera with notes on their ecology. Revised end. *Scient. Publs Freshwat. biol. Ass.* **15**: 1–75, 30 figs.

ULMER, G. 1929. 6. Ordnung: Eintagsfliegen, Ephemeroptera (Agnatha). *Tierwelt Mitteleuropas* **4** (1, 3): 1–43, 150 figs.

Odonata
British species 43

LUCAS, W. J. 1900. "British Dragonflies (Odonata)". 356 pp., 57 figs., 27 pls. Ray Society, London.

LUCAS, W. J. 1930. "The Aquatic (Naiad) Stage of British Dragonflies (Paraneuroptera)". 132 pp., 35 pls. Ray Society, London.

LONGFIELD, C. E. 1949. "The Dragonfiies of the British Isles. 2nd edn. 256 pp., 40 pls., numerous figs. Warne, London.

FRASER, F. C. 1949. Odonata. *Handbk Ident. Br. Insects* **1**(10): 1–48, 24 figs.

GARDNER, A. E. 1954. A key to the larvae of the British Odonata. *Ent. Gaz.* **5**: 157–171, 193–213, 8 + 118 figs.

HAMMOND, C. O. 1977. "The Dragonfiies of Great Britain and Ireland". 115 pp., 23 figs. (compound), 20 pls., 44 maps. Curwen Press, London.
    Includes Gardner's key to the nymphs.

SCHIEMENZ, H. 1953. "Die Libellen unserer Heimat". 154 pp., 30 pls. Urania, Jena.

Thysanoptera
British species 158

MOUND, L. A. et al. 1976. Thysanoptera. *Handbk Ident. Br. Insects* **1**(11): 1–79, 327 figs.

PITKIN, B. R. 1976. The hosts and distribution of British thrips. *Ecological Entomology* **1**: 41–47.

MORISON, G. D. 1947–49. Thysanoptera of the London area. *Lond. Nat.* **26** (suppl.) 1–36, 37–75, 77–131.
PRIESNER, H. 1964. Ordnung Thysanoptera. *Bodenfauna Europas* **2**, 242 pp., 212 figs., 7 pls. Berlin.

Psocoptera
British species 90

FAHY, E. D. 1969. Some features of the nymphs of common species of British Trogiidae (Psocoptera). *Entomologist's mon. Mag.* **105**: 55–59, 2 figs.
GUNTHER, K. K. 1974. Staubläuse. Psocoptera. *Tierwelt Dtl.* **61**: 1–314, ilustr.
NEW, T. R. 1969. The early stages and life histories of some British foliage-frequenting Psocoptera, with notes on the overwintering stages of British arboreal Psocoptera. *Trans. R. ent. Soc. Lond.* **121**: 59–77. 7 figs.
  Includes keys to the immature stages of the British foliage-frequenting species.
NEW, T. R. 1971. An introduction to the natural history of the British Psocoptera. *Entomologist* **104**: 59–97.
  Includes a comprehensive list of references to the earlier literature on British psocids, including references to each species.
NEW, T. R. 1974. Psocoptera. *Handbk Ident. Br. Insects* **1**(7): 1–102, 350 figs.

Phthiraptera (True Lice)
British species about 425

As these have a predominantly host not a geographical distribution, published keys deal with genera on a world basis.

Amblycera, Ischnocera (Biting and Chewing Lice) British species about 400

CLAY, T. 1969. A key to the genera of the Menoponidae (Amblycera: Mallophaga: Insecta). *Bull. Br. Mus. nat. Hist.* (Ent.) **24**: 1–26, 29 figs., 7 pls.
CLAY, T. 1970. The Amblycera (Phthiraptera: Insecta). *Bull. Br. Mus. nat. Hist.* (Ent.) **25**: 75–98, 9 figs., 5 pls.
EICHLER, W. & ZLOTORYCKA, J. 1969. Zeitgenössische Mallophagen-Literatur (I). *Angew. Parasit.* **10**: 53–60, 104–124.
HOPKINS, G. H. E. & CLAY, T. 1952. "A Check List of the Genera and Species of Mallophaga". British Museum (Natural History), London.
KELER, S. VON 1960. Bibliographie der Mallophagen. *Mitt. zool. Mus. Berl.* **36**: 146–403.

Anoplura (Sucking Lice) British species about 25

FERRIS, G. F. 1961. The sucking lice. *Pacific Coast Ent. Soc. Mem.* **1**: ix + 320 pp., 124 pls. San Francisco.
  Keys to Anoplura of the World.
HOPKINS, G. H. E. 1949. The host-association of the lice of mammals. *Proc. zool. Soc. Lond. B* **119**: 387–604.

Hemiptera
British species 1709 approx.

Heteroptera British species 533 approx.

SOUTHWOOD, T. R. E. & LESTON, D. 1959. "Land and water bugs of the British Isles". 436 pp., figs. 1–153, 63 pls. Warne, London.
MASSEE, A. M. 1955. The county distribution of the British Hemiptera-Heteroptera. *Entomologist's mon. Mag.* **91**: 7–27.

HALBERT, J. N. 1935. A list of the Irish Hemiptera (Heteroptera and Cicadina). *Proc. R. Ir. Acad.* **42B** (8): 211–307.
MACAN, T. T. 1965. A revised key to the British water bugs (Hemiptera-Heteroptera) with notes on their ecology. *Scient. Publs Freshwat. biol. Ass.* **16:** 1–77, figs. 1–48.
STICHEL, W. 1955–62. "Illustrierte Bestimmungstabellen der Wanzen. II. Europa (Hemiptera-Heteroptera Europae)". Vol. 1, pp 1–423, Vol. 2, pp. 169–907, figs. 424–932 & 1–978. Vol. 3, pp. 1–428, figs. 1–301, 1–250, 1–222. Vol. 4, pp. 1–838, figs. 1–695, 1–186, 1–747. General Index, pp. 1–110. Hermsdorf, Berlin.
PÉRICART, J. 1972. Hémiptères Anthocoridae, Cimicidae et Microphysidae de l'Ouest-Paléarctique. *Faune de l'Europe et du Bassin Méditerranéen* **7:** 1–402, figs. 1–198
WAGNER, E. & WEBER, H. H. Hétéroptères Miridae. *Faune Fr.* **67:** 1–589, figs. 1–295.
WAGNER, E. 1952. Blindwanzen oder Miriden. *Tierwelt Dtl.* **41:** 1–218, figs. 1–125.
WAGNER, E. 1966. Wanzen oder Heteropteren. I. Pentatomorpha. *Tierwelt Dtl.* **54:** 1–235, figs. 1–149.
WAGNER, E. 1967. Wanzen oder Heteropteren. II. Cimicomorpha. *Tierwelt Dtl.* **55:** 1–179, figs. 1–114.

Homoptera-Auchenorhyncha   British species 351 approx.

EDWARDS, J. 1894–96. "The Hemiptera-Homoptera of the British Isles". 271 pp., 30 pls. Reeve, London.
HAUPT, H. 1935. 2. Unterordnung: Gleichflugler. Homoptera. *Tierwelt Mitteleuropas* **4** (3X): 115–262, figs. 182–560.
   Includes Auchenorhyncha and Psylloidea.
RIBAUT, H. 1936. Homoptères Auchénorhynques. I. Typhlocybidae. *Faune Fr.* **31:** 1–228, figs. 1–629.
RIBAUT, H. 1952. Homoptères Auchénorhynques II. Jassidae. *Faune Fr.* **57:** 1–474, figs. 1–1212.
CHINA, W. E. 1943. New and little-known species of British Typhlocybidae (Homoptera) with keys to the genera *Typhlocyba, Erythroneura, Dikraneura, Notus, Empoasca* and *Alebra. Trans. Soc. Br. Ent.* **8:** 111–153, figs. 1–14.
LE QUESNE, W. J. 1960. Hemiptera, Fulgoromorpha. *Handbk Ident. Br. Insects* **2** (3): 1–68, figs. 1–382.
LE QUESNE, W. J. 1965. Hemiptera, Cicadomorpha (excluding Deltocephalinae and Typhlocybinae). *Handbk Ident. Br. Insects* **2** (2a): 1–64, figs. 1–323.
LE QUESNE, W. J. 1969. Hemiptera, Cicadomorpha, Deltocephalinae. *Handbk Ident. Br. Insects* **2** (2b): 65–148, figs. 324–830.
NAST, J. 1972. "Palaearctic Auchenorhyncha (Homoptera). An annotated check list". 550 pp. Polish Academy of Sciences Institute of Zoology, Warsaw.
KLOET, G. S. & HINCKS, W. D. 1964. "A Check List of British Insects". xv + 119 pp. Royal Entomological Society, London.

Homoptera-Sternorhyncha

Psylloidea   British species 80

EDWARDS, J. see above.
OSSIANNILSSON, F. 1963. Notes on British Psyllids (Hem.-Hom.). *Entomologist* **96:** 249–257, 4 figs.
LOGINOVA, M. M. in Bei-Bienko 1964, pp. 551–608, see above p. 58.
HODKINSON, I. D. 1974. A contribution to the knowledge of some little-known British Psyllids-Homoptera: Psylloidea. *Entomologist's Gaz.* **25:** 75–84, 30 figs.
HAUPT, H. see above.

Aleyrodoidea British species 17
MOUND, L. A. 1966. A revision of the British Aleyrodidae (Hemiptera: Homoptera). *Bull. Br. Mus. nat. Hist.* (Ent.) **17** (9): 397–428, 28 figs.
ZAHRADNIK, J. 1963. 3. Überfamilie der Hemiptera Homoptera: Aleyrodína (Aleurodina), Mottenläuse. *Tierwelt Mitteleuropas* **4** (3Xd): 1–19 + 6 pls.

Aphidoidea British species 552
THEOBALD, F. V. 1926–27, 1929. "The Plant Lice or Aphididae of Great Britain". 3 vols. 1147 pp., 591 figs. Ashford and London.
STROYAN, H. L. G. 1950–72. Recent additions to the British aphid fauna [and similar titles]. *Trans. R. ent. Soc. Lond.* **101**: 89–124; **106**: 283–340; **109**: 311–359; **116**: 29–72; **124**: 37–79.
STROYAN, H. L. G. 1952. The identification of aphids of economic importance. *Plant Path.* **1**: 9–15, 42–48, 92–99, 123–199, many figs.
CARTER, C. I. 1971. Conifer wooly aphids (Adelgidae) in Britain. *Bull. For. Comm.* **42**, 51 pp., 32 figs.
STROYAN, H. L. G. 1978. Aphidoidea: introduction and Chaitophoridae and Callaphididae. *Handbk Ident. Br. Insects* **2** (4a): in press.
HILLE RIS LAMBERS, D. 1938–53. Contributions to a monograph of the Aphididae of Europe. *Temminckia* **3**: 1–44 + 4 pls; **4**: 1–234 + 6 pls; **7**: 179–320 + 7 pls, **8**: 182–323 + 6 pls., **9**: 1–176 + 6 pls. Leiden.
BÖRNER, C. 1952. Europae centralis Aphides. *Mitt. Thüring. bot. Ges., Beih.* **3**: 1–488.
BÖRNER, C. & HEINZE, K. 1957. Aphidoidea. *Handbk. Pfl Krank* (5th edn.) **5**(4): 1–402, 194 figs. P. Parey, Berlin.
HEINZE, K. 1962. Pflanzenschädliche Blattlausarten der Familien Lachnidae, Adelgidae und Phylloxeridae, eine systematisch-faunistische Studie. *Deuts. ent. Z.* (N.F.) **9**: 143–227, 41 figs.
BLACKMAN, R. 1975. "Aphids". 175 pp., 37 figs., 8 pls. Ginn, London.
SHAPOSHNIKOV, R. K. in BEI-BIENKO 1964, pp. 616–799, 273 figs., see above p. 58.

Coccoidea British species 174
NEWSTEAD, R. 1901, 1903. "Monograph of the Coccidae of the British Isles". 2 vols., 476 pp., 75 pls. Ray Society, London.
GREEN E. E. 1927–28. A brief review of the indigenous Coccidae of the British Islands, with emendations and additions [to Febr. 1928]. Suppl. to *Ent. Rec.* **39, 40,** 14 pp., 4 pls.
WILLIAMS, D. J. 1962. The British Pseudococcidae. *Bull. Br. Mus. nat. Hist.* (Ent.) **12** (1): 1–79, 29 figs.
LINDINGER, L. 1912. "Die Schildläuse (Coccidae) Europas, Nordafrikas und Vorderasiens . . ." 388 pp., 32 figs. Eugen Ulmer, Stuttgart.
SCHMUTTERER, H. 1959. Schildläuse oder Coccoidea. *Tierwelt Dtl.* **45**: 1–243, 134 figs., 6 pls.
DANTZIG, E. M. in BEI-BIENKO 1964, pp. 800–850, see above pp. 58.

Neuroptera, Megaloptera and Mecoptera
British species 57 + 6 + 4

FRASER, F. C. 1959. Mecoptera, Megaloptera, Neuroptera. *Handbk. Ident. Br. Insects* **1** (12113): 1–40, figs. 1–15 (compound).
KILLINGTON, F. J. 1936–37. "A monograph of the British Neuroptera". 2 vols. 575 pp., 30 pls. Ray Society, London. (At present being revised.)
KIMMINS, D. E. 1962. Keys to the British species of aquatic Megaloptera and Neuroptera. 2nd edn., revised. *Scient. Publs Freshwat. biol. Ass.* **8**: 1–23, figs.

KIMMINS, D. E. 1963. Notes on two British species of Neuroptera (*Boriomyia mortoni* (McL.) and *B. killingtoni* (Morton), with a description of a new species of the *mortoni* group of *Boriomyia*. *Entomologist's Gaz.* **14**: 140–149, 27 figs.

WARD, L. K. 1970. *Aleuropteryx juniperi* Ohm (Neur. Coniopterygidae) new to Britain feeding on *Carulaspis juniperi* Bouche (Hem. Diaspididae). *Entomologist's mon. Mag.* **106**: 74–78, 3 figs.

ASPÖCK, H. & ASPÖCK, U. 1964. Synopsis der Systematik, Ökologie und Biogeographie der Neuropteren Mitteleuropas im Spiegel der Neuropteren-Fauna von Linz und Oberösterreich, sowie Bestimmungsschlüssel für die mitteleuropäischen Neuropteren. *Naturk. Jb. Stadt Linz* **1964**: 127–282, 155 figs.

ASPÖCK, H. & ASPÖCK, U. 1969. Die Neuropteren Mitteleuropas: ein Nachtrag zur "Synopsis der Sytematik, Ökologie und Biogeographie der Neuropteren Mitteleuropas". *Naturk. Jb. Stadt Linz* **1969**: 17–68, 23 figs.

These two works list the European species of Neuroptera and Megaloptera, with keys and distribution data.

MEINANDER, M. 1972. A revision of the family Coniopterygidae (Planipennia). *Acta zool. fenn.* **136**: 1–357, 223 figs.

A revision of the world species of the family.

WARD, P. H. in preparation. "A revision of the Panorpidae (Scorpion flies) of the Western Palaearctic Region" [or similar title]. British Museum (Natural History), London.

Trichoptera
British species 194

MOSELY, M. E. 1939. "The British Caddis Flies (Trichoptera): a Collector's Handbook". 320 pp., 631 figs., 4 pls. Routledge, London.

HICKIN, N. E. 1967. "Caddis Larvae: larvae of the British Trichoptera". 476 pp., 980 figs. Hutchinson, London.

MACAN, T. T. 1973. A key to the adults of the British Trichoptera. *Scient. Publs Freshwat. biol. Ass.* **28**: 1–151, figs., 5 pls.

BRAY, R. P. 1967. The taxonomy of the larvae and pupae of the British Phryganeidae (Trichoptera). *J. Zool. Lond.* **153**: 223–244, 29 figs.

HILDREW, A. G. & MORGAN, J. C. 1974. The taxonomy of the British Hydropsychidae (Trichoptera). *J. Ent. (B)* **43** (2): 217–229, 51 figs.

LEADER, J. P. 1968. The larva of *Molanna palpata* McLachlan, and some further characters of the larva of *Molanna angustata* Curtis (Trichoptera, Molannidae). *Entomologist's Gaz.* **19**: 21–29, 5 figs.

BARNARD, P. C. 1971. The larva of *Agraylea sexmaculata* Curtis (Trichoptera, Hydroptilidae). *Entomologist's Gaz.* **22**: 253–257, 8 figs.

EDINGTON, J. M. & ALDERSON, R. 1973. The taxonomy of British psychomyiid larvae (Trichoptera). *Freshwat. Biol.* **3**: 463–478, 50 figs., 1 pl.

HILEY, P. D. 1976. The identification of British limnephilid larvae (Trichoptera). *Systematic Entomology* **1**: 147–167, 116 figs.

LEPNEVA, S. G. [Keys to the Insects of the European USSR] 2 Trichoptera **1–2**: 638 + 700 pp., many figs. Israel Program for Scientific Translations, Jerusalem.

Contains descriptions of many European species of Trichoptera larvae and pupae.

BOTOSANEANU, L. 1967. Trichoptera. In "Limnofauna Europaea" (J. Illies, ed.), pp. 285–309. Fischer, Stuttgart.

Distribution of all European species of Trichoptera.

FISCHER, F. C. J. 1960–73. "Trichopterorum Catalogus". 15 vols. and index. Nederlandse Entomologische Vereiniging, Amsterdam.

The world catalogue of taxonomic literature on the Trichoptera.

Lepidoptera
British species about 2500

GENERAL

MEYRICK, E. 1928. "A revised Handbook of the British Lepidoptera". 2nd edn. 914 pp. Watkins & Doncaster, London.
BARRETT, C. G. 1892–1907. "The Lepidoptera of the British Islands". 11 vols. about 300 pp. *per* vol., 469 pls. Lovell Reeve, London.
TUTT, J. W. 1899–1909. "A Natural History of the British Lepidoptera". Vols 1–5, 8–10. 3648 pp. Swann, Sonnenschein, London.
DE WORMS, C. G. M. 1963. Recent additions to the British Macrolepidoptera. *Entomologist's Gaz.* **14**: 101–119, 2 pls. (1 col.).
  Historical data with numerous citations: distributional and biological notes on some species: illustrations of species not included in South 1961 (see below).
MACLEOD, R. D. 1959. "Key to the names of British Butterflies and Moths". vii + 86 pp. Pitman, London.
BEIRNE, B. P. 1941. A list of the Macrolepidoptra of Ireland. *Proc. R. Ir. Acad.* **47**: 53–147.
BRADLEY, J. D., FLETCHER, D. S. & WHALLEY, P. E. S. 1972. In "A Check List of British Insects", G. S. Kloet, and W. D. Hincks, 2nd edn., revised. Part 2, Lepidoptera. *Handbk Ident. Br. Insects* **11** (2), 153 pp.
BRADLEY, J. D., FLETCHER, D. S. & WHALLEY, P. E. S. 1974. Addenda and corrigenda to the Lepidoptera part of Kloet & Hincks Check List of British Insects (Edn 2), 1972. *Entomologist's Gaz.* **25**: 219–222.
BROHMER, P. 1974. See p. 2 (above). Lepidoptera, pp. 381–405.
SEITZ, A. 1906–54. "Macrolepidoptera of the World". Vols. 1–4 and supplements. Rhopalocera and Macro-Heterocera – Fauna Palaearctica. Many pls. A. Kernen, Stuttgart.
FORSTER, W. & WOHLFAHRT, T. A. 1954–60. "Die Schmetterlinge Mitteleuropas". 3 vols. 520 pp., illustr. Franckh'sche, Stuttgart.
BERGMANN, A. 1951–55. "Die Grossschmetterlinge Mittel-deutschlands". 5 vols. about 4000 pp., illustr. adults and habitats. Urania, Jena.
NORDSTRÖM, F., WAHLGREN, E. & TULLGREN, A. 1935–41. "Svenska Fjärilar. Systematisk bearbetning av Sveriges Storfjärilar, Macrolepidoptera". 440 pp., 1800 ilustr., 12 maps. Nordisk Familjeboks, Stockholm (in Swedish).
OPHEIM, M. 1958–72. "Catalogue of the Lepidoptera of Norway". 3 vols. 89 pp., figs., maps. Norsk Lepidopterologisk Selskap, Oslo.
KARSHOLT, O. & NIELSEN, E. S. 1976. "Systematisk fortegnelse over Danmarks sommerfugle. Catalogue of the Lepidoptera of Denmark". 128 pp. Scandinavian Science Press, Klampenborg.
LEMPKE, B. J. 1936–70. Catalogus der Nederlandske Macrolepidoptera. *Tijdschr. Ent.* **79–112**, supplements 1–16, illustr.
LEMPKE, B. J. 1976. "Naamlijst van de Nederlandse Lepidoptera". 99 pp. K. Nederl. Natuurh. Ver., Amsterdam.
LHOMME, L. 1923–49. Catalogue des Lépidoptères de France et de Belgique". 2 vols. 800 + 696 pp. Le Carriol, Lot.

Rhopalocera (butterflies)

FROHAWK, F. W. 1934. "The Complete Book of British Butterflies". 384 pp., figs., 832 col. pls. Ward Lock, London.
SOUTH, R. 1941. "The Butterflies of the British Isles". 212 pp., 127 pls. Warne, London. Reprinted 1943.

HOWARTH, T. G. 1973. "South's British Butterflies". 210 pp., 48 col. pls. Warne, London.
    A complete revision of the original work by Richard South, presented in a new style and format.
HOWARTH, T. G. 1973. "Colour Identification Guide to the British Butterflies". 46 pp., 48 col. pls. Warne, London.
FORD, E. B. 1945. "Butterflies". New Naturalist No. 1. 368 pp., 72 pls. Collins, London.
    Contains historical, distributional and other discursive text.
HIGGINS, L. G. & RILEY, N. D. 1970. "A Field Guide to the Butterflies of Britain and Europe". 380 pp., 60 col. pls., maps. Collins, London.
    Republished in several other European languages.
HIGGINS, L. G. 1976 (1975). "Classification of European Butterflies". 320 pp., 402 figs. Collins, London.
NORDSTRÖM, F. 1955. De fennoskandiska dagfjärilarnas utbredning. Lepidoptera diurna (Rhopalocera och Hesperoidea). *Acta Univ. Lund.* N.F. **51**(1): 176 pp., 119 maps.
ACKERY, P. R. 1975. A guide to the genera and species of Parnasiinae (Lepidoptera, Papilionidae). *Bull. Br. Mus. nat. Hist.* (Ent.) **31:** 71–105, 32 figs., 16 pls.

Macro-Heterocera (larger moths)

SOUTH, R. 1941. "The Moths of the British Isles". New edn. (revised H. M. Edelsten, D. S. Fletcher and R. J. Collins). Vol. 1, 427 pp., 148 pls. Vol. 2, 379 pp., 141 pls. Warne, London.
TUTT, J. W. 1891–92. "The British Noctuae and their varieties". 4 vols. 164 + 180 + 132 + 144 pp. Swan, Sonnenschein, London and Friedländer, Berlin.
    Descriptions of typical forms and of named varieties; no illustrations.
TURNER, H. J. 1926–50. "The British Noctuae and their varieties (J. W. Tutt)". "Supplementary Notes 1–4". Reprinted from *Entomologist's Rec.* Buncle, Arbroath.
CLASSEY, E. W. 1954. Separation characters of some British Noctuid moths. *Proc. S. Lond. ent. nat. Hist. Soc.* **1952–1953:** 64–72, 16 figs., 4 pls.
FORD, E. B. 1955. "Moths". New Naturalist No. 30. 266 pp., 56 pls., 12 maps. Collins, London.
CULOT, J. 1910–20. "Noctuelles et Géomètres d'Europe". 4 vols. about 1000 pp., 81 + 70 pls. Meyrin, Geneva.
JUUL, K. 1948. "Nordens Eupithecier". 147 pp., figs., maps, 13 pls. Gravers Andersen, Aarhus (in Danish, with diagnoses in English).
HOFFMEYER, S. 1960. "De Danske Spindere". Notodontidae etc. 270 pp., 24 col. pls. Universitets forlaget, Aarhus (in Danish).
HOFFMEYER, S. 1962. "De Danske Ugler. Noctuidae". 387 pp., 33 col. pls. Universitets forlaget, Aarhus.
HOFFMEYER, S. 1966. "De Danske Målere. Geometridae". 2nd edn. 361 pp., 25 col. pls. Universitets forlaget, Aarhus.
NORDSTRÖM, F. et al. 1961. De fennoskandiska svärmarnas och spinnarnas utbredning. (Sphinges, Bombycimorpha etc.). *Acta Univ. Lund.* (N.F.) **57**(4): 87 pp., 181 maps.
NORDSTRÖM, F. et al. 1969. "De Fennoskandiska och Danska Nattflynas utbredning (Noctuidae)". 157 pp., 404 maps. Gleerup, Lund.
FIBIGER, M. & KRISTENSEN, N. P. 1974. The Sesiidae (Lepidoptera) of Fennoscandia and Denmark. *Fauna ent. Scand.* **2:** 91 pp., 144 figs., 1 map, col. pls.

Microlepidoptera

HEATH, J. *et al.*, ed. 1976. "The Moths and Butterflies of Great Britain and Ireland". Vol. 1. "Micropterigidae-Heleiozidae". 343 pp., 85 figs., 152 maps, 13 pls. Curwen Press and Blackwell, London. Further vols. in preparation; expected to cover all British Lepidoptera.

BEIRNE, B. P. 1954. "British Pyralid and Plume Moths". 208 pp., 189 figs., 16 col. pls. Warne, London.

WHALLEY, P. E. S. & TWEEDIE, M. W. R. 1963. A revision of the British Scoparias (Lepidoptera: Pyralidae). *Entomologist's Gaz.* **14:** 81–98, 11 pls.

BRADLEY, J. D. 1959. An illustrated list of the British Tortricidae — Part II: Olethreutinae. *Entomologist's Gaz.* **10:** 60–80, 23 figs., 19 pls. Revised nomenclature and systematic arrangement: illustr. 219 species.

BRADLEY, J. D., TREMEWAN, W. G. & SMITH, A 1973. "British Tortricoid Moths. Cochylidae and Tortricidae: Tortricinae". 251 pp., 47 pls. Ray Society, London.

BRADLEY, J. D. *et al.* 1969. Key to the British and French species of *Phyllonorycter* Hübner (Lep., Gracillariidae). *Entomologist's Gaz.* **29:** 3–33, figs.

HANNEMANN, H. J. 1961. Klein-Schmetterlinge oder Micro-lepidoptera. I. Die Wickler (s.str.) (Tortricidae). *Tierwelt Dtl.* **48,** 233 pp., many figs., 22 pls.

HANNEMANN, H. J. 1964. Klein-Schmetterlinge oder Micro-lepidoptera. II. Cochylidae, Carposinidae, Pyraloidea. *Tierwelt Dtl.* **50,** 401 pp., many figs., 22 pls.

HANNEMANN, H. J. 1953. Natürliche Gruppierung der Europäischen Arten der Gattung *Depressaria* s.l. (Lep., Oecophoridae). *Mitt. zool. Mus. Berl.* **29:** 269–373, 130 figs.

OBRAZTSOV, N. S. 1954–68. Die Gattungen der palaearktischen Tortricidae. 8 parts. *Tijdschr. Ent.* **97–111,** numerous figs. and pls.

BLESZYNSKI, S. 1965. "Microlepidoptera Palaearctica". Vol. 1. "Crambinae". 2 parts, 553 pp., 133 pls. G. Fromme, Vienna.

SATTLER, K. 1967. "Microlepidoptera Palaearctica". Vol. 2. "Ethmiidae". 2 parts, 185 pp., 106 pls. Fromme, Vienna.

RAZOWSKI, J. 1970. "Microlepidoptera Palaearctica". Vol. 3. "Cochylidae". 2 parts, 528 pp., 161 pls. Fromme, Vienna.

ROESLER, R. U. 1973. "Microlepidoptera Palaearctica". Vol. 4. "Phycitinae". 2 parts, 752 pp., 170 pls. Fromme, Vienna.

BENTINCK, G. A. & DIAKONOFF, A. 1968. De Nederlandse Bladrollers (Tortricidae). *Monografieën ned. ent. Vereen.* **3:** 200 pp., 99 pls. Amsterdam.

PETERSEN, G. 1969. Beiträge zur Insekten Fauna der DDR: Lepidoptera — Tineidae. *Beitr. Ent.* **19:** 311–388, 205 figs., 2 col. pls.

FRIESE, G. 1969. Beiträge zur Insekten Fauna der DDR: Lepidoptera — Argyresthiidae. *Beitr. Ent.* **19:** 693–752, 34 figs., 2 col. pls.

GAEDIKE, R. 1970. Beiträge zur Insekten Fauna der DDR: Lepidoptera — Acrolepiidae. *Beitr. Ent.* **20:** 209–222, 24 figs., 2 col. pls.

FRIESE, G. 1973. Beiträge zur Insekten Fauna der DDR: Lepidoptera — Ethmiidae. *Beitr. Ent.* **23:** 291–312, 27 figs., 2 col. pls.

PETERSEN, G. 1973. Beiträge zur Insekten Fauna der DDR: Lepidoptera — Galleriidae. *Beitr. Ent.* **23:** 313–324, 14 figs., 2 col. pls.

PATZAK, H. 1974. Beiträge zur Insekten Fauna der DDR: Lepidoptera — Coleophoridae. *Beitr. Ent.* **24:** 153–278, 363 figs., 2 col. pls.

TRAUGOTT-OLSEN, E. & SCHMIDT NIELSEN, E. 1977. The Elachistidae (Lepidoptera) of Fennoscandia and Denmark. *Fauna Ent. Scand.* **6:** 299 pp., genitalia figs., col. pls.

ZAGULYAEV, A. K. 1968. Lepidoptera, Tineidae Part 2 Nemapogoninae. *Fauna SSSR* **4**(2), 436 pp., 385 figs. Israel Program for scientific Translations, Washington.

HERING, E. M. 1957. See p. 59 (above).

GENITALIA

PIERCE, F. N. 1909. "The Genitalia of the Group Noctuidae of the Lepidoptera of the British Isles". 88 pp., 32 pls. Duncan, Liverpool. Reprint 1967. Classey, Feltham.

PIERCE, F. N. 1914. "The Genitalia of the Group Geometridae of the Lepidoptera of the British Isles". 88 pp., 48 pls. Pierce, Liverpool. Reprint 1968, Classey.

PIERCE, F. N. & METCALFE, J. W. 1922. "The Genitalia of the Group Tortricidae of the Lepidoptera of the British Isles". 101 pp., 34 pls. Pierce, Oundle. Reprint 1968, Classey.

PIERCE, F. N. & METCALFE, J. W. 1935. "The Genitalia of the Tineid Families of the Lepidoptera of the British Isles". 116 pp., 58 pls. Pierce, Oundle.

PIERCE, F. N. & METCALFE, J. W. 1938. "The Genitalia of the British Pyrales with the Deltoids and Plumes". 69 pp., 30 pls. Pierce, Oundle. Reprint 1968, Classey.

PIERCE, F. N. & BEIRNE, B. P. 1941. "The Genitalia of the British Rhopalocera and the Larger Moths". 66 pp., 21 pls. Pierce, Oundle. Reprint 1968 Classey, Feltham.

BEIRNE, B. P. 1945. The male genitalia of the British Stigmellidae. *Proc. R. Ir. Acad.* **50:** 191–218, 81 figs.

PIERCE, F. N. 1952. "The Genitalia of the Group Noctuidae of the Lepidoptera of the British Islands. An account of the morphology of the female reproduction organs". 2nd edn. 64 pp., 15 pls. Classey, Feltham.

PETERSEN, G. 1957–58. Die Genitalien der paläarktischen Tineiden (Lepidoptera, Tineidae). *Beitr. Ent.* **7:** 55–176, 338–379, 557–595, 247 figs., 6 pls.; **8:** 111–118, 398–430, 20 figs., 2 pls.

IMMATURE STAGES

BUCKLER, W. 1886–1901. "The larvae of the British Butterflies and Moths". 9 vols. (H. T. Stainton and G. T. Porritt, ed.). Illustr. col. Ray Society, London.

SCORER, A. G. 1913. "The Entomologist's Logbook, and Dictionary of the Life Histories and Food-plants of the British Macrolepidoptera". 374 pp. Routledge, London.

STOKOE, W. J. 1944. "The Caterpillars of the British Butterflies, including the Eggs, Chrysalids and Food-plants based upon "The Butterflies of the British Isles" by Richard South, F.R.E.S." (G. H. T. Stovin, ed.). 288 pp., 32 pls. Warne, London.

STOKOE, W. J. 1949. "The Caterpillars of the British Moths". Vol. 1, 408 pp., 90 pls. Vol. 2, 380 pp., 51 pls. Warne, London.

ALLEN, P. B. M. 1949. "Larval Food Plants". 126 pp. Watkins & Doncaster, London.

FORD, L. T. 1949. "A Guide to the Smaller British Lepidoptera". 230 pp. Also 1958. "Supplement", 15 pp. South London Entomological and Natural History Society.

STAINTON, H. T. 1855–73. "The Natural History of the Tineina". 13 vols. col. pls. J. van Voorst, London.

SPULER, A. 1910. "Die Raupen der Schmetterlinge Europas". Vol. 4. 60 col. pls. E. Schweizerbart'sche, Stuttgart.

Over 2200 excellent coloured pictures of larvae, pupae and some ova.

BLASCHKE, P. 1914. "Die Raupen Europas mit ihren Futter-pflanzen". Vol. 1 "Raupenkalender", 264 pp., 6 col. pls. Vol. 2 "Beschreibung der Futterpflanzen", 75 pp., 28 pls. Graser, Annaberg, Saxony.

WERNER, K. 1958. Die Larvalsystematik einiger Kleinschmetterlingefamilien. *Abh. Larvalsyst. Insekten* **2**, 145 pp., 212 figs.
SWATSCHEK, B. 1958. Die Larvalsystematik der Wickler. Tortricidae. *Abn. Larvalsyst. Insekten.* **3**, 269 pp., 276 figs.
BECK, H. 1960. Die Larvalsystematik der Eulen. Noctuidae. *Abh. Larvalsyst, Insekten.* **4**, 406 pp., 488 figs.
HASENFUSS, I. 1960. Die Larvalsystematik der Zünsler. Pvralidae. *Abh. Larvalsyst. Insekten* **5**, 163 pp., 219 figs.

ECONOMIC

CORBET, A. S. & TAMS, W. H. T. 1943. Keys for the identification of the Lepidoptera infesting stored food products. *Proc. zool. Soc. Lond.* **113:** 55–148, 287 figs., 5 pls.
    Descriptions and illustrations of superficial appearance, wing venation and genitalia structure. Distribution. Larval foods.
HINTON, H. E. 1943. The larvae of the Lepidoptera associated with stored products. *Bull. ent. Res.* **34:** 163–212, 128 figs.
    Morphology, chaetotaxy.
BRITISH MUSEUM (NATURAL HISTORY). 1951. "Clothes Moths and House moths". 5th edn. Economic Series **14**, 28 pp., 12 figs.
BRITISH MUSEUM (NATURAL HISTORY) 1955. "Common Insect Pests of Stored Food Products". 3rd end. Economic Series **15**, 61 pp., 126 figs.
    Keys to identification of adults and larvae.
HINTON, H. E. 1955. The larvae of the species of Tineidae of economic importance. *Bull. ent. Res.* **47:** 251–346, 216 figs.
BALACHOWSKY, A. S. 1966. "Entomologie appliqué à l'Agriculture". Vol. 2. "Lépidoptères". Part 1 (Microlepidoptera) 1057 pp., 373 figs., 4 pls.
BALACHOWSKY, A. S. 1972. "Entomologie appliqué à l'Agriculture". Vol. 2. Lépidotères. (Macrolepidoptera and Pyraloidea). 575 pp., 480 figs.

Coleoptera
British species about 3850

GENERAL

FOWLER, W.W. 1886–91. "The Coleoptera of the British Islands". 5 vols. 120 pls. (in large paper edition). Reeve, London.
FOWLER, W. W. & DONISTHORPE, H. St. J. K. 1913. "The Coleoptera of the British Islands". Vol. 6. (Supplement). 20 pls.
    Keys, descriptions adults; frequency and distribution; some bionomic data.
JOY, N. H. 1932. "A Practical Handbook of British Beetles". 2 vols. xxvii + 622 pp., 169 pls., 1 map. Witherby, London. Reprinted 1976, Classey, Faringdon.
    Keys to species; the only comprehensive British work since Fowler.
AUBER, L. 1960. "Atlas des Coléoptères de France, Belgique, Suisse". Nouvel Atlas d'Entomologie. 2nd edn. 2 vols. 522 pp., 112 figs., 60 pls. (36 col.). Boubée, Paris.
    Keys to major groups; brief description of each species; excellent illustrations.
LINSSEN, E. F. 1959. "Beetles of the British Isles". 2 vols., 595 pp., 71 figs., 126 pls. Warne, London.
BECHYNE, J. 1956. "Beetles". Open Air Guides. 158 pp., 30 figs., 39 pls. (6 col.). Thames & Hudson, London.
DIBB, J. R. 1948. "Field Book of Beetles". xxv + 197 pp., 14 pls. Brown, London and Hull.
    Primary division by bionomic characters.
LANDIN, B.-O. 1970–71. "Coleoptera, Strepsiptera, Hymenoptera. Fältfauna,

Insekter 2". 2 vols. 1053 pp., 1920 figs. Natur och kultur, Stockholm (in Swedish).
Keys Swedish genera.
CROWSON, R. A. 1956. Coleoptera: introduction and keys to families. *Handbk Ident. Br. Insects* **4**(1): 1–59, 118 figs.
FREUDE, H., HARDE, K. W. & LOHSE, G. A. 1965. "Die Käfer Mitteleuropas". Vol. 1. "Einführung in die Käferkunde". 214 pp. 204 figs., 7 col. pls. Goecke & Evers, Krefeld.
General introduction and keys to families. (Series referred to hereafter as *Käfer Mitteleuropas.*)
GÖLLNER-SCHEIDING, U. 1970–71. Bibliographie der Bestimmungstabellen europäischer Insekten (1880–1963). Teil III: Coleoptera und Strepsiptera. *Dt. ent. Z.* **17**: 33–118, 433–476; **18**: 1–84, 287–360.
With index to taxa giving cross-references to authors.
KLOET, G. S. & HINCKS, W. D. 1977. A check list of British insects. 2nd edn. Coleoptera. Revised by R. D. Pope. *Handbk Ident. Br. Insects* **11** (3): i–xiv + 1–105.
BRAKMAN, P. J. 1966. Lijst van Coleoptera uit Nederland en het omliggend gebied. *Monographieën ned. ent. Vereen.* **2**: 1–219.
LINDROTH, C. H. ed. 1960. "Catalogus Coleopterorum Fennoscandiae et Daniae". 478 pp., 1 map. Entomological Society, Lund. Additions and corrections (Norway): Strand, 1970. *Norsk ent. Tidsskr.* **17**: 125–145.
Distribution by provinces, in tabular form.
JOHNSON, W. F. & HALBERT, J. N. 1902. A list of the beetles of Ireland. *Proc. R. Ir. Acad.* (3) **6**: 535–827.

LARVAE

BERTRAND, H. P. I. 1972. "Larves et Nymphes des Coléoptères Aquatiques du Globe". 804 pp., 561 figs. Paris.
Keys genera.
EMDEN, F. I. van 1942. Larvae of British beetles. III. Keys to the families. *Entomologist's mon. Mag.* **78**: 206–226, 253–272, 54 figs.
NIKITSKIY, N. B. 1976. [Morphology of larvae of beetles predaceous on and associated with bark beetles in the north-west Caucasus]. In [Evolutionary morphology of the larvae of Insects] (B. M. Mamaev), pp. 175–201, 22 figs (compound) (in Russian). Science Publishers, Moscow.
VIEDMA, M. G. de 1962–1963. Larvas de coleópteros. *Boln Serv. Plagas for.* **5**: 87–91; **6**: 103–121, 40 figs. Reprinted 1964: *Graellsia* **20**: 245–275.
Keys to 31 families affecting forestry (in Spanish).
KLAUSNITZER, B. in press. "Ordnung Coleoptera (Larven). Bestimmungs bücher zur Bodenfauna Europas". *c*. 400 pp., 1000 figs. Junk, The Hague.

ECONOMIC

HICKIN, N. E. 1963. "The Woodworm Problem". 123 pp., 80 figs., 1 col. pl. Hutchinson, London.
Covers all species affecting converted timber.
HINTON, H. E. 1945. "A Monograph of the Beetles associated with Stored Products". Vol. 1. 443 pp., 505 figs., 55 tabs. British Museum (Natural History), London. Reprinted 1963, Johnson Reprint.
Keys to families, species (adults and larvae). Covers Carabidae, Staphylinidae, Nitidulidae, Lathridiidae, Mycetophagidae, Colydiidae, Murmidiidae (Cerylonidae), Endomychidae, Erotylidae, Anthicidae, Cryptophagidae and Dermestidae.

Caraboidea
LINDROTH, C. H. 1974. Coleoptera, Carabidae. *Handbk Ident. Br. Insects* **4**(2): 1–148, 97 figs.
LINDROTH, C. H. 1961. 9. Skalbaggar, Coleoptera. Sandjägare och jordlöpare. Fam. Carabidae. 2nd edn. *Svensk Insektfauna* **35**: 1–209, 135 figs. (in Swedish).
FREUDE, H. *et al.* 1976. Carabidae. *Käfer Mitteleuropas* **2**: 1–302, many figs.
JEANNEL, R. 1941–49. Coléoptères Carabiques. *Faune Fr.* **39**: 1–571, 213 figs. (1941); **40**: 1–601, 368 figs. (1942); **51**: 1–51, 12 figs., 20 pls. (1949).
BONADONA, P. 1971. Catalogue des Coléoptères Carabiques de France. *Nouv. Revue Ent.* (suppl.) **1**: 177.
SCHWEIGER, H. 1969. Zur Systematik der *Bradycellus*-Arten aus der Verwandtschaft des *harpalinus* Serv. *Ent. Bl. Biol. Syst. Käfer* **65**: 86–101, 5 figs.
BALFOUR-BROWNE, F. 1940 (facsimile reprint 1961). "British Water Beetles". Vol. 1, xxi + 375 pp., 89 figs., 72 maps, 5 pls. Ray Society, London.
Covers Haliplidae, Hygrobiidae, Dysticidae (part).
BALFOUR-BROWNE, F. 1950 (facsimile reprint 1964). "British Water Beetles". Vol. 2, 394 pp., 90 figs., 56 maps. Ray Society, London.
Covers Dytiscidae (part), Gyrinidae.
BALFOUR-BROWNE, F. 1953. Hydradephaga. *Handbk Ident. Br. Insects* **4**(3): 1–33, 44 figs. (compound).
FREUDE, H. *et al.* 1971. Hygrobiidae, Haliplidae, Dytiscidae, Gyrinidae, Rhysodidae. *Käfer Mitteleuropas* **3**: 7–95, many figs.
OCHS, G. 1967. Zur Kenntnis der europäischen *Gyrinus*-Arten. *Ent. Bl. Biol. Syst. Käfer* **63**: 174–186. [Corrections] *Ent. Bl. Biol. Syst. Käfer* **64**: 64.
EMDEN, F. I. van 1942. A key to the genera of larval Carabidae. *Trans. R. ent. Soc. Lond.* **92**: 1–99, 100 figs.
EMDEN, F. I. van 1943. Larvae of British beetles. IV. Various small families. Cicindelidae. Hygrobiidae. *Entomologist's mon. Mag.* **79**: 209–213, 6 figs.
LARSSON, S. G. 1968. Løbebillernes larver. *Danm. Fauna* **76**: 282–433, 76 figs. (in Danish).
LUFF, M. L. 1969. The larvae of the British Carabidae (Coleoptera). I. Carabini and Cychrini. *Entomologist* **102**: 245–263, 75 figs.
LUFF, M. L. 1972. The Larvae of the British Carabidae (Coleoptera). II. Nebriini. *Entomologist* **105**: 161–179, 61 figs.
HOUSTON, W. W. K. & LUFF, M. L. 1975. The larvae of the British Carabidae (Coleoptera). III. Patrobini. *Entomologist's Gaz.* **26**: 59–64, 15 figs.
LUFF, M. L. 1976. The larvae of the British Carabidae (Coleoptera). IV. Notiophilini and Elaphrini. *Entomologist's Gaz.* **27**: 51–67, 47 figs.
GALEWSKI, K. 1963. Immature stages of the Central European species of *Rhantus* Dejean (Coleoptera, Dytiscidae). *Polskie Pismo ent.* **33**: 3–93, 46 pls.
GALEWSKI, K. 1966. Developmental stages of the central european species of *Ilybius* Erichson (Coleoptera, Dytiscidae). *Polskie Pismo ent.* **36**: 117–211, many figs., 93 pls.
GALEWSKI, K. 1973. Some notes on the generic characters of the larvae of the subfamily Colymbetinae (Dytiscidae, Coleoptera) with a key for the identification of the European genera. *Polskie Pismo ent.* **43**: 215–224, 48 figs.
GALEWSKI, K. 1973. Generic characters of the larvae of the subfamily Dytiscinae (Dytiscidae) with a key to the central European genera. *Polskie Pismo ent.* **43**: 491–498, 24 figs.
GALEWSKI, K. 1974. Diagnostic characters of larvae of European species of *Graphoderus* Dejean (Coleoptera, Dytiscidae) with an identification key and some notes on their biology. *Bull. Acad. pol. Sci. Sér. Biol.* **22**: 485–494, 29 figs.

ii. Hydrophiloidea (incl. Hydraenidae).

BALFOUR-BROWNE, F. 1958. "British Water Beetles". Vol. 3, liii + 210 pp., 87 figs., 67 maps. Ray Society, London.

LOHSE, G. A. & VOGT, H. 1971. Hydraenidae, Spercheidae, Hydrophilidae. *Käfer Mitteleuropas* **3**: 95–156, many figs.

KEVAN, D. K. 1966. The British species of the genus *Helophorus* Illiger, subgenus *Helophorus s. str.* (Col., Hydrophilidae). *Entomologist's mon. Mag.* **101** (1965): 254–268, 20 figs.

ANGUS, R. B. 1969. Revisional notes on *Helphorus* F. (Col., Hydrophilidae). 1. General introduction and some species resembling *H. minutus* F. *Entomologist's mon. Mag.* **105**: 1–24, 4 figs., 1 pl.

ANGUS, R. B. 1971. Revisional notes on *Helophorus* F. (Col., Hydrophilidae). 2. The complex round *H. flavipes* F. *Entomologist's mon. Mag.* **106** (1970): 129–148, 2 figs., 1 pl.

ANGUS, R. B. 1971. Revisional notes on *Helophorus* F. (Col., Hydrophilidae). 3. Species resembling *H. strigifrons* Thoms. and some further notes on species resembling *H. minutus* F. *Emtomologist's mon. Mag.* **106** (1970): 238–256, 1 pl.

ANGUS, R. B. 1973. The habitats, life-histories and immature stages of *Helophorus* F. (Coleoptera: Hydrophilidae). *Trans. R. ent. Soc. Lond.* **125**: 1–26, 7 figs., 4 pls. Key to larvae.

ANGUS, R. B. (in press). A re-valuation of the taxonomy and distribution of some European species of *Hydrochus* Leach (Coleoptera, Hydrophilidae). *Entomologist's mon. Mag.*

Histeroidea

HALSTEAD, D. G. H. 1963. Coleoptera Histeroidea. Sphaeritidae and Histeridae. *Handbk Ident. Br. Insects* **4**(10): 1–16, 38 figs.

HINTON, H. E. 1945. The Histeridae associated with stored products. *Bull. ent. Res.* **35**: 309–340, 56 figs. Keys to adults and larvae.

WITZGALL, K. 1971. Histeridae, Sphaeritidae. *Käfer Mitteleuropas* **3**: 156–189, many figs.

Staphylinoidea **(including Sphaeriidae)**
Staphylinidae

PALM, T. 1948–72. Kortvingar, fam. Staphylinidae. *Svensk Insektfauna* **38, 48–53**, 985 pp., many figs. (in Swedish).

LOHSE, G. A. 1964. Staphylinidae I (Micropeplinae bis Tachyporinae). *Käfer Mitteleuropas* **4**: 1–264, many figs.

LOHSE, G. A. *et al.* 1974. Staphylinidae II (Hypocyphtinae und Aleocharinae). *Käfer Mitteleuropas* **5**: 1–304, many figs.

COIFFAIT, H. 1972. Coléoptères Staphylinidae de la région paléarctique occidentale. 1. Généralités, sous-familles Xantholininae et Leptotyphlinae. *Nouv. Revue Ent.* (Suppl.) **2**: 1–651, 219 figs.

TOTTENHAM, C. E. 1954. Staphylinidae (Piestinae to Euaesthetinae). *Handbk Ident. Br. Insects* **4**(8a): 1–79, 196 figs.

ALLEN, A. A. 1969. Notes on some British Staphylinidae (Col.). 1. The genus *Scopaeus* Er., with the addition of *S. laevigatus* Gyll. to our list. *Entomologist's mon. Mag.* **104** (1968): 198–207. 22 figs.

ALLEN, A. A. 1971. Notes on some British Staphylinidae (Col.). 2. Three additions to our species of *Philonthus* Curt. *Entomologist's mon. Mag.* **106** (1970): 157–161, 14 figs.

CAMERON, M. 1944. On the British species of the genus *Tachyporus* Gr. (Col. Staphylinidae). *Entomologist's mon. Mag.* **80**: 16–17.

HAMMOND, P. M. 1971. Notes on British Staphylinidae 2. On the British species of *Platystethus* Mannerheim, with one species new to Britain. *Entomologist's mon. Mag.* **107**: 93–111, 14 figs., 7 maps.
HAMMOND, P. M. 1973. Notes on British Staphylinidae 3. The British species of *Sepedophilus* Gistel *(Conosomus* auctt.). *Entomologist's mon. Mag.* **108** (1972): 130–165, 32 figs., 8 maps.
LAST, H. 1974. *Philonthus mannerheimi* Fauvel (Col., Staphylinidae) and related species. *Entomologist's mon. Mag.* **109** (1973): 85–88, 12 figs.
LUFF, M. L. 1966. The separation of *Stenus impressus* Germar and *S. aceris* Stephens (Col., Staphylinidae). *Entomologist's mon. Mag.* **102**: 49–52, 3 figs.
STEEL, W. O. 1948. The British species of *Staphylinus* subgenus *Ocypus* Steph. (Col., Staphylinidae). *Entomologist's mon. Mag.* **84**: 271–275, 16 figs.
STEEL, W. O. 1957. Notes on the Omaliinae (Col. Staphylinidae). *Entomologist's mon. Mag.* **98**: 157–164, 30 figs.
  Key to *Acrolocha*.
TOTTENHAM, C. E. 1948. A revision of the British species of *Arphirus* Tottenham (subgenus of *Quedius* Stephens) (Col., Staphylinidae). *Entomologist's mon. Mag.* **84**: 241–258, 27 figs.
WELCH, R. C. 1969. Identification of the *Aleochara diversa* (J. Sahlberg) group (Col., Staphylinidae), including a species new to Britain. *Entomologist* **102**: 231–234, 12 figs.
WILLIAMS, S. A. 1969. Notes on the British species of *Ochthephilum* Mulsant & Rey (Col., Staphylinidae). *Entomologist's mon. Mag.* **104** (1968): 261–262, 3 figs.
WILLIAMS, S. A. 1969. The British species of the genus *Amischa* Thomson (Col., Staphylinidae), including *A. soror* Krastz, an addition to the list. *Entomologist's mon. Mag.* **105**: 38–42, 6 figs.
WILLIAMS, S. A. 1970. Notes on the genus *Oligota* Mannerheim (Col., Staphylinidae) and key to the British species. *Entomologist's mon. Mag.* **106**: 54–62, 15 figs.
PUTHZ, V. 1971. Kritische Faunistik der bisher aus Mitteleuropa bekannten *Stenus*-Arten nebst systematischen Bemerkungen und Neubeschreibungen (Coleoptera, Staphylinidae). *Ent. Bl. Biol. Syst. Käfer* **67**: 74–121, 37 figs., 3 maps.
SCHEERPELTZ, O. 1972. Studien an den paläarktischen Arten der Gattung *Myrmecopora* Saulcy (Col., Staphylinidae). *Koleopt. Rdsch.* **50**: 93–109.
KASULE, F. K. 1966. The subfamilies of the larvae of Staphylinidae (Coleoptera), with keys to the larvae of British genera of Steninae and Proteininae. *Trans. R. ent. Soc. Lond.* **118**: 261–283, 92 figs.
KASULE, F. K. 1968. The larval characters of some subfamilies of British Staphylinidae with keys to the known genera. *Trans. R. ent. Soc. Lond.* **120**: 115–138, 116 figs.
KASULE, F. K. 1970. The larvae of Paederinae and Staphylininae (Coleoptera: Staphylinidae) with keys to the known British genera. *Trans. R. ent. Soc. Lond.* **122**: 49–80, 144 figs.
STEEL, W. O. 1966. A revision of the Staphylinid subfamily Proteininae (Coleoptera) I. *Trans. R. ent. Soc. Lond.* **118**: 285–311, 120 figs.
  Key to genera of larvae.
STEEL, W. O. 1970. The larvae of the genera of the Omaliinae (Coleoptera: Staphylinidae) with particular reference to the British fauna. *Trans. R. ent. Soc. Lond.* **122**: 1–47, 191 figs.

Other families

SUNDT, E. 1958. Revision of the Fenno-Scandian species of the genus *Acrotrichis* Motsch., 1848. *Norsk ent. Tidsskr.* **10**: 241–277, 6 figs. See also pp. 173–180.

JOHNSON, C. 1975. Five species of Ptiliidae (Col.) new to Britain, and corrections to the British list of the family. *Entomologist's Gaz.* **26:** 211–223, 13 figs.
FREUDE, H. et al. 1971. Silphidae, Leptinidae, Catopidae, Colonidae, Liodidae, Clambidae, Scydmaenidae, Orthoperidae (= Corylophidae), Sphaeriidae, Ptiliidae, Scaphidiidae. *Käfer Mitteleuropas* **3:** 190–347, many figs.
KEVAN, D. K. 1945. The aedeagi of the British species of the genus *Catops* Pk. (Col., Cholevidae). *Entomologist's mon. Mag.* **81:** 69–72, 13 figs. See also pp. 121–125.
KEVAN, D. K. 1946. The sexual characters of the British species of the genus *Choleva*, including *C. cisteloides*, new to the British list (Col., Cholevidae). *Entomologist's, mon. Mag.* **82:** 122–130, 24 figs.
KEVAN, D. K. 1947. A revision of the British species of the genus *Colon* (Col., Cholevidae). *Entomologist's mon. Mag.* **83:** 249–267, 50 figs.
ZWICK, P. 1968. Zwei neue Catopiden-Gattungen aus Europa (Auflösung der *nigrita*-Gruppe in der Gattung *Catops*). *Ent. Bl. Biol. Syst. Käfer* **64:** 1–16, 17 figs.
PEARCE, E. J. 1957. Pselaphidae. *Handbk Ident. Br. Insects* **4** (9): 1–32, 41 figs.
PEARCE, E. J. 1974. A revised annotated list of the British Pselaphidae (Coleoptera). *Entomologist's mon. Mag.* **110:** 13–26.
JEANNEL, R. 1950. Coléoptères Pselaphides. *Faune Fr.* **53:** 1–421, 169 figs.
BESUCHET, C. 1974. Pselaphidae. *Käfer Mitteleuropas* **5:** 305–362, many figs.

Scarabaeoidea

JANSSENS, A. 1960. "Insectes Coléoptères Lamellicornes". Faune de Belgique. 411 pp., 201 figs., 5 col. pls. Institut royal des Sciences naturelles de Belgique, Brussels.
LANDIN, B.-O. 1957. 9. Skalbaggar, Coleoptera, Bladhorningar. Lamellicornia, fam. Scarabaeidae. *Svensk Insektfauna* **46:** 1–155, 72 figs. (in Swedish).
MACHATSCHKE, J. W. 1969. Lamellicornia. *Käfer Mitteleuropas* **8:** 265–371.
BRITTON, E. B. 1956. Scarabaeoidea (Lucanidae, Trogidae, Geotrupidae, Scarabaeidae). *Handbk Ident. Br. Insects* **5**(11): 1–29, 68 figs.
EMDEN, F. I. van 1941. Larvae of British beetles. II. A key to the British Lamellicornia larvae. *Entomologist's mon. Mag.* **77:** 117–127; 181–192, 19 figs.

Eucinetoidea (Clambidae and Helodidae)

JOHNSON, C. 1966. Clambidae. *Handbk Ident. Br. Insects* **4**(6a): 1–13, 22 figs.
ENDRÖDY-YOUNGA, S. 1971. Clambidae. *Käfer Mitteleuropas* **3:** 266–270, 27 figs.
KEVAN, D. K. 1962. The British species of the genus *Cyphon* Paykull (Col., Helodidae), including three new to the British list. *Entomologist's mon. Mag.* **98:** 114–121, 11 figs.
NYHOLM, T. 1972. Die nordeuropäischen Arten der Gattung *Cyphon* Paykull (Coleoptera). Taxonomie, Biologie, Okologie und Verbreitung. *Entomologica scand.* (Suppl.) **3:** 1–100, 25 figs., 8 maps.
KLAUSNITZER, B. 1975. Zur Kenntnis der Larven der mitteleuropäischen Helodidae. *Dt. ent. Z.* **22:** 61–65, 14 figs.

Byrrhoidea

JOHNSON, C. 1966. The British species of the genus *Byrrhus* L., including *B. arietinus* Steffahny (Col., Byrrhidae) new to the British list. *Entomologist's mon. Mag.* **101** (1965): 111–115, 10 figs.
JOHNSON, C. 1966. Taxonomic notes on British Coleoptera. No. 4 *Simplocaria maculosa* Erichson (Byrrhidae). *Entomologist* **99:** 155–156, 3 figs.
BONADONA, P. 1975. Les *Byrrhus (sensu lato)* de France (Col., Byrrhidae). *Entomologiste* **31:** 193–209, 20 figs.
PAULUS, H. F. 1973. Revision der Familie Byrrhidae I. Zur Systematik und

Faunistik der westpaläarktischen Vertreter der Gattung *Curimopsis* Ganglebauer 1902 (Col., Byrrhidae, Sincalyptinae). *Senckenbergiana biol.* **54:** 353–367, 23 figs.

EMDEN, F. I. van 1958. Über die Larvenmerkmale einige deutscher Byrrhidengattungen. *Mitt. dt. ent. Ges.* **17:** 39–40.

Dryopoidea

BOLLOW, H. 1938–41. Monographie der palaearktischen Dryopidae, mit Berücksichtigung der eventuell transgredierenden Arten (Col.). *Mitt. münch. ent. Ges.* **28:** 147–187, 319–371 (1938); **29:** 109–145 (1939); **30:** 24–71 (1940); **31:** 1–88 (1941), 391 figs., 1 pl.
Includes Psephenidae and Elminthidae.

HOLLAND, D. G. 1972. A key to the larvae, pupae and adults of the British species of Elminthidae. *Scient. Publs Freshwat. biol. Ass.* **26:** 1–58, 29 figs. (some compound), 11 maps.

CLARKE, R. O. S. 1973. Heteroceridae. *Handbk Ident. Br. Insects* **5** (2c): 1–15, 14 figs.

DELACHAMBRE, J. 1963. Faune des Elminthidae de Côte-d'Or (adultes et formes larvaires) (Ins. Coleoptera). *Trav. Lab. Zool. Stn aquic. Grimaldi Dijon* **53:** 1–30, 25 figs.

PIERRE, F. 1945. La larve d'*Heterocerus aragonicus* Kiesw. et son milieu biologique (Col., Heteroceridae). *Revue fr. Ent.* **12:** 166–174, 31 figs.
Key to larvae of *Heterocerus*.

Buprestoidea

SCHAEFER, L. 1949. "Les Buprestides de France. Tableaux analytiques des Coléoptères de la faune franco-rhénane (France, Rhénanie, Belgique, Hollande, Valais, Corse)". 511 pp., 25 pls. E. Le Moult, Paris.

LEVEY, B. 1977. Buprestidae. *Handbk. Ident. Br. Insects* **5**(5a): 1–8, 15 figs.

PALM, T. 1962. Zur Kenntnis der früheren Entwicklungsstadien schwedischer Käfer. 2. Buprestiden-Larven, die in Bäumen leben. *Opusc. ent.* **27:** 65–78, 4 figs. (compound).

Elateroidea

LESEIGNEUR, L. 1972. Coléoptères Elateridae de la faune de France continentale et de Corse. *Bull. mens. Soc. linn. Lyon* **41** (Suppl.): 1–379, 384 figs.

FRANZ, H. 1967. Beiträge zur Systematik der europäischen und nordwestafrikanischen *Agriotes* s. str. (Elateridae). *Ent. Bl. Biol. Syst. Käfer* **63:** 65–86, 22 figs.

FRANZ, H. 1967. Zur Kenntnis der mitteleuropäischen *Hypnoidus*-Arten aus dem Subgenus *Zorochrus* Thoms. *Ent. Bl. Biol. Syst. Käfer* **63:** 32–37, 12 figs.

REITTER, E. 1889. Analytische Tabelle zur Bestimmung der europäischen *Throscus*-Arten. *Wien. ent. Ztg* **8:** 35–37. See also pp. 37–39.

ALLEN, A. A. 1969. Notes on some British serricorn Coleoptera, with adjustments to the list. 1. Sternoxia. *Entomologist's mon. Mag.* **104** (1968): 208–216, 8 figs.
Keys to British Eucnemidae.

FLEUTIAUX, E. 1935. Essai d'un genera [sic!] des Eucnemididae paléarctiques. *Revue fr. Ent.* **2:** 1–18.

KORSCHEFSKY, R. 1941. Bestimmungstabelle der bekanntesten deutschen Elateridenlarven (Coleoptera, Elateridae). *Arb. morph. taxon. Ent. Berl.* **8:** 217–230, 3 pls.

PALM, T. 1972. Die skandinavischen Elateriden-Larven (Coleoptera). *Entomologica scand.* (Suppl.) **2:** 1–63, 31 figs. (compound).

EMDEN, F. I. van 1945. Larvae of British beetles. V. Elateridae. *Entomologist's mon. Mag.* **81**: 13–37, 54 figs.
EMDEN, H. F. van 1956. Morphology and identification of the British larvae of the genus *Elater* (Col., Elateridae). *Entomologist's mon. Mag.* **92**: 167–188, 39 figs.
EMDEN, F. I. van 1943. Larvae of British beetles. IV. Various small families. Eucnemidae. *Entomologist's mon. Mag.* **79**: 218–219, 1 fig.
PALM, T. 1960. Zur Kenntnis der früheren Entwicklungsstadien schwedischer Käfer. I. Bisher bekannte Eucnemiden-Larven. *Opusc. ent.* **25**: 157–169, 11 figs. (compound).

Cantharoidea

FITTON, M. G. (in press). Cantharoidea (Cantharidae, Lampyridae, Lycidae, Drilidae). *Handbk Ident. Br. Insects.*
DAHLGREN, G. 1968. Beiträge zur Kenntnis der Gattung *Rhagonycha* (Col., Cantharidae). *Ent. Bl. Biol. Syst. Käfer* **64**: 93–124, 16 figs. (compound).
FITTON, M. G. 1976. The larvae of the British genera of Cantharidae (Coleoptera). *J. Ent.* (B) **44**: 243–254, 34 figs.
VERHOEFF, K. W. 1923. Zur Kenntnis der Canthariden-Larven. 2. Beitrag. *Arch. Naturgesch.* **89**(1): 110–137.
KORSCHEFSKY, R. 1951. Bestimmungstabelle der bekanntesten deutschen Lyciden-, Lampyriden- und Driliden larven (Coleoptera). *Beitr. Ent.* **1**: 60–64, 3 figs., 1 pl.

Dermestoidea

LEPESME, P. 1949. Révision des *Dermestes* (Col., Dermestidae). *Annls Soc. ent. Fr.* **115** (1946): 37–68, 42 figs.
PEACOCK, E. R. 1976. *Dermestes peruvianus* Cast., *D. haemorrhoidalis* Küst. & other *Dermestes* spp. (Col., Dermestidae). *Entomologist's mon. Mag.* **111** (1975): 1–14, 33 figs., 1 pl.
HINTON, H. E. 1945. The species of *Anthrenus* that have been found in Britain, with a description of a recently introduced species. (Coleoptera, Dermestidae). *Entomologist* **78**: 6–9, 6 figs. See also Hinton, 1945: 234–401 (General Works, economic, above).
HINTON, H. E. 1946. The 'gin traps' of some beetle pupae; a protective device which appears to be unknown. *Trans. R. ent. Soc. Lond.* **97**: 473–496, 27 figs.
Key to pupae of Dermestidae.

Bostrychoidea (Teredilia)

FREUDE, H. *et al.* 1969. Lyctidae, Bostrychidae, Anobiidae, Ptinidae. *Käfer Mitteleuropas* **8**: 7–74, many figs.
JOHNSON, C. 1966. The Fennoscandian, Danish and British species of the genus *Ernobius* Thomson (Col., Anobiidae). *Opusc. ent. Lund* **31**: 81–92, 30 figs.
HINTON, H. E. 1941. The Ptinidae of economic importance. *Bull. ent. Res.* **31**: 331–381, 59 figs.
BÖVING, A. F. 1954. Mature larvae of the beetle-family Anobiidae. *Biol. Meddr* **22**(2): 1–298, 50 pls.
PARKIN, E. A. 1933. The larvae of some wood-boring Anobiidae (Coleoptera). *Bull. ent. Res.* **24**: 33–68, 15 figs. (compound).
HALL, D. W. & HOWE, R. W. 1953. A revised key to the larvae of the Ptinidae associated with stored products. *Ibidem* **44**: 85–96, 92 figs.
EMDEN, F. I. van 1943. Larvae of British beetles. IV. Various small families. Lyctidae, Bostrychidae. *Entomologist's mon. Mag.* **79**: 265–269, 6 figs.

Cleroidea

WINKLER, J. R. 1961. Die Buntkäfer (Cleridae). *Neue Brehm Büch.* **281**: 1–108, 82 figs., 2 pls.
VOGT, H. 1967. Ostomidae [= Trogossitidae]. *Käfer Mitteleuropas* **7**: 14–18, 8 figs.
FAGNIEZ, C. 1946. Étude des *Divales* et *Dasytes* de France et de Corse (Col., Dasytidae). *Revue fr. Ent.* **13**: 19–27.
EVERS, A. M. J. 1971. Über die Paläarktischen Arten der Gattungen *Sphinginus* Rey und *Fortunatius* nov. gen. [Col., Melyridae]. *Ent. Bl. Biol. Syst. Käfer* **67**: 21–41, 4 figs.
EMDEN, F. I. van 1943. Larvae of British beetles. IV. Various small families. Trogositidae, Cleridae. *Entomologist's mon. Mag.* **79**: 214–218, 12 figs.

Lymexyloidea

EMDEN, F. I. van 1943. Larvae of British beetles. IV. Various small families. Lymexylidae. *Entomologist's mon. Mag.* **79**: 259, 261, 2 figs.

Cucujoidea

Clavicornia (*pars*, + Corylophidae)

VOGT, H. *et al.* 1967. Clavicornia. *Käfer Mitteleuropas* **7**: 19–309, many figs.
POPE, R. D. 1953. Coccinellidae and Sphindidae. *Handbk Ident. Br. Insects* **5**(7): 1–12, 23 figs.
POPE, R. D. 1973. The species of *Scymnus* (*s. str.*), *Scymnus* (*Pullus*) and *Nephus* (Col., Coccinellidae) occurring in the British Isles. *Entomologist's mon. Mag.* **109**: 3–39, 30 figs., 9 maps.
FÜRSCH, H. & KREISSL, E. 1967. Revision einiger europäischer *Scymnus* (*s. str.*)- Arten (Col., Coccinellidae). *Mitt. Abt. Zool. Bot. Landesmus. Joanneum* **28**: 207–259, 125 figs.
GOURREAU, J. M. 1974. Systematique de la tribu des Scymnini (Coccinellidae) [de France]. *Annls Zool. Ecol. anim.* (hors Séries): 1–221, 43 pls.
THOMPSON, R. T. 1958. Phalacridae. *Handbk Ident. Br. Insects* **5**(5b): 1–17, 47 figs.
COOMBS, C. W. & WOODROFFE, G. E. 1955. A revision of the British species of the genus *Cryptophagus* (Herbst) (Coleoptera, Cryptophagidae). *Trans. R. ent. Soc. Lond.* **106**: 237–282, 117 figs.
JOHNSON, C. 1967. Additions and corrections to the British list of *Atomaria s. str.* (Col., Cryptophagidae), including a species new to science. *Entomologist* **100**: 39–47, 6 figs.
JOHNSON, C. 1973. The *Atomaria gibbula* group of species. (Coleoptera, Cryptophagidae). *Reichenbachia* **14**: 125–141, 9 figs.
HINTON, H. E. 1941. The Lathridiidae of economic importance. *Bull. ent. Res.* **32**: 191–247, 67 figs.
TOZER, E. R. 1973. On the British species of *Lathridius* Herbst (Col., Lathridiidae). *Entomologist's mon. Mag.* **108** (1972): 193–199, 18 figs., 1 pl.
HALSTEAD, D. G. H. 1973. A revision of the genus *Silvanus* Latreille (Coleoptera, Silvanidae). *Bull. Br. Mus. nat. Hist.* (Ent.) **29**: 39–112, 179 figs.
LOHSE, G. A. 1969. Cisiden Studien IV. *Rhopalodontus perforatus* und seine Verwandten. *Ent. Bl. Biol. Syst. Käfer* **65**: 48–52, 2 figs. (compound).
PEACOCK, E. R. (née Tozer) 1977. Rhizophagidae. *Handbk Ident. Br. Insects* **5**(5a): 1–19, 54 figs.
JOHNSON, C. 1972. *Epuraea adumbrata* Mannerheim and *E. biguttata* (Thunberg) (Col., Nitidulidae) new to Britain. *Entomologist* **105**: 126–129, 10 figs.
KEVAN, D. K. 1967. On the apparent conspecificity of *Cis pygmaeus* (Marsh.) and *C.*

rhododactylis (Marsh.) and on other closely allied species (Col., Ciidae). *Entomologist's mon. Mag.* **102** (1966): 138–144, 5 figs.

ALLEN, A. A. 1970. Revisional notes on the British species of *Orthoperus* Steph. (Col. Corylophidae). *Entomologist's Rec. J. Var.* **82**: 112–120.

EMDEN, F. I. van 1949. Larvae of British beetles. VII. Coccinellidae. *Entomologist's mon. Mag.* **85**: 265–283, 61 figs.

KLAUSNITZER, B. 1970. Zur Larvalsystematik der mitteleuropäischen Coccinellidae (Coleoptera). *Ent. Abh. Mus. Tierk. Dresden* **38**: 55–110, 14 figs. (compound).
　Keys and describes 58 species.

KLAUSNITZER, B. 1973. Bestimmungstabelle für mitteleuropäische Coccinelliden-Larven nach leicht sichtbaren Merkmalen. *Beitr. Ent.* **23**: 93–98, 26 figs.
　Keys 41 species by 'hand lens' characters.

SAVOISKAYA, G. I. & KLAUSNITZER, B. 1973. Morphology and taxonomy of the larvae with keys for their identification. In "Biology of Coccinellidae" (J. Hodek), pp. 36–55, 160 figs. Prague.

Heteromera

KASZAB, Z. 1969. Heteromera. *Käfer Mitteleuropas* **8**: 75–138; 160–264, many figs.

BUCK, F. D. 1954. Lagriidae, Alleculidae, Tetratomidae, Melandryidae, Salpingidae, Pythidae, Mycteridae, Oedemeridae, Mordellidae, Scraptiidae, Pyrochroidae, Rhipiphoridae, Anthicidae, Aderidae and Meloidae. *Handbk Ident. Br. Insects* **5**(9): 1–30, 63 figs.

BRENDELL, M. J. D. 1975. Tenebrionidae. *Handbk Ident. Br. Insects* **5**(10): 1–22, 36 figs.

HALSTEAD, D. G. H. 1967. A revision of the genus *Palorus (sens. lat.)* (Coleoptera, Tenebrionidae). *Bull. Br. Mus. nat. Hist.* (Ent.) **19**: 61–148, 56 figs. (compound), 2 maps.

BONADONA, P. 1971. Les Notoxinae de France (Col., Anthicidae). *Entomologiste* **27**: 132–148, 15 figs.

BONADONA, P. 1974. La classification de Anthicidae de la faune de France (Coleoptera). *Entomologiste* **30**: 101–111, 23 figs.

ALLEN, A. A. 1975. Two species of *Anaspis* (Col., Mordellidae) new to Britain, with a consideration of the status of *A. hudsoni* Donis., etc. *Entomologist's Rec. J. Var.* **87**: 269–274.

EMDEN, F. I. van 1943. Larvae of British beetles. IV. Various small families. Meloidae, Rhipiphoridae, Lagriidae, Synchroidae, Pyrochroidae. *Entomologist's mon. Mag.* **79**: 219–223, 259–265, 7 figs.

EMDEN, F. I. van 1947. Larvae of British beetles. VI. Tenebrionidae. *Entomologist's mon. Mag.* **83**: 154–171, 46 figs. See also **84**: 10.

DUFFY, E. A. J. 1946. Notes on the British species of *Pyrochroa* (Col., Pyrochroidae) with a key to their first-stage larvae. *Entomologist's mon. Mag.* **82**: 92–93, 1 fig.

VIEDMA, M. G. de 1966. Contribución al conocimiento de las larvas de Melandryidae de Europa (Coleoptera). *Eos, Madr.* **41**: 483–506, 52 figs. (in Spanish). See also pp. 507–513.

Chrysomeloidea

Cerambycidae

HARDE, K. W. 1966. Cerambycidae. *Käfer Mitteleuropas* **9**: 7–94, many figs.

DUFFY, E. A. J. 1952. Cerambycidae. *Handbk Ident. Br. Insects* **5**(12): 1–18, 32 figs.

PICARD, F. 1929. Coléoptères Cerambycidae. *Fauna Fr.* **20**: i–vii + 1–166, 71 figs.

VILLIERS, A. 1974. Une nouvelle nomeclature des Lepturines de France (Col., Cerambycidae). *Entomologiste* **30**: 207–217, 34 figs.
　Keys to genera.
DUFFY, E. A. J. 1953. "A Monograph of the Immature Stages of British and Imported Timber Beetles (Cerambycidae)". viii + 350 pp., 292 figs., 8 pls. British Museum (Natural History), London.
DEMELT, C. von 1966. Bockkäfer oder Cerambycidae. 1. Biologie mitteleuropäischer Bockkäfer (Col., Cerambycidae) unter besonderer Berücksichtigung der Larven. *Tierwelt Dtl.* **52**(2): i–vii + 1–115, 97 figs., 9 pls.

Bruchidae

LUKYANOVICH, F. K. & TER-MINASYAN, M. E. 1957. Zhukizernovski (Bruchidae). *Fauna SSSR* **24**(1): 1–209, 209 figs. English translation by P. A. J. Graham, 1971, National Lending Library for Science and Technology, Boston Spa.
HOFFMANN, A. 1945. Coléoptères Bruchides et Anthribides. *Faune Fr.* **44**: 1–184, 382 figs. + illustr. adults.

Chrysomelidae

MOHR, K. H. 1966. Chrysomelidae. *Käfer Mitteleuropas* **9**: 95–280, many figs.
LABOISSIÈRE, V. 1934. Galerucinae de la faune française. *Annls Soc. ent. Fr.* **103**: 1–108, 54 figs.
HINCKS, W. D. 1950. The British species of the genera *Pyrrhalta* Joannis and *Galerucella* Crotch (Col., Chrysomelidae). *J. Soc. Br. Ent.* **3**: 150–156, 9 figs.
KEVAN, D. K. 1963. The British species of the genus *Haltica* Geoffroy (Col., Chrysomelidae). *Entomologist's mon. Mag.* **98** (1962): 189–196, 43 figs.
KEVAN, D. K. 1967. The British species of the genus *Longitarsus* Latreille (Col., Chrysomelidae). *Entomologist's mon. Mag.* **103**: 83–110, 43 figs.
STRAND, A. 1962. Hannens genitalorgan hos de nordiske *Longitarsus*-arter (Col., Chrysomelidae). *Norsk ent. Tiddsskr.* **12**: 25–26, 3 pls. (in Norwegian).
　Photographs of aedeagi of most British species.
SHUTE, S. L. 1976. *Longitarsus jacobaeae* Waterhouse: identity and distribution (Col., Chrysomelidae). *Entomologist's mon. Mag.* **111** (1975): 33–39, 16 figs.
SHUTE, S. L. 1976. A note on the specific status of *Psylliodes luridipennis* Kutschera (Col., Chrysomelidae). *Entomologist's mon. Mag.* **111** (1975): 123–127, 24 figs.
LAMBELET, J. 1975. Les *Phyllodecta* de la faune française (Col., Chrysomelidae). *Entomologiste* **31**: 154–158, 4 figs.
HENRIKSEN, K. L. 1927. Larver. Chrysomelidae. *Danm. Fauna* **31**: 290–376, 21 figs. (in Danish).
PATERSON, N. F. 1931. The bionomics and comparative morphology of the early stages of certain Chrysomelidae (Coleoptera, Phytophaga). *Proc. zool. Soc. Lond.* **1931**: 879–949, 30 figs. (compound), 3 pls.
EMDEN, H. F. van 1962. Key to species of British Cassidinae larvae (Col., Chrysomelidae). *Entomologist's mon. Mag.* **98**: 33–36, 11 figs.

Curculionoidea

HOFFMANN, A. 1950, 1954, 1958. Coléoptères Curculionides. *Faune Fr.* **52**: 1–486, 225 figs.; **59**: 487–1208, 438 figs.; **62**: 1209–1839, 642 figs.
HOFFMANN, A. 1945. Coléoptères Bruchides et Anthribides. *Faune Fr.* **44**: 1–184, 434 figs.
DIECKMANN, L. 1974. Beiträge zur Insektenfauna der DDR: Coleoptera-Curculionidae (Rhinomacerinae, Rhynchitinae, Attelabinae, Apoderinae). *Beitr. Ent.* **24**: 5–54, 103 figs.
ALLEN, A. A. 1964. On the synonymy of *Rhynchites sericeus* Hbst., *ophthalmicus*

Steph. and *olivaceus* Gyll. (Col., Attelabidae). *Entomologist's mon. Mag.* **100:** 49–56.

DIECKMANN, L. 1973. *Apion*-Studien (Coleoptera, Curculionidae). *Beitr. Ent.* **23:** 71–92, 28 figs.

JOHNSON, C. 1965. Taxonomic notes on British Coleoptera. No. 1. *Apion cerdo* Gerst. and its allies (Apionidae). *Entomologist* **98:** 80–82, 11 figs.

KEVAN, D. K. 1960. The British species of the genus *Sitona* Germar (Col., Curculionidae). *Entomologist's mon. Mag.* **95** (1959): 251–261, figs. See also **100:** 91–93, 3 figs.

DIECKMANN, L. 1964. Die mitteleuropäischen Arten aus der Gattung *Bagous* Germ. *Ent. Bl. Biol. Syst. Käfer* **60:** 88–111, 51 figs.

DIECKMANN, L. 1968. Revision der westpaläarktischen Anthonomini (Coleoptera, Curculionidae). *Beitr. Ent.* **17:** 377–564, 114 figs., 4 maps. See also **19:** 679–682.

DIECKMANN, L. 1963. Die palaearktischen Arten der Untergattung *Pseudorchestes* Bedel aus der Gattung *Rhynchaenus* Clairv. (Coleoptera, Curculionidae). *Ent. Abh. Mus. Tierk. Dresden* **29:** 275–327, 66 figs.

DIECKMANN, L. 1972. Beiträge zur Insektenfauna der DDR: Coleoptera-Curculionidae: Ceutorhynchinae. *Beitr. Ent.* **22:** 3–128, 141 figs.

DIECKMANN, L. 1971. *Ceutorhynchus*-Studien (Coleoptera, Curculionidae). *Beitr. Ent.* **21:** 581–595, 28 figs.

DIECKMANN, L. 1966. Die mitteleuropäischen Arten der Gattung *Neosirocalus* Ner. et Wagn. (mit Beschreibung von drei neuen Arten). *Ent. Bl. Biol. Syst. Käfer* **62:** 82–110, 28 figs.

DIECKMANN, L. 1963. *Ceuthorrhynchus interjectus* Schultze und seine Verwandten. *Ent. Bl. Biol. Syst. Käfer* **59:** 161–167, 19 figs.

DIECKMANN, L. 1973. Die westpaläarktischen *Thamiocolus*-Arten (Coleoptera, Curculionidae). *Beitr. Ent.* **23:** 245–273, 51 figs.

DIECKMANN, L. & SMRECZYNSKI, S. 1972. Revision der *Ceutorhynchus nanus*-Gruppe (Coleoptera, Curculionidae). *Acta zool. cracov.* **17:** 325–340, 22 figs.

MORRIS, M. G. 1966. *Ceuthorhynchus unguicularis* C. G. Thomson (Col., Curculionidae) new to the British Isles, from the Suffolk Breckland and the Burren, Co. Clare. *Entomologist's mon. Mag.* **101** (1965): 279–286, 6 figs. Key to *Ceutorhynchus s. str.*

FOLWACZNY, B. 1973. Bestimmungstabelle der paläarktischen Cossoninae (Coleoptera, Curculionidae). *Ent. Bl. Biol. Syst. Käfer* **69:** 65–180, 46 + 37 figs.

BUCK, F. D. 1948. *Pentarthrum huttoni* Woll. (Col., Curculionidae) and some imported Cossoninae. *Entomologist's mon. Mag.* **84:** 152–154, 5 figs.

DUFFY, E. A. J. 1953. Scolytidae and Platypodidae. *Handbk Ident. Br. Insects* **5**(15): 1–20, 40 figs.

MUNRO, J. W. 1926. British bark-beetles. Forestry Commission Bull. No. **8:** 77 pp., 32 figs., 10 pls. Reprinted 1946. H.M.S.O., London.

BALACHOWSKY, A. 1949. Scolytides. *Faune Fr.* **50:** 1–320, 300 figs.

ALLEN, A. A. 1970. *Ernoporus caucasicus* Lind. and *Leperesinus orni* Fuchs (Col., Scolytidae) in Britain. *Entomologist's mon. Mag.* **105** (1969): 245–249.

MICHALSKI, J. 1973. "Revision of the Palearctic Species of the Genus *Scolytus* Geoffroy (Coleoptera, Scolytidae)". 214 pp., 49 pls. Polish Academy of Sciences, Warsaw and Cracow.

EMDEN, F. I. van 1938. On the taxonomy of Rhynchophora larvae (Coleoptera). *Trans. R. ent. Soc. Lond.* **87:** 1–37, 108 figs.

EMDEN, F. I. van 1952. On the taxonomy of Rhynchophora larvae: Adelognatha and Alophinae (Insecta, Coleoptera). *Proc. zool. Soc. Lond.* **122:** 651–795, 153 figs.

SCHERF, H. 1964. Die Entwicklungsstadien der mitteleuropäischen Curculioniden

(Morphologie, Bionomie, Ökologie). *Abh. senckenb. naturforsch. Ges.* **506**: 1–335, 497 figs.
  Key to species based on bionomic characters.
FOWLER, V. W. 1964. The identification of *Otiorrhynchus* larvae from blackcurrant roots with descriptions of the larvae of *O. clavipes* (Bonsd.) and *O. singularis* (L.) (Col., Curculionidae). *Entomologist's mon. Mag.* **99** (1963); 210–212, 4 figs.
KALINA, V. 1970. A contribution to the knowledge of the larvae of European bark beetles (Coleoptera, Scolytidae). *Acta ent. bohemoslovaka* **67**: 116–132.

Stylopoidea

PERKINS, R. C. L. 1918. Synopsis of British Strepsiptera of the genera *Stylops* and *Halictoxenus*. *Entomologist's mon. Mag.* **54**: 67–76. See also pp. 107–108.
KINZELBACH, R. K. 1969. Stylopidae, Fächerflügler (= Ordnung: Strepsiptera). *Käfer Mitteleuropas* **8**: 139–159, many figs.
KINZELBACH, R. K. 1971. Strepsiptera (Fächerflügler). *Handb. Zool.* **4**(2)2/24: 1–68, 57 figs.

Strepsiptera
British species about 16

See Coleoptera, Stylopoidea (immediately above).

Hymenoptera
British species about 6000

GENERAL

RICHARDS, O. W. 1977. Hymenoptera. Introduction and keys to families. 2nd edn. *Handbk Ident. Br. Insects* **6**(1): i–iv + 1–100, 197 + xxii figs.
SCHMIEDEKNECHT, O. 1930. "Die Hymenopteren Nord- und Mitteleuropas". 1062 pp., 127 figs. 2nd edn. G. Fischer, Jena.
  Keys adults genera, species some groups.
CEBALLOS, G. 1941–43. "Las Tribus de los Himenópteros de España". 421 pp., 284 figs. Instituto Español de Entomologia, Madrid (in Spanish).
BISCHOFF, H. 1927. "Biologie der Hymenopteren". 600 pp., 224 figs. J. Springer, Berlin.

Symphyta　　　　　　　　　　　　　　　　　　British species about 480

BENSON, R. B. 1950. An introduction to the natural history of British sawflies (Hymenoptera Symphyta). *Trans. Soc. Br. Ent.* **10**(2): 45–142, 9 figs.
BENSON, R. B. 1951–1958. Hymenoptera Symphyta. *Handbk Ident. Br. Insects* **6** (2a–c): 1–252 + i – vi, 815 figs.
  Subsequent additions mostly recorded in *Entomologist's mon. Mag.*
ENSLIN, E. 1918. "Die Tenthredinoidea Mitteleuropas". 790 pp., 154 figs. Friedländer, Berlin. Originally published in Beihefte, *Dt. ent. Z., 1912–1917*.
LORENZ, H. & KRAUS, M. 1957. Die Larvalsystematik der Blattwespen (Tenthredinoidea und Megalodontoidea). *Abh. Larvalsyst. Insekt.* **1**: i–vii, 1–339, 435 figs.

Apocrita: Parasitica

KERRICH, G. J. 1960. The state of our knowledge of the systematics of the Hymenoptera Parasitica, with particular reference to the British fauna. *Trans. Soc. Br. Ent.* **14**(1): 1–18.

ELLIOT, E. A. & MORLEY, C. 1907. On the hymenopterous parasites of Coleoptera. *Trans. ent. Soc. Lond.* **40:** 7–75.

ELLIOT, E. A. & MORLEY, C. 1911. On the hymenopterous parasites of Coleoptera. First Supplement. *Trans. ent. Soc. London.* **44:** 452–496.

MORLEY, C. & RAIT-SMITH, W. 1933. The hymenopterous parasites of the British Lepidoptera. *Trans. ent. Soc. Lond.* **81:** 133–183.

Ichneumonidae British species over 2000

MORLEY, C. 1903–14. "Ichneumonologia Britannica, the Ichneumons of Great Britain". 5 vols. 1735 pp., few illustr. Keys, Plymouth; H. & W. Brown, London.

Keys, descriptions adults. Very out-of-date but useful for amateurs, especially if Thomson and Schmiedeknecht not available: vol. 1 superseded by Perkins 1959–1960 (see below).

THOMSON, C. G. 1873–97. "Opuscula Entomologica". Vols. 5–22, pp. 455–2452, few illustr. Ohlsson, Lund (in Latin and Swedish).

Keys, diagnoses adults: still very valuable.

SCHMIEDEKNECHT, O. 1902–36. "Opuscula Ichneumonologica". 5 vols. 3332 pp. and Supplements. Blankenburg-i-Thüringen.

Keys, descriptions most species.

TOWNES, H. K., MOMOI, S. & TOWNES, M. 1965. A catalogue and reclassification of the Eastern Palaearctic Ichneumonidae. *Mem. Am. ent. Inst.* **5:** i–v + 1–661.

Keys genera. Needed by more advanced workers for modern concepts, but nomenclature does not follow some Rules and Opinions of the International Commission.

TOWNES, H. K. 1969–1971. The genera of Ichneumonidae 1–4. *Mem. Am. ent. Inst.* **11–13, 17,** 1516 pp., 847 figs.

Comment above applies. The only modern work on world genera (excluding Ichneumoninae).

KERRICH, G. J. 1942. Second review of the literature concerning British Ichneumonidae (Hym.), with notes on Palaearctic species. *Trans. Soc. Br. Ent.* **8:** 43–77, 16 figs.

BEIRNE, B. P. 1941. British species of Diplazonini (Bassini auct.) with a study of the genital and post-genital abdominal sclerites in the male (Hym. Ichneum.). *Trans. R. ent. Soc. Lond.* **91:** 661–712, 11 figs. See also *J. Soc. Br. Ent.* **3**(2): 67–83.

Treats nearly all NW European species.

PERKINS, J. F. 1941. A synopsis of the British Pimplini, with notes on the synonymy of the European species. *Trans. R. ent. Soc. Lond.* **91:** 637–659, 52 figs.

PERKINS, J. F. 1943. Notes on the British species of Adelognathini Roman, with descriptions of two new species (Hym. Ichneumonidae). *Trans. R. ent. Soc. Lond.* **93:** 95–114, 17 figs.

KERRICH, G. J. 1952. A review, and a revision in greater part, of the Cteniscini of the Old World (Hym., Ichneumonidae). *Bull. Br. Mus. nat. Hist.* (Ent.) **2**(6): 305–463, 86 figs., 4 pls. See also *Opusc. ent.* **18:** 151–159; **27:** 45–46; *Polskie Pismo ent.* **45:** 125–128.

PERKINS, J. F. 1959–60. Hymenoptera Ichneumonoidea. Ichneumonidae, key to subfamilies, Ichneumoninae 1–2, Alomyinae, Agriotypinae and Lycorininae. *Handbk Ident. Br. Insects* 7(2a i–ii): 1–213, 758 figs.

HORSTMANN, K. 1969 Typenrevision der europäischen Arten der Gattung *Diadegma* Foerster (syn. *Angitia* Holmgren) (Hymenoptera: Ichneumonidae). *Beitr. Ent.* **19:** 413–472, 122 figs.

HORSTMANN, K. 1971. Revision der europäischen Tersilochinen I (Hymenoptera, Ichneumonidae). *Veröff. Zool. Staatssamml. München* **15:** 45–138, 187 figs.

HORSTMANN, K. 1973. Revision der westpaläarktischen Arten der Gattung *Nemeritis* Holmgren (Hymenoptera, Ichneumonidae). *Opusc. zool. Münch.* **125:** 1–14, 26 figs.
AESCHLIMANN, J.-P. 1973. Révision des espèces ouest-paléarctiques du genre *Triclistus* Foerster (Hymenoptera: Ichneumonidae). *Mitt. schweiz. ent. Ges.* **46:** 219–252, 91 figs.
KASPARYAN, D. R. 1973. [Ichneumon-flies (Ichneumonidae). Subfamily Tryphoninae. Tribe Tryphonini.] *Fauna SSSR* **3**(1) (n.s. part 106): 320 pp., 417 figs. (in Russian).
FITTON, M. G. 1975. A review of the British species of *Tryphon* Fallén (Hym., Ichneumonidae). *Entomologist's mon. Mag.* **110** (1974): 153–171, 41 figs.
GAULD, I. D. 1973. Notes on British Ophionini (Hym., Ichneumonidae) including a provisional key to species. *Entomologist's Gaz.* **24:** 55–65, 6 figs. See also **25:** 147–148.
GAULD, I. D. & MITCHELL, P. A. in press. Hymenoptera Ichneumonoidea. Ichneumonidae, Orthopelmatinae and Anomaloninae. *Handbk Ident. Br. Insects* **7**.
GAULD, I. D. & HUDDLESTON, T. 1976. The nocturnal Ichneumonoidea of the British Isles, including a key to genera. *Entomologist's Gaz.* **27:** 35–49, 20 figs.
SHORT, J. R. T. 1959. A description and classification of the final instar larvae of the Ichneumonidae (Insecta, Hymenoptera). *Proc. U.S. natn. Mus.* **110:** 391–511, 62 figs. See also *Trans. R. ent. Soc. Lond.* **122**(6): 185–210, 16 figs.
FINLAYSON, T. 1975. The cephalic structures and spiracles of final-instar larvae of the subfamily Campopleginae, tribe Campoplegini (Hymenoptera: Ichneumonidae). *Mem. ent. Soc. Can.* **94,** 137 pp., 199 figs.

Braconidae   British species over 600

MARSHALL, T. A. 1885–99. Monograph of British Braconidae. 8 parts. *Trans. ent. Soc. Lond.,* 424 pp., 9 pls.
LYLE, G. T. 1914–24. Contributions to our knowledge of the British Braconidae. (In parts). *Entomologist* **47–57,** 139 pp., 2 pls.
FAHRINGER, J. 1925–37. "Opuscula Braconologica". Vols. 1, 3–4. 1740 pp., few illustr. Fritz Wagner, Vienna.
Treats certain subfamilies only.
NIXON, G. E. J. 1943–49. A revision of the European Dacnusini (Hym. Braconidae, Dacnusinae). 8 parts. *Entomologist's mon. Mag.* **79–86,** 125 pp., 347 figs.
FISCHER, M. 1957–58. Die europäischen Arten der Gattung *Opius* Wesm. (Hym., Braconidae). In parts in different journals: references given by Kerrich 1960 (see above).
FISCHER, M. 1962. Beitrag zur Kenntnis der Wirte von *Opius*-Arten (Hymenoptera, Braconidae). *Entomophaga* **7:** 79–90.
Numerous host records from faunal area.
EADY, R. D. & CLARK, J. A. J. 1964. A revision of the genus Macrocentrus Curtis (Hym., Braconidae) in Europe, with descriptions of four new species. *Entomologist's Gaz.* **15**(3): 97–127, 92 figs.
GRIFFITHS, G. C. D. 1964–68. The Alysiinae (Hym. Braconidae) parasites of the Agromyzidae (Diptera) I–V. *Beitr. Ent.* **14, 16–18,** 516 pp., 185 figs.
NIXON, G. E. J. 1965. A reclassification of the tribe Microgasterini (Hymenoptera: Braconidae). *Bull. Br. Mus. nat. Hist.* (Ent.) Suppl. **2:** 1–284, 346 figs.
NIXON, G. E. J. 1968. A revision of the genus *Microgaster* Latreille (Hymenoptera: Braconidae). *Bull. Br. Mus. nat. Hist.* (Ent.) **22**(2): 31–72, 33 figs.
NIXON, G. E. J. 1970. A revision of the NW European species of *Microplitis* Förster (Hymenoptera: Braconidae). *Bull. Br. Mus. nat. Hist.* (Ent.) **25**(1): 1–30, 29 figs.

NIXON, G. E. J. 1972–76 [Four papers revising the north-western European species of groups of *Apanteles* Förster]. *Bull. ent. Res.* **61, 63–65**, 226 pp., 260 figs.
EADY, R. D. 1969. A new diagnostic character in *Aphidius* (Hymenoptera: Braconidae) of special significance in species on pea aphid. *Proc. R. ent. Soc. Lond.* B **38:** 165–173, 21 figs.
STARY, P. 1966. "Aphid parasites of Czechoslovakia. A review of the Czechoslovak Aphidiidae (Hymenoptera)". 247 pp., 21 pls. Junk, The Hague.
STARY, P. 1973. A review of the Aphidius-species (Hymenoptera, Aphidiidae) of Europe. *Ann. zool. bot. Bratislava* **84:** 1–85, 25 figs. (compound), 3 pls.
HAESELBARTH, E. 1973. Die Blacus-Arten Europas und Zentral-Asiens (Hymenoptera, Braconidae). *Veröff. Zool. Staatssamml. München* **16:** 69–170, 123 figs. on 10 pls.
ACHTERBERG, C. ,van 1976. A revision of the tribus Blacini (Hymenoptera, Braconidae, Helconinae). *Tijdschr. Ent.* **118:** 159–322, 476 figs.
ACHTERBERG, C. van 1976. A preliminary key to the subfamilies of Braconidae (Hymenoptera). *Tijdschr. Ent.* **119:** 33–78, 123 figs.
SHORT, J. R. T. 1952. The morphology of the head of larval Hymenoptera with special reference to the head of Ichneumonoidea, including a classification of the final instar larvae of the Braconidae. *Trans. R. ent. Soc. Lond.* **103:** 27–84 34 figs.

Evanioidea   British species 8

CROSSKEY, R. W. 1951. The morphology, taxonomy and biology of the British Evanioidea (Hymenoptera). *Trans. R. ent. Soc. Lond.* **102:** 247–301, 72 figs.
KIEFFER, J. J. 1912. Evaniidae. *Tierreich* **30,** xiv + 431 pp., illustr.

Chalcidoidea   British species over 1500

NIKOL'SKAYA, M. N. 1952. [Chalcidoidea of the USSR]. *Opred. Faune SSSR* **44:** 1–575, 592 figs. (in Russian).
   Keys families, genera, species in some groups.
PECK, O., BOUČEK, Z. & HOFFER, A. 1964. Keys to the Chalcidoidea of Czechoslovakia (Insecta: Hymenoptera). *Mem. ent. Soc. Can.* **34:** 1–121, 288 figs.
   Keys genera, including almost all British.
FERRIÈRE, C. & KERRICH, G. J. 1958. Hymenoptera Chalcidoidea. Agaontidae, Leucospidae, Chalcididae, Eucharitidae, Perilampidae, Cleonymidae and Thysanidae. *Handbk Ident. Br. Insects* **8**(2a): 1–40, 79 + v figs.
BOUČEK, Z. 1952 (1951). The first revision of the European species of the family Chalcididae (Hymenoptera). *Sborn. ent. Odd. nár. Mus. Praze* Suppl. **1:** 1–108, 17 pls. (150 figs.).
STEFFAN, J. R. 1952. Les espèces françaises du genre *Perilampus* Latr. [Hym. Perilampidae]. *Bull. Soc. ent. Fr.* **52:** 68–74, 12 figs.
HOFFMEYER, E. B. 1931. Beiträge zur Kenntnis der dänischen Callimomiden, mit Bestimmungstabellen der europäischen Arten (Hym. Chalc.). *Ent. Meddr.* **17:** 232–285, 19 figs.
EADY, R. D. 1959. A revision of the nomenclature in the European Torymidae (Hym., Chalcidoidea) with special reference to the Walker types. *Entomologist's mon. Mag.* **94:** 257–271.
CLARIDGE, M. F. 1961. An advance towards a natural classification of the Eurytomid genera (Hym., Chalcidoidea) with special reference to British forms. *Trans. Soc. Br. Ent.* **14**(7): 167–185, 29 figs.
CLARIDGE, M. F. 1961. A contribution to the biology and taxonomy of some Palaearctic species of *Tetramesa* Walker (= *Isosoma* Walk.; = *Harmolita* Motsch.) (Hymenoptera: Eurytomidae), with particular reference to the British fauna. *Trans. R. ent. Soc. Lond.* **113**(9): 175–216, 105 figs.

HEDICKE, H. 1920. Beiträge zu eine Monographie der paläarktischen Isosominen (Hym., Chalc.). *Arch. Naturgesch.* **86**(11): 1–165.
MERCET, R. G. 1921. Himenopteros, fam. Encirtidos. *Trab. Mus. nac. Cienc. nat. Madr.: i–xi* + 1–732, 292 figs. (in Spanish).
Many drawings of whole insects by Gonzalo Ceballos.
GRAHAM, M. W. R. de V. 1958. Notes on some genera and species of Encyrtidae (Hym., Chalcidoidea), with special reference to Dalman's types. *Ent. Tidskr.* **79** (3–4): 147–175.
Key to species of *Bothriothorax* and notes on other genera. See also 1969, *Polskie Pismo ent.* **39**(2): 211–319.
KERRICH, G. J. 1967. On the classification of the Anagyrine Encyrtidae, with a revision of some of the genera (Hymenoptera: Chalcidoidea). *Bull. Br. Mus. nat. Hist.* (Ent.) **20**(5): 141–250, 114 figs., 4 pls.
For genera *Aglyptus* and *Ericydnus*.
GRAHAM, M. W. R. de V. 1969. The Pteromalidae of north-western Europe. *Bull. Br. Mus. nat. Hist.* (Ent.) Suppl. **16**, 908 pp., 686 figs.
FERRIÈRE, C. 1965. Hymenoptera Aphelinidae d'Europe et du Bassin Méditerranéen. *Faune de l'Europe et du Bassin Méditerranéen* **1**: 1–206, 80 figs. Masson, Paris.
FERRIÈRE, C. 1947. Les espèces européenes du genre Elasmus Westw. (Hym. Chalc.). *Mitt. Schweiz. ent. Ges.* **20**: 565–580, 4 figs.
ASKEW, R. R. 1968. Hymenoptera Chalcidoidea. Elasmidae and Eulophidae (Elachertinae, Eulophinae, Euderinae). *Handbk Ident. Br. Insects* **8**(2b): 1–39, 83 + iii figs.
GRAHAM, M. W. R. de V. 1959. Keys to the British genera and species of Elachertinae, Eulophinae, Entedontinae and Euderinae (Hym., Chalcidoidea). *Trans. Soc. Br. Ent.* **13**(10): 169–204, 9 figs.
GRAHAM, M. W. R. de V. 1963. Additions and corrections to the British list of Eulophidae (Hym., Chalcidoidea), with descriptions of some new species. *Trans. Soc. Br. Ent.* **15**(9): 167–275, 59 figs.
GRAHAM, M. W. R. de V. 1971. Revision of British *Entedon* (Hymenoptera: Chalcidoidea), with descriptions of four new species. *Trans. R. ent. Soc. Lond.* **123**(3): 313–358, 27 figs.
BOUČEK, Z. 1958. Revision der europäischen Tetracampidae (Hym. Chalcidoidea) mit einem Katalog der Arten der Welt. *Sborn. ent. Odd. nár. Mus. Praze* **32**: 41–90, 35 figs.
BOUČEK, Z. 1959. A study of Central European Eulophidae, I: Eulophinae (Hymenoptera). *Sborn. ent. Odd. nár. Mus. Praze* **33**: 117–170, 37 figs.
BOUČEK, Z. 1959. A study of Central European Eulophidae, II. *Diaulinopsis* and *Cirrospilus* (Hymenoptera). *Sborn. ent. Odd. nár. Mus. Praze* **33**: 171–194, 6 figs.
BOUČEK, Z. 1963. Studien über europäischen Eulophidae, III: Euderinae (Hymenoptera: Chalcidoidea). *Beitr. Ent.* **13**: 257–281, 22 figs.
BOUČEK, Z. 1965. Studies of European Eulophidae, IV: Pediobius Walk. and two allied genera. *Sborn. ent. Odd. nár. Mus. Praze* **36**: 5–90, 78 figs.
KRYGER, J. P. 1919. The European Trichogramminae. *Ent. Meddr.* **12**: 257–354, 21 figs.
KRYGER, J. P. 1950–51. The European Mymaridae comprising the genera known up to *c*. 1930. *Ent. Meddr.* **26**: 1–97, 45 figs.
HINCKS, W. D. 1950. Notes on some British Mymaridae (Hym.). *Trans. Soc. Br. Ent.* **10**(4): 167–207, 5 figs.
HINCKS, W. D. 1952. The British species of the genus *Ooctonus* Haliday, with a note on some recent work on fairy flies (Hym., Mymaridae). *Trans. Soc. Br. Ent.* **11**(7): 153–163, 8 figs.

HINCKS, W. D. 1959. The British species of the genus *Alaptus* Haliday in Walker (Hym., Chalc., Mymaridae). *Trans. Soc. Br. Ent.* **13**(8): 137–148, 8 figs.

Proctotrupoidea (= Serphoidea) British species about 650

KIEFFER, J. J. 1914–26. Serphidae, Calliceratidae, Diapriidae, Scelionidae. *Tierreich* **42, 44, 48**: 1813 pp., 608 figs.

PSCHORN-WALCHER, H. 1971. Hymenoptera. Heloridae et Proctotrupidae. *Insecta Helvetica Fauna* **4**: 1–63, 103 figs.

NIXON, G. E. J. 1938. A preliminary revision of the British Proctotrupinae. *Trans. R. ent. Soc. Lond.* **87**: 431–466, 71 figs.

NIXON, G. E. J. 1957. Hymenoptera Proctotrupoidea, Diapriidae subfamily Belytinae. *Handbk Ident. Br. Insects* **8** (3d ii): 1–107, 314 figs.
   Includes many NW European species.

NIXON, G. E. J. in preparation. Hymenoptera Proctotrupoidea. Diapriidae subfamily Diapriinae. *Handbk Ident. Br. Insects* **8**.

Cynipoidea British species about 200

DALLA-TORRE, K. W. & KIEFFER, J. J. 1910. Cynipidae. *Tierreich* **24**: xxxv + 891 pp., 422 figs.

WELD, L. H. 1952. "Cynipoidea (Hym.) 1905–1950". 351 pp., 224 figs. Ann Arbor, Michigan.
   Unfortunately very scarce. Keys world genera: reference lists species described since those included in Dalla Torre & Kieffer.

EADY, R. D. & QUINLAN, J. 1963. Hymenoptera Cynipoidea. Key to Families and Subfamilies, and Cynipinae (including Galls). *Handbk Ident. Br. Insects* **8** (1a): 1–81, 371 + vii figs.

HELLÉN, W. 1963. Die Alloxystinen Finnlands (Hymenoptera: Cynipidae). *Fauna fenn.* **15**: 1–24, 1 map.

QUINLAN, J. in press. Hymenoptera Cynipoidea. Eucoilidae. Keys to genera and species. *Handbk Ident. Br. Insects* **8**: 205 figs., 1 pl.

KERRICH, G. J. 1973. On the taxonomy of some forms of *Ibalia* Latreille (Hymenoptera: Cynipoidea) associated with conifers. *J. Linn. Soc. Zool.* **53**: 65–79, 7 figs.
   Includes the only known NW European species.

Apocrita: Aculeata British species 593

GENERAL

OEHLKE, J. 1969. Beiträge zur Insekten-Fauna der DDR: Hymenoptera-Bestimmungstabellen bis zu den Unterfamilien. *Beitr. Ent.* **19**: 753–801, 146 figs.

SAUNDERS, E. 1896. "The Hymenoptera Aculeata of the British Isles". xii + 391 pp., 52 pls. Reeve, London.

STELFOX, A. W. 1927 A list of the Hymenoptera Aculeata *(sensu lato)* of Ireland. *Proc. R. Ir. Acad.* **37**(B), No. 22: 201–355.

STELFOX, A. W. 1933. Some recent records for Irish Aculeate Hymenoptera. *Entomologist's mon. Mag.* **69**: 47–53.

STEP, E. 1932. "Bees, Wasps, Ants and Allied Insects of the British Isles". xxv + 238 pp., 111 pls. Warne, London and New York.

YARROW, I. H. H. 1945. In Hymenopterist's Handbook. *Amateur Ent.* **7**(1943): 13–17, 19–25, 33–35, 55–81.
   Key to genera, biology. References to additions to British list since Saunders (1896), excluding Formicoidea.

LARVAE, NESTS

DANKS, H. V. 1971. Biology of some stem-nesting aculeate Hymenoptera. *Trans. R. ent. Soc. Lond.* **122**(11): 323-399, 17 figs.
   Contains a key to the nests of British aculeate Hymenoptera in *Rubus* stems and their commoner parasites.
LOMHOLDT, O. 1975. The Specidae (Hymenoptera) of Fennoscandia and Denmark. *Fauna ent. Scand.* **4**(1): 41-51, 25 figs.
   Key to genera of Sphecid larvae.
MALYSHEV, S. I. 1936. The nest Habits of Solitary Bees. *Eos, Madr.* **11**: 201-309, 13 pls.
MICHENER, C. D. 1953. Comparative morphological and systematic studies of bee larvae with a key to families of Hymenopterous larvae. *Kans. Univ. Sci. Bull.* **35** (8, pt. 2): 987-1102, 287 figs.

Bethyloidea

LINSENMAIER, W. 1959. Revision der Familie Chrysididae (Hymenoptera). *Mitt. schweiz. ent. Ges.* **32**(1-2): 1-240, 716 figs.
LINSENMAIER, W. 1968. Revision der Familie Chrysididae (Hymenoptera). Zweiter Nachtrag. *Mitt. schweiz. ent. Ges.* **41**: 1-144. 13 figs.
MORICE, F. D. 1900. A revised synoptic table of British Chrysids. *Entomologist's mon. Mag.* **16**: 129-131.
PERKINS, J. F. 1976. Hymenoptera. Bethyloidea (excluding Chrysididae). *Handbk Ident. Br. Insects* **6**(3a): 38 pp., 84 figs.
SPOONER, G. M. 1954. Notes on species of *Omalus* (Hym., Chrysididae) including one new to the British list. *Entomologist's mon. Mag.* **90**: 135-138.
   Contains key to British *Omalus*.

Scolioidea (including Formicidae)

BERNARD, F. 1968. Les Fourmis (Hymenoptera Formicidae) d'Europe Occidentale et Septentrionale. *Faune de l'Europe et du Bassin Méditerranéen* **3**, 411 pp., 379 figs., 46 photos.
BOLTON, B. & COLLINGWOOD, C. A. 1975. Hymenoptera. Formicidae. *Handbk Ident. Br. Insects* **6**(3c): 33 pp., 65 figs.
COLLINGWOOD, C. A. 1963. The *Lasius (Cthonolasius) umbratus* (Hym. Formicidae) species complex in North Europe. *Entomologist* **96**: 145-158, 4 figs., 4 tabs.
DONISTHORPE, H. St. J. K. 1927. "British Ants". xv + 436 pp., 93 figs., 18 pls. Routledge, London.
DONISTHORPE, H. St. J. K. 1927. "The Guests of British Ants, their Habits and Life Histories". xxiii + 244 pp., 55 figs., 16 pls. Routledge, London.
RICHARDS, O. W. in preparation. Hymenoptera Scolioidea (excluding Formicidae), Vespoidea, Sphecoidea. *Handbk Ident. Br. Insects* **6**.
WILSON, E. O. 1955. A monographic revision of the ant genus *Lasius*. *Bull. Mus. comp. Zool. Harv.* **113**(1): 1-199, 17 figs., 2 pls.

Pompiloidea

HAMM, A. H. & RICHARDS, O. W. 1939. The biology of the British Pompilidae (Hymenoptera). *Trans. Soc. Br. Ent.* **6**: 51-114.
WOLF, H. 1972. Hymenoptera: Pompilidae. *Insectà helvetica* **5**, 176 pp., 489 figs.

Vespoidea

BEAUMONT, J. de 1944. Les Guêpes *(Vespa* L. s.l.) de la Suisse. *Bull. Soc. vaud. Sci. nat.* **62** (No. 261): 329-362, 41 figs.

BLÜTHGEN, P. 1961. Die Faltenwespen Mitteleuropas (Hym., Diploptera). *Abh. dt. Akad. Wiss. Berl.* (Chem., Geol., Biol.) **1961**(2), 248 pp., 71 figs.
GUIGLIA, D. 1972. Les Guêpes Sociales (Hymenoptera Vespidae) d'Europe Occidentale et Septentrionale. *Faune de l'Europe et du Bassin Méditerranéen* **6**, viii + 181 pp., 41 figs., 3 pls.
KEMPER, H. & DÖHRING, E. 1967. "Die sozialen Faltwespen Mitteleuropas". 180 pp., 82 figs. P. Parey, Berlin & Hamburg.
LØKEN, A. 1964. Social wasps in Norway (Hymenoptera, Vespidae). *Norsk ent. Tidsskr.* **12**(5–8): 195–218, 24 figs., 2 pls.
RICHARDS, O. W. In preparation. See above.
SPRADBERY, J. P. 1973. "Wasps. An account of the biology and natural history of solitary and social wasps with particular reference to those of the British Isles". xvi + 408 pp., 131 figs., 29 pls. Sidgwick & Jackson, London.

Specoidea

BEAUMONT, J. de 1964. Hymenoptera: Sphecidae. *Insecta helvetica* **3**, 168 pp., 551 figs.
BOHART, R. M. & MENKE, A. S. 1976. "Sphecid Wasps of the World – a generic revision". ix + 695 pp., 190 figs., 1 pl. University of California Press, Berkeley, Los Angeles & London.
LOMHOLDT, O. 1975, 1976. The Sphecidae (Hymenoptera) of Fennoscandia and Denmark. *Fauna ent. scand.* **4**(1): 1–224, figs. 1–272; **4**(2): 225–452, figs. 273–464.
OEHLKE, J. 1970. Beiträge zur Insekten-Fauna der DDR: Hymenoptera–Sphecidae. *Beitr. Ent.* **20**(7–8): 615–812, 387 figs.
RICHARDS, O. W. In preparation. See above.
YARROW, I. H. H. 1969. Some additional and little known British species of the solitary wasp genus *Spilomena* Shuckard (Hym., Specoidea). *Entomologist's Gaz.* **20**(2): 97–104.
YARROW, I. H. H. 1970. Some nomenclatorial problems in the genus *Passaloecus* Shuckard and two species not before recognised as British (Hym., Specidae). *Entomologist's Gaz.* **21**(3): 167–189, 24 figs.

Apoidea

ALFORD, D. V. 1975. "Bumblebees". xii + 352 pp., 210 figs., 27 maps, 56 pls. Davis-Poynter, London.
BUTLER, C. G. 1974. "The World of the Honeybee". New Naturalist No. 29. xii + 226 pp., 42 pls (2 col.). Collins, London.
EBMER, A. W. 1969–71. Die Bienen des Genus *Halictus* Latr. s.l. im Grossraum von Linz (Hymenoptera, Apidae) **1–3**. *Naturk. Jb. Stadt Linz* **1969**: 133–183, figs. 1–36; **1970**: 19–82, figs. 37–64; **1971**: 63–156, figs. 65–127.
FAESTER, K. & HAMMER, K. 1970. Systematik der Mittel- und Nordeuropäischen *Bombus* und *Psithyrus* (Hym., Apidae). *Ent. Meddr* **38**: 257–302, 18 figs.
GUICHARD, K. M. 1974. *Colletes halophila* Verhoeff (Hym., Apidae) and its *Epeolus* parasite at Swanscombe in Kent, with a key to the British species of *Colletes* Latreille. *Entomologist's Gaz.* **25**(3): 195–199.
LØKEN, A. 1973. Studies on Scandinavian bumble bees (Hymenoptera, Apidae). *Norsk ent. Tidsskr.* **20**(1)–218, 99 figs.
NÉHELŸ, L. 1935. "Naturgeschichte der Urbienen". 214 pp., 60 pls. Budapest. (Per Gustav Fischer, Jena).
Revision of *Hylaeus* (= *Prosopis*) of middle Europe.
NOSKIEWICZ, J. 1936. Die Palearktischen *Colletes*-Arten. *Pr. nauk. Wyd. Tow. Nauk. Lwow* **3**: 1–532, 40 figs., 28 pls.

PERKINS, R. C. L. 1919. The British species of *Andrena* and *Nomada*. *Trans. ent. Soc. Lond.* **52**: 218–316, 5 pls.
PERKINS, R. C. L. 1922. The British species of *Halictus* and *Sphecodes*. *Entomologist's mon. Mag.* **58**: 46–174.
PERKINS, R. C. L. 1925. The British species of *Megachile* with descriptions of some new varieties from Ireland, and of a species new to Britain in F. Smith's collection. *Entomologist's mon. Mag.* **61**: 95–101.
PERKINS, R. C. L. 1935. A note on some British species of *Halictus*. *Entomologist's mon. Mag.* **71**: 104–106.
RICHARDS, O. W. 1937. A study of the British species of *Epeolus* Latr. and their races, with a key to the species of *Colletes* (Hymen., Apidae). *Trans. Soc. Br. Ent.* **4**: 89–130, 21 figs., 29 tabs.
WARNCKE, K. 1973. Die Westpaläarktischen Arten der Bienenfamilie Melittidae (Hymenoptera). *Polskie Pismo Ent.* **43**(1): 97–126, 33 figs.
YARROW, I. H. H. 1968. Recent additions to the British bee-fauna, with comments and corrections. *Entomologist's mon. Mag.* **104**: 60–64.
YARROW, I. H. H. 1970. *Hoplitis claviventris* (Thomson 1872) (= *Osmia leucomelana* auctt. nec Kirby) and the identity of *Apis leucomelana* Kirby 1802 (Hymenoptera, Megachilidae). *Entomologist* **103**: 62–69.

Diptera
British species about 6000

The study of the early stages of Diptera has lagged far behind the study of adult flies, and since dipterists are as frequently required to identify larvae as adults, a separate section is given for works relating entirely to early stages (see p.106). Some of the works cited in the main list also include early stages. Where family subheadings are not given, as in the Acalyptratae, the references are grouped roughly according to the classification of the revised Check List of Diptera (1976, *Handbk. Ident. Br. Insects* **11**(5), 139 pp.).

GENERAL

BALACHOWSKY, A. S. & MESNIL, L. 1935–36. "Les Insectes Nuisibles aux Plantes Cultivées". 2 vols. 1921 pp., 1349 figs. Busson, Paris.
  Very useful for adults and larvae of economic species, as far as these were known in 1936.
BEI-BIENKO, G. Y. (see above p. 58).
COLYER, C. N. & HAMMOND, C. O. 1968. "Flies of the British Isles". 2nd edn. 384 pp., 52 pls. Warne, London.
  Excellent general account. Keys to families. Unusually high standard of illustration.
CRAMPTON, G. C. 1942. "Guide to the insects of Connecticut. Part VI. Diptera or True Flies. Fasc. 1: External Morphology". State of Connecticut Public Document No. **47**, pp. 10–165, 14 figs.
EDWARDS, F. W., OLDROYD, H. & SMART, J. 1939. "British Bloodsucking Flies". 156 pp., 64 figs., 45 pls. British Museum (Natural History), London.
  Covers only the flies that suck blood in Britain, whether of man or of other animals: families Culicidae, Ceratopogonidae, Simuliidae, Rhagionidae, Tabanidae, Muscidae (Stomoxydinae). Hippoboscidae, Nycteribiidae. Keys. Biological notes. Out of print.
FAUNE DE FRANCE (Federation française des Sociétés des Sciences naturelles). Lechevalier, Paris.
  Many parts. Covers most, but not all, of British species. Is less comprehensive than Lindner, but for this reason often more convenient to use. The most useful

parts are probably Parent on Dolichopodidae (part 35) and Séguy's big part (28) on Muscidae, Acalypterae and Scatophagidae.

GRIMSHAW, P. H. 1917. Guide to the literature of the British Diptera. *Proc. R. phys. Soc. Edinb.* **20**(2): 78–117.

    Enumerates papers from 1782 to 1916: an invaluable guide to the early literature.

LINDNER, E. 1925 on. "Die Fliegen der Palaearktischen Region". E. Schweitzerbart'sche, Stuttgart.

    Band I, Handbuch, by Lindner himself, contains a history of Dipterology, with sections on morphology, physiology and taxonomy of Diptera, with a key to families and short notes on each. A very large number of subsequent parts covers nearly all the families of Diptera, but even now (1976) parts are still unfinished. This work should always be consulted in dealing with any family of British Diptera; it is only listed by name when it is a major reference for a particular family.

KLOET, G. S. & HINCKS, W. D. 1975. A check list of British insects. 2nd edn. (revised K. G. V. Smith *et al.*). Part 5: Diptera and Siphonaptera. *Handbk Ident. Br. Insects* **11**(5): 1–139.

    Should be consulted for revised nomenclature for all families.

LUNDBECK, W. 1907–12. "Diptera Danica. Genera and species of flies hitherto found in Denmark". 7 vols. Gad, Wesley, Copenhagen and London.

    Covers Brachycera, Aschiza and Tachinidae. Keys sub-families, genera, species; some biological data.

OLDROYD, H. 1970. Diptera: Introduction and key to families. 2nd ed. *Handbk Ident. Br. Insects* **9**(1): 1–104, 150 figs.

OLDROYD, H. 1964. "The Natural History of Flies". 324 pp., 40 figs., 32 pls. Weidenfeld & Nicholson, London.

    An excellent and very readable account.

ROHDENDORF, B. 1974. "The Historical Development of Diptera". xv + 360 pp., 85 figs. University of Alberta Press. English translation of work originally published in Russian, 1964, by Nauka.

    Includes account of and keys to fossil Diptera.

SÉGUY, E. 1950. "La Biologie des Diptères". Encycl. Ent. A. Vol. 26. 609 pp., 225 figs. Lechevalier, Paris.

    Information elaborately classified under 998 headings.

HENNIG, W. 1973. Diptera (Zweiflügler). In KÜKENTHAL, W., see above p. 000. Part 31: 337 pp., 143 figs.

    Very good general account of the Diptera.

SMITH, K. G. V., COGAN, B. H. & PONT, A. C. 1969. A bibliography of James Edward Collin (1876–1968). *J. Soc. Biblphy nat. Hist.* **5**(3): 226–235.

    Lists 212 titles including many key works on Brachycera and Cyclorrhapha by this major British Dipterist.

Nematocera   British species over 2000

COE, R. L., FREEMAN, P. & MATTINGLY, P. F. 1950. Diptera. 2. Nematocera: families Tipulidae to Chironomidae. *Handbk Ident. Br. Insects* **9**(2): 1–126, 199 figs.

Tipulidae and Trichoceridae

COE, R. L. 1950. See above.

EDWARDS, F. W. 1938. British short-palped crane-flies. *Trans. Soc. Br. Ent.* **5**: 1–168, 31 figs. (compound), 5 pls.

HUTSON, A. M. & VANE-WRIGHT, R. I. 1969. Corrections and additions to the list of British Nematocera (Diptera) since Kloet & Hincks' "A Check List of British Insects" (1945). Part 1. Introduction and families Tipulidae, Trichoceridae and

Anisopodidae (Tipuloidea). *Entomologist's Gaz.* **20:** 231–256, 10 figs.
  Supplementary to Coe 1950; see also Hutson & Stubbs, 1974, *Entomologist's Gaz.* **25:** 297 and Stubbs, A. E. & Little, C. J., 1973, *Proc. Br. ent. nat. Hist. Soc.* **6:** 18; **7**(2): 44.
MANNHEIMS, B. 1951 on. In Lindner's Die Fliegen . . .
SAVCHENKO, E. N. 1961–73. Tipulidae. *Fauna SSSR* **2**(3): 1–486, 295 figs; **2**(4): 1–502, 380 figs; **2**(5): 1–281, 160 figs. (in Russian).
STARÝ, J. 1972. European species of the genus *Dicranoptycha* Osten-Sacken (Diptera, Tipulidae). *Acta ent. bohemoslovaca* **69:** 401–416, 15 figs.
STARÝ, J. & ROZKÓSNÝ, R. 1970. A revision of palaearctic species of the subgenera *Protogonomyia* Alexander, *Ellipteroides* Becker and *Ptilostenodes* Alexander (Diptera, Tipulidae: *Gonomyia* Meigen). *Acta ent. bohemoslovaca* **67:** 362–374, 28 figs.
STUBBS, A. E. 1972 on. Introduction to craneflies. *Bull. amat. Ent. Soc.* **31:** 46–54, 83–93; **32:** 14–23, 58–64, 101–107; **33:** 18–23, 142–145, numerous figs. Still appearing.
  Useful introduction to family.
TJEDER, B. 1958. A synopsis of the Swedish Tipulidae. 1. Subfam. Limoniinae: tribe Limoniini. *Opusc. Ent.* **23:** 133–169, 40 figs. 2. Subfam. Limoniinae: tribe Pediciini. *Opusc. Ent.* **24:** 1–9, 9 figs.
LAURENCE, B. R. 1957. The British species of *Trichocera* (Diptera: Trichoceridae). *Proc. R. ent. Soc. Lond., A,* **32:** 132–138, 2 figs.
DAHL, C. 1966. Notes on the taxonomy and distribution of Swedish Trichoceridae (Dipt., Nemat.). *Opusc. ent.* **31:** 93–118, 72 figs.

Ptychopteridae

FREEMAN, P. 1950. See Coe *et al.* (above).

Psychodidae

FREEMAN, P. 1950. See Coe *et al.* (above). See also *Proc. R. ent. Soc. Lond. B* **22:** 69–71 and **25:** 147–156 (1953–1956).
DUCKHOUSE, D. A. 1962. Some British Psychodidae (Diptera, Nematocera): descriptions of species and a discussion on the problems of species pairs. *Trans. R. ent. Soc. Lond.* **114:** 403–436, 17 figs. (compound).
DUCKHOUSE, D. A. 1966. Pscyhodidae (Diptera, Nematocera) of Southern Australia: subfamily Psychodinae. *Trans. R. ent. Soc. Lond.* **118**(6): 153–220, 235 figs.
  Includes some comments on the generic placing of British species.

Dixidae

DISNEY, R. H. L. 1975. A key to British Dixidae. *Scient. Publs Freshwat. biol. Ass.* **31:** 1–78, 23 figs., 2 pls., maps.
  Keys to mature larvae, pupae and adults.
VAILLANT, F. 1969. Les diptères Dixidae des Pyrenées des Alpes et des Carpates. *Annls Linmol.* **5:** 73–84.

Culicidae

MARSHALL, J. F. 1938. "The British Mosquitoes". 341 pp., 172 figs., 20 pls. British Museum (Natural History), London. Reprinted 1966, Johnson Reprint.
MATTINGLY, P. F. 1950. See Coe *et al.* (above).
MARTINI, E. 1929–31. In Lindner's Die Fliegen . . .
NATVIG, L. R. 1948. Contributions to the knowledge of the Danish and Fennoscandian mosquitoes. Culcini. *Norsk ent. Tidsskr.* Suppl. **1,** 567 pp., 148 figs.
STONE, A., KNIGHT, K. L. & STARCKE, H. 1959–70. "A synoptic catalog of the

mosquitoes of the world". Thomas Say Foundation. Vol. 6. Entomological Society of America, Washington, D.C. 358 pp. plus Supplements 1–4 in *Proc. ent. Soc. Wash.* **63**: 29–52; **65**: 117–140; **69**: 197–224; **72**: 137–171. New edn. in preparation by Knight & Stone, scheduled for 1977.

Chironomidae

FREEMAN, P. 1950. See Coe *et al.* (above).
BRUNDIN, L. 1956. Zur Systematik der Orthocladiinae (Dipt., Chironomidae). *Inst. Freshwat. Res. (Drottningholm)* **37**: 5–185, 137 figs.
  Essential for modern generic concepts.
BRUNDIN, L. 1966. Transantarctic relationships and their significance, as evidenced by Chironomid midges with a monograph of subfamilies Podonominae and Aphroteniinae and the Austral Heptagyiae. *K. svenska VetenskAkad. Handl.* **11**(1): 1–472, 638 figs., 30 pls.
  Essential reading: keys, includes some British species.
CRANSTON, P. S. 1975. Corrections and additions to the list of British Chironomidae (Diptera). *Entomologist's mon. Mag.* **110**: 87–95.
  Supplementary to Freeman 1950 (see above).
FITTKAU, E. J. 1962. Die Tanypodinae (Diptera: Chironomidae). *Abh. Larvalsyst. Insekt.* **6**: 1–53, 409 figs.
  Keys to European adults and pupae, with distribution.
FITTKAU, E. J. & LEHMANN, J. 1970. Revision der Gattung *Microcricotopus* Thien. u. Harn. (Dipt., Chironomidae). *Int. Revue Ges. Hydrobiol.* **55**: 391–402, 6 figs. (compound).
HIRVENOJA, K. 1973. Revision der Gattung *Cricotopus* v.d.Wulp und ihrer Verwandten (Diptera, Chironomidae). *Annls zool. fenn.* **10**: 1–363, 216 figs.
  Especially useful for larvae and pupae.
LEHMANN, J. 1969. Die europäischen Arten der Gattung *Rheocricotopus* Thien. und Harn. und drei neue Artvertreter dieser Gattung aus der Orientalis (Diptera, Chironomidae). *Arch. Hydrobiol.* **66**: 348–381, 21 figs.
LEHMANN, J. 1970. Revision der europäischen Arten (Imagines ♂♂) der Gattung *Parachironomus* Lenz (Diptera, Chironomidae). *Hydrobiologia* **33**: 129–158, 21 figs.
LEHMANN, J. 1970. Revision der europäischen Arten (Imagines ♂♂ und Puppen ♂♂) der Gattung *Rheotanytarsus* Bause (Diptera, Chironomidae). *Zool. Anz.* **185**: 344–378, 34 figs.
LEHMANN, J. 1972. Revision der europäischen Arten (Puppen ♂♂ und Imagines ♂♂) der Gattung *Eukiefferiella* Thienemann (Diptera, Chironomidae). *Beitr. Ent.* **22**: 347–405, 89 figs.
SERRA-TOSIO, B. 1964 on. [Series of papers on european Chironomidae and still appearing in *Trav. Lab. Hydrobiol.* **56** on].

Ceratopogonidae

ATCHLEY, W. R., WIRTH, W. W. & GASKINS, C. T. 1975. "A Bibliography and Key Word – In Context Index of the Ceratopogonidae (Diptera) from 1758 to 1973". 300 pp. Texas Technical Press, Lubbock, Texas.
CAMPBELL, J. A. & PELHAM-CLINTON, E. C. 1960. A taxonomic review of the British species of *'Culicoides'* Latreille (Diptera: Ceratopogonidae). *Proc. R. Soc. Edinb. (B)* **67**: 181–302, 291 figs.
CLASTRIER, J. 1961–63. Notes sur les Cératopogonidés (part). *Archs Inst. Pasteur Alger* **39**: 401–437, 20 figs. *(Ceratopogon* and *Alluaudomyia);* **40**: 53–125, 32 figs. *(Bezzia);* **40**: 225–228 *(Palpomyia);* **41**: 41–68, 17 figs. *(Stilobezzia).*
DOWNES, J. A. & KETTLE, D. A. 1952. Descriptions of three species of *Culicoides*

Latreille (Diptera: Ceratopogonidae) new to science, together with notes on, and a revised key to the British species of the *pulicaris* and *obsoletus* groups. *Proc. R. ent. Soc. Lond.* B **21**: 61–78, 8 figs.

EDWARDS, F. W. 1926. On the British biting midges. *Trans. ent. Soc. Lond.* **74**: 389–426, 3 figs., 2 pls.

EDWARDS, F. W. 1939. See Edwards, Oldroyd & Smart (above).

KETTLE, D. S. 1955. Descriptions of two species of *Culicoides* Latreille (Diptera: Ceratopogonidae) new to science. *Proc. R. ent. Soc. Lond.* B. **24**: 37–47, 14 figs.
  Revised couplets to existing keys adults and larvae.

KREMER, M. 1965. Contribution à l'étude de genre *Culicoides* Latreille particulièrement en France. *Encycl. ent.* (A) **39**: 3–299, 479 figs.

Simuliidae

CARLSSON, G. 1962. Studies on Scandinavian black flies (Fam. Simuliidae Latr.). *Opusc. ent.* suppl. **21**: 1–280, 43 figs.

CROSSKEY, R. W. 1970. Simuliidae (Diptera) from the Channel Islands: first records. *Entomologist's Gaz.* **21**: 125–132, 7 figs.
  Keys to adults, larvae and pupae occurring in Jersey.

DAVIES, L. 1966. Taxonomy of British black-flies (Diptera Simuliidae). *Trans. R. ent. Soc. Lond.* **118**: 413–508, 49 figs.

DAVIES, L. 1968. A key to the British species of Simuliidae (Diptera) in the larval, pupal and adult stages. *Scient. Publs Freshwat. biol. Ass.* **24**: 1–126, 49 figs., maps.
  For nomenclatural changes see Crosskey in Kloet & Hincks 1975 (above).

RUBTSOV, I. A. 1959–64. Simuliidae (Melusinidae) in Lindner's Die Fliegen ...

Thaumaleidae

EDWARDS, F. W. 1929. A revision of the Thaumaleidae. *Zool. Anz.* **82**: 121–142, 46 figs.

Bibionidae and Scatopsidae

EDWARDS, F. W. 1925. A synopsis of British Bibionidae and Scatopsidae. *Ann. appl. Biol.* **12**: 263–275, 2 figs (compound).

COLLIN, J. E. 1954. Notes on some British Scatopsidae (Diptera). *J. Soc. Br. Ent.* **5**: 72–75.

COOK, E. F. 1969 on. A synopsis of the Scatopsidae of the Palaearctic. *J. nat. Hist.* **3**: 393–407; **6**: 625–634; **8**: 61–100, many figs. (still appearing).
  Keys to genera and species.

DUDA, P. 1929. Scatopsidae, 1930. Bibionidae. In Lindner's Die Fliegen ...

HUTSON, A. M. 1970. Corrections and additions to the list of British Nematocera (Diptera) since Kloet and Hincks' 'A Check List of British Insects' (1945). Part 2. Scatopsidae. *Entomologist's Gaz.* **21**: 117–123, 2 figs. See also 1972 *Entomologist's mon. Mag.* **108**: 200.

Cecidomyiidae

ASKEW, R. R. & RUSE, J. M. 1974. The biology of some Cecidomyiidae (Diptera) galling the leaves of Birch *(Betula)*, with special references to their Chalcidoid (Hymenoptera) parasites. *Trans. R. ent. Soc. Lond.* **125**: 257–294, 17 figs.
  Illustrations of galls and comparative descriptions, biology.

BAGNALL, R. S. & HARRISON, J. W. H. 1917. A preliminary catalogue of British Cecidomyiidae (Diptera) with special reference to the gall-midges of the North of England. *Trans. ent. Soc. Lond.* **50**: 264–426.

BARNES, H. F. 1946–69. "Gall Midges of Economic Importance". 8 vols. illustr. pls. Crosby Lockwood, London.

Vol. 8 is by W. Nijveldt and contains a chapter on identification, including keys to tribes.

BARNES, H. F. 1954. A new species of *Trotteria* Kieffer (Cedidomyiidae) reared from unopened flower-buds of Privet. *Entomologist's Rec. J. Var.* **66**: 281–283.

BARNES, H. F. *et al.* 1962. The gall midges (Diptera: Cecidomyiidae) of wild ox-eye daisy *(Chrysanthemum leucanthemum* L.) flowers, with the description of a new species. *Trans. Soc. Br. Ent.* **15**: 1–20, 6 figs.

BUHR, H. 1965. See above p. 59.

BUXTON, P. A. & BARNES, H. F. 1953. British Diptera associated with fungi. 1. Gall midges (Cecidomyiidae) reared from the larger fungi. *Proc. R. ent. Soc. Lond. B* **22**: 195–200, 1 fig.

PRITCHARD, A. E. & FELT, E. P. 1958. Itonididae (Cecidomyiidae). In "Guide to the Insects of Connecticut" (G. C. Crampton) (see above p. 91).

DARLINGTON, A. 1968. See above p. 000.

DOCTERS VAN LEEUWEN, W. M. 1957. "Gallenboek". 332 pp. illustr. Thieme, Zutphen (in Dutch).

EDWARDS, F. W. 1938. On the British Lestremiinae, with notes on exotic species. Pts. 1–7: *Proc. R. ent. Soc. Lond. B* **7**: 18–32, 102–108, 173–182, 199–210, 229–243, 253–265, 28 figs. (compound).

Keys to tribes only: diagnoses of genera, sub-genera, species, figures of genitalia. Notes on mounting specimens.

HARDY, D. E. 1960. *Insects Hawaii* **10**: 235–243.

Covers the general discussion of Cecidomyiidae, valuable for students of this family in any region.

HARRIS, K. M. 1966. Gall midge genera of economic importance (Dipt., Cecidomyiidae). Part I: introduction and subfamily Cecidomyiinae supertribe Cecidomyiidi. *Trans. R. ent. Soc. Lond.* **118**: 313–358, 199 figs.

HARRIS, K. M. 1968. A systematic revision and biological review of the cecidomyiid predators (Diptera: Cecidomyiidae) on world Coccoidea (Hemiptera: Homoptera). *Trans. R. ent. Soc. Lond.* **119**: 401–494, 183 figs.

Keys genera predacious on Coccids.

HARRIS, K. M. 1973. Aphidophagous Cecidomyiidae (Diptera): taxonomy, biology and assessments of field populations. *Bull. ent. Res.* **63**: 305–325, 17 figs., 5 tabs.

HARRIS, K. M. 1974. *Massalongia betulifolia* sp.n. (Diptera, Cecidomyiidae) described from leaf galls on *Betula pendula* Roth and *B. pubescens* Erhart. *Entomologist's Gaz.* **25**: 137–139, 6 figs., 1 pl.

PANELIUS, S. 1965. A revision of the European gall midges of the subfamily Porricondylinae (Diptera: Itoniidae). *Acta zool. fenn.* **113**: 1–157, 43 figs.

Illustrated keys to species.

MAMAEV, B. M. 1975. "Evolution of gall forming insects – gall midges". (Translation from the Russian.) 317 pp., 79 figs. Thr British Library, Lending Division, Wetherby, Yorkshire.

Essential preliminary reading for this family.

WYATT, I. J. 1959. A new genus and species of Cecidomyiidae (Diptera) infesting mushrooms. *Proc. R. ent. Soc. Lond. B* **28**: 175–179, 11 figs.

WYATT, I. J. 1961–67. Pupal paedogenesis in the Cecidomyiidae (Diptera). *Proc. R. ent. Soc. Lond. A* **36**: 133–143, 14 figs.; **38**: 136–144, 22 figs.; *Trans. R. ent. Soc. Lond.* **119**(3): 71–98, 52 figs.

Part 3 contains keys to genera of the tribe Heteropezini for adults, larvae, pupae and hemipupae. See also section on immature stages (below).

Mycetophilidae and Sciaridae

EDWARDS, F. W. 1925. British fungus-gnats. *Trans. ent. Soc. Lond.* **57** (1924):

505–670, 230 figs. See also 1941 *Entomologist's mon. Mag.* **77**: 21–32, 67–82, 9 figs. (compound).

FREEMAN, P. 1956. Two new species of Mycetophilidae (Diptera, Nematocera) from Britain. *Proc. R. ent. Soc. Lond. B* **25**: 26–28, 3 figs.

HACKMANN, W. 1970. New species of the genus *Phronia* Winnertz (Diptera, Mycetophilidae) from Eastern Fennoscandia and notes on the synonymies in this genus. *Notul. ent.* **50**: 41–60, 82 figs.

HUTSON, A. M. & KIDD, L. N. 1971. Notes on British Bolitophilinae including three species new to Britain (Diptera: Mycetophilidae). *Entomologist* **104**: 219–226, 11 figs.
  Key to British species.

HUTSON, A. M. & KIDD, L. N. 1975. Notes on British *Bolitophila, Diadocidia* and *Macrocera* (Diptera, Mycetophilidae). *Entomologist's mon. Mag.* **110** (1974): 27–39, 12 figs.
  Partial keys to *Diadocidia* and *Macrocera*.

KIDD, L. N. 1955. A new species of *Mycomyia* (Dipt., Mycetophilidae) taken in Cumberland. *Entomologist's mon. Mag.* **91**: 258, 2 figs.

KIDD, L. N. & ACKLAND, D. M. 1970. *Mycetophila bohemica* Lastovka and *Dynatosoma nigromaculatum* Lundstroem new to Britain, and notes on other little known fungus gnats (Dipt., Mycetophilidae). *Entomologist* **103**: 10–17. See also Kidd, 1969, *Entomologist* **102**: 202; 1955, *Entomologist's mon. Mag.* **91**: 258.

LANDROCK, K. 1940. Zweiflügler oder Diptera VI: Pilzmücken oder Fungivoridae (Mycetophilidae). *Tierwelt Dtl.* **38**: 1–166, 337 figs.

LAŠTOVKA, P. 1963. Beitrag zur Kenntnis der europäischen *Fungivora*-Arten aus der Gruppe *vittipes* (Zett.) (Dipt., Fungivoridae). *Cas. csl. Spol. ent.* **60**: 312–327, 18 figs.

LAŠTOVKA, P. 1972. Holarctic species of *Mycetophila ruficollis*-group (Diptera, Mycetophilidae). *Acta ent. bohemoslovaca* **69**: 275–294, 38 figs. See also under early stages section (below).

LAŠTOVKA, P. & KIDD, L. N. 1975. Review of the British and notes on other species of the *Mycetophila ruficollis*-group, with the description of a new species (Diptera, Mycetophilidae). *Entomologist's mon. Mag.* **110**: 203–214, 40 figs.

LASTOVKA, P. & MATILE, L. 1972. Revision des *Diadocidia* Holarctiques (Dipt., Mycetophilidae). *Annls Soc. ent. Fr.* (N.S.) **8**: 205–223, 28 figs.

MATILE, L. 1971 on. Notes sur les Mycetophilidae (Diptera) de la Faune de France. *Entomologiste* **27**: 64–70; **28**: 74–78; **30**: 26–33, 18 figs.

PLASSMANN, E. 1972. Die Pilzmückengattung *Neoempheria* (Diptera: Fungivoridae). *Senckenberg biol.* **53**: 239–244, 7 figs.

PLASSMANN, E. 1973. Die Pilzmückengattung *Leia* (Diptera:Mycetophilidae). *Senckenberg biol.* **54**: 131–140, 23 figs.

PLASSMANN, E. 1975. Revision der europäischen Arten der Pilzmückengattung *Bolitophila* Meigen (Diptera, Mycetophilidae). *Ent. Scand.* **6**: 145–157, 29 figs.

STEFFAN, W. A. 1966. A generic revision of the family Sciaridae (Diptera) of America north of Mexico. *Univ. Calif. Publs Ent.* **44**: 1–77, 22 figs.

TUOMIKOSKI, R. 1960. Zur Kenntnis der Sciariden (Dipt.) Finnlands. *Ann. zool. Soc. zool. bot. Fennicae 'Vanamu'* **21**(4): 1–164. 33 figs. (compound). *Suomal. eläin-ja kasvit. Seur. van. elain Julk.*
  Keys, figures of male genitalia, wings and palpi.

Brachycera British species nearly 800

VERRALL, G. H. 1909. "British Flies". Vol. 5. "Stratiomyiidae to Cyrtidae". 780 + 34 pp., 407 figs. Gurney & Jackson, London.

Covers all Brachycera except Empididae and Dolichopodidae. Keys adults, very full descriptions: distribution, biological data.

OLDROYD, H. 1969. Diptera Brachycera. *Handbk Ident. Br. Insects* **9**(4): 1–132, 339 figs.

Covers families Stratiomyidae, Xylomyidae, Xylophagidae, Rhagionidae, Tabanidae, Asilidae, Therevidae, Scenopinidae, Acroceridae, Bombyliidae.

CHANDLER, P. J. 1975. An account of the Irish species of two-winged flies (Diptera) belonging to the families of larger Brachycera (Tabanoidea and Asiloidea). *Proc. R. Ir. Acad.* **75B**(2): 81–110.

Irish distribution with some taxonomic comments on these two superfamilies.

LINDNER – Die Fliegen, the relevant volumes should be consulted. The following works are supplementary to these.

Stratiomyiidae, Tabanidae

CHVÁLA, M., LYNEBORG, L. & MOUCHA, J. 1972. "The Horse Flies of Europe (Diptera: Tabanidae)". 499 pp., 164 figs., 8 pls. Entomological Society of Copenhagen.

ROZKOSNY, R. 1973. "The Stratiomyidae (Diptera) of Fennoscandia and Denmark". Fauna Entomologica Scandinavica Vol. I. 152 pp., 456 figs. Klampenborg, Denmark.

Keys, maps, distribution, richly illustrated.

Empididae

COLLIN, J. E. 1961. "British Flies". Vol. 6. "Empididae". 782 pp., 317 figs. Cambridge University Press.

In series with Verrall's two volumes (on Brachycera and Syrphidae). In addition to the keys and descriptions to all known British species there is much critical comment on European species.

ANDREWES, C. 1966. Two species of Empididae (Diptera) new to the British list, from Wiltshire. *Entomologist's mon. Mag.* **102**: 1–2.

CHANDLER, P. J. 1973. *Rhamphomyia (Pararhamphomyia) marginata* Fabricius (Dipt., Empididae) a remarkable addition to the British list. *Proc. Br. ent. nat. Hist. Soc.* **6**(3): 73–76, 1 fig.

CHVÁLA, M. 1969. Revision of the palaearctic species of *Tachydromia* Meig. (= *Tachista* Loew) (Diptera, Empididae). *Sb. ent. Odd. nar. Mus. Praze* **38**: 415–524, 111 figs.

CHVÁLA, M. 1973. European species of the *Platypalpus albiseta*-group (Diptera, Empididae). *Acta ent. bohemoslovaca* **70**: 117–136, 19 figs.

CHVÁLA, M. & KOVALEV, V. G. 1974. Revision of the Palaearctic *Platypalpus nigritarsis*-group (Diptera, Empididae), with special reference to *P. excisus* Beck. *Ibidem* **71**: 250–259, 8 figs.

CHVÁLA, M. 1975. "The Tachydromiinae (Diptera) of Fennoscandia and Denmark". Fauna Entomologica Scandinavica Vol. 3. 336 pp., 790 figs. Klampenborg, Denmark.

Keys, maps, distribution, updates this subfamily as given in Collin 1961.

CHVÁLA, M. 1975. A revision of palaearctic Tachydromiinae genus *Dysaletria* Loew (Diptera: Empididae). *Vestn. csl. Spol. zool.* **39**: 167–172, 4 figs.

SMITH, K. G. V. 1963. *Chersodromia cursitans* Zetterstedt (Dipt., Empididae) reinstated as a British species. *Entomologist's mon. Mag.* **99**: 127–128.

Revised key to some *Chersodromia* species.

SMITH, K. G. V. 1969. *Platypalpus (Cleptodromia) longimana* Corti, new to Britain and the male of *P. altera* (Collin) (Dipt., Empididae). *Entomologist's mon. Mag.* **105**: 108–110, 4 figs.

SMITH, K. G. V. & CHVÁLA, M. 1976. Some British species of *Platypalpus* with one new to science, two new to Britain and new synonymy. *Entomologist's Rec. J. Var.* **88**: 137–144, 9 figs.
    Supplementary to Collin (1961).

Dolichopodidae

VERRALL, G. H. 1904–05. List of British Dolichopodidae with tables and notes. *Entomologist's mon. Mag.* **40**: 164–173, 194–199, 223–228, 241–245; **41**: 51–57, 81–83, 108–112, 167–172, 189–196, 247–252 (no illustr.).
    Concise, and still largely reliable, though a number of species have been added to the British List since its publication. Keys mostly apply to males only.
COLLIN, J. E. 1941. The British species of the Dolichopodid genus *Medeterus* Fisch. *Entomologist's mon. Mag.* **77**: 68–75, 142–148, 1 fig.
COLLIN, J. E. 1943. A revised table of the British species of *Argyra* Macq. (Dipt., Dolichopodidae). *Entomologist's mon. Mag.* **79**: 114–117.
FONSECA, E. C. M. d'A. 1976. Four new species of Palaearctic Dolichopodidae (Diptera) including two from Britain. *Entomologist's mon. Mag.* **111**: 23–27, 12 figs.
FONSECA, E. C. M. d'A (in press). Dolichopodidae. *Handbk Ident. Br. Insects*
NEGROBOV, O. P. 1973. Zur Kenntnis einiger palaearktischer Arten der Gattung *Asyndetus* Loew (Diptera, Dolichopodidae). *Beitr. Ent.* **23**: 157–167.
PARENT, O. 1938. In *Faune de France* **35** (see above).
STACKELBERG, A. V. (& NEGROBOV, O. P.) 1930. Dolichopodidae. In Lindner's "Die Fliegen..."
THUNEBORG, E. 1955. A revision of the Palaearctic species of the genus *Medetera* Fischer (Dipt., Dolichopodidae). *Ann. ent. fenn.* **21**: 130–157, 50 figs. See also *Entomologist's mon. Mag.* **97**: 100.

Cyclorrhapha—Aschiza   British species about 650

Lonchopteridae
ANDERSSON, H. 1966. The Swedish species of *Lonchoptera* Meig. (Dipt., Lonchopteridae) with lectotype designations. *Opusc. Ent.* **31**: 77–80.
ANDERSSON, H. 1971. Notes on north european *Lonchoptera* (Dipt., Lonchopteridae) with lectotype designations. *Ent. Tdskr.* **91**: 42–45, 2 figs.
SMITH, K. G. V. 1969. Lonchopteridae. *Handbk Ident. Br. Insects* **10**(2): 1–9, 14 figs.

Phoridae
SCHMITZ, H. 1929. "Revision der Phoriden". 212 pp., 49 figs., 2 pls. Dummlers, Bering and Bonn.
SCHMITZ, H. (& BEYER, E. M. & DELAGE, F. A.) 1938 on. Phoridae. In Lindner's "Die Fliegen" **4**: 1–608 (still appearing).
COLYER, C. N. 1952–60. In *Entomologist's mon. Mag.* **88**: 135–139; **90**: 108–112, 121–128; *J. Soc. Br. Ent.* **5**: 91–94; *Broteria Cienc. Nat.* **28**: 19–23; **29**: 3–6, figs.
    Short papers mostly treating a few species.
COLYER, C. N. 1957. A new species of *Plastophora* (Dipt., Phoridae) from England; a short discussion of the evolution of the present concept of the genus and a key for the identification of the world species. *Broteria, Cienc. Nat.* **26**: 75–89, 21 figs.
BORGMEIER, T. 1968, 1971. A catalogue of the Phoridae of the world (Diptera, Phoridae). *Studia ent.* **11**: 1–367; **14**: 177–224.
    Contains original citations of world species and world bibliography.
SMITH, K. G. V. 1977. Notes on some British Phoridae (Diptera) including two

species of *Megaselia* Rondani new to science. *Entomologist's Rec. J. Var.* **89:** 5 figs. (in press).
  Includes key to *Citrago* species.

Platypezidae, Pipunculidae, Syrphidae and Conopidae

VERRALL, G. H. 1901. "British Flies". Vol. 8. "Platypezidae, Pipunculidae, Syrphidae". 683 pp., 458 figs. Gurney & Jackson, London. Reprinted 1969, Classey, Faringdon.

BANKOWSKA, R. 1963. Syrphiden. *Klucze Oznacz. Owad. Pol.* **27:** 1–236.

CHANDLER, P. J. 1973. The flat-footed flies (Diptera, Aschiza-Platypezidae) known to occur in Kent. With a key to the genera and species so far recorded from the British Isles. *Trans. Kent Fld. Club* **5**(1): 15–44, 1 fig.

CHANDLER, P. J. 1974. Additions and corrections to the British list of Platypezidae (Diptera), incorporating a revision of the palaearctic species of *Callomyia* Meigen. *Proc. Trans. Br. ent. nat. Hist. Soc.* **7**(1): 1–32, 34 figs.

COE, R. L. 1953. Syrphidae. *Handbk Ident. Br. Insects* **10**(1): 1–98, 46 figs. (compound).
  See Kloet & Hincks 1975 (above) for revised nomenclature.

CROW, P. N. 1969. *Eriozona syrphoides* Fallén (Diptera, Syrphidae) in North Wales – a new British species and genus. *Entomologist's Rec. J. Var.* **81:** 237–238, 1 fig.

DUŠEK, J. & LASKA, P. 1967. Versuch zum Aufbau eines natürlichen Systems mitteleuropäischer Arten der Unterfamilie Syrphinae (Diptera). *Acta sci. nat. Brno* **1:** 349–390, illustr.

GOELDLIN de TIEFENAU, P. 1976. Revision du genre *Paragus* (Dipt., Syrphidae) de la région palearctique occidentale. *Mitt. Schweiz. ent. Ges.* **49:** 79–108, 37 figs.

HIPPA, H. 1968. A generic revision of the genus *Syrphus* and allied genera (Diptera, Syrphidae) in the Palaearctic region, with descriptions of the male genitalia. *Acta ent. fenn.* **25:** 1–94, 331 figs.

HIPPA, H. 1968. Classification of the palaearctic species of the genera *Xylota* Meigen and *Xylotomima* Shannon (Dipt., Syrphidae). *Acta ent. fenn.* **34**(4): 179–197, 23 figs.

SÉGUY, E. 1961. Diptères Syrphides de l'europe occidentale. *Mem. Mus. natn. Hist. nat. Paris* (A) **23:** 1–248, 48 figs.

SPEIGHT, M. C. D. 1973. British species of *Sphaerophoria* (Diptera, Syrphidae) confused with *S. menthastri* (L.), including a key to the males of the seven species of *Sphaerophoria* found in the British Isles. *Entomologist* **106:** 228–233, 4 figs.

SPEIGHT, M. C. D., CHANDLER, P. J. & NASH, R. 1975. Irish Syrphidae (Diptera); notes on the species and an account of their known distribution. *Proc. R. Ir. Acad.* **75B**(1): 1–80, 2 figs.
  Includes key to European genera of tribe Syrphini and key to *Parasyrphus* species.

SPEIGHT, M. C. D. & SMITH, K. G. V. 1975. A key to males of the British species of *Neocnemodon* Goffe (Dipt., Syrphidae). *Entomologist's Rec. J. Var.* **87:** 150–153, 1 fig. (compound).

VOCKEROTH, J. R. 1969. A revision of the genera of the Syrphini (Diptera: Syrphidae). *Mem. ent. Soc. Can.* **6:** 1–176, 100 figs.

VOCKEROTH, J. R. 1971. The identity of some holarctic and old world species of *Sphaerophoria* (Dipt., Syrphidae). *Can. Ent.* **103:** 1627–1635, 7 figs.

COE, R. L. 1966. Pipunculidae. *Handbk Ident. Br. Insects* **10**(26): 1–83, 192 figs., 1 pl.

COLLIN, J. E. 1956. Scandinavian Pipunculidae. *Opusc. Ent.* **21:** 149–169, 19 figs.

CHVÁLA, M. 1961. Czechoslovak species of the subfamily Conopinae (Diptera: Conopidae). *Acta Univ. Carol. Biologica* **1961**(2): 103–145, 31 figs., maps, tabs.

CHVÁLA, M. 1963. A review of the Conopid flies of the genus *Sicus* Scop. (Diptera, Conopidae). *Acta. Univ. Carol. Biologica* **1963**(3): 275–282, 7 figs.
CHVÁLA, M. 1965. Czechoslovak species of the subfamilies Myopinae and Dalmanniinae (Diptera, Conopidae). *Acta Univ. Carol. Biologica* **1965**(2): 93–149, 33 figs., tabs., maps.
    The keys in the above three works cover central Europe but are of value for more northern territories. See also Lyneborg in the following section.
SMITH, K. G. V. 1969. Conopidae. *Handbk Ident. Br. Insects* **10**(3a): 1–19, 34 figs.
SMITH, K. G. V. 1970. The identity of *Myopa polystigma* Rondani, and an additional British and continental species of the genus (Diptera: Conopidae). *Entomologist* **103**: 186–189, 1 pl.

Cyclorrhapha–Acalyptratae British species over 1200

In this group the family limits are often ill-defined and the literature is scattered. All works relevant to the British fauna are listed together, but grouped into families so far as possible. Important European works are also included and the relevant sections of Lindner's Die Fliegen should also be consulted.
SÉGUY, E. In *Faune de France* **28**.
COLLIN, J. E. 1910–11. Additions and corrections to the British list of Muscidae Acalyptratae. *Entomologist's mon. Mag.* **46**: 47–48, 124–129, 169–178; **47**: 145–153, 182–187, 229–234, 253–256.
    Partly out of date but still useful.
COGAN, B. H. & DEAR, J. P. 1975. Additions and corrections to the list of British acalypterate Diptera. *Entomologist's mon. Mag.* **110** (1974): 173–181, 8 figs.
LYNEBORG, L. 1962–64. Danske acalyptrate fluer. 1. Conopidae, Micropezidae, Calobatidae, Megamerinidae og Tanypezidae. *Ent. Meddr.* **31**: 249–264; Danske acalyptrate fluer. 2. Psilidae, Platystomidae og Otitidae (Diptera). *Ent. Meddr.* **32**: 367–388, 22 figs. (in Danish).
ZUSKA, J. & LAŠTOVKA, P. 1965. A review of the Czechoslovak species of the family Piophilidae with special reference to their importance to food industry (Diptera, Acalyptrata). *Acta ent. bohemoslovaca* **62**(2): 141–157, 11 figs.
ZUSKA, J. 1965. Notes on the Palearctic species of the genus *Nemopoda* Robineau-Desvoidy (Diptera, Sepsidae). *Acta ent. bohemoslovaca* **62**(4): 308–313, 16 figs. See also Andrewes, *Entomologist's mon. Mag.* **98**: 8; Laurence, *Entomologist's mon. Mag.* **88**: 81.
SHORROCKS, B. 1972. "Invertebrate Types. *Drosophila*". 144 pp., 53 figs., 8 pls. Ginn, London.
    A useful introduction to the principal genus of this important family. Taxonomy, biology, genetics. Keys to the commonest species (22) of *Drosophila*, but care should be taken to avoid confusion with the equally common drosophilid genus *Scaptomyza*.
FONSECA, E. C. M. d'A. 1965. A short key to the British Drosophilidae (Diptera) including a new species of *Amiota*. *Trans. Soc. Br. Ent.* **16**: 233–244.
BASDEN, E. B. 1954. The distribution and biology of Drosophilidae (Diptera) in Scotland, including a new species of '*Drosophila*'. *Trans. R, Soc. Edinb.* **62**: 603–654.
    Keys to adults of species occurring in Scotland.
HACKMANN, W. 1955. On the genera *Scaptomyza* Hardy and *Parascaptomyza* Duda (Dipt., Drosophilidae). *Notul. ent.* **35**: 74–91, 32 figs.
HACKMANN, W. et al. 1970. On the biology and karyology of *Chymomyza costata* Zetterstedt, with reference to the taxonomy and distribution of various species of *Chymomyza* (Dipt., Drosophilidae). *Ann. ent. fenn.* **36**: 1–9, 21 figs., 3 maps.

EGGLISHAW, H. J. 1960. Studies on the family Coelopidae (Diptera). *Trans. R. ent. Soc. Lond.* **112**: 109–140, 24 figs.
   Systematics and biology, descriptions and illustrations of larvae.
BURNET, B. 1960. The European species of the genus *Coelopa* (Dipt., Coelopidae). *Entomologist's mon. Mag.* **96**: 8–13, 3 figs.
COLLIN, J. E. 1930. Some species of the genus *Meonura* (Diptera). *Entomologist's mon. Mag.* **66**: 82–89, 11 figs. See also *Entomologist's mon. Mag.* **73**: 250–252.
COLLIN, J. E. 1933. Five new species of Diptera. *Entomologist's mon. Mag.* **69**: 272–275. 10 figs.
   Keys to Camillidae.
COLLIN, J. E. 1943. The British species of Helomyzidae (Diptera). *Entomologist's mon. Mag.* **79**: 234–251. See also *J. Soc. Br. Ent.* **4**: 37–39.
HACKMANN, W. 1970. Trixoscelidae from southern Spain. *Ent. Scand.* **1**: 127–139, 36 figs.
   Includes key to European species.
SABROSKY, C. W. 1956. Additions to the knowledge of the old world Asteiidae. *Revue fr. Ent.* **23**: 216–243, 9 figs.
COLLIN, J. E. 1944. The British species of Anthomyzidae (Diptera). *Entomologist's mon. Mag.* **80**: 265–272, 1 fig.
ANDERSSON, H. 1976. Revision of the *Anthomyza* species of Northwest Europe. I. The *gracilis* group. *Ent. Scand.* **7**: 41–52, 48 figs.
COLLIN, J. E. 1944. The British species of Psilidae (Diptera). *Entomologist's mon. Mag.* **80**: 214–224, 2 figs.
WAKERLEY, S. B. 1959. A new species of *Psila* Meigen (Diptera: Psilidae) from Northern England. *Proc. R. ent. Soc. Lond.* B **28**: 107–108, 8 figs.
COLLIN, J. E. 1945. The British species of Opomyzidae (Diptera). *Entomologist's Rec. J. Var.* **57**: 13–16. See also Andrewes, *Entomologist's mon. Mag.* **100**: 167.
HACKMANN, W. 1958. The Opomyzidae of eastern Fennoscandia. *Notul. ent.* **38**: 114–126, 13 figs.
COLLIN, J. E. 1945. British Micropezidae (Diptera). *Entomologist's Rec. J. Var.* **57**: 115–119.
COLLIN, J. E. 1947. The British genera of Trypetidae (Dipt.) with notes on a few species. *Entomologist's Rec. J. Var.* **59**: 1–14. See also *Entomologist's Rec. J. Var.* **59**: 39 and Stubbs, A. E., *Proc. Br. ent. nat. Hist. Soc.* **7**(4): 103.
COLLIN, J. E. 1948. A short synopsis of the British Sapromyzidae (Diptera). *Trans. R. ent. Soc. Lond.* **99**: 225–242, 6 figs. See also *Entomologist* **99**: 144.
COLLIN, J. E. 1949. The Palaearctic species of the genus *Aphaniosoma* Beck. (Diptera, Chiromyidae). *Ann. Mag. nat. Hist.* (12)**2**: 127–147, 12 figs.
COLLIN, J. E. 1952. On the European species of the genus *Odinia* Robineau-Desvoidy (Diptera: Odiniidae). *Proc. R. ent. Soc. Lond.* B **21**: 110–116.
COGAN, B. H. 1969. Two species of the genus *Odinia* R.-D. (Dipt., Odiniidae) new to Britain, one of which is new to science. *Entomologist's mon. Mag.* **104**: 252–254, 2 figs.
COLLIN, J. E. 1953. A new species of *Clusiaria* Diptera, Clusiidae). *Clusiaria apicalis* Zett., new to Britain. *J. Soc. Br. Ent.* **4**: 138–140.
COLLIN, J. E. 1960. British Tethinidae (Diptera). *Entomologist* **93**: 191–193. See also 1966, *Boll. Mus. civ. Stor. nat. Venezia* **16**: 19–32.
ANDERSSON, H. 1977. Taxonomic and phylogenetic studies on Chloropidae (Diptera) with special reference to old world genera. *Entomologica Scand.* suppl. **8**: 1–200.
COLLIN, J. E. 1966. A revision of the British species of *Cetema* Hendel (Diptera, Chloropidae), with two species new to science. *Entomologist* **99**: 116–120.
COLLIN, J. E. 1946. The British genera and species of Oscinellinae (Diptera,

Chloropidae). *Trans. R. ent. Soc. Lond.* **97**: 117–148, 6 figs.
ZUSKA, J. 1960. Bemerkungen über einige paläarktische Arten der Gattung *Chlorops* Meigen und Beschreibung einer neuen Art aus der Tschechoslowakei (Diptera, Chloropidae). *Cas. ceské Spol. ent.* **57**: 387–397, 12 figs.
SMITH, K. G. V. 1965. The immature stages of *Gaurax* (= *Botanobia*) *dubius* Macquart (Dipt., Chloropidae), with notes on the specific status of *G. fascipes* Becker. *Entomologist's mon. Mag.* **100** (1974): 237–239, 8 figs.
CHVÁLA, M., DOSKOCIL, J., MOOK, J. H. & POKORNY, V. 1974. The genus *Lipara* Meigen (Diptera, Chloropidae), systematics, morphology, behaviour and ecology. *Tijdschr. Ent.* **117**: 1–25, 22 figs.
ANDERSSON, H. 1971. The European species of *Limnellia* (Dipt., Ephydridae). *Ent. Scand.* **2**: 53–59, 16 figs.
COLLIN, J. E. 1964. The British species of *Ephydra* (Dipt., Ephydridae). *Entomologist's mon. Mag.* **99** (1963): 147–152, 3 figs.
  Use in conjunction with Wirth (1975), see below.
COLLIN, J. E. 1930. Some new species of the Dipterous genus *Scatella* Dsv. and the differentiation of *Stictoscatella* gen. nov. (Ephydridae). *Entomologist's mon. Mag.* **66**: 133–139, 7 figs.
COLLIN, J. E. 1966. A contribution towards the knowledge of the male genitalia of speces of *Hydrellia*. *Boll. Mus. civ. Stor. nat. Venezia* **16**: 7–18, 26 pls.
COLLIN, J. E. 1943. The British species of *Psilopa* Fln. and *Discocerina* Mcq. (Dipt. Ephydridae). *Entomologist's mon. Mag.* **79**: 145–151.
PARMENTER, L. 1952. *Coenia curvicauda* Mg. (Diptera, Ephydridae) — an overlooked species. *J. Soc. Br. Ent.* **4**: 89–90.
WIRTH, W. W. 1975. A revision of the Brine flies of the genus *Ephydra* of the Old World (Diptera, Ephydridae). *Ent. Scand.* **6**: 11–44, 58 figs.
KNUTSON, L. V. & LYNEBORG, L. 1965. Danish acalypterate flies. 3. Sciomyzidae (Diptera). *Ent. Meddr.* **34**: 61–101, 56 figs.
  Includes all genera and species known from the British Isles. See also *Entomologist's Rec. J. Var.* **78**: 227–230.
COLLIN, J. E. 1953. A revision of the British (and notes on other) species of Lonchaeidae (Diptera). *Trans. Soc. Br. Ent.* **11**: 181–207, 24 figs.
  Use in conjunction with Hackmann and Morge, see below.
HACKMANN, W. 1956. The Lonchaeidae (Dipt.) of eastern Fennoscandia. *Notul. ent.* **36**: 89–115, illustr.
MORGE, G. 1959–62. Monographie der palaearktischen Lonchaeidae. *Beitr. Ent.* **9**: 1–371, 909–945; **12**: 381–434, illustr.
MORGE, G. 1963–67. Die Lonchaeidae und Pallopteridae Österreichs und der agrenzenden Gebiete. *Naturk. J. Stadt Linz* **1963**: 123–312; **1967**: 141–212, 241 figs.
RICHARDS, O. W. 1930. The British species of Sphaeroceridae (Borboridae, Diptera). *Proc. zool. Soc. Lond.* **1930**: 261–345, 23 figs., 1 pl. See also *J. Soc. Br. Ent.* **5**: 152–178; *Entomologist's mon. Mag.* **88**: 81.
HACKMANN, W. 1965. On the genus *Copromyza* Fallén (Dipt., Sphaeroceridae). with special reference to the Finnish species. *Notul. ent.* **45**: 33–46, 39 figs.
SMITH, K. G. V. 1963. A short synopsis of British Chamaemyiidae (Dipt.). *Trans. Soc. Br. Ent.* **15**: 103–115, 12 figs.
COLLIN, J. E. 1966. The British species of *Chamaemyia* Mg. *(Ochtiphila* Fln.*)*. *Trans. Soc. Br. Ent.* **17**: 121–128, 9 figs.
ANDREWES, C. 1967. *Acrometopia wahlbergi* (Zett.) (Diptera, Chamaemyiidae), a genus and species of fly new to Britain. *Entomologist's mon. Mag.* **103**: 208.
McALPINE, J. F. 1971. A revision of the subgenus *Neoleucopis* (Diptera: Chamaemyiidae). *Can. Ent.* **103**: 1851–1874, 40 figs.

TANASIYCHUK, V. N. 1968. Palaearctic species of *Parochthiphila*. *Ent. rev., Wash.* **47**: 388–399, 13 figs.
TANASIYCHUK, V. N. 1970. Palaearctic species of the genus *Chamaemyia* Panzer. *Ent. rev., Wash.* **49**: 128–140, 11 figs.
  Both the above originally published in Russian in *Ent. Obozr.*
SPENCER, K. A. 1972. Agromyzidae. *Handbk Ident. Br. Insects* **10**(5g): 1–136, 360 figs.
SPENCER, K. A. 1976. The Agromyzidae (Diptera) of Fennoscandia and Denmark. *Fauna ent. Scand.* **5**: 606 pp., 922 figs.
GRIFFITHS, G. C. D. 1974. Studies on boreal Agromyzidae (Diptera). V. On the genus Chromatomyia Hardy, with revision of Caprifoliaceae-mining species. *Quaest. ent.* **10**: 35–69, illustr.

Cyclorrhapha-Calyptratae — British species nearly 1000

Muscidae

HENNIG, W. 1955–64. In Linder's "Die Fliegen"...
FONSECA, E. C. M. d'A. 1968. Muscidae. *Handbk Ident. Br. Insects* **10**(4b): 1–119, 16 figs. (compound), 6 pls.
PONT, A. C. 1970. *Myospila hennigi* Gregor & Povolny, 1958 (Dipt., Muscidae), new to Britain, and notes on the european species of *Myospila* Rondani, 1856. *Entomologist's mon. Mag.* **106**: 111–113.

Anthomyiidae

HENNIG, W. 1966–76. Anthomyiidae. In Lindner's "Die Fliegen..."
  There is no comprehensive work on the British fauna but the following papers will be found useful. Those of Collin should only be used in conjunction with Hennig above because of outdated nomenclature.
ACKLAND, D. M. 1964. Two new British species of Anthomyiidae (Dipt.) with taxonomic notes on related pests of conifers. *Entomologist's mon. Mag.* **100**: 136–144.
ACKLAND, D. M. 1970. Notes on the Palaearctic species of *Egle* R.-D. (Dipt., Anthomyiidae) with descriptions of two new species. *Entomologist's mon. Mag.* **105**: 185–192, 22 figs.
COLLIN, J. E. 1943. The British species of *Prosalpia* Pok. (Dipt., Anthomyidae). *Entomologist's mon. Mag.* **79**: 83–86. See also *J. Soc. Br. Ent.* **4**: 40–41, 169–177; **5**: 94–100; *Proc. R. ent. Soc. Lond. B* **23**: 95–102; *Entomologist* **96**: 277–283.
COLLIN, J. E. 1953. Some additional British Anthomyiidae (Diptera). *J. Soc. Br. Ent.* **4**: 169–177.
COLLIN, J. E. 1954. The genus *Chiastochaeta* Pokorny (Diptera, Anthomyiidae). *Proc. R. ent. Soc. Lond. B.* **23**: 95–102, 3 figs. (compound).
COLLIN, J. E. 1955. Genera and species of Anthomyiidae allied to *Chirosia* (Diptera). *J. Soc. Br. Ent.* **5**: 94–100.
COLLIN, J. E. 1967. Notes on some British species of *Pegohylemyia* (Dipt., Anthomyiidae) with descriptions of four new species. *Entomologist's mon. Mag.* **102** (1966): 181–191, 4 figs. (compound).
FONSECA, E. C. M. d'A. 1952. A survey of the Swedish species of *Hydrophoria* and *Acroptena* by O. Ringdahl. *J. Soc. Br. Ent.* **4**: 75–82.
  Translated from the Swedish and keys modified to include all British species.
FONSECA, E. C. M. d'A. 1954. Translations of Ringdahl's Muscid Tables, additions and corrections. *J. Soc. Br. Ent.* **5**(1): 17–22.

FONSECA, E. C. M. d'A. 1956. A review of the British sub-families and genera of the family Muscidae. *Trans. Soc. Br. Ent.* **12:** 113–128.
Includes key to genera of Anthomyiidae.
FONSECA, E. C. M. d'A. 1966. Eight undescribed species of Muscidae (Diptera) from Britain. *Entomologist's mon. Mag.* **101:** 269–278, 7 figs. (compound).
SMITH, K. G. V. 1971. *Eustalomyia hilaris* Fallén (Diptera: Anthomyiidae) confirmed as British, with notes on other species in the genus. *Entomologist's Gaz.* **22:** 55–60, 8 figs.
Keys, biology, distribution.

Scatophagidae

ANDERSSON, H. 1971. Revision of the North European species of *Cosmetopus* Becker (Dipt., Scatophagidae). *Ent. Scand.* **5:** 95–102, 23 figs.
COLLIN, J. E. 1958. A short synopsis of the British Scatophagidae (Diptera). *Trans. Soc. Br. Ent.* **13:** 37–56.
HACKMANN, W. 1956. The Scatophagidae (Dipt.) of eastern Fennoscandia. *Fauna fenn.* **2:** 1–67.

Calliphoridae, Sarcophagidae and Tachinidae

In LINDNER'S "Die Fliegen..." fasc. **64.** "Larvaevoridae", several authors.
DAY, C. 1948. "Keys to the British Tachinidae". 150 pp., 217 figs. Buncle, Arbroath. Reprinted from *N. West. Nat.* 1946–47.
EMDEN, F. I. van 1954. Tachinidae and Calliphoridae. *Handbk Ident. Br. Insects* **10**(4a): 1–133, 42 figs. (compound).
Nomenclature of the above two works is now out of date and they should be used in conjunction with Mesnil in Lindner's "Die Fliegen" ... and papers by Herting and Mesnil for which see *Zool. Rec.*
CROSSKEY, R. W. 1974. The British Tachinidae of Walker and Stephens (Diptera). *Bull. Br. Mus. nat. Hist.* (Ent.) **30**(5): 269–308.
Clarifies many of the early names used in this family.
DAY, C. D. & FONSECA, E. C. M. d'A. 1955. A key to the females of the British species of *Sarcophaga* (Dipt., Calliphoridae). *J. Soc. Br. Ent.* **5:** 119–123.
MIHALYI, F. 1976. Contribution to the knowledge of the genus *Pollenia* R.-D. (Diptera: Calliphoridae). *Acta zool. hung.* **22:** 327–333, 18 figs.
PATTON, W. S. & WAINWRIGHT, C. J. 1935–37. The British species of the subfamily Sarcophaginae, with illustrations of the male and female terminalia. *Ann. trop. Med. Parasit.* **29:** 73–90, 517–532; **30:** 187–201, 337–350; **31:** 303–31, illustr.
PEUS, F. 1960. Zur Kenntnis der ornithoparasitischen Phormiinen (Diptera, Calliphoridae). *Dt. ent. Z.* **7**(3): 193–235.
ROHDENDORF, B. B. 1937. Sarcophagidae. *Fauna SSSR* (19)**1:** 1–500, 535 figs.
SCHUMANN, H. 1964. Revision der Gattung *Onesia* Robineau-Desvoidy, 1830 (Dipt., Calliphoridae). *Beitr. Ent.* **14:** 915–938, 28 figs.
SCHUMANN, H. 1971. Merkblätter über angewandte Parasitenkunde und Schädlingsbekämpfung. 18. Die Gattung *Lucilia* (Goldfliegen). *Angew. Parasit.* **12**(4): 1–20, 20 figs.
SCHUMANN, H. 1973. Revision der palaearktischen *Melinda*-Arten (Diptera: Calliphoridae). *Dt. ent. Z.* **20:** 293–314, 13 figs.
SCHUMANN, H. 1973. Bemerkungen zum Status der Gattungen *Onesia, Melinda* und *Bellardia* (Diptera, Calliphoridae). *Mitt. zool. Mus. Berl.* **49:** 333–344, 6 figs.
SCHUMANN, H. 1974. Revision der palaearktischen *Ballardia*-Arten (Diptera, Calliphoridae). *Dt. ent. Z.* **21:** 231–299, 82 figs.

SMITH, K. G. V. 1961. *Eucarcelia intermedia* Herting (Dipt., Tachinidae) in Britain. *Entomologist's mon. Mag.* **96:** 117.
SPENCE, T. 1954. A taxonomic study of the females of the British *Lucilia* species (Diptera: Calliphoridae). *Proc. R. ent. Soc. Lond. B* **23:** 29–55, 2 figs. (compound).
Provides the first key to females of *Lucilia*.

Pupipara

SMART, J. 1939. In Edwards *et al.* (see above p. 91).

Hippoboscidae

THEODOR, O. & OLDROYD, H. 1964. In Lindner's "Die Fliegen . . ."
HILL, D. S. 1962. Revision of the British species of *Ornithomyia* Latr. *Proc. R. ent. Soc. Lond. B* **31:** 11–18, 5 figs.
HILL, D. S. 1962. A study of the distribution and host preferences of three species of *Ornithomyia* in the British Isles. *Proc. R. ent. Soc. Lond. A* **37:** 37–48, 5 figs.
HILL, D. S. 1963. The life history of the British species of *Ornithomyia* (Diptera: Hippoboscidae). *Trans. R. ent. Soc. Lond.* **115:** 381–407, 7 figs.
MAA, T. C. 1963. Genera and species of Hippoboscidae, types, synonymy, habitats and natural groupings. *Pacif. Insects Monogr.* **6:** 1–186, 55 figs.
MAA, T. C. 1969. A revised check list and concise host index of Hippoboscidae (Diptera). *Pacif. Insects Monogr.* **20:** 261–299.

Nycteribiidae and Streblidae

THEODOR, O. 1954. In Lindner's "Die Fliegen . . ."
HUTSON, A. M. 1971. Ectoparasites of British bats. *Mammal Rev.* **1:** 143–150, 7 figs.
THEODOR, O. 1966. "An illustrated Catalogue of the Nycteribiidae (Diptera Pupipara) in the Rothschild Collection and the British Museum (Natural History)". 506 pp., 898 figs., 5 pls, 6 maps. Cambridge University Press.
THOMPSON, G. B. 1972. An annotated bibliography of British Nycteribiidae. *Angew. Parasit.* **13**(2): 106–113.
MAA, T. C. 1971. An annotated bibliography of batflies (Diptera: Streblidae; Nycteribiidae). *Pacif. Insects Monogr.* **28:** 119–211.

EARLY STAGES

The following list is a small selection of recent papers dealing with or relevant to the region. Works earlier than Hennig (1943–52) are only included where they are comprehensive studies or series. Works inlcuded in the adult list that also include early stages are not repeated here.

BRAUNS, A. 1954. "Terricole Dipterenlarven und Puppen terricoler Dipterenlarven". 2 vols. 355 pp., 171 figs. Berlin.
Very useful guide to soil and leaf-litter larvae. Key to families.
BRINDLE, A. 1963. Terrestrial Diptera larvae. *Entomologist's Rec. J. Var.* **75:** 47–62, 19 figs.
A summary with illustrated keys to families.
BRINDLE, A. 1961 on. Taxonomic notes on the larvae of British Diptera. *Entomologist* **94** on.
18 illustrated papers have so far appeared in this series.
CLAUSEN, C. P. 1940, reprint 1972 (see p. 59 above).
HENNIG, W. 1948–52. "Die Larvenformen der Dipteren". 3 vols. Akademie-Verlag, Berlin.
Covers world literature in immature stages up to about 1949. Some keys and figures facilitating identification to family level.

JAMES, M. T. 1947. The flies that cause myiasis in man. *U.S. Dept. Agric. Misc. Publ.* **631:** 175 pp., 96 figs.
JOHANSSEN, P. A. 1934–37. Aquatic Diptera. Part I. Nematocera, excluding Chironomidae and Ceratopogonidae. *Bull Cornell Univ. agric. Exp. Sta.* **164,** 77 pp., 218 figs. Part II. Orthorrhapha, Brachycera and Cyclorrhapha, **177,** 62 pp., 132 figs. Part III. Chironomidae, subfamilies Tanypodinae, Diamesinae, Orthocladiinae, **205,** 84 pp., 274 figs. Part IV. Chironomidae, subfamily Chironominae; and Part V. Ceratopogonidae (L. C. Thomsen), **210,** 80 pp. Reprint 1969, Classey, Faringdon.
KRIVOSHEINA, N. P. & MAMAEV, B. M. 1967. [Classification key to Diptera larvae of arboricole insects]. 367 pp., 154 figs. Izvestia Nauka, Moscow (in Russian).
MALLOCH, J. R. 1917. A preliminary classification of Diptera exclusive of Pupipara, based upon larval and pupal characters, with keys to imagines in certain families. Part I. *Bull. Illinois State Lab.* **12:** 161–407, 29 pls.
OLDROYD, H. & SMITH, K. G. V. In Smith, K. G. V., ed. 1973 (see above p. 59). Eggs and larvae of flies pp. 289–323, 15 figs. (compound).
Keys third instar larvae of medical importance.
ZUMPT, F. 1964. "Myiasis in Man and Animals in the Old World". 267 pp., 346 figs. Butterworth, London.

Nematocera

ACTON, A. B. 1956. The identification and distribution of the larvae of some species of *Chironomus* (Diptera). *Proc. R. ent. Soc. Lond. A* **31:** 161–164.
Banding patterns of chromosomes. Other refs given.
BRINDLE, A. 1958. Notes on the identification of *Limnophila* larvae (Diptera-Tipulidae). *Trans. Soc. Br. Ent.* **13:** 57–68, 23 figs.
BRINDLE, A. 1960. The larvae and pupae of the British Tipulinae (Diptera: Tipulidae). *Trans. Soc. Br. Ent.* **14:** 63–114, 179 figs.
BRINDLE, A. & BRYCE, A. 1960. The larvae of the British Hexatomini (Dipt., Tipulidae). *Entomologist's Gaz.* **11:** 207–224, 13 figs. (compound). See also *Entomologist's mon. Mag.* **91:** 149–152.
CHISWELL, J. R. 1956. A taxonomic account of the last instar larvae of some British Tipulinae (Diptera-Tipulidae). *Trans. R. ent. Soc. Lond.* **108:** 409–484, 110 figs.
DAHL, C. 1973. Trichoceridae (Dipt.) of Spitsbergen. *Ann. ent. fenn.* **39**(2): 49–59, 35 figs.
Keys all known larvae of the family.
KEILEN, D. & TATE, P. 1940. The early stages of the families Trichoceridae and Anisopodidae (= Rhyphidae) (Diptera: Nematocera). *Trans. R. ent. Soc. Lond.* **90:** 39–62, 87 figs.
KETTLE, D. S. & LAWSON, J. W. H. 1952. The early stages of British biting midges *Culicoides* Latreille (Diptera: Ceratopogonidae) and allied genera. *Bull. ent. Res.* **43:** 421–467, 6 pls.
LAŠTOVKA, P. 1971. A study on the last instar larvae of some Czechoslovak *Mycetophila* (Diptera, Mycetophilidae). *Acta Univ. Carol. Biol.* **1970:** 137–176, 75 figs.
LAŠTOVKA, P. 1972. A contribution to the larval morphology of the genera *Platurocypta* and *Dynatosoma* (Diptera, Mycetophilidae). *Entomologist* **105:** 59–76, 56 figs.
MADWAR, S. 1937. Biology and morphology of the immature stages of Mycetophilidae. *Phil. Trans. Roy. Soc. Lond. B.* **227:** 1–110, 392 figs.
MAMAEV, B. M. & KRIVOSHEINA, N. P. 1965. [Larvae of gall midges (Diptera, Cecidomyiidae): comparative morphology, biology and identification tables]. 278

pp., 94 figs. (compound). Izdatelstvo Nauka, Moscow (in Russian).
MORRIS, R. M. 1921–22. The larval and pupal stages of the Bibionidae. *Bull. ent. Res.* **12:** 221–232, 17 figs.; **13:** 189–195, 10 figs., 1 pl.
PLASSMANN, E. 1972. Morphologisch-taxonomische Untersuchungen an Fungivoridenlarven. *Dt. Ent. Z.* **19:** 73–99, 15 figs. (compound).
SATCHELL, G. H. 1947. The larvae of the British species of *Psychoda* (Diptera: Psychodidae). *Parasitology* **38:** 51–69, 84 figs.
SATCHELL, G. H. 1949. The early stages of the British species of *Pericoma* Walker (Diptera, Psychodidae). *Trans. R. ent. Soc. Lond.* **100:** 411–447, 26 figs. (compound).
SAUNDERS, L. G. 1924. On the life history and the anatomy of the early stages of *Forcipomyia* (Diptera, Ceratopogonidae). *Parasitology* **16:** 164–212, 26 figs., 3 pls.
THEOWALD, B. 1957. Die Entwicklungstadien der Tipuliden (Diptera, Nematocera), insbesondere der West-Palaearktischen Arten. *Tijdschr. Ent.* **100:** 195–308, 329 figs.
WYATT, I. J. 1964. Immature stages of Lestremiinae (Diptera: Cecidomyiidae) infesting cultured mushrooms. *Trans. R. ent. Soc. Lond.* **116:** 15–28, 36 figs.

Brachycera

DYTE, C. E. 1959. Some interesting habitats of larval Dolichopodidae (Diptera). *Entomologist's mon. Mag.* **95:** 139–143, 2 figs.
DYTE, C. E. 1967. Some distinctions between the larvae and pupae of the Empididae and Dolichopodidae (Diptera). *Proc. R. ent. Soc. Lond. A* **42:** 119–128, 11 figs.
HOBBY, B. M. & SMITH, K. G. V. 1961–62. [Papers on larvae and pupae of British Empididae and Rhagionidae] in *Entomologist's mon. Mag.* **97–98,** illustr.
McFADDEN, M. W. 1967. Soldier fly larvae in America north of Mexico. *Proc. U.S. natn. Mus.* **121:** 1–72, 156 figs.
MELIN, D. 1923. Contributions to the biology, metamorphosis and distribution of the Swedish Asilids. *Zool. Bidr. Uppsala* **8:** 1–316, 295 figs.
NAGATOMI, A. 1958–62. Studies in the aquatic snipe flies of Japan (Diptera, Rhagionidae). *Mushi* **32:** 46–67; **33:** 1–3; **35:** 11–27, 29–38; **36:** 103–149, illustr.
Useful for illustrated descriptions of eggs, larvae and pupae. Keys.

Cyclorrhapha

ALLEN, P. 1956–58. [Series of papers on Agromyzid larvae] in *Proc. R. ent. Soc. Lond. A* **31–33,** illustr.
BEDDING, R. 1973. The immature stages of Rhinophorinae (Diptera: Calliphoridae) that parasitise British woodlice. *Trans. R. ent. Soc. Lond.* **125**(1): 27–44, 63 figs.
BROOKS, A. R. 1951. Identification of the root maggots (Diptera: Anthomyiidae) attacking cruciferous garden crops in Canada, with notes on biology and control. *Can. Ent.* **83:** 109–120, 32 figs.
CHANDLER, A. E. F. 1968. A preliminary key to the eggs of some of the commoner aphidophagous Syrphidae (Diptera) occurring in Britain. *Trans. R. ent. Soc. Lond.* **120:** 199–218, 4 figs. (compound).
DIXON, T. J. 1960. Key to and descriptions of the third instar larvae of some species of Syrphidae (Diptera) occurring in Britain. *Trans. R. ent. Soc. Lond.* **112:** 345–379, 8 figs. (compound).
EGGLISHAW, H. J. 1960–61. [Series of papers on Cyclorrhaphous flies breeding in seaweed] in *Entomologist's mon. Mag.* **96** and *Entomologist* **93–94,** illustr.
FOOTE, B. A., BERG, C. O., NEFF, S. E. & KNUTSON, L. 1959 on. [Series of well illustrated papers published independently or jointly on larvae of Holarctic Sciomyzidae in various American and British Journals: refs. in *Zool. Rec.*]
GOELDLIN de TIEFENAU, P. 1974. Contribution à l'étude systématique et écolo-

gique des Syrphidae (Dipt.) de la Suisse occidentale. *Mitt. Schweiz. ent. Ges.* **47**: 151–252, 116 figs.
  Some 30 species of aphidophagous larvae described and illustrated.
HARTLEY, J. C. 1961. A taxonomic account of the larvae of some British Syrphidae. *Proc. zool. Soc. Lond.* **163**: 505–573, 117 figs.
HERING, E. M. 1954–57. Die Larven der Agromyziden (Diptera) 1–3. *Tijdschr. Ent.* **97**: 115–136; **98**: 257–281; **100**: 73–94, illustr. See also *Tijdschr. Ent.* **98**: 1–27 for register of larvae described earlier by de Meijere.
KEILIN, D. 1917. Recherches sur les Anthomyidae à larves carnivores. *Parasitology* **9**: 325–450, 15 pls.
KEILIN, D. & TATE, P. 1930. On certain semi-carnivorous Anthomyid larvae. *Parasitology* **22**: 168–180, 5 figs., 1 pl.
KEILIN, D. 1951. Recherches sur les larves de Diptères Cyclorrhaphes. *Bull. Sci. Fr. Belg.* **49**: 15–198, 16 pls.
LYNEBORG, L. 1970. Taxonomy of European *Fannia* larvae (Diptera, Fanniidae). *Stuttg. Beitr. Naturk.* **215**: 1–28, 20 figs.
OKELY, E. F. 1974. Description of the puparia of twenty-three British species of Sphaeroceridae (Diptera, Acalyptratae). *Trans. R. ent. Soc. Lond.* **126**(1): 41–56, 61 figs.
  Keys to genera and species.
OSBORNE, P. 1961. Comparative external morphology of *Psila rosae* (F.) and *P. nigricornis* Mg. (Dipt., Psilidae), third instar larvae and puparia. *Entomologist's mon. Mag.* **97**: 124–127, 4 figs. (compound).
PHILLIPS, V. T. 1946. The biology and identification of Trypetid larvae (Diptera: Trypetidae). *Mem. Am. ent. Soc.* **12**: 1–161, 192 figs.
SCHUMANN, H. 1963. Zur Larvalsystematik der Muscinae nebst Beschreibung einiger Musciden- und Anthomyidenlarven. *Dt. ent. Z.* **10**: 134–151, 12 pls.
SKIDMORE, P. 1973. Notes on the biology of palaearctic Muscids (1). *Entomologist* **106**: 25–48, 14 figs. (compound).
SMITH, K. G. V. 1966. The larvae of *Thecophora occidensis* with comments upon the biology of Conopidae (Dipt.). *J. Zool. Lond.* **149**: 263–276, 6 figs., 1 pl.
  Keys, reviews, biology of world species.
STEYSKAL, G. C. 1964. Larvae of Micropezidae (Diptera), including two species that bore in ginger roots. *Ann. ent. Soc. Am.* **57**: 292–296, 14 figs.
THOMSON, R. C. M. 1937. Observations on the biology and larvae of the Anthomyiidae. *Parasitology* **29**: 237–358, 157 figs.
ZUSKA, J. 1963. The puparia of the European species of the family Larvaevoridae (Diptera). 1. (Subfamily Salmaciinae, part 1). *Sborn. ent. Odd. nár. Mus. Praze* **35**: 333–372, 85 figs.

Siphonaptera (fleas)

CLAASENS, A. J. M. & O'ROURKE, F. J. 1966. The distribution and general ecology of the Irish Siphonaptera. *Proc. R. Ir. Acad.* **64B**(23): 413–463, 2 maps.
SMIT, F. G. A. M. 1957. The recorded distribution and hosts of Siphonaptera in Britain. *Entomologist's Gaz.* **8**(1): 45–75.
SMIT, F. G. A. M. 1957. Siphonaptera. *Handbk Ident. Br. Insects* **1**(16): 1–94, figs. 1–200.
SMIT, F. G. A. M. 1975. Siphonaptera. In Kloet & Hincks 1975, see above p. 92.
SMIT, F. G. A. M. 1962. Catalogus der Nederlandse Siphonaptera. *Tijdschr. Ent.* **105**(3): 45–96, figs. 1–8.
SMIT, F. G. A. M. 1968. De vlooien (Siphonaptera) van de Benelux-landen. *Wet. Meded. K. ned. natuurh. Veren.* **72**. 1–48, figs. 1–170.

SMIT. F. G. A. M. 1954. Lopper. *Danm. Fauna* **60:** 1–125, figs. 1–182.
SMIT, F. G. A. M. 1969. A catalogue of the Siphonaptera of Finland with distribution maps of all Fennoscandian species. *Ann. Zool. fenn.* **6**(1): 47–86. figs. 1–60, 1 map.
BRINCK-LINDROTH, G. & SMIT, F. G. A. M. 1971. The Kemner collection of Siphonaptera in the Entomological Museum, Lund, with a check-list of the fleas of Sweden. *Ent. scand.* **2**(4): 269–286, figs. 1–13.
BEAUCOURNU, J. C. 1968. Catalogue provisoire des Siphonaptères de la faune française. *Ann. Soc. ent. Fr.* (N.S.) **4**(3): 615–635.
BEAUCOURNU, J. C. & GILOT, B. 1971. Additions au catalogue provisoire des Siphonaptères de la faune française. *Bull. Soc. ent. Fr.* **76**(1–2): 46–48.
PEUS, F. 1967. Zur Kenntnis der Flöhe Deutschlands. I. Zur Taxonomie der Vogelflöhe (Insecta, Siphonaptera). *Dt. Ent. Z.* (N.F.) **14** (I–II): 81–108, figs. 1–25.
PEUS, F. 1968. Zur Kenntnis der Flöhe Deutschlands. II. Faunistik und Ökologie der Vogelflöhe (Insects, Siphonaptera). *Zool. Jb. Syst.* **95**(4): 571–633.
PEUS, F. 1970. Zur Kenntnis der Flöhe Deutschlands (Insects, Siphonaptera). III. Faunistik und Ökologie der Säugetierflöhe. Insectivora, Lagomorpha, Rodentia. *Zool. Jb., Syst.* **97**: 1–54.
PEUS, F. 1972. Zur Kenntnis der Flöhe Deutschlands (Schluss) (Insecta, Siphonaptera). IV. Faunistik und Ökologie der Säugetierflöhe. *Zool. Jb., Syst.* **99**(3): 408–504, maps 1, 2.

TARDIGRADA
British species about 76

OUÉNOT, L. 1932. Tardigrades. *Faune Fr.* **24:** 1–96, 98 figs.
HALLAS, T. E. 1969. Danmarks Tardigrader. *Natur. Mus., Aarhus* **13** (4): 1–18, 19 figs.
LE GROS, A. E. 1958. How to begin the study of tardigrades. *Countryside* (N.S.) **18** (8): 1–11, 31 figs.
MARCUS, E. 1936. Tardigrada. *Tierreich* **66:** xvii + 340 pp., 306 figs.
MAY, R. M. 1948. "La Vie des Tardigrades". 132 pp., 40 pls. Gallimard, Paris.
MORGAN, C. I. 1975. Some notes on the Tardigrada of the Mullet Peninsula, including four additions to the Irish fauna and a key to the Irish species. *Ir. Nat. J.* **18:** 165–177, 1 fig.
MORGAN, C. I. 1976. Studies on the British tardigrade fauna; some zoogeographical and ecological notes. *J. nat. Hist.* **10:** 607–632, 6 figs.
MORGAN, C. I. & KING, P. E. 1976. British Tardigrads. *Synopses Br. Fauna* (N.S.): **9,** vi + 132 pp., 28 figs., 5 maps.
MURRAY, J. 1911. Scottish Tardigrada; a review of our present knowledge. *Ann. Scot. nat. Hist.* **78:** 88–95, 4 figs.
MURRAY, J. 1911. Clare Island Survey. Arctiscoida. *Proc. R. Ir. Acad.* **31** (37): 1–16, 3 pls.
PILATO, G. 1969. Schema per una nuova sistemazione della famiglie e dei generi degli Eutardigrada. *Boll. Accad. gioenia Sci. nat.* (IV) **10:** 181–193 (in Italian).
POLLOCK, L. W. 1971. On some British marine Tardigrada, including two new species of *Batillipes*. *J. mar. biol. Ass. U.K.* **51:** 93–103, 3 figs.
RENAUD-MORNANT, J. & POLLOCK, L. W. 1971. A review of the systematics and ecology of marine Tardigrada. *Smithson. Contr. Zool.* **76:** 109–117, 8 figs.
RICHTERS, F. 1903. Nordische Tardigraden. *Zool. Anz.* **27:** 168–172, 2 figs.
THULIN, G. 1911. Beiträge zur Kenntnis der Tardigradenfauna Schwedens. *Ark. Zool.* **7**(16): 1–60, 31 figs.

THULIN, G. 1928. Über die Phylogenie und das System der Tardigraden. *Hereditas* **11**: 207–266, 29 figs.
VAN DER LAND, J. 1963. The Tardigrada of the Netherlands. A Review of records from literature and a revision of the Loman collection. *Zool. Meded., Leiden* **38**: 195–206, 10 figs.

MOLLUSCA
About 800 British species

GENERAL

FORBES, E. & HANLEY, S. 1848–53. "A History of British Molluscs and their Shells". J. van Voorst, London.
    Vol. 1 pp. 57–477. Bivalvia and 59 plates of species in all molluscan groups.
    Vol. 2 pp. 1–557. Bivalvia, Pteropoda, Prosobranchia and Chitons.
    Vol. 3 pp. 1–616. Prosobranchia and Opisthobranchia.
    Vol. 4 pp. 1–293. 132 plates of shells; mainly Pulmonata and Cephalopoda but also notes on all molluscan groups.
JEFFREYS, J. C. 1862–69. "British Conchology". J. van Voorst, London.
    Vol. 1, 114 pp. of introduction; pp. 1–341, 8 pl. Land and Freshwater; Bivalvia, Prosobranchia, Pulmonata.
    Vol. 2, 14 pp. of introduction; pp. 27–465, 8 pl. Marine: Bivalvia.
    Vol. 3, pp. 1–393, 8 pl. Marine: Bivalvia, Scaphopoda, Amphineura, Gastropoda.
    Vol. 4, pp. 1–486, 8 pl. Marine: Gastropoda.
    Vol. 5, pp. 1–258, 102 pl. Marine: Opisthobranchia, Cephalopoda, and supplement.
JUTTING, T. van BENTHEM 1933. Gastropoda Prosobranchia et Pulmonata. *Fauna Nederl.* **7**: 1–387, 297 figs.
JUTTING, T. van BENTHEM 1943. Lamellibranchia. *Fauna Nederl.* **12**: 1–477, 144 figs.
McMILLAN, N. F. 1968. "British Shells". xii + 196 pp., 2 figs., 80 pl. Warne, London.
MOORE, R. C. Ed. 1960–71. "Treatise on Invertebrate Palaeontology". Kansas.
    1960 Part I, Mollusca 1. xiii + 351 pp., 216 figs. Mollusca – general features, Scaphopoda, Amphineura, Monoplacophora, Gastropoda – general features, Archaeogastropoda and some Caenogastropoda and Opisthobranchia.
    1969 Part N, Vol. 1 (of 3). Mollusca 6. Bivalvia. pp. xxxvii + 1–490, 300 figs.
    1969 Part N, Vol. 2 (of 3). Mollusca 6. Bivalvia. pp. ii + 491–952, 310 figs.
    1971 Part N, Vol. 3 (of 3). Mollusca 6. Bivalvia. pp. iv + 953–1224, 153 figs.
WENZ, W. 1938. Allgemeiner Teil und Prosobranchia. Gastropoda Part I. In "Handbuch der Paläozoologie" (O. H. Schindewolf, ed.), vol. 6, xii + 1639 pp., 4211 figs. Berlin.
ZILCH, A. 1959. Euthyneura. Gastropoda Part II. in "Handbuch der Paläozoologie". (O. H. Schindewolf, ed.), vol. 6, xii + 834 pp., 2515 figs. Berlin.
THIELE, J. 1929–34. "Handbuch der systematischen Weichtierkunde". Vol. 1. Class Loricata, pp. 1–22, 12 figs.; Class Gastropoda, pp. 23–778, 782 figs. Vol. 2. Class Scaphopoda, pp. 779–782, 4 figs. Class Bivalvia, pp. 782–984, 81 figs.; Class Cephalopoda, pp. 948–995, 26 figs. + 15 pp. additions and corrections, pp. 995–1010.

This list is intended only to provide an entry into the literature. Papers of more local interest will be found in the following journals:
Archiv für Molluskenkunde, Frankfurt.
Basteria.
Bulletin de la Societe Malacologique de France, Paris.
Haliotis.
Journal of Conchology, London.

MOLLUSCA: MARINE
GENERAL

JUTTING, T. van BENTHEM. 1936. Gastropoda Opisthobranchia; Amphineura et Scaphopoda. *Fauna Nederl.* **8:** 1–106, 38 figs.
NIERSTRASZ, H. F. & HOFFMANN, H. 1929. Aculifera. *Tierwelt N.-u. Ostsee* **9a:** 1–64, 58 figs.
SARS, G. O. 1878. "Bidrag til Kundskaben om Norgen Arktiske Fauna. 1. Mollusca regionis Arcticae Norvegiae". 466 pp., 52 pl. Christiania (Oslo).
WINCKWORTH, R. 1932. The British marine Mollusca. *J. Conch. Lond.* **19:** 211–252, figs.
WINCKWORTH, R. 1951. A list of the marine mollusca of the British Isles: additions and corrections. *J. Conch. Lond.* **23:** 131–134.

GASTROPODA

ANKEL, W. E. 1936. Prosobranchia. *Tierwelt N. u. Ostsee* **9b:** 1–240, 222 figs.
DALES, R. P. 1951. Heteropoda. *Fich. Ident. Zooplancton* **66:** 4 pp., 12 figs.
FRETTER, V. & GRAHAM, A. 1962. "British Prosobranch Mollusca. Their functional anatomy and ecology". 755 pp., 317 figs. Ray Society, London.
FRETTER, V. & PILKINGTON, M. C. 1970. Prosobranchia. Veliger larvae of Taenioglossa and Stenoglossa. *Fich. Ident. Zooplancton* **129–132,** 26 pp., 35 figs.
GRAHAM, A. British Prosobranchs. *Synopsis Br. Fauna* (n.s.) **2,** 114 pp., 119 figs.
HADFIELD, G. M. 1964. Opisthobranchia. The veliger larvae of the Nudibranchia. *Fich. Ident. Zooplancton* **106,** 3 pp., 9 figs.
HELLER, J. 1975. The taxonomy of some British *Littorina* species with notes on their reproduction (Mollusca: Prosobranchia). *J. Linn. Soc. Zool.* **56:** 131–151, 10 figs., 2 pls.
HOFFMANN, H. 1926. Opisthobranchia, Pteropoda. *Tierwelt N.- u. Ostsee* **9c:** 1–66, 42 figs.
HUNNAM, P. & BROWN, G. 1975. Sublittoral nudibranch mollusca (sea slugs) in Pembrokeshire waters. *Fld Stud.* **4:** 131–159, 14 figs.
MORTON, J. E. 1957. Opisthobranchia. Order: Gymnosomata. Families: Pneumodermalidae, Cliopsidae. *Fich. Ident. Zooplancton* **79,** 4 pp., 5 figs.
MORTON, J. E. 1957. Opisthobranchia. Order: Gymnosomata. Family: Clionidae. *Fich. Ident. Zooplancton* **80,** 4 pp., 5 figs.
NORDSIECK, F. 1968. "Die europäischen Meeres-Gehauseschnecken (Prosobranchia) vom Eismeer bis Kapverden und Mittelmeer". 273 pp., 31 pls. Gustav Fischer, Stuttgart.
NORDSIECK, F. 1972. "Die europäischen Meeresschnecken (Opisthobranchia mit Pyramidellidae, Rissoacea)". Vom Eismeer, Kapverden, Mittelmeer und Schwarzesmeer. 1–327, 14 pls. Gustav Fischer, Stuttgart.
PRUVOT-FOL, A. 1954. Mollusques Opisthobranches. *Faune Fr.* **58:** 1–460, 173 figs., 1 pl.

SPOEL, S. van der 1967. 'Euthecosomata". 375 pp., 366 figs. Noordyn & Zn. Gorinchem.
SPOEL, S. van der 1972. Pteropoda. Thecosomata. *Fich. Ident. Zooplancton* **140–142,** 12 pp., 57 figs.
THIRIOT-QUIEVREUX, C. 1973. Heteropoda. *Oceanogr. Mar. Biol. Ann. Rev.* **11:** 237–261, 11 figs.
THOMPSON, T. E. 1976. "Biology of Opisthobranch Molluscs". Vol. 1. 207 pp., 106 figs. Ray Society, London.
THOMPSON, T. E. & BROWN, G. H. 1976. British opisthobranch molluscs. *Synopsis Br. Fauna* (n.s.) **8,** vi + 204 pp., 105 figs., 1 pl.

BIVALVIA

ALLEN, J. A. 1954. A comparative study of the British species of *Nucula* and *Nuculana. J. mar. biol. Ass. U.K.* **33:** 457–472, 8 figs., 1 pl.
BOWDEN, J. & HEPPELL, D. 1966. Revised list of British Mollusca. 1. Introduction: Nuculacea – Ostreacea. *J. Conch. Lond.* **26:** 99–124.
BOWDEN, J. & HEPPELL, D. 1968. Revised list of British Mollusca. 2. Unionacea – Cardiacea. *J. Conch. Lond.* **26:** 237–272.
JENSEN, A. S. & SPARCK, R. 1934. Bløddyr II. Saltvandsmuslinger. *Danm. Fauna* **40:** 1–208, 175 figs. (in Danish).
HØPNER PETERSEN, G. & RUSSELL, P. J. C. 1971. *Cardium hauniense* compared with *C. exiguum* and *C. glaucum. Proc. malac. Soc. Lond.* **39:** 409–420, 2 figs., 3 pls.
LEWIS, J. R. & SEED, R. 1969. Morphological variations in *Mytilus* from S.W. England in relation to the occurrence of *M. galloprovincialis* (Lmk). *Cah. Biol. Mar.* **10:** 231–253, 9 figs., 2 pls.
NORDSIECK, F. 1969. "Die europäischen Meeresmuscheln (Bivalvia) von Eismeer bis Kapverden, Mittelmeer und Schwarzes Meer". 256 pp., 25 pls. Gustav Fischer, Stuttgart.
REES, C. B. 1950. The identification and classification of lamellibranch larvae. *Hull Bull. mar. Ecol.* **3:** 73–104, 4 figs., 5 pls.
RUSSELL, P. J. C. 1971. A reappraisal of the geographical distribution of the cockles, *Cardium edule* L. and *C. glaucum* Bruguière. *J. Conch.* **27:** 225–234.
TEBBLE, N. 1976. "British Bivalve Seashells. A handbook for identification". 2nd edn. 212 pp., 110 figs., 12 pls. HMSO, Edinburgh.
URK, R. M. van 1964. The genus *Ensis* in Europe. *Basteria* **28:** 13–44, 13 figs.
URK, R. M. van 1973. Systematical notes on *Cardium edule* L. and *C. glaucum* Brug. in the Netherlands. *Basteria* **37:** 95–112, 14 figs.

POLYPLACOPHORA

MATHEWS, G. 1953. A key for use in the identification of British Chitons. *Proc. malac. Soc. Lond.* **29:** 241–248, 6 figs.
MUUS, B. J. 1959. Skallus, Søtaender, Blaksprutter. *Danm. Fauna* **65:** 71–239, figs. 44–117 (in Danish).
    A comprehensive survey including descriptions of most British species with excellent illustrations.

APLACOPHORA

SALVINI-PLAWEN, L. von 1975. Mollusca: caudofoveata. *Mar. Invert. Scand.* **4,** 55 pp., 59 figs.

SCAPHOPODA

MUUS, B. J. 1959. (see above).

CEPHALOPODA

ROBSON, G. C. 1929, 1932. "A Monograph of the Recent Cephalopoda". Vol. 1. xi + 595 pp., 89 figs. 7 pls. Vol. 2. xi + 359 pp., 79 figs., 6 pls. British Museum (Natural History), London.
JAECKEL, G. A. von SIEGFRIED 1958. Cephalopoden. *Tierwelt N.- u. Ostsee* **9**: 479–723, 86 figs.
MUUS, B. J. 1959. (see above).
MUUS, B. J. 1963. Cephalopoda, Sepioidae. *Fich. Ident. Zoplancton* **94**, 5 pp., 11 figs.
MUUS, B. J. 1963. Teuthoidea. *Fich. Ident. Zooplancton* **95**, 3 pp., 14 figs. **96**, 6 pp., 10 figs. **97**, 5 pp., 5 figs.
MUUS, B. J. 1963. Octopoda. *Fich. Ident. Zooplancton* **98**, 4 figs.

MOLLUSCA: NON-MARINE

GENERAL

ADAM, W. 1960. Mollusques I. Mollusques terrestres et dulcicoles. *Faune Belg.* 402 pp., 163 figs., 4 col. pl.
EHRMANN, P. 1956. Mollusca. *Tierwelt Mitteleur.* **2** (1), 264 pp., 147 figs., 13 pls. (Supplement by A. Zilch, and S. G. A. Jaeckel 1962. 294 pp., 9 pls.). Leipzig.
ELLIS, A. E. 1951. Census of the distribution of British non-marine Mollusca. *J. Conch. Lond.* **23** (6/7): 171–244 with maps. Supplement by M. P. Kerney 1966. Issued as supplement to *J. Conch. Lond.* **25,** 8 pp.
GERMAIN, L. 1930–31. Mollusques terrestres et fluviatiles. *Faune Fr.* **21–22,** 897 pp. + xiv pp., 860 figs., 26 pls.
JANUS, H. 1958. "Unsere Schnecken und Muscheln". 124 pp., 154 figs., 4 pls. Stuttgart. Translated into English as "The Young Specialist looks at Land and Freshwater Molluscs". 1965. 179 pp., 154 figs., 4 pls. Burke, London.
KENNARD, A. S. & WOODWARD, B. B. 1926. "Synonymy of British non-marine Mollusca". xxiv + 447 pp. British Museum (Natural History), London.
LICKHAREV, I. M. & RAMMEL'MEIER, E. S. 1962. "Terrestrial molluscs of the fauna of the U.S.S.R.". 574 pp., 420 figs. Israel Program for scientific translations, Washington.
MANDAHL-BARTH, G. 1949. Bløddyr III. Ferskvandsbløddyr. *Danm. Fauna* **54**: 1–249, 134 figs. (in Danish).
SOÓS, L. 1943. "Magyarország Tarmészetrajza. I Allattani Rész. A Kárpát-medence Mollusca-faunája". 478 pp., 22 figs., 30 pl. Budapest (in Hungarian).

GASTROPODA

BONDESEN, P. 1950. A comparative morphological-biological analysis of the egg capsules of freshwater pulmonate gastropods Hygrophila, Basommatophora Pulmonata. *Natura Jutl.* **3**: 1–208, 69 figs.
CAIN, A. J. & WILLIAMSON, M. H. 1958. Variation and specific limits in the *Arion ater* aggregate. *Proc. malac. Soc. Lond.* **33** (2): 72–86, 5 figs.
ELLIS, A. E. 1969. "British Snails". 2nd edn. 298 pp., figs., 14 pl. Clarendon Press, Oxford.

FORCART, L. 1957. Taxonomische Revision paläarktischer Zonitinae, I. *Arch. Molluskenk.* **86** (4/6): 101–136, 19 figs.
FORCART, L. 1959. Die palaearktischen Arten des genus *Columella* (Moll., Styll., Pupillidae). *Verh. naturf. Ges. Basel* **70:** 7–18, 4 pl.
FORCART, L. 1959. Taxonomische Revision paläarktischer Zonitinae, II. *Arch. Molluskenk.* **88** (1/3): 7–34, 12 figs., 3 pl.
FORCART, L. 1960. Taxonomische Revision paläarktischer Zonitinae, III-V. *Arch. Molluskenk.* **89** (1/3): 1–22, 4 figs., 2 pl.
GITTENBERGER, E., BACKHUYS, W. & RIPKEN, T. E. 1970. "De Landslakken van Nederland". 177 pp., 192 figs., 87 maps. Amsterdam (in Dutch).
CAMERON, R. A. D. & REDFERN, M. 1976. British land snails. *Synopsis Br. Fauna* (n.s.) **6,** 64 pp., 31 figs.
GROSSU, A. V. 1955. Mollusca: Gastropoda Pulmonata. *Fauna Repub. pop. rom.* **3** (1): 1–520, 283 figs. (in Romanian).
HUBENDICK, B. 1949. "Våra Snäckor. Snäckor i söh ock bräckt vatten". 100 pp., 172 figs., 4 pl. Stockholm (in Swedish).
KERNEY, M. P. & CAMERON, R. A. D. (in preparation). "A Field Guide to the Land Mollusca of N.W. Europe". Collins, London.
LOHMANDER, H. 1937. Über die nordischen Formen von *Arion circumscriptus* Johnston. *Acta soc. Fauna Flora Fenn.* **60:** 90–112, 16 figs.
MACAN, T. T. & COOPER, R. D. 1969. A key to the British fresh- and brackish-water gastropods with notes on their ecology. 3rd edn. *Scient. Publs Freshwat. biol. Ass.* **13,** 46 pp.
ØKLAND, F. 1925. "Die Verbreitung der Landgastropoden Norwegens". 168 pp., 61 figs. Oslo.
QUICK, H. E. 1933. The anatomy of British Succineae. *Proc. malac. Soc. Lond.* **20** (6): 295–318, 18 figs., 3 pls.
QUICK, H. E. 1960. British slugs (Pulmonata; Testacellidae, Arionidae, Limacidae). *Bull. Br. Mus. nat. Hist.* (Zool.) **6** (3): 105–226. 19 figs., 1 pl., 20 maps.
PAUL, C. R. C. 1975. *Columella* in the British Isles. *J. Conch. Lond.* **28** (16): 371–383, 6 figs., 1 pl.
RIEDEL, A. 1966. Zonitidae (excl. Daudebardiinae) dar Kaukasusländer (Gastropoda). *Annls zool. Warsz.* **24** (1): 1–304, 24 figs., 6 pl. and 18 maps.
STEENBERG, C. M. 1911. Blöddyr I. Landsnegle. *Danm. Fauna* **10:** 1–221, 181 figs. (in Danish).
WALDEN, H. W. 1955. The land gastropoda of the vicinity of Stockholm. *Ark. Zool.* **7:** 391–448, 15 figs., 1 pl.
WALDEN, H. W. 1966. Einige Bemerkungen zum Ergänzungsband zu Ehrmann's "Mollusca" in "Die Tierwelt Mitteleuropas". *Arch. Molluskenk.* **95** (1–2): 49–68, 6 figs.

BIVALVIA

ELLIS, A. E. 1962. British freshwater bivalve molluscs, with keys and notes for the identification of the species. *Synopsis Br. Fauna* **13:** 1–92, 38 figs., 16 pls.

BRACHIOPODA

British species 15–20

DAVIDSON, T. 1886–88. A monograph of recent Brachiopoda. *Trans. Linn. Soc. Lond. Zool.* (2) **4:** 1–248, 30 pls.

HELMCKE, J. G. 1940. Die Brachiopoden der deutschen Tiefsee-Expedition. *Wiss. Ergebn. dt. Tiefsee-Exped. Valdivia,* 1898–99, **25** (3): 255–316, 43 figs.

MASSY, A. L. 1925. The Brachiopoda of the coast of Ireland. *Proc. R. Ir. Acad.* **37B**(6): 37–46.
    Eleven species listed, eight of which also occur off coasts of Great Britain (no figs.).

THOMSON, J. A. 1927. Brachiopod morphology and genera (Recent and Tertiary). *N.Z. Board Sci. and Art, Manual* **7**, 338 pp., 2 pls.

ATKINS, D. 1959. A new species and genus of Brachiopoda from the Western Approaches and the growth stages of the lophophore. *J. mar. biol. Ass. U.K.* **39**: 71–89, 14 figs., 1 pl.

ATKINS, D. 1959. The growth stages of the lophophore of the brachiopods *Platidia davidsoni* (Eudes Deslongchamps) and *P. anomioides* (Philippi), with notes on the feeding mechanism. *J. mar. biol. Ass. U.K.* **38**: 103–132, figs. 1–23.

ATKINS, D. 1959. The early growth stages and adult structure of the lophophore of *Macandrevia cranium* (Müller) (Brachiopoda, Dallinidae). *J. mar. biol. Ass. U.K.* **38**: 335–350, 2 figs.

ATKINS, D. 1959. The growth stages of the lophophore and loop of the brachiopod *Terabratalia transversa* (Sowerby). *J. Morph.* **105**: 401–426, figs.

ATKINS, D. 1961. The generic position of the brachiopod *Megerlia echinata* (Fischer & Oehlert). *J. mar. biol. Ass. U.K.* **41**: 89–94, 4 figs.

ATKINS, D. 1961. A note on the growth-stages and structure of the adult lophophore of the brachiopod *Terebratella (Waltonia) inconspicua* (G. B. Sowerby). *Proc. zool. Soc. Lond.* **136**: 255–271, 10 figs.

ATKINS, D. 1961. The growth stages and adult structure of the lophophore of the brachiopods *Megerlia truncata* (L.) and *M. echinata* (Fischer & Oehlert). *J. mar. biol. Ass. U.K.* **41**: 95–111, 16 figs.

FOSTER, M. W. 1974. Recent antarctic and subantarctic brachiopods. *Antarctic Res. Ser.* **21**, ix + 189 pp., 39 figs.

RUDWICK, M. J. S. 1970. "Living and Fossil Brachiopods". 199 pp., 99 figs. Hutchinson, London.

WILLIAMS, A. 1965. In "Treatise on Invertebrate Paleontology" (R. C. Moore, ed.), Part H, pp. 524–927, figs. 398–746. Geological Society of America and University of Kansas Press.

BRYOZOA (ECTOPROCTA)

GENERAL

EGGLESTON, D. 1975. The marine fauna of the Cullercoats district. 3a, Ectoprocta. *Rep. Dove mar. Lab.* **3**(18): 5–30.

MOORE, P. G. 1973. Bryozoa as a community component on the north east coast of Britain. In "Living and Fossil Bryozoa" (G. P. Larwood, ed.), pp. 21–36, 3 figs. Academic Press, London and New York.

RYLAND, J. S. 1970. "Bryozoans". 175 pp., 21 figs. Hutchinson, London.

RYLAND, J. S. 1974. A revised key for the identification of intertidal Bryozoa (Polyzoa). *Fld Stud.* **4**: 77–86, 4 figs.

RYLAND, J. S. 1976. Physiology and ecology of marine Bryozoans. *Adv. mar. Biol.* **14**: 285–443, 44 figs.

FOULING AND SETTLEMENT

RYLAND, J. S. 1965. "Catalogue of Main Marine Fouling Organisms". Vol. 2. "Polyzoa". 83 pp., 38 figs. O.E.C.D., Paris.
RYLAND, J. S. 1965. Polyzoa (Bryozoa) order Cheilostomata, Cyphonautes larvae. *Fich. Ident. Zooplancton* **107**, 5 pp.
RYLAND, J. S. 1972. Bryozoa and marine fouling. In "Marine Borers, Fungi and fouling organisms of wood" (G. Jones and S. K. Eltringham, eds.), pp. 137–154. *Proc. O.E.C.D.* 1968. O.E.C.D., Paris.

PHYLACTOLAEMATA

BUSHNELL, J. H. 1968. Aspects of architecture, ecology and zoogeography of freshwater Ectoprocta. In "Proc. 1st International Conference on Bryozoa" (E. Annoscia, ed.). *Atti Soc. ital. Sci. nat.* **108**: 129–151.
BUSHNELL, J. H. 1973. The freshwater Ectoprocta ... in "Living and Fossil Bryozoa" (G. P. Larwood, ed.) pp. 503–522, 6 figs. Academic Press, London and New York.
LACOURT, A. W. 1968. A monograph of the freshwater Bryozoa – Phylactolaemata. *Zool. Verh. Leiden* **93**: 1–159, 13 figs., 18 pls.
PRENANT, M. & BOBIN, G. 1956. Bryozoaires, Pt. 1. *Faune Fr.* **60**: 1–398, 151 figs.

GYMNOLAEMATA

MARCUS, E. 1940. Mosdyr (Bryozoa eller Polyzoa). *Danm. Fauna* **46**: 1–401, 221 figs. (in Danish).
PRENANT, M. & BOBIN, G. 1966. Bryozoaires, Pt. 2. *Faune Fr.* **68**: 1–647, 210 figs.
RYLAND, J. S. 1963. The species of *Haplopoma* (Polyzoa). *Sarsia* **10**: 9–18, 4 figs.
RYLAND, J. S. 1963. Systematics and biological studies on Polyzoa(Bryozoa) from western Norway. *Sarsia* **14**: 1–59, 14 figs.
RYLAND, J. S. & HAYWARD, P. J. 1977. British Anascan Bryozoans. *Synopsis Br. Fauna, n.s.* **10**, vi + 188 pp. 85 figs.

STENOLAEMATA

HARMELIN, J.-G. 1973. Morphological variation and ecology of the Recent Cyclostome Bryozoan *Idmonea atlantica* ... In "Living and Fossil Bryozoa" (G. P. Larwood, ed.), pp. 95–106, 6 figs. Academic Press, London and New York.
HARMER, S. F. 1891. On the British species of *Crisia*. *Q. Jl micr. Sci.* **32**: 127–180, 1 pl.
HARMER, S. F. 1896. On the development of *Lichenopora verrucaria*. *Q. Jl micr. Sci.* **39**: 71–144, 2 figs., 3 pls.
HARMER, S. F. 1898. On the development of *Tubulipora,* and on some British and Northern species of this genus. *Q. Jl micr. Sci.* **41**: 73–158, 3 pls.
NIELSEN, C. 1970. On metamorphosis and ancestrula formation in Cyclostomatous Bryozoans. *Ophelia* **7**(2): 217–256, 41 figs.
RYLAND, J. S. 1967. Crisiidae (Polyzoa) from western Norway. *Sarsia* **29**: 269–282, 5 figs.

PHORONIDEA

British species at least 4

CORI, C. J. 1932. Phoronidea. *Tierwelt Nord- u. Ostsee* **7c:** 101–132, 24 figs.
FORNERIS, L. 1957. Phoronidea, Phoronidae, Actinotrocha larvae. *Fich. Ident. Zooplancton* **69,** 4 pp.
SELYS-LONGCHAMPS, M. de 1907. Phoronia. *Fauna Flora Golf Neapel.* **30:** 1–280, 1 fig., 12 pls (1 col.).

ECHINODERMATA

British species about 170

MORTENSEN, Th. 1927. "Handbook of the Echinoderms of the British Isles". 471 pp., 69 figs. Oxford University Press.
BELL, F. J. 1892. "Catalogue of the British Echinoderms in the British Museum (Natural History)". xvi + 202 pp., figs., 16 pls. British Museum (Natural History), London.
CHADWICK, H. C. 1914. Echinoderm larvae of Port Erin. *Proc. Trans. biol. Lpool. biol. Soc.* **28** (22): 467–498, 9 pls.
BREHAUT, R. N. 1966. The Echinodermata of Guernsey. *Rep. Trans. Soc. guernés.* **18:** 54–57.
BUCHANAN, J. B. 1966. The marine fauna of the Cullercoats district: Echinodermata. *Rep. Dove mar. Lab.* **15**(3): 21–39.
CLARK, A. M. 1970. Echinodermata: Crinoidea. *Mar. Invert. Scand.* **3:** 1–55, 19 figs.
ROWE, F. W. E. 1970. A note on the British species of cucumarians, involving the erection of two nominal genera. *J. mar. Biol. Ass. U.K.* **50:** 683–687.
ROWE, F. W. E. 1971. The marine flora and fauna of the Isles of Scilly: Echinodermata. *J. nat. Hist.* **5:** 233–238.

HEMICHORDATA

British species

ENTEROPNEUSTA

ADULTS

HORST, C. F. van der 1925. Enteropneusta. *Tierwelt N.- u. Ostsee* **7a:** 1–12, 7 figs.
HORST, C. F. van der 1927–29. Enteropneusta. *Bronn's Kl. Ordn. Tierreichs* **4**(4), 2(2): 601–737, figs. 683–733.
BURDON-JONES, C. 1956. Observations on the Enteropneust, *Protoglossus koehleri* (Caullery and Mesnil). *Proc. zool. Soc. Lond.* **127:** 35–38, 19 figs., 1 pl.
BURDON-JONES, C. & McINTYRE, A. D. 1960. *Sterobalanus*, a genus new to the Old World. *Nature, Lond.* **186:** 491–492, 1 fig.
BURDON-JONES, C. & PATIL, A. M. 1960. A revision of the genus *Saccoglossus* (Enteropneusta) in British waters. *Proc. zool. Soc. Lond.* **134:** 635–645, 3 figs.

LARVAE

BURDON-JONES, C. 1952. Development and biology of the larva of *Saccoglossus horsti* (Enteropneusta). *Phil. Trans. R. Soc. Lond.* (B), **236:** 553.
BURDON-JONES, C. 1957. Ptychoderidae, Tornaria larvae. *Fich. Ident. Zooplancton* **70,** 6 pp., 16 figs.

CHORDATA

TUNICATA   British species over 75

GENERAL

BERRILL, N. J. 1950. "The Tunicata, with an account of the British Species". iii + 354 pp., 120 figs. Ray Society, London.
ROWE, F. W. E. 1972. The marine flora and fauna of the Isles of Scilly: Enteropneusta, Ascidiacea, Thaliacea, Larvacea and Cephalochordata. *J. nat. Hist.* **6:** 207–213.

Ascidiacea

THOMPSON, H. 1930–34. The Tunicata of the Scottish area. parts I-IV. *Sci. Invest. Fish. Scotl.* **1930** (3); **1931** (1); **1932** (2); **1934** (1), 177 pp., 41 pls., 56 maps.
LAFARGUE, F. 1977. Révision taxonomique des Didemnidae des côtes de France (Ascidies composées: synthèse des resultats principaux. *Annls. Inst. océanogr.* **53,** 176 pp.
MILLAR, R. H. 1960. "The Fauna of the Clyde Sea area: Ascidiacea, with a Key to the Species". 16 pp., 9 figs. Scottish Marine Biological Association, Millport.
MILLAR, R. H. 1966. Tunicata: Ascidiacea. *Mar. Invert. Scand.* **1:** 1–123, 86 figs., maps.
MILLAR, R. H. 1970. British Ascidians. *Synopsis Br. Fauna* **1:** 1–88, 60 figs.
ALDER, J. & HANCOCK, A. 1905, 1907, 1912. "The British Tunicata. An unfinished Monograph" (J. Hopkinson, ed.). Vol. 1, xvi + 146 pp., 20 pls. Vol. 2. xxviii + 164 pp., 30 pls. Vol. 3. xii + 113 pp., 16 pls. Ray Society, London.
HARTMEYER, R. 1915. Alder und Hancocks Britische Tunicaten. Eine Revision. *Mitt. Zool. Mus. Berl.* **7** (3): 305–344.

Thaliacea and Appendicularia

BUCKMANN, A. 1926. Copelata. *Tierwelt N.- u. Ostsee* **12a:** 1–20, 17 figs.
IHLE, J. E. W. 1927. Thaliacea. *Tierwelt N.- u. Ostsee* **12a** 21–48, 12 figs.
BUCKMANN, A. 1930. Manteltiere oder Tunicata. *Tierwelt Dtl.* **17:** 143–163, 16 figs.
FRASER, J. H. 1949. The distribution of Thaliacea (Salps and Doliolids) in Scottish waters, 1920–1939. *Sci. Invest. Fish. Scotl.* **1949** (1): 1–44, 16 figs.

CEPHALOCHORDATA   British species 1

WEBB, J. E. 1956. On the populations of *Branchiostoma lanceolatum* and their relations with the West African Lancelets. *Proc. zool. Soc. Lond.* **127:** 125–140.

VERTEBRATA

Pisces
About 350 British species

GENERAL

ANDERSSON, K. A. 1942 (later editions also). "Fiskar och Fiske i Norden". 2 vols. 1064 pp., many figs., 574 pls. Stockholm (in Swedish).

DUNCKER, G. 1960. Die Fische der Nordmark. *Abt. naturw. Ver. Hamburg* N.F. **Suppl. 3:** 1–432, 145 figs., 1 map.

JOENSEN, J. S. & TANING, A. V. 1970. Marine and freshwater fishes. *Zoology Faroes* **62:** 1–241.

NIJSSEN, H. 1968. Zeevissen. *Wet. Meded. K. ned. natuurh. Veren.* **65:** 1–72, 118 pls (in Dutch).

WHEELER, A. 1969. "The Fishes of the British Isles and north west Europe". xvii + 613 pp., figs., maps. Macmillan, London.

FRESHWATER

BERG, L. S. 1962–65. "Freshwater fishes of the U.S.S.R. and adjacent countries". 3 vols. vii + 504; viii + 496; viii + 510 pp., figs. (English ed.). Israel Programme for Scientific Translations, Jerusalem, Nos 741, 742, 743.

LADIGES, W. & VOGT, D. 1965. "Die Susswasserfische Europas, bis zum Ural und Kaspischen Meer". 250 pp., 44 pls., maps. P. Parey, Berlin.

MAITLAND, P. S. 1972. Key to British freshwater fishes. *Scient. Publs Freshwat. biol. Ass.* **27:** 1–139, 64 figs., 1 pl., 55 maps.

MUUS, B. J. & DAHLSTRØM, P. 1971. "The Freshwater Fishes of Britain and Europe". 222 pp., figs, many pls. Collins, London.

POTTER, I. C. & OSBORNE, T. S. 1975. The systematics of British larval lampreys. *J. Zool. Lond.* **176:** 311–329, 7 figs., 1 pl.

SPILLMANN, C. J. 1961. Poissons d'eau douce. *Faune Fr.* **65:** 1–303, 98 figs.

MARINE

ANDRIASHEV, A. P. 1964. "Fishes of the Northern Seas of the U.S.S.R.". 566 pp., 300 figs. English edn. Israel Programme for Scientific Translations, Jerusalem, No. 836.

CROSS, T. F. & LYES, M. C. 1974. A first north-eastern Atlantic record of the bluefish *Pomatomus saltatrix* (L., 1758) (Faun. Pomatomidae). *J. Fish Biol.* **6:** 659–660, 1 pl.

HUREAU, J. C. & MONOD, T. (eds.), 1973. "Check-list of the Fishes of the north-eastern Atlantic and of the Mediterranean". 2 vols. UNESCO, Paris.

MILLER, P. J. 1969. Systematics and biology of the leopard-spotted goby, *Gobius ephippiatus* (Teleostei: Gobiidae), with description of a new genus and notes on the identity of *G. macrolepis* Kolombatovic. *J. mar. biol. Ass. U.K.* **49:** 831–855, 7 figs., 1 pl.

MILLER, P. J. 1974. A new species of *Gobius* (Teleostei: Gobiidae) from the western English Channel, with a key to related species in the British and Irish fauna. *J. Zool. Lond.* **174:** 467–480, 4 figs., 1 pl.

MILLER, P. J. & EL-TAWIL, M. Y. 1974. A multidisciplinary approach to a new species of *Gobius* (Teleostei: Gobiidae) from southern Cornwall. *J. Zool. Lond.* **174:** 539–574, 8 figs., 2 pls.

POLL, M. 1947. "Faune de Belgique. Poissons Marins". 452 pp., 267 figs., 3 maps.

TREWAVAS, E. & INGHAM, S. E. 1972. A key to the species of Mugilidae (Pisces) in the Northeastern Atlantic and Mediterranean, with explanatory notes. *J. Zool. Lond.* **167:** 15–29, 2 figs.

WHEELER, A. 1970. *Gobius cruentatus* – a fish new to the northern European fauna. *J. Fish Biol.* **2**: 59–67, 2 figs.

WHEELER, A., de GROOT, S. J. & NIJSSEN, H. 1974. The occurrence of a second species of *Lophius* in northern European waters. *J. mar. Biol. Ass. U.K.* **54**: 619–623, 1 fig., 1 pl.

WHEELER, A. & DUNNE, J. 1975. *Tripterygion atlanticus* sp.nov. (Teleostei – Tripterygiidae) the first record of a tripterygiid fish in North-Western Europe. *J. Fish. Biol.* **7**: 639–649, 2 figs., 1 pl.

Amphibia and Reptilia

SMITH, M. A. 1973. "The British Amphibians and Reptiles". 5th edn. xiv + 366 pp., 88 figs., 37 pls. Collins, London.

ARNOLD, E. N., BURTON, J. A. & OVENDEN, D. W. 1978. "A Field Guide to the Reptiles and Amphibians of Britain and Europe". 272 pp., figs., 40 pls. Collins, London.

GISLÉN, T. & KAURI, H. 1959. Zoogeography of the Swedish amphibians and reptiles with notes on their growth and ecology. *Acta Vertebr.* **1**(3): 197–397, 69 figs.

ANGEL, F. 1946. Reptiles et amphibiens. *Faune Fr.* **45**, 204 pp., figs.

WITTE, G. F. de 1948. "Amphibiens et reptiles". 2nd edn. *Faune Belg.*, 321 pp., figs., pls.

MERTENS, R. 1975. "Kriechtiere und Lurche". 6th edn. 104 pp., 105 figs., 54 pls. Kosmos, Stuttgart.

BUND, C. F. van de 1964. "De verspreising van de reptielen en amphibieën in Nederland. Nederlandse Vereniging voor Herpetologie en Terrariumkunde". 72 pp., text-illust. (In Dutch, with English summary).

THORN, R. 1968. "Les Salamandres d'Europe, d'Asie et d'Afrique du Nord". 376 pp., 56 figs., 16 pls. 11 maps. Lechevalier, Paris.

BRONGERSMA, L. D. 1967. "British Turtles. Guide for the identification of stranded turtles on British coasts". viii + 23 pp., 19 figs. British Museum (Natural History), London.

FRETEY, J. 1975. "Guide des Reptiles et Batraciens de France". 239 pp., 54 figs., 32 pls. Hatier, Paris.

Aves

425 breeding species in the British Isles, including irregular visitors.

BIBLIOGRAPHY

IRWIN, R. 1951. "British Bird Books: an Index to British Ornithology from A.D. 1481 to 1948". xix + 398 pp. Grafton, London.

FIELD GUIDES

BRUUN, B. & SINGER, A. 1974 (1970). "The Hamlyn Guide to Birds of Britain and Europe". 319 pp., col. pls. Hamlyn, London.

Every species figured in colour opposite a tabloid description and distribution map.

CAMPBELL, B. & FERGUSON-LEES, J. [with the assistance of H. MAYER-GROSS]. 1972. "A Field Guide to Birds' Nests". xiii + 545 pp., 8 phot. pls., bird drawings by D. I. M. Wallace, distribution maps.

A comprehensive guide to nest finding.

FITTER, R. S. R. & RICHARDSON, R. A. 1952. "The Pocket Guide to British Birds". xvi + 240 pp., numerous figs., 64 col. and 48 black and white pls. Collins, London.

Follows an 'ecological' not systematic arrangement.

FITTER, R. S. R., [assisted by CHARTERIS, G., illustr. RICHARDSON, R. A.] 1954. "The Pocket Guide to Nests and Eggs". iv + 172 pp., 40 col. + 8 black and white pls. Collins, London.
Companion volume to the above, following same 'ecological' arrangement of species.
HARRISON, C. 1975. "A Field Guide to the Nests, Eggs and Nestlings of British and European Birds, with North Africa and the Middle East". 432 pp. including 64 col. pls. Collins, London.
Excellent, comprehensive handbook with 16 plates of nestlings (by Philip Burton) and 48 plates of eggs. Identification keys to nests, eggs, young nestlings and chicks.
HEINZEL, H., FITTER, R. S. R. & PARSLOW, J. 1972. "The Birds of Great Britain and Europe, with North Africa and the Middle East". 320 pp. + 16 pp. distribution maps for Britain and Ireland. Col. illust. Collins, London.
Every species and some subspecies figured in colour opposite a tabloid description and distribution map.
PETERSON, R., MOUNTFORT, G. & HOLLOM, P. A. D. 1954. "A Field Guide to the Birds of Britain and Europe". xxxiv + 318 pp., 64 pls, mostly col., black and white drawings and maps. Collins, London.
One of the early field-guides, still unsurpassed.
SVENSSON, L. 1970. "Identification Guide to European Passerines". Naturhistoriska Museet, Stockholm.
Plumage descriptions of sex and age groups, wing formulae and measurements; many drawings of diagnostic characters. An excellent, detailed guide very suitable for bird-ringers.

GENERAL

BANNERMAN, D. A. 1953–63. "The Birds of the British Isles". 12 vols. Each vol. has about 400 pp. and 50 col. pls by George E. Lodge. Oliver and Boyd, Edinburgh.
The most comprehensive work on British birds ever published.
CAMPBELL, B. & WATSON, D. 1964. "The Oxford Book of Birds". xvi + 207 pp., figs., 96 cols. pls. Oxford University Press, Oxford.
Text descriptions and excellent colour plates on facing pages.
COWARD, T. A. (J. A. G. BARNES, ed.) 1969. "Birds of the British Isles and Their Eggs". xvi + 359 pp., 177 col. and phot. Pls. Warne, London.
A condensation, with revised text of T. A. Coward's famous 3-vol. work.
HOLLOM, P. A. D. 1952. "The Popular Handbook of British Birds". xxiv + 511 pp., 150 pls. (136 col.). H. F. & G. Witherby, London.
An abridged version of "The Handbook of British Birds", dealing with regularly occurring species.
HOLLOM, P. A. D. 1960. "The Popular Handbook of Rarer British Birds". xiv + 133 pp., 39 col. + 1 black and white pls. H. F. & G. Witherby, London.
Abridged descriptions of rarities from "The Handbook of British Birds".
HUDSON, R., ed. 1971. "A Species List of British and Irish Birds". 20 pp. British Trust for Ornithology, Tring.
A useful systematic list for report compilers, etc.
VARIOUS AUTHORS. 1969. "Book of British Birds". 472 pp. Drive Publications, London.
Species descriptions; also sections on identification, distribution, evolutionary history, biology, etc. Many col. illust. by Raymond Harris Ching and others.
WITHERBY, H. F., JOURDAIN, F. C. R., TICEHURST, N. F. & TUCKER, B. W. 1938 (reprinted 1948). "The Handbook of British Birds". 5 vols. lxxxv + 1882 pp.,

147 pls., mostly col., black and white figures and maps. H. F. & G. Witherby, London.

The definitive scientific work on British birds, with detailed descriptions of all plumage phases and digest of information on status, behaviour, migration, etc.

SHARROCK, J. T. R. 1976. "The Atlas of Breeding Birds in Britain and Ireland". 447 pp, numerous maps. British Trust for Ornithology and Irish Wildbird Conservancy, Tring.

Full page texts and maps for 209 species breeding in Britain and Ireland. Also shorter texts for 21 species (ten of which have quarter-page maps) which have bred sporadically or in feral groups during the survey period 1968–1972. Past distribution maps are given for 25 species for which intensive surveys have been carried out in the past.

YEATMAN, L., ed. 1976. "Atlas des Oiseaux Nicheurs de France". xvi + 282 pp., numerous maps and vignettes by Y. Ridel. Société Ornithologique de France, Ministère de la Qualité de la Vie Environnement, Paris.

Texts and half-page maps for 264 species currently breeding, and for a further 23 which did so formerly; 12 species are new colonists since 1936, since when 18 species have ceased to breed.

DYBBRO, T. 1976. "De Dansk Yaglefugles udbredelse". Pp. 293, numerous maps and vignettes by Jon Fjeldsa. Dansk Ornithologisk Forening, Copenhagen (in Danish).

The systematic section gives texts and quarter-page maps for 189 species breeding between 1971 and 1974.

SPECIAL GROUPS

CRAMP, S., BOURNE, W. R. P. & SAUNDERS, D. 1974. "The Seabirds of Britain and Ireland". 287 pp., 4 col. + 8 phot. pls + 32 pp. of distribution maps. Collins, London.

A definitive work on seabird numbers and distribution, from "Operation Seafarer 1969–70" research.

OGILVIE, M. A. 1975. "Ducks of Britain and Europe". 208 pp., 16 col. pls + 80 drawings by Carol Ogilvie, 24 distribution maps. T. & A. D. Poyser, Berkhamsted.

Deals with the 42 species and subspecies of ducks on the British list.

PORTER, R. F., WILLIS, I., CHRISTENSEN, S. & NIELSEN, B. P. 1974. "Flight identification of European Raptors". 184 pp., 80 photographs plus numerous drawings of raptors in flight. T. & A. D. Poyser, Berkhamsted.

The most comprehensive work on the field identification of a notoriously difficult order. Includes all 24 British species.

WILLIAMSON, K. 1960–64 (with revisions). "Identification for Ringers". No. 1, 1960 (revised 1968), The Genera *Cettia, Locustella, Acrocephalus* and *Hippolais,* 78 pp., 8 phots; No. 2, 1962 (revised 1967), The Genus *Phylloscopus,* 88 pp., 1 col. and 4 phot. pls; No. 3, 1964 (revised 1968), The Genus *Sylvia,* 75 pp., 4 phot. pls., maps. British Trust for Ornithology, Tring.

Systematic appraisal, descriptions, tables of measurements, moult, distribution, etc.

STATUS

PARSLOW, J. 1973. "Breeding Birds of Britain and Ireland: a Historical Survey". 272 pp. including 50 pp. of species distribution maps, text-figs. T. & A. D. Poyser, Berkhamsted.

Comprehensive survey of present distributions and changes during last 200 years.

SNOW, D. W., ed. 1971. "the Status of Birds in Britain and Ireland". 333 pp., figs. British Ornithologists' Union, London.
    The most up-to-date 'official' list of birds of the British Isles.
SHARROCK, J. T. R. 1974. "Scarce Migrant Birds in Britain and Ireland". 192 pp., 12 phot. pls., numerous maps and histograms. T. & A. D. Pyser, Berkhamsted.
    A careful analytical study of regional and seasonal variations in occurrence of scarce migrants and American vagrants.

Mammalia
About 60 non-marine and 30 marine species in Britain.
About 95 non-marine and 34 marine species in NW Europe.

GENERAL

CORBET, G. B. & SOUTHERN, H. N. (eds.), 1977. "The Handbook of British Mammals". 2nd edn. 520 pp., 184 illustr. Blackwell, Oxford. (First edn. H. N. Southern, 1964).
    Deals with all species, terrestrial and marine, including vagrant bats, seals and cetaceans, established introductions and species that have become extinct in historic times. Guide to identification in form of tables and keys. Most species illustrated.
CORBET, G. B. 1976. "Finding and Identifying Mammals in Britain". 56 pp., many figs., 4 col. pls. British Museum (Natural History), London.
    A checklist and illustrated guide to all species except cetaceans.
LEVER, C. 1977. See p. 2.
LYNEBORG, L. 1971. "Mammals in Colour". 247 pp. Blanford, London.
    Coloured illustrations of all British and W. European species, with many details of structure illustrated.
OVENDEN, D. W., ARNOLD, E. N. & CORBET, G. B. (In press). "The Wild Animals of Britain and Europe". Collins, London.
    Fully comprehensive, with coloured illustrations and maps for all species.

Cetacea

FRASER, F. C. 1976. "British Whales, Dolphins and Porpoises: a guide for the identification and reporting of stranded whales, dolphins and porpoises on the British coasts". 5th edn. x + 34 pp., 31 figs. British Museum (Natural History), London.

Artiodactyla

PAGE, F. J. T. 1971. "Field Guide to British Deer". 2nd edn. 83 pp. illustr. Blackwell, Oxford.

FUNGI

British species about 12,000

The Fungi are now usually treated as a Kingdom in their own right independent of the plants (Plantae) and animals (Animalia). Two main divisions are recognized, the Myxomycota for plasmodial types and Eumycota for non-plasmodial (mainly mycelial) types. For practical reasons the lichen-forming fungi are treated separately below (pp. 151–157) although they belong in the Eumycota.

GENERAL

For details of publications cataloguing new taxa see Hawksworth (1974).

AINSWORTH, G. C. 1971. "Ainsworth & Bisby's Dictionary of the Fungi". 6th edn. x + 663 pp. Commonwealth Mycological Institute, Kew.
  Notes on genera, major literature, terms, etc.; an essential handbook; includes lichenized fungi.
AINSWORTH, G. C., SPARROW, F. K. & SUSSMAN, A. S., eds. 1973. "The Fungi. An advanced treatise". Vols. IV A-B. Academic Press, New York and London.
  Includes keys to most accepted genera and extensive literature lists; the standard multi-authored reference work **to be used for all groups of non-lichenized fungi treated here.**
VON ARX, J. A. 1974. "The Genera of Fungi Sporulating in Pure Culture". 2nd edn. 315 pp. J. Cramer, Vaduz.
  Keys to genera.
BESSEY, E. A. 1950. "Morphology and Taxonomy of Fungi". 791 pp. Constable, London. Reprint 1964. Hafner, New York.
BIBLIOGRAPHY OF SYSTEMATIC MYCOLOGY 1947 on. Commonwealth Mycological Institute, Kew.
  Twice-yearly listing of publications on systematic mycology.
BULLETIN OF THE BRITISH MYCOLOGICAL SOCIETY 1967 on. British Mycological Society, London.
  Twice-yearly; includes keys and literature lists from time to time.
CLEMENTS, F. E. & SHEAR, C. L. 1931. "The Genera of Fungi". iv + 496 pp. Hafner, New York. Reprint 1965. Hafner, New York.
  Keys to genera.

GAMS, W., VAN DER AA, H.A., VAN DER PLAATS-NITERINK, A. J., SAMSON, R. A. & STALPERS, J. A. 1975. "CBS Course in Mycology". 104 pp. Centraalbureau voor Schimmelcultures, Baarn.
   Includes useful literature lists.
HAWKSWORTH, D. L. 1974. "Mycologist's Handbook. An introduction to the principles of taxonomy and nomenclature in the Fungi and Lichens". 231 pp. Commonwealth Mycological Institute, Kew.
HOLDEN, M. 1975. Guide to the literature for the identification of British fungi. 3rd ed. *Bull. Br. mycol. Soc.* **9:** 67–106.
   Extensive bibliography which should be consulted in conjunction with that presented here.
MYCOLOGICAL PAPERS 1925 on. Commonwealth Mycological Institute, Kew.
   Includes monographs of many groups of microfungi.
MYCOTAXON 1974 on. Mycotaxon, Ithaca, N.Y.
   A quarterly journal of systematic mycology.
PERSOONIA 1959 on. Rijksherbarium, Leiden.
   A journal of systematic mycology including monographs and revisions of many groups.
RABENHORST'S KRYPTOGAMEN-FLORA VON DEUTSCHLAND, ÖSTERREICH UND DER SCHWEIZ. 1881–1920. Vol. 1. Akademie Verlag, Leipzig.
   Detailed multi-authored monograph in German issued in many parts, with keys.
STEVENS, R. B., ed. 1974. "Mycology Guidebook". xxiv + 703 pp. University of Washington Press, Seattle & London.
   Guide to techniques and methods of study in most groups.
STUDIES IN MYCOLOGY 1972 on. Centraalbureau voor Schimmelcultures, Baarn.
   Monographs of microfungi (mainly growing in culture).
TALBOT, P. H. B. 1971. "Principles of Fungal Taxonomy". 274 pp. Macmillan, London & Basingstoke.
TRANSACTIONS OF THE BRITISH MYCOLOGICAL SOCIETY 1897 on. Cambridge University Press, London & New York.
   The journal of the British Mycological Society; bimonthly.
WEBSTER, J. 1970. "Introduction to Fungi". viii + 424 pp. Cambridge University Press, London.

HABITAT KEYS AND LISTS

Works dealing with particular taxonomic groups in restricted habitats are listed only under their group and not in this section.

Animals and Man

AINSWORTH, G. C. & AUSTWICK, P. K. C. 1973. "Fungal Diseases of Animals". 2nd edn. vii + 216 pp. Commonwealth Agricultural Bureaux, Farnham Royal.
EMMONS, C. W., BINFORD, C. H. & UTZ, J. P. 1970. "Medical Mycology". 2nd edn. 508 pp. Kimpton.
LARONE, D. H. 1976. "Medically Important Fungi. A guide to identification". 156 pp. Harper & Row. Hagerstown, Md, etc.
"NOMENCLATURE OF FUNGI PATHOGENIC TO MAN AND ANIMALS". 1977. 4th edn. v + 26 pp. Medical Research Council, London.
REVIEW OF MEDICAL AND VETERINARY MYCOLOGY 1943 on. Commonwealth Mycological Institute, Kew.
   A comprehensive abstracting journal.

Biodeteriogenic Fungi

INTERNATIONAL BIODETERIORATION BULLETIN 1965 on. University of

Aston Biodeterioration Centre, Birmingham.
LOVELOCK, D. W. & GILBERT, R. J., eds. 1975. "Microbial Aspects of the Deterioration of Materials". xiii + 261 pp. Society for Applied Bacteriology Technical series No. 7. Academic Press, London, New York & San Francisco.

Bryophytic Fungi

RACOVITZA, A. 1959. Étude systematique et biologique des champignons bryophiles. *Mém. Mus. natn. Hist. Nat., Paris*, n.s., B **10**: 1–288, pls. I–LXXXIV.

Coprophilous Fungi

RICHARDSON, M. J. & WATLING, R. 1975. "Keys to Fungi on Dung". 2nd edn. 36pp. British Mycological Society, London. [Originally published in *Bull. Br. mycol. Soc.* **2–3** (1969).]

Entomogenous Fungi

LEATHERDALE, D. 1958–66. A host catalogue of British entomogenous fungi. *Entomologist's mon. Mag.* **94**: 103–105; **97**: 226–227; **101**: 163–164.
LEATHERDALE, D. 1970. The arthropod hosts of entomogenous fungi in Britain. *Entomophaga* **15**: 419–435.
PETCH, C. 1948. A revised list of British entomogenous fungi. *Trans. Br. mycol. Soc.* **31**: 286–304.

Freshwater Fungi

See JONES 1976 (p. 127), INGOLD 1975 (p. 151), SPARROW 1960 (p. 130) and under CHYTRIDIOMYCETES (p. 130) and OOMYCETES (p. 130).

Fungi on Fungi

NICOT, J. 1966. Clé pour la détermination des espèces banales de champignons fongicoles. *Revue mycol.* **31**: 393–399.

Hypogeous Fungi

HAWKER, L. E. 1954. British hypogeous fungi. *Phil. Trans. R. Soc.*, B **237**: 429–546.
HAWKER, L. E. 1974. Revised annotated list of British hypogeous fungi. *Trans. Br. mycol. Soc.* **63**: 67–76.

Lichenicolous Fungi

CLAUZADE, G. & ROUX, C. 1976. "Les Champignons Lichénicoles non Lichénisés". 110 pp. Institut de Botanique, Montpellier.
HAWKSWORTH, D. L. 1975–78. Notes on British lichenicolous fungi, I. *Kew Bull.* **30**: 183–203. II. *Notes R. bot. Gdn Edinb.* **36**: in press.
  Includes a synopsis of British literature.
KEISSLER, K. A. von 1930. Die Flechtenparasiten. *Rabenh. Krypt.-Fl.* **8**: i – ix + 1–712.
VOUAUX, L. l'Abbé 1912–14. Synopsis des champignons parasites de lichens. *Bull. Soc. mycol. Fr.* **28**: 177–256; **29**: 33–128, 399–494; **30**: 135–198, 281–329.

Marine Fungi

JOHNSON, T. W. & SPARROW, F. K. 1961. "Fungi in Oceans and Estuaries". xxii + 668 pp. J. Cramer, Weinheim.
JONES, E. B. G., ed. 1976. "Recent Advances in Aquatic Mycology". 749 pp., illustrated. Elek Science, London.
  Includes authoritative reviews of many aspects of this subject.
KOHLMEYER, J. & KOHLMEYER, E. 1971. "Synoptic Plates of Higher Marine Fungi". 3rd edn. 88 pp. J. Cramer, Lehre.

Myxomyceticolous Fungi

ING, B. 1974. Mouldy myxomycetes. *Bull. Br. mycol. Soc.* **8:** 25–30.

Plant Pathogenic Fungi

DESCRIPTIONS OF PLANT PATHOGENIC FUNGI AND BACTERIA 1964 on. Commonwealth Mycological Institute, Kew.
 Loose-leaf detailed descriptions; 40 issued each year.
MOORE, W. C. 1959. "British Parasitic Fungi". 430 pp. Cambridge University Press, London.
PLANT PATHOLOGIST'S POCKETBOOK 1968. 267 pp. Commonwealth Mycological Institute, Kew.
REVIEW OF PLANT PATHOLOGY 1970 on. [formerly REVIEW OF APPLIED MYCOLOGY 1922–1969.] Commonwealth Mycological Institute, Kew.
 A comprehensive abstracting journal; monthly.

Predacious Fungi

COOKE, R. C. & GODFREY, B. E. S. 1964. A key to the nematode destroying fungi. *Trans. Br. mycol. Soc.* **47:** 61–74.
DOLFUS, R. P. 1946. "Parasites (animaux et végétaux) des Helminthes". 482 pp. Lechevalier, Paris.

Soil Fungi

BARRON, G. L. 1968. See p. 150.
DOMSCH, K. H. & GAMS, W. 1970. "Pilze aus Agarboden". 2nd edn. xi + 222 pp. G. Fischer, Stuttgart. English translation by H. J. Hudson 1972. Longman Group, London.
 New much extended version in preparation.
GILMAN, J. C. 1957. "A Manual of Soil Fungi". 2nd edn. xi + 450 pp. Iowa State College Press, Ames, Iowa.

Thermophilic Fungi

COONEY, D. G. & EMERSON, R. 1964. "Thermophilic Fungi". xii + 188 pp. W. H. Freeman, San Francisco & London.

MYXOMYCOTA (MYCETOZOA)

This taxon comprises plasmodial and aggregative organisms showing both fungal and protozoan affiinities. They have been included at different times in the plant, protistan, animal or fungal kingdoms, but, for convenience, are here treated as a phylum of the Fungi, with the major divisions as classes. A valuable discussion of the taxonomic position and the phylogeny of the group is given by L. S. Olive (1975 see below p. 129), who also lists the extensive literature on the biology of these organisms.

MYXOMYCETES (MYXOGASTRES)   British species 300
Plasmodial slime fungi

ALEXOPOULOS, C. J. 1973. In Ainsworth *et al.* (see p. 125) vol. 4B, pp. 39–60.
ING, B. 1965. An introduction to the study of the Myxomycetes. *News Bull. Br. mycol. Soc.* **24:** 13–21.
 Keys to genera; figures.

ING, B. 1968. "A Census Catalogue of British Myxomycetes". 24 pp. British Mycological Society, London.
    A check-list with details of British distribution by vice-county.

KRZEMIENIEWSKA, H. 1960. "Sluzowce Polski". 315 pp. Warsaw.
    Keys, descriptions; the standard work on Polish species.

LISTER, G. 1925. "Monograph of the Mycetozoa". 3rd edn. xxxii + 296 pp. British Museum (Natural History), London.
    A comprehensive account, now much out of date, but still valuable for its beautiful plates.

MARTIN, G. W. & ALEXOPOULOS, C. J. 1969. "The Myxomycetes". 561 pp., 41 col. pls. University of Iowa Press, Ames, Iowa.
    The standard world monograph, with keys and descriptions. The plates are inferior to those in Lister (1925) but the taxonomic content is of great critical value.

NANNENGA-BREMEKAMP, N. E. 1975 (1974). "De Nederlandse Myxomyceten". 440 pp. K.N.N.V., Zutphen.
    Excellent account of the Dutch species, most of which occur in Britain, and very clear illustrations of all the taxa described. Keys and full descriptions and clear diagnostic details. In Dutch.

The works listed above include the single British species of *Ceratiomyxa*, which may be placed in a separate class, CERATIOMYXOMYCETES, which has links with the next class.

PROTOSTELIOMYCETES (PROTOSTELIA)

British species 2

OLIVE, L. S. 1975. "The Mycetozoans". x + 293 pp. Academic Press, New York & London.

DICTYOSTELIOMYCETES (DICTYOSTELIA)
Cellular slime moulds

British species about 5

OLIVE, L. S. 1975. See above.

ACRASIOMYCETES (ACRASEA)
Acrasid slime moulds

British species 2

OLIVE, L. S. 1975. See above.
RAPER, K. B. 1973. In Ainsworth *et al.* (see p. 125) vol. 4B, pp. 9–36.

LABYRINTHULOMYCETES (LABYRINTHULINA)
Net plasmodial moulds

British species about 6

ARCHER, W. 1875. On *Chlamydomyxa labyrinthuloides. Q. Jl microsc. Sci., n.s.* **15**: 107–130.

GOLDSTEIN, S. 1973. Zoosporic marine fungi (Thraustochytriaceae and Dermocystidiaceae). *A. Rev. Microbiol.* **27**: 13–26.

JOHNSON, T. W. & SPARROW, F. K. 1961. "Fungi in Oceans and Estuaries". xxii + 668 pp. J. Cramer, Weinheim.

OLIVE, L. S. 1975. See above.

HYDROMYXOMYCETES
Plasmodial water moulds

British species about 4

CASH, J. & HOPKINSON, J. 1905. "The British Freshwater Rhizopoda and Heliozoa". Vol. 1. Ray Society, London.
JAHN, E. 1928. Hydromyxomycetes. In "Die natürlichen Pflanzenfamilien" (A. Engler and K. Prantl, eds.), 2nd edn., vol. 2, pp. 304–339. Engelman, Leipzig.

This group is best regarded as part of the rhizopod Protozoa.

PLASMODIOPHOROMYCETES (PLASMODIOPHORINA)
Club-root fungi

British species about 10

KARLING, J. S. 1968. "The Plasmodiophorales". 2nd edn. (revised). Hafner, New York.

This group is often included as a class of Mastigomycotina (see below).

EUMYCOTA
MASTIGOMYCOTINA AND ZYGOMYCOTINA
(Phycomycetes)
GENERAL

FITZPATRICK, H. M. 1930. "The Lower Fungi, Phycomycetes". xi + 331 pp. McGraw-Hill, New York & London.
RAMSBOTTOM, J. 1916. A list of British Phycomycetes. *Trans. Br. mycol. Soc.* **5:** 301–317.
SPARROW, F. K. 1960. "Aquatic Phycomycetes". 2nd edn. 1187 pp. University of Michigan Press, Ann Arbor.
SPARROW, F. K. 1973. In Ainsworth *et al.* (see p. 125) vol. 4B, pp. 61–73.

CHYTRIDIOMYCETES

CANTER H. M. 1946–71. Studies on British chytrids I-XXXI. *Trans. Br. mycol. Soc.* **29–56.**
CANTER, H. M. 1953. Annotated list of British aquatic chytrids. *Trans. Br. mycol. Soc.* **36:** 278–303.
GOLDSTEIN, S. 1973. Zoosporic marine fungi (Thraustochytriaceae and Dermocystidiaceae). *A. Rev. Microbiol.* **27:** 13–26.
KARLING, J. S. 1942. "The Simple Holocarpic Biflagellate Phycomycetes". x + 123 pp. New York.
KARLING, J. S. 1964. "*Synchytrium*". xviii + 470 pp. Academic Press, New York & London.
PERROT, P. E. T. 1955. The genus *Monoblepharis*. *Trans. Br. mycol. Soc.* **38:** 247–282.
SPARROW, F. K. 1973. In Ainsworth *et al.* (see p. 125) vol. 4B, pp. 85–110.

OOMYCETES

CEJP, K. 1959. Oomycetes I. *Flora ČSR* **2B.** 475 pp. Czechoslovak Academy of Sciences, Prague.

COKER, W. C. 1923. "The Saprolegniaceae with notes on other Water Molds". 201 pp. University of North Carolina Press, Chapel Hill. Reprint 1968. J. Cramer, Lehre.
DICK, M. W. 1973. In Ainsworth *et al.* (see p.125) vol. 4B, pp. 113–158.
GÄUMANN, E. 1923. Beiträge zur einer Monographie der Gattung *Peronospora*. *Beitr. Kryptfl. schweiz.* **5**(4): 1–360.
GUSTAVSSON, A. 1959. Studies on Nordic *Peronospora*'s I. Taxonomic revision. *Op. bot. Soc. bot. Lund* **3**(1), 1–271.
JOHNSON, T. W. 1956. "The Genus *Achlya:* Morphology and Taxonomy". 180 pp. University of Michigan Press, Ann Arbor.
SCOTT, W. S. 1961. A monograph of the genus *Aphanomyces*. *Tech. Bull. Va agric. Exp. Stn* **151**: 1–95.
SEYMOUR, R. L. 1970. The genus *Saprolegnia*. *Nova Hedwigia* **19**: 1–160.
WATERHOUSE, G. M. 1968. The genus *Pythium* Pringsheim. *Mycol. Papers* **110**: 1–203.
WATERHOUSE, G. M. 1970. The genus *Phytophthora* de Bary. 2nd edn. *Mycol. Papers* **122**: 1–59.
WATERHOUSE, G. M. 1973. In Ainsworth *et al.* (see p. 125) vol. 4B, pp. 165–183.

TRICHOMYCETES

LICHTWARDT, R. W. 1973. In Ainsworth *et al.* (see p. 125) vol. 4B, pp. 237–243.

ZYGOMYCETES

BENJAMIN, R. K. 1959–65. The merosporangiferous Mucorales. *Aliso* **4**: 321–433; **5**: 11–19, 273–322; **6**: 1–10. Reprint as one volume 1967. J. Cramer, Lehre.
GERDEMANN, J. L. & TRAPPE, J. M. 1974. The Endogonaceae in the Pacific North West. *Mycologia, Mem.* **5**: 1–76.
HESSELTINE, C. W. 1955. Genera of Mucorales with notes on their synonymy. *Mycologia* **47**: 344–363.
HESSELTINE, C. W. & ELLIS, J. J. 1973. In Ainsworth *et al.* (see p. 125) vol. 4B, pp. 187–217.
INUI, T., TAKEDA, Y. & IIZUKA, N. 1965. Taxonomical studies on the genus *Rhizopus*. *J. gen. appl. Microbiol.* **11**: Suppl., 122 pp.
LENDNER, A. 1908. "Les Mucorinées de la Suisse". 180 pp. K.-J. Wyss, Berne.
MIL'KO, A. A. 1974. "Opredelitel' Mukoral'nykh Gribov". 303 pp. 'Naukova Dumka, Kiev.
NAUMOV, N. A. 1939. "Clés des Mucorinées (Mucorales)". 137 + xxxvi pp. P. Lechevalier, Paris.
NOTTEBROCK, H., SCHOLER, H. J. & WALL, M. 1974. Taxonomy and identification of mucormycosis-causing fungi. I. Synonymity of *Absidia ramosa* with *Absidia corymbifera*. *Sabouraudia* **12**: 64–74.
SCHIPPER, M. A. A. 1973. A study on variability in *Mucor hiemalis* and related species. *Stud. mycol., Baarn* **5**: 1–40.
SCHIPPER, M. A. A. 1975. On *Mucor mucedo, Mucor flavus* and related species. *Stud. mycol., Baarn* **10**: 1–33.
SCHIPPER, M. A. A. 1976. On *Mucor circinelloides, Mucor racemosus* and related species. *Stud. mycol., Baarn* **12**: 1–40.
WATERHOUSE, G. M. 1973. In Ainsworth *et al.* (see p. 125) vol. 4B, pp. 219–229.
WATERHOUSE, G. M. 1975. Key to the species *Entomophthora*. *Bull. Br. mycol. Soc.* **9**: 15–41.
ZYCHA, H., SIEPMANN, R. & LINNEMANN, G. 1970 (1969). "Mucorales". 355 pp. J. Cramer, Lehre.

ASCOMYCOTINA (ASCOMYCETES)

GENERAL

DENNIS, R. W. G. 1968. "British Ascomycetes". xxxii + 456 pp. J. Cramer, Lehre.
   The standard text with descriptions, keys to genera, and 71 plates (40 coloured); should be consulted for all groups of Ascomycotina; a new edition is promised for 1977.

MOSER, M. 1963. "Kleine Kryptogamenflora". Vol. 2a. "Ascomyceten". 147 pp. G. Fischer, Stuttgart.
   Keys, some line drawings.

HEMIASCOMYCETES

Ascoideales

BATRA, L. R. 1973. "Nematosporaceae (Hemiascomycetidae): Taxonomy, pathogenicity, distribution, and vector relations". Technical Bulletin No. 1469. 71 pp. U.S. Department of Agriculture, Washington DC.

Endomycetales (Yeasts, etc.)

VON ARX, J. A., RODRIGUES DE MIRANDA, L., SMITH, M. T. & YARROW, D. 1977. The genera of yeasts and yeast-like fungi. *Stud. mycol., Baarn* **14**: 1–42.

BARNETT, J. A. & PANKHURST, R. J. 1974. "A New Key to the Yeasts". 273 pp. North Holland Publishing, Amsterdam & London.
   Keys based mainly on cultural and physiological characters; to be used with the following. Includes descriptions since Lodder.

KREGER-VAN RIJ, N. J. W. 1973. In Ainsworth *et al.* (see p. 125) vol. 4A, pp. 11–32.

LODDER, J., ed. 1970. "The Yeasts: a Taxonomic Study". 2 vols. 1385 pp. North Holland Publishing, Amsterdam.
   The standard work.

Protomycetales

REDDY, M. S. & KRAMER, C. L. 1975. A taxonomic revision of the Protomycetales. *Mycotaxon* **3**: 1–50.

Taphrinales

HENDERSON, D. M. 1954. The genus *Taphrina* in Scotland. *Notes R. bot. Gdn Edinb.* **21**: 165–180.

MIX, A. J. 1949. A monograph of the genus *Taphrina*. *Univ. Kansas Sci. Bull.* **33**: 1–167. Reprint 1968. J. Cramer, Lehre.

PLECTOMYCETES

APINIS, A. E. 1964. Revision of British Gymnoascaceae. *Mycol. Papers* **96**: 1–56.

BOOTH, C. 1961. Studies of Pyrenomycetes VI. *Thielavia* with notes on some allied genera. *Mycol. Papers* **83**: 1–15.

DODGE, C. W. 1929. The higher Plectascales. *Annls mycol.* **27**: 145–184.

FENNELL, D. I. 1973. In Ainsworth *et al.* (see p. 125) vol. 4A, pp. 45–68.

MALLOCH, D. & CAIN, R. F. 1970. Five new genera in the new family Pseudeurotiaceae. *Can. J. Bot.* **48**: 1815–25.

MALLOCH, D. & CAIN, R. F. 1974. The Trichocomaceae (Ascomycetes): synonyms in recent publications. *Can. J. Bot.* **51**: 1647–1648.

PITT, J. I. 1974. A synoptic key to the genus *Eupenicillium* and to sclerotigenic *Penicillium* species. *Can. J. Bot.* **52**: 2231-2236.
STOLK, A. C. & SAMSON, E. A. 1972. The genus *Talaromyces*. *Stud. mycol., Baarn* **2**: 1-65.

PYRENOMYCETES

GENERAL

VON ARX, J. A. & MÜLLER, E. 1954. Die Gattungen der amerosporen Pyrenomyceten. *Beitr. Kryptfl. Schweiz* **11**(1): 1-434.
BARR, M. E. 1959. Northern Pyrenomycetes I. Canadian eastern arctic. *Contr. Inst. bot. Univ. Montreal* **73**: 1-98.
BISBY, G. R. & MASON, E. W. 1940. List of Pyrenomycetes recorded for Britain. *Trans. Br. mycol. Soc.* **24**: 127-243.
BUTTERFILL, G. 1969. "Keys to the Genera of amerospored and didymospored Pyrenomycetes". 53 pp. Commonwealth Mycological Institute, Kew.
English translation of keys in v. Arx & Müller 1954 and Müller & v. Arx 1962.
MÜLLER, E., & VON ARX, J. A. 1962. Die Gattungen der didymosporen Pyrenomyceten. *Beitr. Kryptfl. Schweiz* **11**(2): 1-922.
MÜLLER, E. & VON ARX, J. A. 1973. In Ainsworth *et al.* (see p. 125) vol. 4A, pp. 87-132.
MUNK, A. 1957. Danish Pyrenomycetes. *Dansk bot. Ark.* **17**: 1-491.

Coronophorales

FITZPATRICK, H. M. 1923. Monograph of the *Nitschkiae*. *Mycologia* **15**: 23-67.
NANNFELDT, J. A. 1975. Stray studies in the Coronophorales (Pyrenomycetes) 4-8. *Svensk bot. Tidskr.* **69**: 289-335.

Erysiphales (Powdery mildews)

BLUMER, S. 1967. "Echte Mehltaupilze (Erysiphaceae). Ein Bestimmungsbuch für die in Europa vorkommenden Arten". 436 pp. G. Fischer, Jena
JUNELL, L. 1967. Erysiphaceae of Sweden. *Symb. bot. upsal.* **19**(1): 1-117.
YARWOOD, C. E. 1973. In Ainsworth *et al.* (see p. 125) vol. 4A, pp. 71-86.

Hypocreales

ARNOLD, G. R. W. 1976. "Internationale Bibliographie der Hypomycetaceae". Bibliographische Mitteilungen der Universität Jena No. 25. 129 pp. Jena.
Bibliography 595 papers with species index.
BOOTH, C. 1959. Studies of Pyrenomycetes: IV. *Nectria* (Part I). *Mycol. Papers* **73**: 1-115.
DOI, Y. 1972. Revision of the Hypocreales with cultural observations IV. The genus *Hypocrea* and its allies in Japan. *Bull. natn. Sci. Mus., Tokyo* **15**: 649-751.
KOBAYASI, Y. 1941. The genus *Cordyceps* and its allies. *Sci. Rept. Tokyo Bunrika Daighaku* B **84**: 53-260.
PERRIN, R. 1976. Clef de détermination des *Nectria* d'Europe. *Bull. Soc. mycol. Fr.* **92**: 335-347.
PETCH, T. 1938. British Hypocreales. *Trans. Br. mycol. Soc.* **21**: 243-305.
ROGERSON, C. T. 1971. The Hypocrealan fungi. *Mycologia* **62**: 865-910.

Sphaeriales

AMES, L. M. 1963 (1961). "A Monograph of the Chaetomiaceae". U.S. Army Research and Development Series No. 2. ix + 125 pp. U.S. Army, Washington. Reprint 1969. J. Cramer, Lehre.

VON ARX, J. A. 1975. On *Thielavia* and some similar genera of Ascomycetes. *Stud. mycol., Baarn* **8**: 1–28.
BARRON, G. L., CAIN, R. F. & GILMAN, J. C. 1961. The genus *Microascus*. *Can. J. Bot.* **39**: 1609–1631.
CAILLEUX, R. 1971. Recherches sur la mycoflore coprophile Centrafricaine. Les genres *Sordaria, Gelasinospora, Bombardia*. *Bull. Soc. mycol. Fr.* **87**: 461–626.
CAIN, R. F. 1934. Studies of coprophilous Sphaeriales in Ontario. *Univ. Toronto Stud., biol. ser.* **38**: 1–126.
CROXALL, H. E. 1950. Studies of British Pyrenomycetes III. The British species of the genus *Diatrypella*. *Trans. Br. mycol. Soc.* **33**: 45–73.
DOGUET, G. 1955. Le genre *Melanospora*. *Botaniste* **39**: 1–313.
FRANCIS, S. M. 1975. *Anthostomella* Sacc. (Part I). *Mycol. Papers* **139**: 1–97.
HAWKSWORTH, D. L. & WELLS, H. 1973. Ornamentation on the terminal hairs in *Chaetomium* Kunze ex Fr. and some allied genera. *Mycol. Papers* **134**: 1–24.
Includes useful bibliography on the Chaetomiaceae *s. lat.*
HUNT, J. 1956. Taxonomy of the genus *Ceratocystis*. *Lloydia* **19**: 1–58.
LUNDQVIST, N. 1972. Nordic Sordariaceae *s. lat*. *Symb. bot. upsal.* **20**(1): 1–374.
MALLOCH, D. 1970. New concepts in the Microascaceae illustrated by two new species. *Mycologia* **62**: 727–740.
MALLOCH, D. & CAIN, R. F. 1973. The genus *Thielavia*. *Mycologia* **65**: 1055–1077.
MILLER, J. H. 1961. "A Monograph of the World Species of *Hypoxylon*". xii + 158 pp. University of Georgia Press, Athens.
MIRZA, J. H. & CAIN, R. F. 1969. Revision of the genus *Podospora*. *Can. J. Bot.* **47**: 1999–2048.
OLCHOWECKI, A. & REID, J. 1974. Taxonomy of the genus *Ceratocystis* in Manitoba. *Can. J. Bot.* **52**: 1675–1711.
Includes keys to the world's known species.
SCHRANTZ, J. P. 1960. Recherches sur les Pyrénomycètes de l'ordre des Diatrypales sensu Chadefaud. *Bull. Soc. mycol. Fr.* **76**: 305–407.
WEHMEYER, L. E. 1933. "The Genus *Diaporthe* Nitschke and its Segregates". x + 349 pp. University of Michigan Press, Ann Arbor.
WEHMEYER, L. E. 1941. "A Revision of *Melanconis, Pseudovalsa, Prosthecium* and *Titania*". viii + 162 pp. University of Michigan Press, Ann Arbor.
WHALLEY, A. J. S. & GREENHALGH, G. N. 1973. Numerical taxonomy of *Hypoxylon* II. A key for the identification of British species of *Hypoxylon*. *Trans. Br. mycol. Soc.* **61**: 455–459.

DISCOMYCETES

GENERAL

BOUDIER, E. 1907. "Histoire et Classification des Discomycètes d'Europe". 223 pp. Klincksieck, Paris. Reprint 1968. Asher, Amsterdam.
ERIKSSON, B. 1970. On ascomycetes on Diapensiales and Ericales in Fennoscandia I. Discomycetes. *Symb. bot. upsal.* **19**(4): 1–71.
KIMBROUGH, J. W. 1970. Current trends in the classification of the Discomycetes. *Bot. Rev.* **36**: 91–161.
KORF, R. P. 1973. In Ainsworth *et al.* (see p. 125) vol. 4A, pp. 249–319.
LE GAL, M. 1973. "Les Discomycètes de Madagascar". 465 pp. Muséum National d'Histoire Naturelle, Paris.
NANNFELDT, J. A. 1932. Studien über die Morphologie und Systematik der nicht-lichenisierten inoperculaten Discomyceten. *Nova Acta R. Soc. scient. upsal., ser. 4*, **8**(2): 1–368.

RAMSBOTTOM, J. & BALFOUR-BROWNE, F. L. 1951. List of Discomycetes recorded for Britain. *Trans. Br. mycol. Soc.* **34:** 38–137.
VELENOVSKÝ, J. 1934. "Monographia Discomycetum Bohemiae". 2 vols. 436 pp. Prague.
The second volume comprises 31 plates.

Helotiales

AEBI, B. 1972. Untersuchungen über Discomyceten der Gruppe *Tapesia-Trichobelonium*. *Nova Hedwigia* **23:** 49–112.
BUCKWALD, N. F. 1947. Sclerotiniaceae Daniae. *Friesia* **3:** 235–330.
DENNIS, R. W. G. 1949. A revision of the British Hyaloscyphaceae with notes on related European species. *Mycol. Papers* **32:** 1–97.
DENNIS, R. W. G. 1956. A revision of the British Helotiaceae in the herbarium of the Royal Botanic Gardens, Kew, with notes on related European species. *Mycol. Papers* **62:** 1–216.
DENNIS R. W. G. 1964. Remarks on the genus *Hymenoscyphus* S. F. Gray. *Persoonia* **3:** 29–80.
ECKBLAD, F.-E. 1963. Contributions to the Geoglossaceae of Norway. *Nytt Mag. Bot.* **10:** 137–158.
GREMMEN, J. 1954–57. Taxonomic notes on Mollisiaceous fungi I–V. *Fungus* **24:** 1–8; **25:** 1–12; **26:** 28–31, 32–37; **27:** 30–33.
JOHANSEN, G. 1949. The Danish species of the genus *Pezicula*. *Dansk bot. Ark.* **13**(3): 1–26.
KORF, R. P. 1951. A monograph of the Arachnopezizeae. *Lloydia* **14:** 129–180.
RAITVIÍR, A. 1970. Synopsis of the Hyaloscyphaceae. 115 pp. [Scripta Mycologica no. 1]. Academy of Sciences of the Estonian S.S.R., Tartu.
SCHÜEPP, H. 1959. Untersuchungen über Pseudopezizoideae sensu Nannfeldt. *Phytopath. Z.* **36:** 213–269.
SVRČEK, M. 1954. Revise Velenovského druhů rodu *Orbilia* (Discomycetes). *Sb. nár. mus. Praze* **10B**(1): 1–23.

Pezizales

DISSING, H. 1966. The genus *Helvella* in Europe. *Dansk bot. Ark.* **25:** 1–172.
ECKBLAD, F.-E. 1968. The genera of the operculate Discomycetes. *Nytt Mag. Bot.* **15:** 1–191.
KORF, R. 1972. Synoptic key to the genera of the Pezizales. *Mycologia* **64:** 937–994.
MAAS GEESTERANUS, R. A. 1967–69. De fungi van Nederland II. Pezizales I–II. *Wet. Meded. K. ned. natuurh. Vereen.* **69:** 1–72; **80:** 1–84.
RIFAI, M. A. 1968. The Australian Pezizales in the herbarium of the Royal Botanic Gardens, Kew. *Verh. K. ned. Akad. Wet.*, III, **57**(3): 1–295.
SVRČEK, M. 1948. Ceské druhy podceledi Lachneoideae (cel. Pezizaceae). *Sb. nár. mus. Praze* **4B**(6): 1–95. In English.
VAN BRUMMELEN, J. 1967. A world monograph of the genera *Ascobolus* and *Saccobolus*. *Persoonia, Suppl.* **1:** 1–260.

Phacidiales

DARKER, G. D. 1967. A revision of the genera of the Hypodermataceae. *Can. J. Bot.* **45:** 1399–1444.
TEHON, L. R. 1935. A monographic rearrangement of *Lophodermium*. *Ill. Biol. Monogr.* **13**(4): 1–151.
TERRIER, C.-E. 1942. Essai sur la systématique des Phacidiales (Fr.) sensu Nannfeldt (1932). *Beitr. Kryptfl. Schweiz* **9**(2): 1–99.

Tuberales

ECKBLAD, F.-E. 1954. Studies in the hypogean fungi of Norway I. *Endogone* and Tuberales. *Nytt Mag. Bot.* **3**: 35–41.
ECKBLAD, F.-E. 1962. Studies in the hypogean fungi of Norway II. Revision of the genus *Elaphomyces*. *Nytt Mag. Bot.* **9**: 199–210.
HAWKER, L. E. 1954. See p. 127 above.
HAWKER, L. E. 1974. See p. 127 above.
LANGE, M. 1956. Danish hypogeous macromycetes. *Dansk bot. Ark.* **16**: 1–84.

LABOULBENIOMYCETES

BALAZUC, J. 1971. Bibliographie des Laboulbeniales. *Bull. mens. Soc. linn. Lyon* **40**: 134–149.
BALAZUC, J. 1973–74. Laboulbeniales de France. *Bull. mens. Soc. linn. Lyon* **42**: 244–256, 280–285; **43**: 12–21, 57–64, 73–79, 252–262, 295–315, 346–368.
BENJAMIN, R. K. 1973. In Ainsworth *et al.* (see p. 125) vol. 4A, pp. 223–246.
SUGIYAMA, K. 1973. Species and genera of the Laboulbeniales (Ascomycetes) in Japan. *Ginkgoana* **2**: 1–97.
THAXTER, R. 1896–1931. Contribution towards a monograph of the Laboulbeniaceae. Parts I-V. *Mem. Am. Acad. Arts Sci.* **12**: 187–429; **13**: 217–469; **14**: 309–426; **15**: 427–580; **16**: 1–435. Reprint in 2 vols. (with valuable new introduction and supplement by R.K. Benjamin) 1971. J. Cramer, Lehre.

LOCULOASCOMYCETES

See also under Pyrenomycetes (General)

AHMED, S. I. & CAIN, R. F. 1972. Revision of the genera *Sporormia* and *Sporormiella*. *Can. J. Bot.* **50**: 419–477.
VON ARX, J. A. 1959. Beiträge zur Kenntnis der Gattung *Mycosphaerella*. *Sydowia* **3**: 22–100.
VON ARX, J. A. & MÜLLER, E. 1975. A re-evaluation of the bitunicate Ascomycetes with keys to families and genera. *Stud. mycol., Baarn* **9**: 1–159.
BARR, M. E. 1968. The Venturiaceae in North America. *Can. J. Bot.* **46**: 799–864.
BARR, M. E. 1972. Preliminary studies on the Dothideales in temperate North America. *Contr. Univ. Mich. Herb.* **9**: 523–638.
BATISTA, A. C. 1959. Monografia dos fungos Micropeltaceae. *Publs. Inst. Mic. Recife* **56**: 1–520.
BISBY, G. R. 1944. British Hysteriales. *Trans. Br. mycol. Soc.* **27**: 20–28.
BOSE, S. K. 1961. Studies on *Massarina* Sacc. and related genera. *Phytopath. Z.* **41**: 121–213.
CHESTERS, C. G. C. & BELL, A. 1970. Studies in the Lophiostomataceae Sacc. *Mycol. Papers* **120**: 1–55.
ELLIS, J. P. 1976. British *Microthyrium* species and similar fungi. *Trans. Br. mycol. Soc.* **67**: 381–394.
HOLM, L. 1957. Études taxonomiques sur les Pléosporacées. *Symb. bot. upsal.* **14**(3): 1–188.
HUGHES, S. J. 1976. Sooty moulds. *Mycologia* **68**: 693–820.
LUCAS, M. T. & WEBSTER, J. 1967. Conidial states of British species of *Leptosphaeria*. *Trans. Br. mycol. Soc.* **50**: 85–121.
LUTTRELL, E. S. 1951. Taxonomy of the Pyrenomycetes. *Univ. Missouri Stud.* **24**: 1–120. Reprint 1967. J. Cramer, Lehre.
LUTTRELL, E. S. 1973. In Ainsworth *et al.* (see p. 125) vol. 4A, pp. 135–219.

WEBSTER, J. 1952–57. Graminicolous Pyrenomycetes III-VI. *Trans. Br. mycol. Soc.* **34:** 318–321; **35:** 208–214; **38:** 347–365; **40:** 509–522.
WEHMEYER, L. E. 1961. "A World Monograph of the genus *Pleospora* and its Segregates". xi + 451 pp. University of Michigan Press, Ann Arbor.
ZOGG, H. 1962. Die Hysteriaceae s. str. und Lophiaceae. *Beitr. Kryptfl. Schweiz* **11**(3): 1–190.

BASIDIOMYCOTINA (BASIDIOMYCETES)

TELIOMYCETES

GENERAL

BLUMER, S. 1963. "Rost- und Brandpilze auf Kulturpflanzen". 379 pp. G. Fischer, Jena.

Uredinales (Rusts)

CUMMINS, C. B. 1959. "Illustrated Genera of Rust Fungi". ii + 131 pp. Burgess Publishing, Minneapolis.
CUMMINS, C. B. 1971. "The Rust Fungi of Cereals, Grasses and Bamboos". xv + 570 pp. Springer, Berlin.
GÄUMANN, E. 1959. Die Rostpilze Mitteleuropas. *Beitr. Kryptfl. Schweiz* **12:** 1–1407.
KERN, F. D. 1973. "A Revised Taxonomic Account of *Gymnosporangium*". 134 pp. Pennsylvania State University Press, University Park and London.
LAUNDON, G. F. 1973. In Ainsworth *et al.* (see p. 125) vol. 4B, pp. 247–279.
WILSON, M. & HENDERSON, D. M. 1966. "British Rust Fungi". 384 pp. Cambridge University Press, London.
The standard British work.

Ustilaginales (Smuts)

AINSWORTH, G. C. & SAMPSON, K. 1950. "The British Smut Fungi". 137 pp. Commonwealth Mycological Institute, Kew.
The standard British work.
DURÁN, R. 1973. In Ainsworth *et al.* (see p. 125) vol. 4B, pp. 281–300.
DURÁN, R. & FISCHER, W. G. 1961. "The Genus *Tilletia*". v + 138 pp. Washington State University.
LINDEBERG, B. 1959. Ustilaginales of Sweden. *Symb. bot. upsal.* **16**(2): 1–175.
ZUNDEL, G. L. 1953. "The Ustilaginales of the World". xi + 410 pp. Pennsylvania State College, School of Agriculture, Philadelphia.

HYMENOMYCETES

GENERAL

HAAS, H. 1969. "The Young Specialist Looks at Fungi". 240 pp. Burke Publishing.
HEIM, R. 1969. "Les Champignons d'Europe". 2nd edn. 680 pp. Boubée & Cie, Paris.
LANGE, M. & HORA, F. B. 1965. "Collins' Guide to Mushrooms & Toadstools". 2nd edn. 257 pp., col. pls. Collins, London.
MICHAEL, E. & HENNIG, B. 1958–70. "Handbuch für Pilzfreunde. 5 vols. Many col. pls. G. Fisher, Jena.
MOSER, M. 1967. Die Röhrlinge und Blätterpilze (Agaricales). In "Kleine Kryptogamenflora". 2nd edn. (H. Gams, ed.) **2b**(2): 1–443. G. Fischer, Stuttgart.

REID, D. A. 1955–75. New or interesting records of British Hymenomycetes I-VI. *Trans. Br. mycol. Soc.* **38**: 387–399; **41**: 419–445; **48**: 513–537; **55**: 413–441; *Persoonia* **7**: 293–303; *Beih. Nova Hedwigia* **51**: 199–206.

RINALDI, A. & TYNDALO, V. 1974. "Mushrooms and other Fungi". 333 pp. Hamlyn, London.
    Well illustrated in colour; valuable for all macromycetes; first published in Italian in 1972.

ROMAGNESI, H. 1956–67. "Nouvelle Atlas des Champignons". 4 vols. Bordas, Paris.
    Also issued in 3 small volumes in 1962.

SMITH, A. H. & SHAFFER, R. L. 1964. "Keys to Genera of Higher Fungi". iv + 120 pp. University of Michigan Press, Ann Arbor.

WAKEFIELD, E. M. & DENNIS, R. W. G. 1950. "Common British Fungi". 290 pp., 111 col. pls. Gawthorn, London.
    Very valuable but long out of print; nomenclature dated.

WATLING, R. 1973. "Identification of the Larger Fungi". 218 pp. Hulton Educational, Amersham.

Agaricales

General

BRESINSKY, A. 1976. Gattungsschlüssel für Blätte- und Röhrenpilze nach mikroscopischen Merkmalen. *Beih. Z. Pilzkde* **1**: 1–42.
    Keys to genera based on microscopic characters.

COOKE, M. C. 1881–91. "Illustrations of British Fungi (Hymenomycetes)". 8 vols. Williams & Norgate, London.
    Valuable for its 1198 coloured plates; updated names are listed in *Trans. Br. mycol. Soc.* **20**: 33–95 (1936).

DENNIS, R. W. G., ORTON, P. D. & HORA, F. B. 1960. New check list of British Agarics and Boleti. *Trans. Br. mycol. Soc.* **43**, Suppl., 225 pp. Reprint 1974. J. Cramer, Lehre.

HENDERSON, D. M., ORTON, P. D. & WATLING, R. 1968. "British Fungus Flora: Agarics and Boleti. Introduction". 58 pp. H.M.S.O., Edinburgh.
    Keys to genera.

HORA, F. B. 1960. New check list of British Agarics and Boleti. Part IV. Validations, new species and critical notes. *Trans. Br. mycol. Soc.* **43**: 440–459.

KONRAD, P. & MAUBLANC, A. 1924–37. "Icones Selectae Fungorum". 6 vols. P. Lechevalier, Paris.
    Valuable for its 500 coloured plates.

KÜHNER, R. & ROMAGNESI, H. 1953. "Flore analytique des Champignons Superiéurs". 557 pp. Mason & Cie, Paris.
    The standard European flora essential to all serious students of Agaricales; 5 supplements published in *Bull. Soc. mycol. Fr.* **69**: 361–388 (1953) (*Lactarius*); **71**: 169–201 (1955) (*Inocybe*); **72**: 181–249 (1956) *(Pluteus, Volvariella); Bull. Soc. nat. Oyonnax* **1954**: 73–131 (Pleurotaceae, Marasmiaceae, Tricholomataceae); **1955**: 3–95 *(Inocybe);* **1956**: 3–94 (Naucoriaceae, Coprinaceae, Lepiotaceae); *Bull. mens. Soc. linn. Lyon* **1955**: 39–54 *(Cortinarius); Revue mycol.* **19**: 3–46 (1954); **20**: 196–230 (1955) *(Rhodophyllus).*

LANGE, J. E. 1935–40. "Flora Agaricana Danica". 5 vols. Copenhagen.
    Includes 500 fine coloured plates; in English.

ORTON P. D. 1960. New check-list of British Agarics and Boleti. Part III. Notes on genera and species in the list. *Trans. Br. mycol. Soc.* **43**: 159–439.
    Includes keys to *Crepidotus, Flammulaster, Hygrophorus, Naucoria, Nolanea* and *Pluteus.*

ORTON, P. D. 1965, 1969. Notes on British Agarics II-III. *Notes R. bot. Gdn Edinb.* **26**: 43–65; **29**: 75–127.

PILÁT, A. & UŠÁK, O. 1958. "Mushrooms". 220 pp. Spring Books, London.
PILÁT, A. & UŠÁK, O. 1961. "Mushrooms and other Fungi". 160 pp. P. Nevill, London.
REID, D. A. 1966–72. Coloured illustrations [icones] of rare and interesting fungi. Parts 1–5. *Nova Hedwigia, Suppls.*
RICKEN, A. 1910–15. "Die Blätterpilze (Agaricaceae)". 2 vols. T. O. Weigel, Leipzig.
SINGER, R. 1975. "The Agaricales in Modern Taxonomy". 3rd edn. 912 pp. J. Cramer, Vaduz. Specialist use only.
SMITH, A. H. 1973. In Ainsworth *et al.* (see p. 125) vol. 4B, pp. 421–450.
WATLING, R. 1967. Keys to the families and genera of agarics known to contain species with brown or ochre spore prints. *Bull. Br. mycol. Soc.* **1**: 65–80.

Monographs

Note. Up to date keys to British species of treated genera are included in the series of papers by D. N. PEGLER & T. W. K. YOUNG on basidiospore form in *Kew Bull.* **26**: 499–537 (1972) *(Inocybe);* **27**: 483–500 (1972) *(Galerina* and *Kuehneromyces);* **27**: 311–323 (1972) *(Crepidotus);* **28**: 365–379 (1973) (Leucopaxilleae); **29**: 659–667 (1974) *(Lepista* and *Ripartites);* **30**: 19–32 (1975) *(Clitopilus, Rhodocybe* and *Rhodotus);* **30**: 225–240 (1975) *(Naucoria, Phaeogalera* and *Simocybe).*

Agaricus (Psalliota)

BOHUS, G. 1961–76. *Agaricus [Psalliota]* Studies I-VI. *Annls hist.-nat. Mus. natn. hung.* **53**: 187–195; **61**: 151–157; **63**: 78–82; **66**: 17–85; **67**: 37–40; **68**: 45–49.
ESSETTE, H. 1964. "Les Psalliotes". Atlas mycologique No. **1**. 136 pp. P. Lechevalier, Paris.
KÜHNER, R. 1974. Agaricales de la zone alpine. Genre *Agaricus. Trav. scient. Parc natn. Vanoise* **5**: 131–147.
MÖLLER, F. H. 1950–52. Danish *Psalliota* species. *Friesia* **4**: 1–60, 135–220.
PILÁT, A. 1951. The Bohemian species of the genus *Agaricus. Acta Mus. nat. Prague* **7B**(1): 1–42.

Amanita

BAS, C. 1962. Het geslacht *Amanita* in Nederland I-II. *Coolia* **9**: 40–44, 57–59.
BAS, C. 1969. Morphology and subdivision of *Amanita* and a monograph of its section *Lepidella. Persoonia* **5**: 285–579.
HEINEMANN, P. 1964. Les Amanitées. *Naturalistes belg.* **45**: 1–22.
JOLY, P. 1967. Clé des principales Amanites de la flore française. *Revue mycol.* **32**: 162–175.
PARROT, A. G. 1960. "Amanites de sud-ouest de la France". 73 pp. Centre d'Études et de Recherches Scientifiques, Biarritz.

Boletus s. lat.

BLUM, J. 1962. "Les Bolets". Études mycologiques No. **1**. 168 pp. P. Lechevalier, Paris.
HEINEMANN, P. 1961. Les Boletinées. *Naturalistes belg.* **42**: 333–362.
LECLAIR, A. & ESSETTE, H. 1968. "Les Bolets". 148 pp. P. Lechevalier, Paris.
PILÁT, A. & DERMEK, A. 1974. "Hríbovite Huby". 207 pp., 103 col. pls. Slovenskj Akademia, Bratislava.
SINGER, R. 1965–67. "Die Röhrlinge". 2 vols. J. Klinkhardt, Bad Heilbrunn.
WATLING, R. 1970. "British Fungus Flora. Part 1. Boletaceae: Gomphidiaceae: Paxillaceae". 125 pp. H.M.S.O., Edinburgh.

Chroogomphus

MILLER, O. K. 1964. Monograph of *Chroogomphus* (Gomphidiaceae). *Mycologia* **56:** 526–549.

MILLER, O. K. 1970. A new *Chroogomphus* with loculate hymenium and a revised key to the section *Floccigomphus*. *Mycologia* **62:** 831–836.

Cantharellus s. lat.

CORNER, E. J. H. 1966. "A Monograph of Cantharelloid Fungi". 255 pp. Oxford University Press, London.

PERREAU, J. 1970. Chanterelles et craterelles. *Revue mycol.* **35:** 280–286.

Clitocybe

HARMAJA, H. 1969. The genus *Clitocybe* (Agaricales) in Fennoscandia. *Karstenia* **10:** 5–168.

Conocybe

kits van waveren, e. 1970. The genus *Conocybe* subgenus *Pholiotina* I. The European annulate species. *Persoonia* **6:** 119–165.

KÜHNER, R. 1935. "Le Genre *Galera*". Encyclopédie mycologiques No. 7. 240 pp. P. Lechevalier, Paris.

WATLING, R. 1971. The genus *Conocybe* subgen. *Pholiotina* II. Some European exannulate species and North American annulate species. *Persoonia* **6:** 313–339.

Coprinus

KITS VAN WAVEREN, E. 1968. The "*stercorarius* group" of the genus *Coprinus*. *Persoonia* **5:** 131–176.

LANGE, M. 1952. Species concept in the genus *Coprinus*. *Dansk bot. Archiv* **14:** 1–164.

LANGE, M. & SMITH, A. H. 1953. The *Coprinus ephemerus* group. *Mycologia* **45:** 747–780.

LOCQUIN, M. 1955. Recherches sur les Coprines. *Bull. Soc. mycol. Fr.* **71:** 5–18.

ORTON, P. D. 1957. Observations on the genus *Coprinus*. *Trans. Br. mycol. Soc.* **40:** 263–276.

ORTON, P. D. 1972. Notes on British Agarics IV. *Notes R. bot. Gdn Edinb.* **32:** 135–150.

WATLING, R. 1967–72. Notes on some British Agarics I-III. *Notes R. bot. Gdn Edinb.* **28:** 39–56; **31:** 359–364; **32:** 127–133.

Cortinarius

MOSER, M. 1960. "Die Gattung *Phlegmacium*". 442 pp. J. Klinkardt, Bad Heilbrunn.

ORTON, P. D. 1955, 1958. *Cortinarius* I-II. *Naturalist, Hull, Suppl.* 149 pp.

Crepidotus

HESLER, L. R. & SMITH, A. H. 1965. "North American species of *Crepidotus*". 168 pp. Hafner, New York.

PILÁT, A. 1948. "Monographie des Espèces Européenes du genre *Crepidotus* Fr." Atlas des Champignons de l'Europe No. 6. 84 pp. Prague.

Cystoderma

HEINEMANN, P. & THOEN, D. 1973. Observations sur le genre *Cystoderma*. *Bull. Soc. mycol. Fr.* **89:** 5–34.

SMITH, A. H. & SINGER, R. 1945. A monograph of the genus *Cystoderma*. *Pap. Mich. Acad. Sci.* **30:** 71–124.

THOEN, D. 1967. Les Cystodermes. *Naturalistes belg.* **48:** 285–297.

Galerina s. lat.

KÜHNER, R. 1935. See p. 140 above.
KÜHNER, R. 1972. Agaricales de la zone alpine. Genre *Galerina* Earle. *Bull. Soc. mycol. Fr.* **88:** 41–118.
KÜHNER, R. 1972. Agaricales de la zone alpine. Genre *Galera* Earle et *Phaeogalera* gen. nov. *Bull. Soc. mycol. Fr.* **88:** 119–153.
SMITH, A. H. & SINGER, R. 1964. "A Monograph of the Genus *Galerina*". 384 pp. Hafner, New York and London.

Gerronema

SINGER, R. 1964. Die Gattung *Gerronema*. *Nova Hedwigia* **7:** 52–92.

Gomphidius

MILLER, O. K. 1971. The genus *Gomphidius* with a revised description of the Gomphidiaceae and a key to the genera. *Mycologia* **63:** 1129–1163.

Hebeloma

BOHUS, G. 1972. *Hebeloma* studies I. *Annls hist.-nat. Mus. natn. hung.* **64:** 71–78.
BRUCHET, G. 1970. Contribution à l'étude de genre *Hebeloma* (Fr.) Kummer; partie spéciale. *Bull. mens. Soc. linn. Lyon* **39:** Suppl. **6:** 132 pp.
MOSER, M. 1970. Beiträge zur Kenntnis der Gattung *Hebeloma*. *Z. Pilzk.* **36:** 61–75.

Hygrophorus s. lat.

BON, M. 1974. Hygrophores du centre-est de la France étudiés au salon du Museum 1971. *Bull. mens. Soc. linn. Lyon* **43:** 333–343.
BON, M. 1976. Clé monographique des Hygrophoraceae Roze. *Docums mycol.* **7:** 1–24.
HESLER, L. R. & SMITH, A. H. 1963. "North American species of *Hygrophorus*". 416 pp. University of Tennessee Press, Knoxville.
KÜHNER, R. 1976. Agaricales de la zone alpine. Genre *Hygrocybe* (Fr.) Kummer. *Bull. Soc. mycol. Fr.* **92:** 455–515.
MOSER, M. 1967. Beitrag zur Kenntnis verschiedener Hygrophoreen. *Z. Pilzk.* **33:** 1–21.

Inocybe

HEIM, R. 1931. "Le Genre *Inocybe*". Encyclopédie mycologique No. 1. 430 pp. P. Lechevalier, Paris.
PEARSON, A. A. 1954. The genus *Inocybe*. *Naturalist, Hull* **1954:** 117–140.
STANGL, J. 1971–74. Über einige Risspilze Sudbayerns. I-II. *Z. Pilzkde* **37:** 19–32; **39:** 191–202.
STANGL, J. & VESELSKÝ, J. 1971–75. Beiträge zur Kenntnis seltenerer *Inocybe*-Arten. *Česká mykol.* **25:** 1–9; **27:** 11–25; **29:** 65–78.

Lactarius

BABOS, M. 1959. Notes on occurrence in Hungary of *Lactarius* species with regard to their range in Europe. *Annls hist.-nat. Mus. natn. hung.* **51:** 171–196.
BLUM, J. 1966. Lactaires et Russules au salon du champignons de 1965. *Revue mycol.* **31:** Suppl. 85–106.
BLUM, J. 1976. "Les Lactaires". Études mycologiques No. 3. 371 pp., 94 figs., 16 col. pl. P. Lechevalier, Paris.
HEIM, R. & LECLAIR, A. 1950. Les Lactaires à lait rouge. *Revue mycol.* **15:** 65–79.
HEINEMANN, P. 1960. Les Lactaires. 2nd ed. *Naturalistes belg.* **41:** 133–156.

NEUHOFF, W. 1956. "Die Milchlinge". 248 pp. Klinkhardt, Bad Heilbrunn.
PEARSON, A. A. 1950. The genus *Lactarius*. *Naturalist, Hull* **1950**: 81–91.

Lentinellus

MILLER, O. K. & STEWART, L. 1971. The genus *Lentinellus*. *Mycologia* **63**: 333–369.

Lentinus

PILÁT, A. 1946. "Atlas de Champignons de l'Europe". Vol. 5 *"Lentinus"*. 46 pp. Prague.

Lepiota (including Leucocoprinus)

BABOS, M. 1958–74. Studies on Hungarian *Lepiota* species I-IV. *Annls nat.-hist. Mus. natn. hung.* **50**: 87–92; **53**: 195–199; **61**: 157–164; **66**: 65–75.
BON, M. & BOIFFARD, J. 1972. Lépiotes des dunes Vendéennes. *Bull. Soc. mycol. Fr.* **88**: 15–28.
BON, M. & BOIFFARD, J. 1974. Lépiotes de Vendée et de la Côte Atlantique française I. *Bull. Soc. mycol. Fr.* **90**: 287–306.
HUIJSMAN, H. S. C. 1960. Observations sur les *Lepioteae* Fayod. *Persoonia* **1**: 325–329.
LOCQUIN, M. 1951–52. Les espèces françaises du genre *Leucocoprinus*. Première partie: sectio *Procerae*. *Revue mycol.* **16**: 213–234; **17**: 47–54.
LOCQUIN, M. 1956. Quelques Lépiotes nouvelles ou critiques. *Friesia* **5**: 292–296.

Lepista

BIGELOW, H. E. & SMITH, A. H. 1969. The status of *Lepista*, a new section of *Clitocybe*. *Brittonia* **21**: 144–177.

Leptonia

LARGENT, D. L. 1977. "The genus *Leptonia* on the Pacific Coast of the United States". Bibliotheca mycologica No. 55. 286 pp., 94 figs. J. Cramer, Vaduz.
LARGENT, D. L. & BENEDICT, R. G. 1970. Studies in the Rhodophylloid fungi II. *Alboleptonia*, a new genus. *Mycologia* **62**: 437–452.

Leucopaxillus

SINGER, R. & SMITH, A. H. 1943. A monograph of the genus *Leucopaxillus* Boursier. *Pap. Mich. Acad. Sci.* **28**: 85–132.

Marasmius

GILLIAM, M. S. 1976. The genus *Marasmius* in the northeastern United States and adjacent Canada. *Mycotaxon* **4**: 1–144.

Melanoleuca

MÉTROD, G. 1948. Essai sur le genre *Melanoleuca* Patouillard emend. *Bull. Soc. mycol. Fr.* **64**: 141–165.
SINGER, R. 1935. Étude systematique sur les *Melanoleuca* d'Europe et clé des espèces observées en Catalogne. *Cavanillesia* **7**: 122–132.

Mycena

KÜHNER, R. 1938. "Le Genre *Mycena*". Encyclopédie mycologique No. 10. 710 pp. P. Lechevalier, Paris.
PEARSON, A. A. 1955. *Mycena*. *Naturalist, Hull* **1955**: 41–63.
SMITH, A. H. 1947. "North American Species of *Mycena*". 522 pp. University of Michigan Press, Ann Arbor.

Naucoria
ROMAGNESI, H. 1963. Les *Naucoria* du groupe *Centunculus (Ramicola* Velen.). *Bull. Soc. mycol. Fr.* **78**: 337–358.

Omphalina
BIGELOW, H. E. 1970. *Omphalina* in North America. *Mycologia* **62**: 1–32.
CEJP, K. 1936. "Atlas des Champignons de l'Europe". Vol. 4 *"Omphalia* (Fr.) Quél". 152 pp. Prague.

Oudemansiella
MOSER, M. 1955. Studien zur Gattung *Oudemansiella* Speg., Schleim- und Sammetrüblinge. *Z. Pilzkde* **19**: 4–11.

Panaeolus
HORA, F. B. 1957. The genus *Panaeolus* in Britain. *Naturalist, Hull* **1957**: 77–88.
O'LAH, G. N. 1969. Le genre *Panaeolus*. *Revue mycol., Mém. ser.* **10**: 1–273.

Panellus
MILLER, O. K. 1970. The genus *Panellus* in North America. *Michigan Bot.* **9**: 18–30.

Phaeocollybia
SMITH, A. H. 1957. Contribution towards a monograph of *Phaeocollybia*. *Brittonia* **9**: 195–217.

Phaeomarasmius
SINGER, E. 1956. Versuch einer Zusammenstellung der Arten der Gattung *Phaeomarasmius. Schweiz. Z. Pilzkde* **34**: 53–65.

Pholiota
SMITH, A. H. & HESLER, L. R. 1968. "The North American Species of *Pholiota*". 402 pp. Hafner, New York.

Pleurotus
PILÁT, A. 1935. "Atlas des Champignons de l'Europe". Vol. 2 *"Pleurotus* Fries". 193 pp. Prague.

Pluteus
SINGER, R. 1956. Contribution towards a monograph of the genus *Pluteus*. *Trans. Br. mycol. Soc.* **39**: 145–232.

Psathyrella
KITS VAN WAVEREN, E. 1971–72. Notes on the genus *Psathyrella* I-III. *Persoonia* **6**: 249–280, 295–312; **7**: 23–54.
SMITH, A. H. 1972. The North American species of *Psathyrella*. *Mem. N.Y. bot. Gdn* **24**: 1–633.

Psilocybe
ORTON, P. D. 1969. Notes on British Agarics. III. *Notes R. bot. Gdn Edinb.* **29**: 75–127.

Rhodocybe
KÜHNER, R. & LAMOURE, D. 1971. Agaricales de la zone alpine. Genre *Rhodocybe* R. Maire. *Bull. Soc. mycol. Fr.* **77**: 15–23.

Ripartites

HUIJSMAN, H. S. C. 1960. Observations sur le genre *Ripartites*, *Persoonia* **1**: 335–339.

Russula

BLUM, J. 1962. "Les Russules". Encyclopédie mycologique No. 32. 236 pp. Lechevalier, Paris.
CRAWSHAY, R. 1930. "The Spore Ornamentation of the Russules". 180 pp. Baillière, Tindal & Cox, London.
HEINEMANN, P. 1962. Les Russules. 4th edn. *Naturalistes belg.* **43**: 1–32.
KÜHNER, R. 1975. Agaricales de la zone alpine. Genre *Russula* Pers. ex S. F. Gray. *Bull. Soc. mycol. Fr.* **91**: 313–390.
RAYNER, R. W. 1968–70. Keys to the British species of *Russula* I-III. *Bull. Br. mycol. Soc.* **2**: 76–109; **3**: 89–120; **4**: 19–46. Also issued separately; additions and corrections in **10**: 69–73, 1976.
ROMAGNESI, H. 1967. "Les Russules de l'Europe et d'Afrique du Nord". 998 pp. Bordas, Paris.
SCHAEFFER, J. 1952. "*Russula* Monographie". 296 pp. Klinkhardt, Bad Heilbrunn.
SCHWOBEL, H. 1974. Die Täublinge. – Beiträge zur ihrer Kenntnis und Verbreitung II-III. *Z. Pilzkde* **39**: 175–190; **40**: 145–158.

Squamanita

BAS, C. 1965. The genus *Squamanita*. *Persoonia* **3**: 331–359.

Tricholoma

BON, M. 1967–69. Révision des Tricholomes. *Bull. Soc. mycol. Fr.* **83**: 324–335; **85**: 475–492.
BON, M. 1974. Tricholomes de France et d'Europe Occidentale 1–2. *Docums mycol.* **3**(12): 1–53; **4**(14): 55–110.
GULDEN, G. 1972. "Musseronflora. Slekten *Tricholoma* (Fr. ex Fr.) Kummer *sensu lato*", 96 pp. Universitetforlaget, Oslo, Bergen & Tromsø.

Volvariella

ORTON, P. D. 1974. The European species of *Volvariella* Spegazzini. *Bull. mens. Soc. linn. Lyon, num. spec.* **1974**: 313–326.

Xeromphalina

MILLER, O. K. 1968. A revision of the genus *Xeromphalina*. *Mycologia* **60**: 156–188.

Aphyllophorales

General

BOURDOT, H. & GALZIN, A. 1928. "Hyménomycètes de France. Hetérobasidiés – Homobasidiés gymnocarpes". iv + 761 pp. Sceaux, Paris. Reprint 1969. Cramer, Lehre.
CHRISTIANSEN, M. P. 1960. Danish resupinate fungi. Part II. Homobasidiomycetes. *Dansk bot. Ark.* **19**: 57–388.
DONK, M. A. 1954–62. Notes on resupinate Hymenomycetes I-VI. *Reinwardtia* **2**: 425–434; **3**: 363–379; *Fungus* **26**: 3–24; **27**: 1–29; **28**: 16–36; *Persoonia* **2**: 217–238.
DONK, M. A. 1964. A conspectus of the families of Aphyllophorales. *Persoonia* **3**: 199–324.

ERIKSSON, J. 1958. Studies in the Hetero- and Homobasidiomycetes—Aphyllophorales in the Muddus National Park in north Sweden. *Symb. bot. upsal.* **16**(1): 1–172.
TALBOT, P. H. B. 1973. In Ainsworth *et al.* (see p. 125) vol. 4B, pp. 327–349.
WAKEFIELD, E. M. 1917. Notes on British Thelephoraceae. *Trans. Br. mycol. Soc.* **5**: 474–481.
WAKEFIELD, E. M. 1952. New or rare British Hymenomycetes (Aphyllophorales). *Trans. Br. mycol. Soc.* **35**: 34–65.

Clavariaceae

CORNER, E. J. H. 1950. "A Monograph of *Clavaria* and allied Genera". xv + 740 pp. Oxford University Press, London.
CORNER, E. J. H. 1970. Supplement to "A Monograph of *Clavaria* and allied Genera". *Beih. Nova Hedwigia* **33**: 1–299.
PERREAU, J. 1969. Les Clavaires. *Revue mycol.* **33**: 396–415.
PETERSEN, R. H. 1973. In Ainsworth *et al.* (see p. 125) vol. 4B, pp. 351–368.
SCHILD, E. 1971. "Clavariales". Fungorum rariorum icones coloratae No. 5. 44 pp. Cramer, Lehre.

Corticiaceae

General

ERIKSSON, J. & RYVARDEN, L. 1973–76. "The Corticiaceae of North Europe". Vols. 2, 3 and 4 only so far published. Fungiflora, Oslo.
JÜLICH, W. 1971. Einige neue oder unbekannte Corticiaceae (Basidiomycetes). *Willdenowia* **6**: 215–224.
JÜLICH, W. 1972. Monographie der Athelieae (Corticiaceae, Basidiomycetes). *Willdenowia Beih.* **7**: 1–284.
JÜLICH, W. 1973. Studien an resupinaten Basidiomyceten I-II. *Persoonia* **7**: 3–8, 381–388.
JÜLICH, W. 1974. The genera of the Hyphodermoideae (Corticiaceae). *Persoonia* **8**: 59–97.
PARMASTO, E. 1968. "Conspectus systematis Corticiacearum". 261 pp. Academy of Sciences of the Estonian SSR, Tartu.
WAKEFIELD, E. M. 1913. Notes on British species of *Corticium*. *Trans. Br. mycol. Soc.* **4**: 113–121.

Aleurodiscus

LEMKE, P. A. 1964. The genus *Aleurodiscus* (sensu stricto) in North America. *Can. J. Bot.* **42**: 213–282.
LEMKE, P. A. 1964. The genus *Aleurodiscus* (sensu lato) in North America. *Can. J. Bot.* **42**: 723–768.
PILÁT, A. 1926. Monographie der mitteleuropäischen Aleurodiscineen. *Annls mycol.* **24**: 202–230.

Athelia

JÜLICH, W. 1972. See above.
LIBERTA, A. E. 1962. A taxonomic analysis of section *Athele* of the genus *Corticium* II. *Mycologia* **53**: 443–450.

Botryobasidium

ERIKSSON, J. 1958. Studies in Corticiaceae (*Botryohypochnus* Donk, *Botryobasidium* Donk and *Gloeocystidiellum* Donk). *Svensk bot. Tidskr.* **52**: 1–17.

ERIKSSON, J. & HJØRTSTAM, K. 1969. Studies in the *Botryobasidium vagum* complex. *Friesia* **9:** 1–17.

Hyphodontia

ERIKSSON, J. & HJØRTSTAM, K. 1969. Four new taxa of *Hyphodontia* (Basidiomycetes). *Svensk bot. Tidskr.* **63:** 217–232.
Includes key to species.

Leucogyrophana

JÜLICH, W. 1974. Notes on cyanophily of spores with a discussion of the genus *Leucogyrophana* (Corticiaceae). *Persoonia* **8:** 51–58.

Merulius

GINNS, J. H. 1976. *Merulius* s.s. and s.l., taxonomic dispositions and identification of species. *Can. J. Bot.* **54:** 100–167.

Paullicorticium

HJØRTSTAM, K. 1971. The genus *Paullicorticium* (Basidiomycetes) in Sweden. *K. Göteborgs Svampklubb* **1971:** 6–13.

LIBERTA, A. E. 1962. The genus *Paullicorticium* (Thelephoraceae). *Brittonia* **14:** 219–223.

Pellicularia s. lat.

TALBOT, P. H. B. 1965. Studies of *"Pellicularia"* and associated genera of Hymenomycetes. *Persoonia* **3:** 371–406.

Peniophora

BOIDIN, J. 1961. Hetérobasidiomycètes saprophytes et Homobasidiomycètes résupinés VIII. *Peniophora* Cke à dendrophyses. *Revue mycol.* **26:** 153–172.

BOIDIN, J. 1965. Le genre *Peniophora* sensu-stricto en France (Basidiomycètes). *Bull. mens. Soc. linn. Lyon* **34:** 161–169, 213–219.

ERIKSSON, J. 1950. *Peniophora* Cke, sect. *Coloratae* Bourd. & Galz. *Symb. bot. upsal.* **10**(5): 1–76.

SLYSH, A. R. 1960. "The Genus *Peniophora* in New York State and adjacent regions". Technical Publication No. 83. 95 pp. University State College of Forestry, Syracuse, N.Y.

Trechispora

LIBERTA, A. E. 1973. The genus *Trechispora* (Basidiomycetes, Corticiaceae). *Can. J. Bot.* **51:** 1871–1892.

Tubulicrinis s. lat.

OBERWINKLER, F. 1966. Die Gattung *Tubulicrinis* Donk s.l. (Corticiaceae). *Z. Pilzkde* **31:** 12–48.

WERESUB, L. K. 1953. Studies of Canadian Thelephoraceae X. Some species of *Peniophora*, section *Tubuliferae. Can. J. Bot.* **31:** 760–778.

Xenasma

LIBERTA, A. E. 1962. A taxonomic analysis of section *Athele* of the genus *Corticium*. 1. Genus *Xenasma. Mycologia* **52:** 884–914.

Cyphellaceae

AGERER, R. 1973. *Rectipilus,* eine neue Gattung cyphelloider Pilze. *Persoonia* **7:** 389–436.
Incl. key *Henningsomyces* spp.

AGERER, R. 1975. *Flagelloscypha,* Studien an cyphelloiden Basidiomyceten. *Sydowia* **27**: 131–265.
COOKE, W. B. 1961. The cyphellaceous fungi. *Sydowia, Beih.* **4**: 1–144.
DONK, M. A. 1959–62. Notes on Cyphellaceae I-II. *Persoonia* **1**: 25–110; **2**: 331–348.
PILÁT, A. 1924. Beiträge zur Kenntnis der Thelephoraceen I. Die Cyphellaceen Bonner. *Annls mycol.* **22**: 204–218.
PILÁT, A. 1925. Zweiter Beiträge zur Kenntnis der tschechoslowakischen Cyphellaceen. *Annls mycol.* **23**: 144–173.

Hydnaceae

JAHN, H. 1965. Die Stachelbarte (*Hericium, Creolophus*) und ihr Vorkommen in Westfälen. *Westfälische Pilzbriefe* **5**: 90–100.
MAAS GEESTERANUS, R. A. 1975. Die terrestrischen Stachelpilze Europas (The terrestrial hydnums of Europe). *Verh. K. ned. Akad. Wet., naturk.* (3) **65**: 1–127, 40 col. pls.

Polyporaceae s. lat.

BONDARTSEV, A. S. 1971. "The Polyporaceae of the European U.S.S.R. and Caucasia". 896 pp. Israel Program for Scientific Translations, Jerusalem. (Originally published in Russian in 1953).
DOMANSKI, S. 1972. "Fungi, Polyporaceae I (resupinatae), Mucronoporaceae I (resupinatae)". 234 pp. U.S. Department of Commerce National Technical Information Service, Springfield, Va.
DOMANSKI, S., ORLOS, H. & SKIRGIELLO, A. 1973. "Fungi, Polyporaceae II (pileatae), Mucronoporaceae II (pileate), Ganodermataceae, Bondarzewiaceae, Boletopsidaceae, Fistulinaceae". 330 pp. U.S. Department of Commerce National Information Service, Springfield, Va.
DONK, M. A. 1974. Check list of European Polypores. *Verh. K. ned. Akad. Wet., naturk.* (3) **62**: 1–469.
JAHN, H. 1963. Mitteleuropäische Porlinge. *Westfälische Pilzbriefe* **4**: 1–143.
JAHN, H. 1967. Die resupinaten *Phellinus*-Arten in Mitteleuropa mit Hinweisen auf die resupinaten *Inonotus*-Arten. *Westfälische Pilzbriefe* **6**: 37–124.
JAHN, H. 1971. Resupinate Porlinge, *Poria* s. lat. in Westfälen und in Nordlichen Deutschland. *Westfälische Pilzbriefe* **8**: 41–68.
KREISEL, H. 1963. Über *Polyporus brumalis* und verwandte Arten. *Feddes Repert.* **68**: 129–138.
LOWE, J. L. 1957. The genus *Fomes*. Technical Publication No. 80. 97 pp. University State College of Forestry, Syracuse, N.Y.
LOWE, J. L. 1966. The genus *Poria*. Technical Publication No. 90. 183 pp. University State College of Forestry, Syracuse, N.Y.
LOWE, J. L. 1975. Polyporaceae of North America: The genus *Tyromyces*. *Mycotaxon* **2**: 1–83.
OVERHOLTS, O. L. 1953. "The Polyporaceae of the United States, Alaska and Canada". 466 pp. Michigan State University Press, Ann Arbor.
PEGLER, D. N. 1964. A survey of the genus *Inonotus*. *Trans. Br. mycol. Soc.* **47**: 175–195.
PEGLER, D. N. 1973. The polypores. *Bull. Br. mycol. Soc.* **7**: *Suppl.* 43 pp.
PEGLER, D. N. 1973. In Ainsworth *et al.* (see p. 125) vol. 4B, pp. 397–420.
PEGLER, D. N. & YOUNG, T. W. K. 1973. Basidiospore form in the British species of *Ganoderma*. *Kew Bull.* **28**: 351–364.
PILÁT, A. 1936–42. "Atlas des Champignons de l'Europe". Vol. 3 "Polyporaceae". 2 vols. Prague.
RYVARDEN, L. 1976. "The Polyporaceae of North Europe I. *Albatrellus—Incrustoporia*". 214 pp. Fungiflora, Oslo.

STEYAERT, R. L. 1967. Considerations générales sur le genre *Ganoderma* et plus specialement sur les espèces Européenes. *Bull. Soc. r. bot. Belg.* **100:** 189–211.

Stereaceae

JAHN, H. 1968. Die Schichtpilze (*Stereum* s. lato). *Schweiz Z. Pilzkde* **46:** 65–74.
LENTZ, P. L. 1955. "*Stereum* and allied genera of fungi in the Upper Mississippi Valley". U.S.D.A. Agricultural Monograph No. 24. 74 pp. U.S. Department of Agriculture, Beltsville.
PILAT, A. 1930. Monographie der europäischen Stereaceen. *Hedwigia* **70:** 10–132.
REID, D. A. 1965. A monograph of the stipitate Stereoid fungi. *Beih. Nova Hedwigia* **18:** 1–384.

Thelephoraceae s. lat.

COOKE, W. B. 1957. The genera *Serpula* and *Meruliopsis*. *Mycologia* **49:** 197–225.
CORNER, E. J. H. 1968. A monograph of *Thelephora*. *Beih. Nova Hedwigia* **27:** 1–100.
LARSEN, M. J. 1968. "Tomentelloid fungi of North America". Technical Publication No. 93. 157 pp. State University College of Forestry, Syracuse, N.Y.
LARSEN, M. J. 1973. The genus *Pseudotomentella*. *Nova Hedwigia* **22:** 599–620.
LARSEN, M. J. 1974. A contribution to the taxonomy of the genus *Tomentella*. *Mycologia Mem.* **4:** 1–145.
SVRČEK, M. 1958. Contribution to the taxonomy of the resupinate Thelephoraceous fungi. *Česká mykol.* **12:** 66–77.
SVRČEK, M. 1960. Tomentelloideae Cechoslovakiae. Genera resupinata familiae Thelephoraceae s. str. *Sydowia* **14:** 170–245.
WAKEFIELD, E. M. 1969. Tomentelloideae in the British Isles. *Trans. Br. mycol. Soc.* **53:** 161–206.

Exobasidiales

SAVILE, D. B. O. 1959. Key to the North American species of *Exobasidium*. *Can. J. Bot.* **37:** 641–656.

Tremellales s. lat.

BOURDOT, H. & GALZIN, A. 1928. "Hyménomycètes de France. Hetérobasidiés—Homobasidiés gymnocarpes". iv + 761 pp. Sceaux, Paris. Reprint 1969. Cramer, Lehre.
CHRISTIANSEN, M. P. 1959. Danish resupinate fungi part I. Ascomycetes and Heterobasidiomycetes. *Dansk bot. Ark.* **19:** 7–55.
DONK, M. A. 1966. Check list of European hymenomycetous Heterobasidiae. *Persoonia* **4:** 145–335.
DONK, M. A. 1974. Check list of European hymenomycetous Heterobasidiae. Supplement and corrections. *Persoonia* **8:** 35–50.
LUCK-ALLEN, E. R. 1960. The genus *Heterochaetella*. *Can. J. Bot.* **38:** 559–569.
LUCK-ALLEN, E. R. 1963. The genus *Basidiodendron*. *Can. J. Bot.* **41:** 1025–1052.
McNABB, R. F. R. 1965. Some auriculariaceous fungi from the British Isles. *Trans. Br. mycol. Soc.* **48:** 187–192.
McNABB, R. F. R. 1973. In Ainsworth *et al.* (see p. 125) vol. 4B, pp. 303–317.
MARTIN, G. W. 1952. Revision of the north-central Tremellales. *Stud. nat. Hist. Iowa Univ.* **19** (3): 1–122. Reprint 1969. Cramer, Lehre.
NEUHOFF, W. 1931. Die europäischen Arten der Gattung *Tremella*. *Z. Pilzkde* **10:** 70–75.

NEUHOFF, W. 1936. Die Gallertpilze Schwedens (Tremellaceae, Dacrymycetaceae, Tulasnellaceae, Auriculariaceae). *Ark. Bot.* **28A** (1): 1–57.
OBERWINKLER, A. 1963. Niedere Basidiomyceten aus Sudbayern III. die Gattung *Sebacina* Tul. s.l. *Ber. bayer. bot. Ges.* **36**: 41–55.
PILÁT, A. 1957. Übersicht der europäischen Auriculariales und Tremellales unter besonderer Berücksichtigung der tschechoslowakischen Arten. *Acta Mus. nat. Prague* **13b** (4): 1–210.
REID, D. A. 1974. A monograph of the British Dacrymycetales. *Trans. Br. mycol. Soc.* **62**: 433–494.
ROGERS, D. P. 1933. A taxonomic review of the Tulasnellaceae. *Annls mycol.* **31**: 181–203.
TORKELSEN, A. E. 1968. The genus *Tremella* in Norway. *Nytt Mag. Naturvid.* **15**: 225–239.
WELLS, K. 1959. Studies of some Tremellaceae III. The genus *Bourdotia*. *Mycologia* **51**: 541–564.
WELLS, K. 1961. Studies of some Tremellaceae IV. *Exidiopsis*. *Mycologia* **53**: 317–370.
WELLS, K. 1974. Studies of some Tremellaceae V. A new genus, *Efibulobasidium*. *Mycologia* **67**: 147–156.

GASTEROMYCETES

See also under Ascomycotina (Tuberales) for Hymenogastrales.

BRODIE, H. J. 1975. "The Bird's Nest Fungi". 198 pp. University of Toronto Press, Toronto.
DEMOULIN, V. 1969. Les Gasteromycètes. *Naturalistes belge.* **50**: 225–270.
DISSING, H. & LANGE, M. 1961–62. The genus *Geastrum* in Denmark. *Bot. Tidsskr.* **57**: 1–27; **58**: 64–67.
DRING, D. M. 1973. In Ainsworth *et al.* (see p. 125) vol. 4B, pp. 451–478.
ECKBLAD, F.-E. 1955. The Gasteromycetes of Norway, the epigeaen genera. *Nytt mag. Bot.* **4**: 19–86.
GUZMAN, G. 1970. Monografia del genero *Scleroderma*. *Darwiniana* **16**: 233–407.
HAWKER, L. 1955. Hypogeous fungi IV and V. *Trans. Br. mycol. Soc.* **38**: 73–77. (*Rhizopogon*).
KREISEL, H. 1962. Die Lycoperdaceae der DDR. *Feddes Repert.* **64**: 1–114. Reprint 1973. Cramer, Lehre.
KREISEL, H. 1967. Taxonomische-pflanzengeographische Monographie der Gattung *Bovista*. *Beih. Nova Hedwigia* **25**: 1–244.
PALMER, J. T. 1955. Observations on Gasteromycetes 1–3. *Trans. Br. mycol. Soc.* **38**: 317–334. (*Geastrum*).
PALMER, J. T. 1968. A chronological catalogue to the literature of the British Gasteromycetes. *Nova Hedwigia* **15**: 65–178.
PERDECK, A. C. 1950. Revision of the Lycoperdaceae of the Netherlands. *Blumea* **6**: 480–516.
PILÁT, A., ed. 1958. "Gasteromycetes". Flora ČSR **B1**. 864 pp. Czechoslovak Academy of Sciences, Prague.
SOEHNER, E. 1962. Monographie der Gattung Hymenogaster. *Beih. Nova Hedwigia* **2**: 1–114.
ZELLER, S. M. 1949. Keys to the orders, families and genera of the Gasteromycetes. *Mycologia* **41**: 36–58.

DEUTEROMYCOTINA (FUNGI IMPERFECTI)

GENERAL

BARNETT, H. L. & HUNTER, B. B. 1972. "Illustrated Genera of Imperfect Fungi". 3rd edn. 241 pp. Burgess Publishing, Minneapolis.
KENDRICK, W. B., ed. 1971. "Taxonomy of Fungi Imperfecti". 309 pp. University of Toronto Press, Toronto.

BLASTOMYCETES (Yeasts p.p.)

See also p. 132 under Ascomycotina—Endomycetales.
DERX, H. G. 1930. Étude sur les Sporobolomycètes. *Annls mycol.* **28:** 1–23.
NYLAND, G. 1950. The genus *Tilletiopsis*. *Mycologia* **42:** 487–496.
TUBAKI, K. 1952. Studies in the Sporobolomycetaceae in Japan. *Nagaoa* **1:** 26–31.

COELOMYCETES

VON ARX, J. A. 1957. Die Arten der Gattung *Colletotrichum* Cda. *Phytopath. Z.* **29:** 413–468.
VON ARX, J. A. 1970. "A Revision of the Fungi classified as *Gloeosporium*". 203 pp. 2nd edn. Cramer, Lehre.
BESTAGNO BIGA, M. L., CIFFERI, R. & BESTAGNO, G. 1959. Ordinamento artificiale delle specie del genere *Coniothyrium*. *Sydowia* **12:** 258–320.
GROVE, W. B. 1932, 1937. "British Stem- and Leaf-Fungi (Coelomycetes)". 2 vols. Cambridge University Press, Cambridge. Reprint 1967. J. Cramer, Lehre.
   Still useful although now very dated; includes host indices.
GUBA, E. F. 1961. "Monograph of *Monochaetia* and *Pestalotia*". 342 pp. Harvard University Press, Cambridge, Mass.
JØRSTAD, I. 1965. "*Septoria* and Septorioid Fungi on Dicotyledons in Norway". 110 pp. Oslo University Press, Oslo.
MORGAN-JONES, G., NAG RAJ, T. R. & KENDRICK, W. B. 1972–75. "Icones Generum Coelomycetum I-VII". University of Waterloo Biology Series, Waterloo.
PETRAK, F. & SYDOW, H. 1926–27. Die Gattungen der Pyrenomyceten, Sphaeropsideen und Melanconieen I. *Beih. Feddes Repert.* **42:** 1–551.
SUTTON, B. C. 1961–77. Coelomycetes I-VI. *Mycol. Papers* **80:** 1–16 *(Pestalotiopsis);* **88:** 1–50 *(Neobarclaya* etc.); **97:** 1–42 *(Seimatosporium* etc.); **123:** 1–46 *(Harknessia* etc.); **138:** 1–224 *(Coryneum);* **141:** 1–253 (Generic names).
SUTTON, B. C. 1973. In Ainsworth *et al.* (see p. 125), vol. 4A, pp. 513–582.
VAN DER AA, H. A. 1973. Studies in *Phyllosticta*. *Stud. mycol., Baarn* **5:** 1–110.

HYPHOMYCETES

BARRON, G. L. 1968. "The Genera of Hyphomycetes from Soil". 346 pp. Williams & Wilkins, Baltimore. Reprint 1972. R. E. Krieger Publishing, Huntington, New York.
BOOTH, C. 1966. The genus *Cylindrocarpon*. *Mycol. Papers* **104:** 1–56.
BOOTH, C. 1971. "The Genus *Fusarium*". 237 pp. Commonwealth Mycological Institute, Kew.
BOOTH, C. 1977. "*Fusarium*. Laboratory guide to the Identification of the Major Species". 58 pp. Commonwealth Mycological Institute, Kew.
CHUPP, C. 1954. "A Monograph of the Fungus Genus *Cercospora*". 667 pp. C. Chupp, Ithaca, N.Y.

DE HOOG, G. S. 1972. The genera *Beauveria, Isaria, Tritirachium* and *Acrodontium*. *Stud. mycol., Baarn* **1**: 1–41.

DE HOOG, G. S. 1974. The genera *Blastobotrys, Sporothrix, Calicarisporium* and *Calicarisporiella* gen. nov. *Stud. mycol., Baarn* **7**: 1–84.

ELLIS, M. B. 1971. "Dematiaceous Hyphomycetes". 608 pp., 419 figs. Commonwealth Mycological Institute, Kew.

This and the following title together include almost all British brown pigmented Hyphomycetes.

ELLIS, M. B. 1976. "More Dematiaceous Hyphomycetes". 507 pp., 383 figs. Commonwealth Mycological Institute, Kew.

GAMS, W. 1971. "*Cephalosporium*-artige Schimmelpilze (Hyphomycetes)". x + 262 pp. G. Fischer, Stuttgart.

GAMS, W. & HOLUBOVÁ-JECHOVÁ, V. 1976. *Chloridium* and some other dematiaceous Hyphomycetes growing on decaying wood. *Stud. mycol., Baarn* **13**: 1–99.

INGOLD, C. T. 1975. Guide to aquatic Hyphomycetes. *Scient. Publs Freshwat. biol. Ass.* **30**, 96 pp.

KENDRICK, W. B. & CARMICHAEL, J. W. 1973. In Ainsworth *et al.* (see p. 125) vol. 4 A, pp. 323–509.

Well-illustrated.

MORRIS, E. F. 1963. "Synnematous Genera of Fungi Imperfecti". Series in Biological Sciences No. 3. 143 pp. Western Illinois University.

NAG RAJ, T. R. & KENDRICK, G. 1976. "A Monograph of *Chalara* and allied genera". 200 pp. Wilfrid Laurier University Press, Waterloo.

RAPER, K. B. & FENNELL, D. I. 1965. "The Genus *Aspergillus*". 686 pp. Williams & Wilkins, Baltimore.

RAPER, K. B. & THOM, C. 1949. "Manual of the *Penicillia*". 875 pp. Williams and Wilkins, Baltimore. Reprint 1968. Hafner, New York.

RIFAI, M. A. 1969. A revision of the genus *Trichoderma*. *Mycol. Papers* **116**: 1–56.

SAMSON, R. A. 1974. *Paecilomyces* and some allied Hyphomycetes. *Stud. mycol., Baarn* **6**: 1–119.

SAMSON, R. A., STOLK, A. C. & HADLOCK, R. 1976. Revision of the subsection *Fasciculata* of *Penicillium* and some allied species. *Stud. mycol., Baarn* **11**: 1–47.

SUBRAMANIAN, C. V. 1972. "Hyphomycetes". 930 pp. I.C.A.R., New Delhi.

SUTTON, B. C. 1973. Hyphomycetes from Manitoba and Saskatchewan. *Mycol. Papers* **132**: 1–143.

WAKEFIELD, E. M. & BISBY, G. R. 1941. List of Hyphomycetes recorded for Britain. *Trans. Br. mycol. Soc.* **25**: 49–126, 427–428.

LICHENES

British species about 1380

This is not a homogeneous systematic group but comprises Fungi (mainly Ascomycotina) united in a common method of nutrition (*i.e.* symbiosis with algae). The names of lichens refer, for nomenclatural purposes, to their fungal components so that the included algae can bear independent scientific names. As no entirely satisfactory system incorporating both the non-lichenized and lichen-forming fungi exists at the present time, works relevant to the lichen-forming fungi are listed separately here.

GENERAL

AINSWORTH, G. C. 1971. See above p. 125.

Includes lichen terms, genera, etc.

ALVIN, K. L. 1977. "The Observer's Book of Lichens". 2nd edn, 188 pp. F. Warne, London.
   An introductory guide, well illustrated, many illustrations in full colour.
DUNCAN, U. K. (assisted by P. W. James). 1970. "Introduction to British Lichens". lxxiv + 292 pp. Buncle, Arbroath.
   The standard British lichen flora; illustrated by line drawings.
HALE, M. E. 1974. "The Biology of Lichens". 2nd edn. 181 pp. E. Arnold, London.
   The standard English introduction to the biology of the group.
HAWKSWORTH, D. L. 1974. See above p. 126.
HAWKSWORTH, D. L. & ROSE, F. 1976. "Lichens as Pollution Monitors". Studies in Biology No. 66. 64 pp. E. Arnold, London.
   Includes brief notes with some illustrations of species used in air pollution survey work.
HENSSEN, A. & JAHNS, H. M. 1973 (1974). "Lichenes. Eine Einführung in die Flechtenkunde". xii + 467 pp. G. Thieme, Stuttgart.
   Detailed well-illustrated accounts of higher taxa; the orders and sub-orders used in this Bibliography follow this work.
LICHENOLOGIST 1958 on. Academic Press, London, New York and San Francisco.
   The journal of the British Lichen Society including many papers on systematics; twice yearly.
SMITH, A. L. 1918, 1926. "A Monograph of the British Lichens." 2nd edn. 2 vols. British Museum (Natural History), London.
   Detailed descriptions; some plates; now dated and in need of an extensive revision.

HABITAT KEYS

FERRY, B. W. & SHEARD, J. W. 1969. Zonation of supralittoral lichens on rocky shores around the Dale peninsula, Pembrokeshire (with key for their identification). *Fld Stud.* **3:** 41–67.
FLETCHER, A. 1975. Key for the identification of British marine and maritime lichens I-II. *Lichenologist* **7:** 1–52, 73–115.
JAMES, P. W. 1970. The lichen flora of shaded acid rock crevices and overhangs in Britain. *Lichenologist* **4:** 309–322.
LAUNDON, J. R. 1962. The taxonomy of sterile crustaceous lichens in Britain. 1. Terricolous species. *Lichenologist* **2:** 57–67.
LAUNDON, J. R. 1963. The taxonomy of sterile crustaceous lichens in Britain. 2. Corticolous and lignicolous species. *Lichenologist* **2:** 101–151.

LISTS

JAMES, P. W. 1965. A new check-list of British lichens. *Lichenologist* **3:** 95–153.
JAMES, P. W. 1966. A new check-list of British lichens: Additions and corrections 1. *Lichenologist* **3:** 242–247.

BIBLIOGRAPHY

HAWKSWORTH, D. L. 1970. Guide to the literature for the identification of British lichens. *Bull. Br. mycol. Soc.* **4:** 73–95.
   Also available separately.
HAWKSWORTH, D. L. 1977. A bibliographic guide to the lichen floras of the world. In "Lichen Ecology" (M. R. D. Seaward, ed.): 437–502. Academic Press, London, New York and San Francisco.
   Titles arranged by country.
HAWKSWORTH, D. L. & SEAWARD, M. R. D. 1977. "Lichenology in the British Isles 1568–1975. An historical and bibliographical survey". 244 pp. Richmond Publishing, Richmond, Surrey.

Includes citations of about 2,700 publications indexed by vice-county.

MITCHELL, M. E. 1971. "A Bibliography of Books, Pamphlets and Articles relating to Irish Lichenology, 1727–1970". 76 pp. Privately printed, Galway.

422 publications indexed by vice-county.

FOREIGN WORKS

Floras of particular value in the identification of British lichens. For foreign monographs of particular groups of lichens including British species see pp. 154–157.

ANDERS, J. 1928. "Die Strauch- und Laubflechten Mitteleuropas". 217 pp. G. Fischer, Jena. Reprinted 1975. Asher, Amsterdam.

Useful for its plates.

DAHL, E. & KROG, H. 1973. "Macrolichens of Denmark, Finland, Norway and Sweden". 184 pp. Universitetsforlaget, Oslo, Bergen and Tromsø.

Keys, in English, with some illustrations; includes most British macrolichens. An extremely useful book to be strongly recommended.

ERICHSEN, C. F. E. 1957. "Flechtenflora von Nordwestdeutschland". xxiv + 411 pp. G. Fischer, Stuttgart.

Keys and short descriptions.

GALLØE, O. 1927–72. "Natural History of the Danish Lichens". 10 vols. H. Aschehoug, Copenhagen.

Includes 1,397 plates and 7,010 figures, many in colour; index in vol. 10.

GAMS, H. 1967. "Kleine Kryptogamenflora". Vol. 3. "Flechten (Lichenes)". viii + 244 pp. G. Fischer, Jena.

Keys; some line drawings.

HILLMANN, J. & GRUMMANN, V. 1957. Flechten. *Krypt.-Fl. Mark Brandenb.* **8:** i–x + 1–898. Borntraeger, Berlin-Nikolassee.

Keys and detailed descriptions.

OZENDA, P. & CLAUZADE, G. 1970. "Les Lichens. Étude Biologique et Flore Illustrée". 801 pp. Masson & Cie, Paris.

Keys; numerous excellent line drawings and photographs.

POELT, J. 1969. "Bestimmungsschlüssel europäischer Flechten." (1)–(71) + 757 pp. J. Cramer, Lehre.

Keys to most European lichens; the standard European text. Supplements in the course of preparation.

RABENHORST'S KRYPTOGAMEN-FLORA VON DEUTSCHLAND, ÖSTERREICH UND DER SCHWEIZ. 1933–60. Vol. 9. Die Flechten. Akademie Verlag, Leipzig.

Detailed but incomplete multi-authored monograph issued in parts with keys (see Hawksworth, 1977, above for contents of parts).

VAINIO, E. A. 1921–27, 1934. Lichenographia fennica I-IV. *Acta Soc. Fauna Flora fenn.* **49**(2): 1–274; **53**(1): 1–340; **57**(1): 1–138; **57**(2): 1–531. I and II reprinted 1975. O. Koeltz, Koenigstein.

Detailed but incomplete monograph covering many traditionally "difficult" taxonomic groups including pyrenocarpous lichens, Caliciales, Lecideaceae, etc.

DISTRIBUTION

BRITISH LICHEN SOCIETY 1973 on. Distribution maps of lichens in Britain. *Lichenologist* **5:** 464–480; **6:** 169–199; **7:** 180–192; **9:** 175–187.

A continuing series; includes notes on ecology and systematics.

COPPINS, B. J. 1976. Distribution patterns shown by epiphytic lichens in the British Isles. In "Lichenology: Progress and Problems" (D. H. Brown, D. L. Hawksworth & R. H. Bailey, eds.), pp. 249–278. Academic Press, London, New York and San Francisco.

DEGELIUS, G. 1935. Das ozeanische Element der Strauch- und Laubflechtenflora von Skandinavien. *Acta phytogeogr. suec.* **7**: i–xii + 1–411.
HAWKSWORTH, D. L., COPPINS, B. J. & ROSE, F. 1974. Changes in the British lichen flora. In "The Changing Flora and Fauna of Britain" (D. L. Hawksworth, ed.), pp. 47–78. Academic Press, London & New York.
MITCHELL, M. E. 1961. L'élément eu-oceanique dans la flore lichenique du sud-ouest de l'Irlande. *Revta Biol.* **2**: 177–256.

MONOGRAPHS

Caliciales

NÁDVORNIK, J. 1942. Systematische Übersicht der mitteleuropäischen Arten der Flechtenfamilie Caliciaceae. *Studia bot. čsl.* **5**: 6–40.
SCHMIDT, A. 1970. Anatomische-taxonomische Untersuchungen an europäischen Arten der Flechtenfamilie Caliciaceae. *Mitt. Staatsinst. allg. Bot. Hamburg* **13**: 111–166.
TIBELL, L. 1971. The genus *Cyphelium* in Europe. *Svensk bot. Tidskr.* **65**: 138–164.
TIBELL, L. 1975. The Caliciales of boreal North America. *Symb. bot. upsal.* **21**(2): 1–128.
TOBOLEWSKI, Z. R. 1966. Rodzina Caliciaceae w Polsce. *Pozn. Tow. Przyj. Nauk, Prace Kom. Biol.* **24**(5): 1–105. In Polish.

Lecanorales

Lecanorineae

AHTI, T. 1961. Taxonomic studies on reindeer lichens *(Cladonia,* subgenus *Cladina). Suomal. eläin-ja kasvit. Seur. van. kasvit. Julk.* **32**(1): 1–160.
AHTI, T. 1966. *Parmelia olivacea* and the allied non-isidiate and non-sorediate corticolous lichens in the Northern Hemisphere. *Acta bot. fenn.* **70**: 1–68.
BITTER, G. 1901. Zur Morphologie und Systematik von *Parmelia,* Untergattung *Hypogymnia. Hedwigia* **40**: 171–274.
BRODO, I. M. & HAWKSWORTH, D. L. 1977. *Alectoria* and allied genera in North America. *Op. bot. Soc. bot. Lund* **42**: 1–164.
CULBERSON, W. L. & CULBERSON, C. F. 1968. The lichen genera *Cetrelia* and *Platismatia* (Parmeliaceae). *Contr. U.S. natn. Herb.* **34**: 449–558.
DEGELIUS, G. 1954. The lichen genus *Collema* in Europe. *Symb. bot. upsal.* **13**(2): 1–499.
EIGLER, G. 1969. Studien zur Gliederung der Flechtengattung *Lecanora. Diss. Bot., Lehre* **4**: 1–195.
HAKULINEN, R. 1954. Die Flechtengattung *Candelariella* Müller Argoviensis. *Suomal. eläin-ja kasvit. Seur. van. kasvit. Julk.* **27**(3): i–vi + 1–127.
HALE, M. E. 1965. A monograph of *Parmelia* subgenus *Amphigymnia. Contr. U.S. natn. Herb.* **36**: 193–358.
HALE, M. E. 1965. Studies on the *Parmelia borreri* group. *Svensk bot. Tidskr.* **59**: 37–48.
HALE, M. E. & KUROKAWA, S. 1964. Studies on *Parmelia* subgenus *Parmelia. Contr. U.S. natn. Herb.* **36**: 121–191.
HAWKSWORTH, D. L. 1972. Regional studies on *Alectoria* (Lichenes) II. The British species. *Lichenologist* **5**: 181–261.
HEDLUND, T. 1892. Kritische Bemerkungen über einige Arten der Flechtengattungen *Lecanora* (Ach.), *Lecidea* (Ach.) und *Micarea* (Fr.). *Bih. K. svenska VetenskAkad. Handl.* **18**, 3(3): 1–102.
HENNIPMAN, E. 1968. De Nederlandse *Cladonia's* (Lichenes). *Wet. Meded. K. ned. natuurh. Veren.* **79**: 1–53. In Dutch; well illustrated.

HERTEL, H. 1967. Revision einiger calciphiler Formenkreis der Flechtengattung *Lecidea*. *Beih. Nova Hedwigia* **24**: 1–155.
HERTEL, H. 1968–75. Beiträge zur Kenntnis der Flechtenfamilie Lecideaceae I-VI. *Herzogia* **1**: 25–39, 321–329; **2**: 37–62, 231–261, 479–515; **3**: 365–406.
HERTEL, H. 1975. Ein vorläufiger Bestimmungsschlüssel für die kryptothallinen, schwarzfrüchtigen, saxicolen Arten der Sammelgattung *Lecidea* (Lichenes) in der Holarktis. *Decheniana* **127**: 37–78.
JAHNS, H. M. 1970. Remarks on the taxonomy of the European and North American species of *Pilophorus* Th. Fr. *Lichenologist* **4**: 199–213.
JAMES, P. W. 1971. New or interesting British lichens: 1. *Lichenologist* **5**: 114–148.
KERSHAW, K. A. 1960. The genus *Stereocaulon* Schreb. in the British Isles. *Lichenologist* **1**: 184–203.
KERSHAW, K. A. 1961. The genus *Umbilicaria* in the British Isles. *Lichenologist* **1**: 251–265.
KOFLER, L. 1956. Remarques sur les *Lecanora* corticoles du groupe *subfusca*. *Revue bryol. lichén.* **25**: 167–182.
KROG, H. & JAMES, P. W. 1977. The genus *Ramalina* in Fennoscandia and the British Isles. *Norw. J. Bot.* **24**: 15–43.
LLANO, G. A. 1950. "A Monograph of the Lichen Family Umbilicariaceae in the Western Hemisphere". Navexos P-831. 281 pp. Office of Naval Research, Washington, D.C.
MAAS GEESTERANUS, R. A. 1948. Revision of the lichens of the Netherlands I. Parmeliaceae. *Blumea* **6**: i–viii + 1–199.
MAGNUSSON, A. H. 1952. Lichens from Torne Lappmark. *Ark. Bot., ser. 2*, **2**: 45–249.
MAGNUSSON, A. H. 1952. Key to the species of *Lecidea* in Scandinavia and Finland I-II. *Svensk bot. Tidskr.* **46**: 178–198, 313–323.
POELT, J. 1958. Die lobaten Arten der Flechtengattung *Lecanora* Ach. sensu ampl. in der Holarktis. *Mitt. bot. StSamml., Münch.* **2**: 411–589.
RUNEMARK, H. 1956. Studies in *Rhizocarpon* I-II. *Op. bot. Soc. bot. Lund* **2**(1): 1–152; 2(2): 1–150.
SIERK, H. A. 1964. The genus *Leptogium* in North America north of Mexico. *Bryologist* **67**: 245–317.
TAVARES, C. N. 1965. The genus *Pannaria* in Portugal. *Port. Acta biol., B* **8**: 1–16.
THOMSON, J. W. 1967. Notes on *Rhizocarpon* in the arctic. *Nova Hedwigia* **14**: 421–481.
THOMSON, J. W. 1968 (1967). "The Lichen Genus *Cladonia* in North America". 172 pp. University of Toronto Press.

Lichineae

FORSSELL, K. B. J. 1885. Beiträge zur Kenntnis der Anatomie und Systematik der Gloeolichen. *Nova Acta R. Soc. Scient. upsal., ser. 3*, **13**(6): 1–118.
HENSSEN, A. 1963. Eine Revision der Flechtenfamilien Lichinaceae und Ephebaceae. *Symb. bot. upsal.* **18**(1): 1–123.

Peltigerineae

THOMSON, J. W. 1950. The species of *Peltigera* of North America north of Mexico. *Am. Midl. nat.* **44**: 1–68.
WETMORE, C. M. 1960. The lichen genus *Nephroma* in north and middle America. *Publs Mich. St. Univ. Mus., ser. biol.* **1**: 369–452.
YOSHIMURA, I. 1971. The genus *Lobaria* of eastern Asia. *J. Hattori bot. Lab.* **34**: 231–364.

Teloshistineae

LAUNDON, J. R. 1974. *Leproplaca* in the British Isles. *Lichenologist* **6**: 102–105.
NORDIN, I. 1972. "*Caloplaca,* sect. *Gasparrinia* i Nordeuropa". 184 pp. Skriv Service, Uppsala. In Swedish; illustrated.
POELT, J. 1954. Die galappten Arten der Flechtengattung *Caloplaca* in Europa mit besonderer Berücksichtigung Mitteleuropas. *Mitt. bot. StSamml., Münch.* **2**: 11–31.
POELT, J. 1965. Über einige Arten-gruppen der Flechtengattungen *Caloplaca* und *Fulgensia. Mitt. bot. StSamml., Münch.* **5**: 571–607.
WADE, A. E. 1965. The genus *Caloplaca* Th. Fr. in the British Isles. *Lichenologist* **3**: 1–28.
WUNDER, H. 1974. Schwarzfrüchtige, saxicole Sippen der Gattung *Caloplaca* (Lichenes, Teloschistaceae) in Mitteleuropa, dem Mittelmeergebiet und Vorderasien. *Blthca Lich., Lehre* **3**: 1–186.

Physciineae

FREY, E. 1963. Beiträge zu einer Lichenenflora der Schweiz II. III. Die Familie Physciaceae. *Ber. schweiz. bot. Ges.* **73**: 389–503.
KUROKAWA, S. 1962. A monograph of the genus *Anaptychia. Beih. Nova Hedwigia* **6**: 1–115.
MOBERG, R. 1977. The lichen genus *Physcia* and allied genera in Fennoscandia. *Symb. bot. upsal.* **22**(1): i–vii + 1–108.
POELT, J. 1966. Zur Kenntnis der Flechtengattung *Physconia. Nova Hedwigia* **12**: 107–135.
SHEARD, J. W. 1964. The genus *Buellia* de Notaris in the British Isles (excluding section *Diploica* (Massal.) Stiz.). *Lichenologist* **2**: 225–262.
SHEARD, J. W. 1967. A revision of the lichen genus *Rinodina* (Ach.) Gray in the British Isles. *Lichenologist* **3**: 328–367.
THOMSON, J. W. 1963. The lichen genus *Physcia* in North America. *Beih. Nova Hedwigia* **7**: 1–172.
WADE, A. E. 1960. The British *Anaptychiae* and *Physciae. Lichenologist* **1**: 126–144.

Pertusariineae

HERTEL, H. 1969. Die Flechtengattung *Trapelia* Choisy. *Herzogia* **1**: 111–130.
HØEG, O. 1923. The corticolous Norwegian Pertusariaceae and Thelotremaceae. *Nyt Mag. Naturvid.* **61**: 139–178.
HOWARD, G. E. 1970. The lichen genus *Ochrolechia* in North America north of Mexico. *Bryologist* **73**: 93–130.
OSHIO, M. 1968. Taxonomical studies on the family Pertusariaceae of Japan. *J. Sci. Hiroshima Univ.,* B(2) **12**: 81–163.

Gyalectales

JAMES, P. W. 1975. The genus *Gyalideopsis* Vězda in Britain. *Lichenologist* **7**: 155–161.
LETTAU, G. 1932–37. Monographische Bearbeitung einiger Flechtenfamilien. *Beih. Feddes Repert.* **69**: 1–250.
VĚZDA, A. 1966. Flechtensystematische Studien IV. Die Gattung *Gyalidea* Lett. *Folia geobot. phytotax., Praha* **1**: 311–340.
VĚZDA, A. 1968. Flechtensystematische Studien VI. Die Gattung *Sagiolechia* Massal. *Folia geobot. phytotax., Praha* **2**: 383–396.

Ostropales

NAKANISHI, M. 1966. Taxonomical studies on the family Graphidaceae of Japan. *J. Sci. Hiroshima Univ.,* B(2) **11**: 41–126.

SALISBURY, G. 1972. *Thelotrema* Ach. sect. *Thelotrema* 1. The *T. lepadinum* group. *Lichenologist* **5**: 262–274.

Sphaeriales, Verrucariales and Pleosporales (Pyrenocarpous Lichens)

HARRIS, R. C. 1973. The corticolous pyrenolichens of the Great Lakes region. *Mich. Bot.* **12**: 1–68.
SANTESSON, R. 1939. Amphibious pyrenolichens 1. *Ark. Bot.* **29A**(10): 1–67.
SERVÍT, M. 1954. "Československé Lišejníky Čeledi Verrucariaceae". 249 pp. Nakladatelství Československé Akademie Věd, Prague. In Czech and Latin.
SWINSCOW, T. D. V. 1960–71. Pyrenocarpous lichens: 1–15. *Lichenologist* **1**: 169–178, 242–250; **2**: 6–56, 156–166, 276–283; **3**: 42–54, 55–64, 72–83, 233–235, 415–417, 418–422; **4**: 34–54, 218–233; **5**: 92–112.

Arthoniales

ALMQUIST, S. 1880. Monographia Arthoniarum Scandinaviae. *K. svenska VetenskAkad. Handl.* **17**(6): 1–69.

PLANTAE

ALGAE

British species about 10,000

For a comprehensive list of keys to the smaller algae see:
GEORGE, E. A. 1976. A guide to algal keys (excluding seaweeds). *Br. phycol. J.* **11**: 49–55.

FRESHWATER

BELCHER, J. H. & SWALE, E. M. F. 1976. "A Beginner's Guide to Freshwater Algae". 48 pp. HMSO, London.

BOURRELLY, P. 1966–70. "Les Algues d'Eau Douce". 3 vols. Boubée & Cie, Paris:
  1. 1966. "Les Algues Vertes". 511 pp.
  2. 1968. "Les Algues Jaunes et Brunes". 438pp.
  3. 1970. "Les Algues Bleues et Rouges". 512 pp.
  Keys to and descriptions of genera, illustrations of several species. World-wide basis.

HINDÁK, F., KOMÁREK, J., MARVIN, P. & RŮŽIČKA, J. 1975. "Klic na Urcovanie Yytrosnych Rastlin". Vol. 1. 397 pp. Bratislava. In Czech.

HUBER-PESTALOZZI, G. 1938–72. "Das Phytoplankton des Süsswassers". In "Die Binnengewasser" (A. Thienemann, ed.). Vol. 16. Schweizerbart'sche, Stuttgart:
  Part 1. 1938. "Blaualgen, Bakterien, Pilze". 342 pp.
  Part 2(i). 1941. "Chrysophyceen, Farblose Flagellaten, Heterokonten". 365 pp.
  Part 3. 1968. "Cryptophyceen, Chloromonadinen, Peridineen". 2nd edn. (G. Huber-Pestalozzi & B. Fott). ix + 322pp.
  Part 4. 1955. "Euglenophyceen". ix + 606 pp., 114 pls.
  Part 5. 1961. "Chlorophyceae (Grünalgen), Ordnung Volvocales". xii + 744 pp., 158 pls.
  Part 6. 1972. "Chlorophyceae (Grünalgen), Ordnung Tetrasporales". x + 116 pp., 47 pls.
  Descriptions and keys to species. World-wide coverage.

PASCHER, A. 1913–32. "Die Süsswasser-Flora Deutschlands, Österreichs und der Schweiz". G. Fischer, Jena:
  Part 1. 1914. "Flagellatae 1" (A. Pascher and E. Lemmermann). iv + 138 pp.
  Part 2. 1913. "Flagellatae 2" (A. Pascher and E. Lemmermann). iv + 192 pp.

Part 3. 1913. "Dinoflagellatae (Peridineae)" (A. J. Schilling). iv + 66 pp.
Part 4. 1927. "Volvocales—Phytomonadinae" (A. Pascher). Flagellatae 4—Chlorophyceae. 1. vi + 506 pp.
Part 5. 1915. "Chlorophyceae" 2 (E. Lemmermann, J. Brunnthaler and A. Pascher). iv + 250 pp.
Part 6. 1914. "Chlorophyceae 3" (W. Heering). iv + 250 pp.
Part 7. 1921. "Chlorophyceae 4" (W. Heering). iv + 103 pp.
Part 9. 1913. "Zygnemales" (O. Borge and A. Pascher). iv + 51 pp. * 2nd edn. 1932 (V. Czurda). v + 232 pp.
Part 10. 1930. "Bacillariales (Diatomeae)" (H. von Schönfeldt). iv + 187 pp. *2nd edn. 1930 (F. Hustedt). viii + 466 pp.
Part 11. 1925. "Heterokontae, Phaeophyta, Rhodophyta, Charophyta" (A. Pascher, J. Schiller and W. Migula). iv + 250 pp.
Part 12. 1925. "Cyanophyceae" (L. Geitler); "Cyanochloridinae—Chlorobacteriaceae" (L. Geitler and A. Pascher). viii + 481 pp.
*The two parts of the second edition have the title: Süsswasser-Flora Mitteleuropas.

PRESCOTT, G. W. 1962. "Algae of the Western Great Lakes area with an illustrated key to the genera of Desmids and Freshwater Diatoms". Revised edn. 977 pp. W. C. Brown, Dubuque, Iowa.

RABENHORST's KRYPTOGAMEN-FLORA VON DEUTSCHLAND, ÖSTERREICH UND DER SCHWEIZ. 1890–1966. Vols. 5, 7, 10–14. Akademie Verlag, Leipzig. Includes:-
  5. 1890–97. "Die Characeen" (W. Migula).
  7. 1927–66 (unfinished). "Die Kieselalgen" (F. Hustedt).
  10(2). 1930. "Silicoflagellatae" (K. Gemeinhardt). "Coccolinthineae" (J. Schiller).
  10(3) 1931–37. "Dinoflagellatae" (J. Schiller).
  11. 1937–39. "Heterokontae" (A. Pascher).
  12(4). 1938–40. "Oedogoniales" (K. Gemeinhardt).
  13(1). 1933–39. "Desmidiaceae" (W. Krieger) (incomplete).
  13(2). 1941–44. "Zygnemales" (R. Kolkwitz and H. Krieger).
  14(2). 1930–32. "Cyanophyceae" (L. Geitler).

Descriptions, keys generic and specific, distribution foreign only, general biological data; a well-illustrated account in German for advanced students.

SMITH, G. M. 1933. "The Freshwater Algae of the United States". 716 pp. Illustrated. MacGraw-Hill, New York & London. 2nd edn. 1950.

WEST, G. S. & FRITSCH, F. E. 1927. "A Treatise on the British Freshwater Algae". 534 pp. University Press, Cambridge.

Keys generic only, distribution British only, biological data, descriptions of genera and a few species.

MARINE

BARRETT, J. H. & YONGE, C. M. 1958. See above p. 3.

Algae pp. 219–252; keys and descriptions; ecology; a very useful early beginner's book.

BUTCHER, R. W. 1959–67. An introductory account of the smaller algae of British coastal waters. *Fishery Invest., Lond.*, ser. 4.
  Part 1. 1959. Introduction and Chlorophyceae. 74 pp., 14 pls.
  Part 4. 1967. Cryptophyceae. vi + 54 pp., 20 pls.
  Part 5. 1964. Bacillariophyceae (Diatoms) (N. I. Hendey). xxii + 317 pp., 45 pls.
  Part 8. 1961. Euglenophyceae—Euglineae. 17 pp., 3 pls.

Descriptions, keys to genera and species (genera only for diatoms). Many new species in other groups.

CAMPBELL, A. C. 1976. See p. 3.
DICKINSON, C. I. 1963. "British Seaweeds". 232 pp. The Kew Series. Eyre & Spottiswoode, London. Out of print.
JONES, W. E. 1962. A key to the genera of the British seaweeds. *Fld Stud.* 1(4): 1–32. Reprinted 1964 with revisions.
 Systematic keys to genera, and in some cases to species. In process of revision but still useful at all levels.
NEWTON, L. 1931. "A Handbook of British Seaweeds". xiii + 478 pp., 270 text-figs. British Museum (Natural History), London. Reprinted 1958.
 Still a useful handbook; a complete revision is in progress (Dixon & Irvine, 1977).
PANKOW, H. 1971–76. "Algenflora der Ostsee". Vol. 1, "Benthos". 419 pp. Vol. 2, "Plankton" (V. Kell & B. Martens). 493 pp. G. Fischer, Stuttgart.
PARKE, M. W. & DIXON, P. W. 1976. Checklist of British marine Algae—Third revision. *J. Mar. biol. Ass. U.K.* **56.** 527–594.
PRUD'HOMME VAN REINE, W. J. & HARRISON, M. C. 1956. "Plants and Animals of the Sea-shore. A Handy Guide containing Drawings and Descriptions of over 450 spp. of birds, shellfish, seaweeds, fish etc". vi + 138 pp., 34 pls. Murray, London.

CYANOPHYTA

DESIKACHARY, T. V. 1959. "Cyanophyta". x + 686 pp., 139 pls. Indian Council of Agricultural Research, New Delhi.
DROUET, F. 1968. Revision of the classification of the Oscillatoriaceae. *Monogr. Acad. nat. Sci. Philad.* **15:** 1–370.
DROUET, F. 1973. "Revision of the Nostocaceae with cylindrical trichomes". xii + 292 pp. Hafner Press, New York.
DROUET, F. & DAILY, W. A. 1956. Revision of the Coccoid Myxophyceae. *Bot. Stud. Butler Univ.* **12:** 1–218.
 Distributional and habitat data, including Britain, taxonomy, with keys to genera, species and occasionally, forms; many figures. Additions and corrections to the original paper in *Trans. Am. microsc. Soc.* **76:** 219–222 (1957).

RHODOPHYTA

DIXON, P. W. & IRVINE, L. M. 1977. "The Seaweeds of the British Isles". Vol. 1. "Rhodophyta. Part 1. Introduction, Nemaliales, Gigartinales". xi + 250 pp., 90 figs. British Museum (Natural History), London.
 Descriptions of species, and distribution in Britain. To be followed by treatment of all other British seaweeds.
ISRAELSON, G. 1942. The freshwater Florideae of Sweden. *Symb. bot. upsal.* **6**(1): 1–135.
KYLIN, H. 1956. "Die Gattungen der Rhodophyceen". xv + [1] + 673 pp., 458 figs. CWK Gleerups Förlag, Lund.

CHROMOPHYTA

Bacillariophyceae
CLEVE-EULER, A. 1951–55. Die Diatomeen von Schweden und Finnland. *K. svenska VetenskAkad. Handl.,* ser. 4, **2**(1): 1–163. 1951. **3**(3): 1–153. 1952. **4**(1): 1–158. 1953. **4**(5): 1–255. 1954. **5**(4): 1–232. 1955.

HENDEY, N. I. 1964. "An Introductory account of the Smaller Algae of British coastal waters". Part 5. "Bacillariophyceae (Diatoms). xxii + 317 pp., 45 pls. HMSO, London.
LEBOUR, M. V. 1930. "The Planktonic Diatoms of Northern Seas". ix + 244 pp., 181 text-figs., 4 pls. Ray Society, London.
PATRICK, R. & REIMER, C. W. 1966–75. The Diatoms of the United States exclusive of Alaska and Hawaii. *Monogr. Acad. nat. Sci. Philad.* **13**: vol. 1. xi + 688 pp., vol. 2(1) ix + 213pp.

Freshwater only. Descriptions and figures of all species, keys to genera and species.

Chrysophyceae

BOURRELLY, P. 1957. Recherches sur les Chrysophycées. Morphologie, phylogénie, systématique. *Revue algol., Mém., hors-sér.* **1**: 1–412.

Keys and descriptions of genera, and of some species. World-wide treatment.

Xanthophyceae

BLUM, J. L. 1972. Vaucheriaceae. *N. Am. Fl., ser.* 3, **8**: 1–64.

Keys and descriptions of species. World-wide treatment.

Phaeophyceae

See also under Marine (pp. 160–161).
HAMEL, G. 1931–39. "Phéophycées de France". xlvii + 431 pp., 10 pls. Paris.

EUGLENOPHYTA

LEEDALE, G. 1967. "Euglenoid Flagellates". xiii + 24 pp. Prentice-Hall, London.

CHLOROPHYTA

Ulvales

BLIDING, C. 1963. A critical survey of european taxa in Ulvales. *Op. bot. Soc. bot. Lund* **8**(3): 1–160.

Useful survey of most aspects of the biology of the Ulvales, including British species. Taxonomy, but no keys. Useful descriptions and photographs.

Cladophora

VAN DEN HOEK, C. 1963. "Revision of the European species of *Cladophora*". vii + 1–248 pp., 55 pls. E. J. Brill, Leiden.

All aspects of the genus in Europe; key to species and varieties.
SÖDERSTRÖM, J. 1963. Studies in *Cladophora*. *Acta Hort. gothoburg* **26**(1): 1–147, 125 figs.

Concerns the genus in the European Atlantic; maps; most aspects of its biology; key to species.

Desmidiaceae

WEST, W. & G. S. & CARTER, N. 1904–23. "A Monograph of the British Desmidiaceae". 5 vols. 1198 pp., 167 pls. Ray Society, London.

Keys, generic and specific; distribution British and foreign; biological data very scanty; a very useful monograph with good illustrations.

Charophyceae (Charophyta; Stoneworts; see also p. 169).

ALLEN, G. O. 1950. "British Stoneworts (Charophyta)". 52 pp. Buncle, Arbroath.
   A short introduction to the group, with keys and descriptions.
GROVES, J. & BULLOCK-WEBSTER, F. R. 1924. "The British Charophyta". 2 vols. 280 pp. Ray Society, London.
   Descriptions, illustrations, keys generic and specific, distribution British and foreign, biological data fairly full; a useful monograph with good illustrations.
WOOD, R. D. & IMAHORI, K. 1964–65. "Monograph of the Characeae". 2 vols. xxiv + 904 pp., 395 pls. & figs. Cramer, Weinheim.
   World-wide treatment with descriptions and keys to species.

BRYOPHYTA

British species about 980

GENERAL

WATSON, E. V. 1968. "British Mosses and Liverworts". 2nd edn. 495 pp., illustr. Cambridge University Press.
   Illustrated descriptions of and keys to many British bryophytes.
SMITH, A. J. E., ed. 1963 on. Distribution maps of British and Irish Bryophytes. *Trans. Br. bryol. Soc.* **4–6** 1963–1971; *J. Bryol.* **7** 1972 on.
AUGIER, I. 1966. "Flora des Bryophytes". Encyclopédie biologique No. 4. 702 pp. P. Lechavalier, Paris.
GAMS, H. 1973. "Kleine Kryptogamenflora". Vol. 4. "Die Moos- und Farnpflanzen". 5th edn. 240 pp. Fischer, Stuttgart.

HEPATICAE (HEPATICOPSIDA AND ANTHOCERTOPSIDA)
(Liverworts)   British species about 290

GENERAL

MACVICAR, S. M. 1926. "The Student's Handbook of British Hepatics". 2nd edn. 464 pp. Sumfield, Eastbourne. Reprinted 1960. Wheldon & Wesley, Codicote.
JONES, E. W. 1952. Advances in the knowledge of British Hepatics since 1926. *Trans. Br. bryol. Soc.* **2:** 1–10.
JONES, E. W. 1958. An annotated list of British hepatics. *Trans. Br. bryol. Soc.* **3:** 353–374.
   Check list with references, critical remarks, etc.
PATON, J. A. 1965. "Census Catalogue of British Hepatics". 4th edn. 50 pp. British Bryological Society, Ipswich.
   Full British and Irish distribution by vice-counties: nomenclature corrected: now the British standard check list. For species added to the British list since 1965 see *Trans. Br. bryol. Soc.* **5–6** 1965–1971; *J. Bryol.* **7** 1972 on.
MÜLLER, K. 1951. Die Lebermoose Deutschlands, Oesterreichs und der Schweiz. 3rd edn. *Rabenh. Krypt.-Fl.* **6**(1): 1–756.
   Ed. 1 (1906–1911) is superior in some respects to Ed. 3 and should be consulted.
VAN DEN BERGEN, C. 1955–57. "Flora Générale de Belgique". "Bryophytes" Vol. 1(1–3). Ministère de l'Agriculture, Bruxelles.
ARNELL, S. 1956. "Illustrated Moss Flora of Fennoscandia". Vol. 1. Hepaticae. 308 pp. Gleerups, Lund.

SCHUSTER, R. M. 1953. Boreal Hepaticae. A manual of the liverworts of Minnesota and adjacent regions. *Am. Midl. Nat.* **42:** 257–684.
Well illustrated.

SCHUSTER, R. M. 1958. Annotated key to the orders, families and genera of the Hepaticae of America north of Mexico. *Bryologist* **61:** 1–66.

SCHUSTER, R. M. 1966–75. "The Hepaticae and Anthocerotae of North America east of the Hundredth Meridian". 3 vols. Columbia University Press, New York.
An exhaustive and lavishly illustrated work of which two further volumes are still to appear.

MONOGRAPHS OF SPECIAL GROUPS

Ricciaceae

PATON, J. A. 1967. *Riccia crystallina* L. and *R. cavernosa* Hoffm. in Britain. *Trans. Br. bryol. Soc.* **5:** 222–225.

Riccardiaceae

LITTLE, E. R. B. 1968. The oil bodies of the genus *Riccardia* Gray. *Trans. Br. bryol. Soc.* **5:** 536–540.

Fossombroniaceae

PATON, J. A. 1973. Taxonomic studies on the genus *Fossombronia* Raddi. *J. Bryol.* **7:** 243–252.

Calypogeiaceae

PATON, J. A. 1962. The genus *Calypogeia* in Britain. *Trans. Br. bryol. Soc.* **4:** 221–229.

Lophoziaceae

FITZGERALD, J. W. & FITZGERALD, R. D. 1962. *Barbilophozia atlantica* (Kaal.) K. Müll. in Britain. *Trans. Br. bryol. Soc.* **4:** 214–220.

GROLLE, R. 1960. Beitrag zur Kenntnis von *Barbilophozia,* insbesondere *B. floerkii* und *B. hatcheri. Nova Hedwigia* **2:** 555–566.

Scapaniaceae

BUCH, H. 1928. Die Scapanien Nord-europas und Sibiriens. II Systematischer Teil. *Soc. Sci. Fennica, Commentat. biol.* **3**(1): 1–177.

Lejeuneaceae

GREIG-SMITH, P. 1954. Notes on Lejeuneaceae. II. A quantitative assessment of criteria used in distinguishing some British species of *Lejeunea. Trans. Br. bryol. Soc.* **2:** 458–469.

BUCH, H. 1924. Muscinées recoltés dans le nordouest de la Péninsule Ibérique. *Revue bryol. lichén.* **7:** 238–248.

MUSCI (MOSSES) British species about 690

GENERAL

BRAITHWAITE, R. 1887–1905. "The British Moss Flora". 3 vols. Reeve, London.

DIXON, H. N. 1924. "The Student's Handbook of British Mosses". 580 pp. Illustrated. 3rd edn. Sumfield, Eastbourne. Reprint 1954. Wheldon & Wesley, Codicote.

Descriptions of and keys to all taxa known in Britain in 1924; nomenclature and classification now out of date.

RICHARDS, P. W. & WALLACE, E. C. 1950. Annotated list of British Mosses. *Trans. Br. bryol. Soc.* **1,** *Suppl.* 31 pp.
  Check-list with references to species recorded since Dixon, H. N. (1924), critical notes, references to relevant literature, etc.

SMITH, A. J. E. 1978. "The Moss Flora of Britain and Ireland." 705 pp., illustrated. Cambridge University Press, Cambridge.
  A fully comprehensive modern flora.

WARBURG, E. F. 1963. "A Census Catalogue of British Mosses". 3rd edn. 88 pp. British Bryological Society, Ipswich.
  Full British and Irish distribution by vice-counties; nomenclature now out of date. For species added to the British list since 1963 see *Trans. Br. bryol. Soc.* **4–6** 1963–1971; *J. Bryol.* **7** 1972 on.

CRUNDWELL, A. C. 1957. Some neglected British moss records. *Trans Br. bryol. Soc.* **3**: 174–179.

LIMPRICHT, K. G. 1890–1904. Die Laubmoose Europas. *Rabenh. Krypt.-Fl.* **4**(1): 1–836, (2): 1–854, (3): 1–864, *1–79*.

MÖNKEMEYER, W. 1927. Die Laubmoose Europas. *Rabenh. Krypt.-Fl.* **4** (Ergänzungsband): 1–960. Reprint 1963. Cramer, Weinheim.

PODPĚRA, J. 1954. "Conspectus Muscorum Europaeorum". 697 pp. Československé Akademie Ved, Prague.

NYHOLM, E. 1954–69. "Illustrated Moss Flora of Fennoscandia. II. Musci". 6 fascicles. Gleerups, Lund.

LYE, K. A. 1968. "Moseflora". 144 pp. Universitetsforlaget, Oslo.

BOESEN, D. F. *et al.* 1973. "Dansk Mosflora. Die Pleurokarpe bladmosser". 97 pp. University of Copenhagen.

LANDWEHR, J. & BARKMAN, J. J. 1966. "Atlas von Nederlandse Bladmossen". Koninlijke Nederlandse Naturhistorische Vereniging.

DE SLOOVER, J. 1968. "Flora Générale de Belgique". "Bryophytes". Vol. 3(1). Ministère de l'Agriculture, Brussels.

DEMARET, F. & CASTAGNE, E. 1959–64. "Flora Générale de Belgique". "Bryophytes". Vol. 2 (1–3). Ministère de l'Agriculture, Brussels.

GROUT, A. J. 1928–40. "Moss Flora of North America North of Mexico". 3 vols. Newfane, Vermont.

MONOGRAPHS OF SPECIAL GROUPS

Sphagnales (Sphagnopsida)

DUNCAN, U. K. 1962. An illustrated key to *Sphagnum* mosses. *Trans. Proc. bot. Soc. Edinb.* **29**: 290–301.

FEARNSIDES, M. 1938. Graphic keys for the identification of *Sphagna*. *New Phytol.* **37**: 409–420.

HILL, M. O. 1975. *Sphagnum subsecundum* Nees and *S. auriculatum* Schimp. in Britain. *J. Bryol.* **8**: 435–441.

HILL, M. O. 1976. A key for the identification of British *Sphagna* using macroscopic characters. *Bull. Br. bryol. Soc.* **27**: 22–31.

MAASS, H. S. G. 1965. *Sphagnum dusenii* and *S. balticum* in Britain. *Bryologist* **68**: 211–217.

PROCTOR, M. C. F. 1955. A key to the British species of *Sphagnum*. *Trans. Br. bryol. Soc.* **2**: 552–560.

TALLIS, J. H. 1962. The identification of *Sphagnum* spores. *Trans. Br. bryol. Soc.* **4**: 209–213.

ÅBERG, G. 1937. Untersuchen über die *Sphagnum*-Arten der Gruppe *Subsecunda* in Europa. *Ark. Bot.* **29A**(1): 1–77.

Andreaeales (Andreaeopsida)

SCHULTZE-MOTEL, W. 1970. Monographie der Laubmoosgattung *Andreaea* I. Die costaten Arten. *Willdenowia* **6**: 25–110.

Bryales (Bryopsida)

Polytrichaceae

ALBRECHT, J. H. 1934. Synopsis of the European species of *Pogonatum* and *Polytrichum. J. Bot., Lond.* **72**: 75–90, 104–110.

NYHOLM, E. 1971. Studies on the genus *Atrichum* P. Beauv. *Lindbergia* **1**: 1–33.

Fissidentaceae

NORKETT, A. H. 1956. Notes on *Fissidens. Trans. Br. bryol. Soc.* **3**: 69–71.

SMITH, A. J. E. 1970. *Fissidens viridulus* Wahlenb. and *F. minutulus* Sull. *Trans. Br. bryol. Soc.* **6**: 56–68.

SMITH, A. J. E. 1975. Key to British and Irish species of Fissidentaceae. *Bull. Br. bryol. Soc.* **26**: 26–27.

SMITH, A. J. E. & WARBURG, E. F. 1961. *Fissidens crassipes* Wils. ex B., S. & G., *F. mildeanus* Schimp. and *F. rufulus* B., S. & G. *Trans. Br. bryol. Soc.* **4**: 204–205.

POTIER DE LA VARDE, R. 1938. "Le genre *Fissidens* dans la Manche." 30 pp. Imprimerie René Jaqueline, St Lô.

Keys and critical notes; figures most of the British species.

Archidiaceae

SNIDER, J. A. 1975. A revision of the genus *Archidium* (Musci). *J. Hattori bot. Lab.* **39**: 105–201.

Dicranaceae

AHTI, T., ISOVIITA, P. & MAASS, W. S. G. 1965. *Dicranum leioneurum* new to the British Isles and Labrador. *Bryologist* **68**: 197–201.

BRIGGS, D. 1965. Experimental taxonomy of some British species of the genus *Dicranum. New Phytol.* **64**: 366–386.

CORLEY, M. F. V. 1976. The taxonomy of *Campylopus pyriformis* (Schultz) Brid. and related species. *J. Bryol.* **9**: 193–212.

CORLEY, M. F. V. 1976. Nerve sections in the Dicranales I. *Campylopus* and *Dicranodontium. Bull. Br. bryol. Soc.* **28**: 14–15.

CRUNDWELL, A. C. 1960. Notes on the British species of *Cynodontium. Trans. Br. bryol. Soc.* **3**: 706–712.

LAWTON, E. 1961. A revision of the genus *Rhabdoweisia. Bryologist* **64**: 140–156.

RICHARDS, P. W. & SMITH, A. J. E. 1975. A progress report on *Campylopus introflexus* (Hedw.) Brid. and *C. polytrichoides* De Not. in Britain and Ireland. *J. Bryol.* **8**: 293–298.

Pottiaceae

CHAMBERLAIN, D. F. 1969. New combinations in *Pottia starkeana. Notes R. bot. Gdn Edinb.* **29**: 403–404.

CRUNDWELL, A. C. & NYHOLM, E. 1962. Notes on the genus *Tortella.* I. *T. inclinata, T. densa, T. flavovirens* and *T. glareicola. Trans. Br. bryol. Soc.* **4**: 187–193.

CRUNDWELL, A. C. & NYHOLM, E. 1972. A revision of *Weissia*, subgenus *Astomum*. I. The European species. *J. Bryol.* **7**: 7–19.

DELGADILLO, M. C. 1975. Taxonomic revision of *Aloina, Aloinella* and *Crossidium* (Musci). *Bryologist* **78:** 245–303.
JONES, E. W. 1949. Notes on British *Barbulas. Trans. Br. bryol. Soc.* **1:** 190–193.
WARBURG, E. F. 1958. The *Cinclidotus* of the River Teme. *Trans. Br. bryol. Soc.* **3:** 383–385.

Grimmiaceae

CRUNDWELL, A. C. 1952. *Grimmia homodictyon. Trans. Br. bryol. Soc.* **2:** 15–18.
CRUNDWELL, A. C. 1959. *Grimmia trichodon* in Britain. *Trans. Br. bryol. Soc.* **3:** 558–562.
JONES, E. W. & WARBURG, E. F. 1950. *Grimmia andreaeoides* Limpr. *Trans. Br. bryol. Soc.* **1:** 367–368.
LOESKE, L. 1930. Monographie der europäischen Grimmiaceen. *Biblthca bot.* **25:** 1–236.
POELT, J. 1953. Zur Kenntnis der *gracile*-Formen der Sammelart *Schistidium apocarpum* (L.) Br. Eur. *Svensk bot. Tidskr.* **47:** 248–262.
SMITH, A. J. E. 1975. Key to the British genera and species of the Grimmiaceae. *Bull. Br. bryol. Soc.* **25:** 21–24.

Funariaceae

CRUNDWELL, A. C. & NYHOLM, E. 1974. *Funaria muhlenbeckii* and related European species. *Lindbergia* **2:** 222–229.
DUCKER, B. E. T. & WARBURG, E. F. 1961. *Physcomitrium eurystomum* Sendtn. in Britain. *Trans. Br. bryol. Soc.* **4:** 95–97.
LOESKE, L. 1914–19. "Die Laubmoose Europas". Vol. 2. "Funariaceae". viii + 120 pp. Illustrated. Berlin.

Ephemeraceae

BRYAN, V. S. & ANDERSON, L. E. 1957. The Ephemeraceae in North America. *Bryologist* **60:** 67–172.
DOUIN, C. 1907. Étude sur l'*Ephemerum serratum* et remarques sur les *Ephemerum* européens. *Bull. Soc. bot. Fr.* **54:** 242–251, 306–326.

Bryaceae

CRUNDWELL, A. C. & NYHOLM, E. 1964. The European species of the *Bryum erythrocarpum* complex. *Trans. Br. bryol. Soc.* **4:** 597–637.
IWATSUKI, Z. & KOPONEN, T. 1972. On the taxonomy and distribution of *Rhodobryum roseum* and a related species (Bryophyta). *Acta bot. fenn.* **96:** 1–22.
MARGADANT, W. D. & MEIJER, W. 1950. Preliminary remarks on *Orthodontium* in Europe. *Trans. Br. bryol. Soc.* **1:** 266–274.
PODPERA, J. 1942–53. *Bryum* generis monographiae prodromus. I. Species Eurasiae Septentrionalis. *Acta Soc. Sci. nat. Moravo-Silesacae* **14–17.**
SMITH, A. J. E. 1973. On the differences between *Bryum creberrimum* Tayl. and *B. pallescens* Schleich. ex Schwaegr. *J. Bryol.* **7:** 333–337.
SYED, H. 1973. A taxonomic study of *Bryum capillare* Hedw. and related species. *J. Bryol.* **7:** 265–326.
WILCZEK, R. & DEMARET, F. 1976. Les espèces du "complexe *Bryum bicolor*" (Musci). *Bull. Jard. bot. natn. Belg.* **46:** 511–541.

Mniaceae

KOPONEN, T. 1968. Generic revision of Mniaceae Mitt. (Bryophyta). *Ann. bot. fenn.* **5:** 117–151.
KOPONEN, T. 1968. The moss genus *Rhizomnium* (Roth.) Kop. with description of

Rhizomnium perssonii, species nova. *Mem. Soc. Fauna Fl. fenn.* **44**: 33–50.

KOPONEN, T. 1971. A monograph of *Plagiomnium* sect. *Rosulata* (Mniaceae). *Ann. bot. fenn.* **8**: 305–367.

Bartramiaceae

DISMIER, C. 1908. Essai monographique sur les *Philonotis* de France. *Mém. Soc. Sci. nat. Math. Cherbourg* **36**: 367–428.

FIELD, J. H. 1963. Notes on the taxonomy of the genus *Philonotis* by means of vegetative characters. *Trans. Br. bryol. Soc.* **4**: 429–433.

Orthotrichaceae

MALTA, N. 1926. Die Gattung *Zygodon*. *Acta hort. bot. Univ. Latv.* **1**: 1–184.

RHODES, P. G. M. 1926. The European varieties of *Zygodon viridissimus*. *Rep. Br. bryol. Soc.* **1**: 200–202.

SMITH, A. J. E. & HILL, M. O. 1975. A taxonomic investigation of *Ulota bruchii* Hornsch. ex Brid., *U. crispa* (Hedw.) Brid. and *U. crispula* Brid. I. European material. *J. Bryol.* **8**: 423–434.

VITT, D. H. 1973. "A Revision of the Genus *Orthotrichum* in North America north of Mexico". Bibliotheca Bryophytorum No. 1. J. Cramer, Lehre.

Fontinalaceae

WELCH, W. H. 1960. "A Monograph of the Fontinalaceae". 357 pp. Martinus Nijhoff, The Hague.

Leskeaceae

LAWTON, E. 1957. Revision of the genus *Lescuraea* in Europe and N. America. *Bull. Torrey bot. Club* **84**: 281–307.

Thuidiaceae

TALLIS, J. H. 1961. The distributions of *Thuidium recognitum* Lindb., *T. philibertii* Limpr. and *T. delicatumum* Mitt. in Britain. *Trans. Br. bryol. Soc.* **4**: 102–106.

Amblystegiaceae

CRUNDWELL, A. C. & NYHOLM, E. 1961. A study of *Campylium hispidulum* and related species. *Trans. Br. bryol. Soc.* **4**: 194–200.

LODGE, E. 1960. Studies of variation in British material of *Drepanocladus fluitans* and *D. exannulatus*. I. An analysis of the variation. *Svensk bot. Tidskr.* **54**: 368–386.

Brachytheciaceae

BRIZI, U. 1896. Saggio monographico del genero *Rhynchostegium*. *Malpighia* **10**: 227–257.

CRUNDWELL, A. C. 1959. A revision of the British material of *Brachythecium glaciale* and *B. starkei*. *Trans. Br. bryol. Soc.* **3**: 565–567.

WIGH, K. 1974. The European genera of the family Brachytheciaceae (Bryophyta) and chromosome numbers published in the genus *Brachythecium*. *Bot. Notiser* **127**: 89–103.

Plagiotheciaceae

CRUNDWELL, A. C. 1959. *Plagiothecium laetum* in Britain. *Trans. Br. bryol. Soc.* **3**: 563–564.

GREENE, S. W. 1957. The British species of the *Plagiothecium denticulatum-sylvaticum* group. *Trans. Br. bryol. Soc.* **3**: 181–190.

Hypnaceae
DOIGNON, P. & GUILLAMOT, M. 1950. Les *Stereodon* de l'Europe. *Revue bryol. lichén.* **20**: 263-288.
GREENE, S. W. & GREENE, D. N. 1960. An assessment of some characters distinguishing *Pylaisia polyantha* (Hedw.) B. & S. from *Hypnum cupressiforme* Hedw. var. *resupinatum* (Wils.) Schp. *Trans. Br. bryol. Soc.* **3**: 715-723.

PTERIDOPHYTA
(Ferns and Fern Allies)
British species about 80

HOOKER, W. J. 1861. "The British Ferns". 66 col. pls. Reeve, London.
  Descriptions, no keys or biological data, British distribution in general terms; useful for its good illustrations.
MOORE, T. 1859-60. "The Nature Printed British Ferns. 2 vols. 620 pp. Bradbury & Evans, London.
  Descriptions, illustrations, no keys, detailed British distribution: no biological data; out-of-date but still useful.
NEWMAN, E. 1854. "A History of British Ferns". 343 pp. J. van Voorst, London.
  Descriptions, illustrations, no keys; British and foreign distribution; some biological data.
STEP, E. 1949. "Wayside and Woodland Ferns". New edn. (by A. B. Jackson). 144 pp. Warne, London.
  Descriptions, illustrations, no keys, British and foreign distribution.
TAYLOR, P. G. 1960. "British Ferns and Mosses". The Kew Series. 231 pp. Eyre & Spottiswoode, London.
  Descriptions, illustrations and keys; ecological but no cytological data; includes fern allies and a few mosses.
HYDE, H. A., WADE. A. E. & HARRISON, S. G. 1969. "Welsh Ferns, Clubmosses, Quillworts and Horsetails". 5th edn. 178 pp. National Museum of Wales, Cardiff.
  Descriptions, keys, British and foreign distribution, cytological data, etc.
LUERSSEN, C. 1889. Die Farnpflanzen. *Rabenh. Krypt.-Fl.* **3**: 1-906.
  Descriptions, illustrations, generic and specific keys, overseas distribution only (often inaccurate), scanty biological data: the best book for serious students, but some British species not included.
KENT, D. H. 1967. See p. 170 below.

SPERMATOPHYTA
(Flowering Plants and Conifers)
British species about 2000, excluding microspecies of certain genera.

GENERAL
Many of the books listed include Charophyceae (see also p. 163) and Pteridophyta (see also above). Though some of the works cited are out-of-date as regards classification and nomenclature they remain useful.

BABINGTON, C. C. 1922. "Manual of British Botany". 10th edn. (revised by A. J. Wilmott). liv + 612 pp. Gurney & Jackson, London.
BENTHAM, G. 1947. "Handbook of the British Flora". 7th edn. (revised by A. B. Rendle) (reprinted). lxi + 606 pp. L. Reeve, London.
BUTCHER, R. W. 1961. "A New Illustrated British Flora". 2 vols., 1825 figs. L. Hill, London.
BUTCHER, R. W. & STRUDWICK, F. E. 1946. "Further Illustrations of British Plants". 2nd edn. iv + ii + 476 pp., 485 figs. L. Reeve, London.
CLAPHAM, A. R., TUTIN, T. G. & WARBURG, E. F. 1962. "Flora of the British Isles". 2nd edn. xlviii + 1269 pp., 84 figs. Cambridge University Press.
  The standard British flora.
CLAPHAM, A. R., TUTIN, T. G. & WARBURG, E. F. 1957–65. "Flora of the British Isles". "Illustrations by S. J. Roles". 4 vols., 1910 figs. Cambridge University Press.
CLAPHAM, A. R., TUTIN, T. G. & WARBURG, E. F. 1968. "Excursion Flora of the British Isles". 2nd edn. xxxv + 586 pp. Cambridge University Press.
DAVIS, P. H. & CULLEN, J. 1965. "The Identification of Flowering Plant Families". 122 pp. Oliver & Boyd, Edinburgh & London.
DAVIS, P. H. & HEYWOOD, V. H. 1963. "Principles of Angiosperm Taxonomy". xx + 556 pp. Oliver & Boyd, Edinburgh & London.
DRUCE, G. C. 1948. "Hayward's Botanists' Pocket-Book". 19th edn. (reprinted). xlv + 310 pp. S. Bell, London.
FITCH, W. H. & SMITH, W. G. 1946. "Illustrations of the British Flora". 5th edn. (reprinted). xxvii + 338 pp., 1315 figs. L. Reeve, London.
FITTER, R., FITTER, A. & BLAMEY, M. 1974. "The Wild Flowers of Britain and Northern Europe". 2nd edn. 336 pp., 2900 figs. Collins, London.
HOOKER, J. D. 1937. "The Student's Flora of the British Isles". 3rd edn. (reprinted). xxiii + 563 pp. Macmillan, London.
HUTCHINSON, J. 1959. "The Families of Flowering Plants". 2nd edn. Oxford University Press.
KENT, D. H. 1967. "Index to Botanical Monographs and Taxonomic Papers relating to Phanerogams and Vascular Cryptogams found Growing Wild in the British Isles". xi + 163 pp. Academic Press, London & New York.
McCLINTOCK, D. & FITTER, R. S. R. 1956. "The Pocket Guide to Wild Flowers". xii + 340 pp., 1400 figs. Illustrated. Collins, London. [Suppl. by D. McClintock (1957) ix + 89 pp. Platt, Kent: privately printed.]
MARTIN, W. K. 1969. "The Concise British Flora in Colour". 2nd edn. (revised D. H. Kent). 254 pp., 1486 figs. Ebury Press & M. Joseph, London.
MOSS, C. E. 1914–20. "The Cambridge British Flora". Vols. 2 and 3 only. Illustrated. Cambridge.
ROSS-CRAIG, S. 1948-74. "Drawings of British Plants". 31 vols. + index. 1317 figs. Bell, London.
STACE, C. A., (ed.). 1975. "Hybridization and the Flora of the British Isles". xiii + 626 pp. Academic Press, London, New York & San Francisco.
SYME, J. T. BOSWELL. 1863–86. "English Botany; or coloured figures of British Plants". 12 vols. R. Hardwicke, London. [Suppl. to vols. 1–4 (1891) 1892 compiled by N. E. Brown, London].
TUTIN, T. G. *et al.*, eds. 1964 on "Flora Europaea". 4 vols to date. Cambridge University Press.
  Authoritative treatments of all genera planned; with keys; essential for all advanced students.
WEBB, D. A. 1977. "An Irish Flora". 6th edn. (revised). xxxi + 276 pp., 100 figs. Dundalgan Press, Dundalk.

LISTS

HANBURY, F. J. 1925. "The London Catalogue of British Plants". 11th edn. 55 + 3 pp. London.
DRUCE, G. C. 1928. "British Plant List". 2nd edn. xi + ii + 154 pp. T. Buncle, Arbroath.
CLAPHAM, A. R. 1946. Check-list of British vascular plants. *J. Ecol.* **33:** 308–347.
DANDY, J. E. 1958. "List of British Vascular Plants". xvi + 176 pp. British Museum (Natural History) and Botanical Society of the British Isles, London.
DANDY, J. E. 1969. Nomenclatural changes in the "List of British Vascular Plants". *Watsonia* **7:** 157–178.
EHRENDORFER, F. 1973. "Liste der Gefasspflanzen Mitteleuropas". 2nd edn. xii + 318 pp. G. Fischer, Stuttgart.

FOREIGN BOOKS USEFUL IN THE IDENTIFICATION OF FLOWERING PLANTS IN BRITAIN

ASCHERSON, P. & GRAEBNER, P. 1896–1939. "Synopsis der mitteleuropäischen Flora". 8 vols. W. Engelmann, Leipzig.
BAILEY, L. H. 1949. "Manual of Cultivated Plants". 2nd edn. 1116 pp. Macmillan, New York & London.
BINZ, A. & THOMMEN, E. 1953. "Flore de la Suisse". 2nd edn. xxxvi + 450 pp. F. Rouge, Lausanne.
BONNIER, G. E. M. & DOUIN, R. 1911–35. "Flore complète de France, Suisse et Belgique". 12 vols. 721 col. pls. Librarie Générale de l'Enseignement . . ., Paris.
BOOM, B. K. & RUYS, J. D. 1950. "Flora der Gekweekte, Kruidachtige Gewassen". 450 pp. H. Veenman, Wageningen.
BRIQUET, J. & LITARDIÈRE, R. 1910–55. "Prodrome de la Flore Corse". 3 vols. Incomplete. Georg, Geneva.
COSTE, l'ABBÉ H. 1937. "Flore Descriptive et Illustrée de la France". 3 vols. Reprinted. Illustrated. P. Klincksieck, Paris. Also Suppls. by P. Jovet & R. de Vilmorin (1972) **1:** lxi + 88 pp.; (1974) **2:** 89–173 pp.; (1975) **3:** 174–337. A. Blanchard, Paris.
COUTINHO, A. X. P. 1939. "Flora de Portugal". 2nd edn. (by R. T. Palhinha). 933 pp. Bertrand, Lisbon.
FIORI, A. 1923–29. "Nuova Flora Analitica d'Italia". 2 vols. Ricci, Florence.
FIORI, A. & PAOLETTI, G. 1933. "Iconographia Florae Italicae". 3rd edn. Florence.
FOURNIER, P. 1961. "Les Quatre Flores de la France". (Corrected reprint.) xlviii + 1105 pp., 8075 figs. P. Lechevalier, Paris.
FRANCO, J. M. A. P. do AMARAL 1971. "Nova Flora de Portugal (Continente e Açores)". 1 vol. (to date). xxiv + 648 pp. Astoria, Lisbon.
GARCKE, F. A. 1972. "Illustrierte Flora Deutschland und angrenzender Gebiete". 23rd edn. (edited by K. von Weihe). xx + 1607 pp. Illustrated. P. Parey, Berlin & Hamburg.
HEGI, G. 1906–31. "Illustrierte Flora von Mittel-Europa". 8 vols. Illustrated. Lehmann, Munich. 2nd edn. 1936–1971 7 vols. Hanser, Munich & Berlin.
HERMANN, F. 1956. "Flora von Nord- und Mitteleuropa". xii + 1154 pp. G. Fischer, Stuttgart.
HESS, H. E., LANDOLT, E. & HIRZEL, R. 1967–72. "Flora der Schweiz und agrenzender Gebiete". 3 vols. Birkhäuser, Stuttgart.
HEUKELS-OOSTROOM, S. J. VAN 1975. "Flora van Nederland". 18th edn. 912 pp., 1038 figs. P. Noordhoff, Groningen.

HYLANDER, N. 1953–66. "Nordisk Kärlväxtflora". 2 vols. Almqvist & Wiksell, Stockholm.
KOMAROV, V. L. et al. 1934–64. "Flora S.S.S.R." 30 vols. Illustrated. Akademiya Nauk SSSR., Moscow & Leningrad.
LANGHE, J.-E. DE, et al. 1967, "Flora de la Belgique, du Nord de la France et des Regiones voisines . . . Redigée à l'initiative de William Mullenders". xliv + 749 pp. Éditions Desoer, Liège.
LID, J. 1963. "Norsk og Svensk Flora". 4th edn. 800 pp., 434 figs. Norske Samlaget, Oslo.
LÖVE, Á. 1970. "Íslensk-Ferdaflóra". 428 pp. Illustrated. Almenna Bókaf élagi à, Reykjavik. (In Icelandic).
MANSFIELD, R. 1959. Prodromus enumerationis specierum plantarum agri- et horticulturae. *Kulturpflanzen Beih.* **2:** i–v + 1–659.
POLUNIN, O. 1969. "Flowers of Europe. A Field Guide". 642 pp., 1926 col. photographs, 50 figs. Oxford University Press, London.
POLUNIN, O. & HUXLEY, A. J. 1965. "Flowers of the Mediterranean". xi + 257 pp., 439 figs. Chatto & Windus, London.
POLUNIN, O. & SMYTHIES, B. E. 1973. "Flowers of South-West Europe". xv + 480 pp. Illustrated. Oxford University Press, London.
ROBYNS, W., ed. 1952 on. "Flora Générale de Belgique. Spermatophytes". 4 vols. to date by A. Lawalrée. Illustrated. Jardin Botanique de l'État, Brussels.
ROSTRUP, E. 1953. "Den Danske Flora". 18th edn. lxiv + 527 pp., 154 figs. Gylderdalske Boghandel, Copenhagen.
ROTHMALER, W. 1962–63. "Excursionsflora von Deutschland. Spermatophyta". 3rd edn. Vols. 2–4. Illustrated. Volk & Wisson, Berlin.
ROUY, G. & FOUCAUD, J. 1893–1913. "Flore de France". 14 vols. Asnières (Seine), Paris & Rochefort.
SAMPAIO, G. 1947. "Flora Portuguesa". 2nd edn. (by A. P. de Lima). xliii + 792 pp. Impressiona Moderna, Porto.
SCHINZ, H. & KELLER, R. 1923. "Flora der Schweiz". 4th edn. xxxvi + 792 pp. Illustrated. A. Ranstein, Zurich.
WEEVERS, Th. et al., eds. 1948 on. "Flora Neerlandica". 7 parts to date. Illustrated. De Vereeniging, Amsterdam.
WEIMARCK, H. 1963. "Skånes Flora". xxiv + 720 pp. Corona, Lund.
WILLKOMM, M. & LANGE, J. 1861–93. "Prodromus Florae Hispanicae". 3 vols. and Suppl. E. Schweizerbart, Stuttgart.

MONOGRAPHS OF SPECIAL GROUPS

Trees and Shrubs

BARBER, P. & PHILLIPS, C. E. 1975. "The Trees Around Us". 191 pp. Illustrated. Weidenfeld & Nicolson, London.
BOOM, B. K. 1975. "Nederlandse Dendrologie". 9th edn. 454 pp., 134 figs. H. Veenman, Wageningen.
DALLIMORE, W. & JACKSON, A. B. 1966. "A Handbook of Coniferae and Ginkgoaceae". 4th edn. (by S. G. Harrison). xix + 729 pp. Illustrated. E. Arnold, London.
DEBAZAC, E. F. 1964. "Manuel des Conifères". 172 pp. Illustrated. École National des Eaux et Forêts, Nancy.
DEN OUDEN, P. & BOOM, B. K. 1965. "Manual of Cultivated Conifers hardy in the cold- and warm-temperate zone". xii + 526 pp. Illustrated. M. Nijhoff, The Hague.
ELWES, H. J. & HENRY, A. 1906–13. "The Trees of Great Britain and Ireland". 7 vols. Illustrated. Privately printed, Edinburgh.

GILBERT-CARTER, H. 1932. "Our Catkin-bearing Plants; an introduction". 2nd edn. xii + 61 pp. Illustrated. Oxford University Press, London.
GILBERT-CARTER, H. 1936. "British Trees and Shrubs Including those Commonly Planted; a Systematic Introduction to our Conifers and Woody Dicotyledons". xv + 291 pp. Illustrated. Clarendon Press, Oxford.
GURNEY, R. 1958. "Trees of Britain". 228 pp. Illustrated. Faber, London.
HOLBROOK, A. W. 1966. "The Country Life Pocket Guide to Trees in Britain". 5th edn. (revised). 248 pp. Illustrated. Country Life, London.
KRÜSSMANN, G. 1960–62. "Handbuch der Laubgehölze". 2 vols. Illustrated. P. Parey, Berlin & Hamburg.
KRÜSSMANN, G. 1968. "Die Bäume Europas". 140 pp. Illustrated. P. Parey, Berlin and Hamburg.
KRÜSSMANN, G. 1970–71. "Handbuch der Nadelgehölze". 366 pp. Illustrated. P. Parey, Berlin and Hamburg.
MAKINS, F. K. 1948. "The Identification of Trees and Shrubs". 2nd edn. vii + 375 pp., 128 figs. Dent, London.
MEIKLE, R. D. 1958. "British Trees and Shrubs". Kew Series. 244 pp., 84 figs., 15 col. pls. Eyre & Spottiswoode, London.
MITCHELL, A. 1974. "A Field Guide to the Trees of Britain and Northern Europe". 415 pp., 640 figs., 40 col. pls. Collins, London.
NICHOLSON, B. E. & CLAPHAM, A. R. 1975. "The Oxford Book of Trees". 216 pp. Illustrated. Oxford University Press, London.
PRIME, C. T. & DEACOCK, R. J. 1951. "Trees and Shrubs: their identification in summer and winter". 110 pp. Illustrated. W. Heffer, Cambridge.
REHDER, A. 1940. "Manual of Cultivated Trees and Shrubs hardy in North America". 2nd edn. xxx + 996 pp. + map. Macmillan, New York.
SCHNEIDER, C. K. 1906–12. "Illustriertes Handbuch der Laubholzkunde". 2 vols. and index. Illustrated. G. Fischer, Jena.
WARD, H. M. 1904–09. "Trees: A Handbook of Forest-Botany for the Woodlands and the Laboratory". 5 vols. Illustrated. Cambridge University Press.

Water Plants

COOK, C. D. K. *et al.* 1974. "Water Plants of the World. A Manual for the Identification of the Genera of the Freshwater Macrophytes". viii + 561 pp. Illustrated. W. Junk, The Hague.
FASSETT, N. C. 1972. "A Manual of Aquatic Plants". 2nd. edn. 405 pp. Illustrated. Madison.
HASLAM, S. M., SINKER, C. A. & WOLSELEY, P. O. 1975. British water plants. *Fld Stud.* **4:** 243–351.
 Also available separately; illustrated keys.
MUENSCHER, W. C. 1967. "Aquatic Plants of the United States". Reprinted. x + 374 pp., 154 figs. Constable, London.
ROE, C. D. 1967. "A Manual of Aquarium Plants". 111 pp. Illustrated. Shirley Aquatics, Solihull.
STODOLA, J. 1967. "Encyclopedia of Water Plants". 368 pp. Illustrated. T.F.H. Publications, New York.
WIT, H. C. DE 1964. "Aquarium Plants". 255 pp. Illustrated. English edn. prepared by V. Higgins. Blanford Press, London.

Sedges and Grasses (Cyperaceae and Gramineae)

ARMSTRONG, S. F. 1937. "British Grasses and their Employment in Agriculture". 3rd edn. ix + 350 pp., 194 figs. Cambridge University Press.
HITCHCOCK, A. S. 1950. "Manual of the Grasses of the United States". 2nd edn.

(revised A. Chase). 1051 pp. Illustrated. U.S. Department of Agriculture Publication No. 200, Washington, D.C.

HUBBARD, C. E. 1968. "Grasses: A Guide to their Structure, Identification, Uses, and Distribution in the British Isles". 2nd edn. 463 pp. Illustrated. Penguin Books, Harmondsworth.

JERMY, A. C. & TUTIN, T. G. 1968. "British Sedges. A Handbook to the species of *Carex* found growing in the British Isles". 199 pp. Illustrated. Botanical Society of the British Isles, London.

PARNELL, R. 1842–45. "The Grasses of Britain". 3 vols. Illustrated. Blackwood, Edinburgh & London.

Orchids (Orchidaceae)

BROOKE, B. J. 1950. "The Wild Orchids of Britain". 139 pp., 40 col. pls. Bodley Head, London.

DANESCH, E. & DANESCH, O. 1969. "Orchideen Europas: Südeuropa". 256 pp., 184 col. pls. Hallwag, Stuttgart.

DANESCH, O. & DANESCH, E. 1962. "Orchideen Europas: Mitteleuropas". 264 pp., 165 figs. Hallwag, Stuttgart.

DUPERREX, A. 1961. "Orchids of Europe". xiii + 235 pp., 120 figs., 32 col. pls. English edn. by A. J. Huxley. Blandford Press, London.

GODFREY, M. J. 1933. "Monograph & Iconograph of the Native British Orchidaceae". xiv + 259 pp., 57 col. pls. Cambridge University Press.

SUMMERHAYES, V. S. 1968. "Wild Orchids of Britain with a key to the Species". 2nd edn. xviii + 366 pp., 72 col. pls. Collins, London.

SUNDERMANN, H. 1975. "Europäische und mediterrane Orchideen. Eine Bestimmungsflora mit Berücksichtigung der Ökologie". 2nd edn. 243 pp. Illustrated. Brücke-Verlag Kurt Schmersow, Hildesheim.

DISTRIBUTION IN BRITISH ISLES

DRUCE, G. C. 1932. "The Comital Flora of the British Isles". xxxii + 407 pp. + map. T. Buncle, Arbroath.

PERRING, F. H. & SELL, P. D. 1968. "Atlas of the British Flora. Critical Supplement". viii + 159 pp. Nelson, London.

PERRING, F. H. & WALTERS, S. M., eds. 1976. "Atlas of the British Flora". 2nd edn. xxvi + 432 pp. EP Publishing, Wakefield.

PRAEGER, R. L. 1934. "The Botanist in Ireland". xii + 587 pp. Illustrated. Hodges & Figgis, Dublin.

WATSON, H. C. 1883. "Topographical Botany: Being Local and Personal Records toward showing the Distribution of British Plants Traced through the 112 Counties and Vice-Counties of England, Wales and Scotland". 2nd edn. by J. G. Baker & W. W. Newbould. xlv + 612 pp. London. Suppls. by A. Bennett (1905) *J. Bot., Lond.* **43:** *Suppl.* 14 pp. and A. Bennett, C. E. Salmon & J. R. Matthews (1929–30), *J. Bot., Lond.* **67–68:** *Suppl.* 96 pp.

SCANNELL, M. J. P. & SYNNOTT, D. M. 1972. "Census Catalogue of the Flora of Ireland". xvi + 127 pp. National Museum of Ireland, Dublin.

BIBLIOGRAPHY

Abstracts from literature relating to British (and European) plants are compiled by D. H. Kent for *B.S.B.I. Abstracts* (1971 on). Comprehensive annual lists of world vascular plant literature are provided by *The Kew Record of Taxonomic Literature* (1974 [for 1971] on. HMSO, London).

BLAKE, S. F. 1961. Geographical Guide to the Floras of the World. Part 2. *Misc. Publs U.S. Dept. Agric.* **797:** 1–797 pp.

BRUMMITT, R. K. 1966–70. Index to European taxonomic literature for 1965. *Regnum Vegetabile* **45**: 1–166. 1970. *Ibid.* **70**: 1–189 (for 1968).
BRUMMITT, R. K. & FERGUSON, I. K. 1968–69. Index to European taxonomic literature for 1966. *Regnum Vegetabile* **53**: 1–245: (1968); *Ibid.* **61**: 1–202 (1969) [for 1967].
KENT, D. H. 1963. Progress in the study of the British flora since World War 2. *Webbia* **18**: 129–150.
KENT, D. H. 1975. Progress in the study of the British flora, 1961–71. *Mem. Soc. Broteriana* **24**: 353–375.
KENT, D. H., KOVANDA, M. & BRUMMITT, R. K. 1971. Index to European taxonomic literature for 1969. *Regnum Vegetabile* **80**: 1–160.
SIMPSON, N. D. 1960. "A Bibliographical Index of the British Flora". xix + 429 pp. Bournemouth.

HISTORY

GODWIN, H. 1975. "The History of the British Flora". 2nd edn. x + 541 pp. Cambridge University Press.
PENNINGTON, W. 1974. "The History of British Vegetation". 2nd ed. viii + 152 pp. English Universities Press, London.

GLOSSARY

GILBERT-CARTER, H. 1964. "Glossary of the British Flora". 3rd edn. xxiv + 96 pp. Cambridge University Press.
JACKSON, B. D. 1949. "A Glossary of Botanic Terms with their Derivation and Accent". 4th edn. (reprinted). x + 481 pp. London.
STEARN, W. T. 1973. "Botanical Latin". 2nd edn. xiv + 566 pp. David & Charles, Newton Abbot.
Vocabulary pp. 377–548.

ANATOMY AND MORPHOLOGY

ARBER, A. 1920. "Water Plants. A Study of Aquatic Angiosperms". xvi + 436 pp. Illustrated. Cambridge University Press.
ARBER, A. 1925. "Monocotyledons". xvi + 258 pp. Illustrated. Cambridge University Press.
ARBER, A. 1950. "The Natural Philosophy of Plant Form". xiv + 247 pp. Illustrated. Cambridge University Press.
BIERHORST, D. W. 1971. "Morphology of Vascular Plants". xii + 560 pp. Illustrated. Macmillan, London & New York.
BOLD, H. C. 1973. "Morphology of Vascular Plants". 3rd edn. xv + 668 pp. Illustrated. Harper & Row, New York.
BOULTON, E. H. B. & JAY, B. A. 1946. "British Timbers, their Properties, Uses and Identification". 2nd edn. Black, London.
CARLQUIST, S. 1961. "Comparative Plant Anatomy". xii + 146 pp. Illustrated. Holt, Rinchart & Winston, New York.
CHALK, L. & RENDLE, B. J. 1929. "British Hardwoods, their Structure and Identification". *Forest Products Res. Bull.* **3**: vi + 53 pp. HMSO, London.
EAMES, A. J. 1961. "Morphology of the Angiosperms". ix + 518 pp. Illustrated. McGraw Hill, New York.
FAHN, A. 1974. "Plant Anatomy". 2nd edn. viii + 611 pp. Illustrated. Pergamon Press, Oxford, New York, etc.
GREGUSS, P. 1959. "Holzanatomie der europäischen Laubhölzer und Sträucher". 2nd edn. Budapest.
KIRCHNER, O. VON, LOEW, E. & SCHRÖTER, C. 1904–38. "Lebensgeschichte

der Blütenpflanzen Mitteleuropas". Illustrated. 4 vols. E. Ulmer, Stuttgart.
METCALFE, C. R. 1960. "Anatomy of the Monocotyledons: 1. Gramineae". lxii + 731 pp. Clarendon Press, Oxford.
METCALFE, C. R. & CHALK, L. 1950. "Anatomy of the Dicotyledons". 2 vols. Clarendon Press, Oxford.
PANSHIN, A. J., ZEEUW, C. DE & BROWN, H. P. 1964. "Textbook of Wood Technology. 1. Structure, Identification, Uses and Properties of the Commercial Woods of the United States". 2nd edn. xiv + 643 pp. Illustrated. McGraw Hill, New York.
SOLEREDER, H. 1908. "Systematic Anatomy of the Dicotyledons". 2 vols. (Translated into English by L. A. Brodle & G. E. Fritsch; revised by D. H. Scott.) Clarendon Press, Oxford.
SOLEREDER, H. & MEYER, F. J. 1928–33. "Systematische Anatomie der Monokotyledonen". Vols. 1, 3, 4 and 6. (Never completed.) Berlin.

POLLEN AND SPORE IDENTIFICATION

BEUG, H.-J. 1961. "Leitfaden der Pollenbestimmung für Mitteleuropa und angrenzende Gebiete". xiv + 63pp., 8 pls. Gustav Fischer, Stuttgart.
BOROS, Á. and JÁRAI-KOMLÓDI, M. 1975. "An Atlas of Recent European Moss Spores". 466 pp., 237 pls. Akadémiai Kiadó, Budapest.
ERDTMAN, G. 1954. "An Introduction to Pollen Analysis". xv + 239 pp. Revised printing. Illustrated. Chronica Botanica, Waltham, Mass.
ERDTMAN, G. 1957–65. "Pollen and Spore Morphology/Plant Taxonomy. Gymnospermae, Pteridophyta, Bryophyta. An Introduction to Palynology". Vols. 2–3. Almqvist & Wiksell, Stockholm.
ERDTMAN, G. 1969. "Handbook of Palynology. Morphology-Taxonomy-Ecology. An Introduction to the Study of Pollen Grains and Spores". 486 pp. Illustrated. Munksgaard, Copenhagen.
ERDTMAN, G. 1971. "Pollen Morphology and Plant Taxonomy. An Introduction to Palynology Vol. 1. New edn. xii + 553 pp. Illustrated. Hafner, New York & London.
ERDTMAN, G., BERGLUND, B. & PRAGLOWSKI, J. 1961–63. "An Introduction to a Scandinavian Pollen Flora". 2 vols. Almqvist & Wiksell, Stockholm.
ERDTMAN, G. & SORSA, P. 1971. "Pollen and Spore Morphology/Plant Taxonomy, Pteridophyta (Text and additional illustrations)". An Introduction to Palynology Vol. 4. 302 pp. Illustrated. Almqvist & Wiksell, Stockholm.
FAEGRI, K. & IVERSEN, J. 1975. "Textbook of Pollen Analysis". 3rd edn. (by K. Faegri). 295 pp. Illustrated. Munksgaard, Copenhagen.
JANSEN, C. R., *et al.* 1974 on. The northwest European pollen flora. *Rev. Palaeobot. Polynology* **17** (3/4) on: *Suppls.*
PUNT, W., ed. 1976. "The Northwest European Pollen Flora". Vol. I. 145 pp. Elsevier Scientific Publications, Amsterdam, Oxford and New York.
    Separate issue of earlier parts of the preceeding in one volume; will eventually be a comprehensive pollen flora.

PROKARYOTES

For the Blue-Green Algae (Cyanophyta) see p. 161.

BACTERIA

GENERAL
BUCHANAN, R. E. & GIBBONS, N. E., eds. 1974. "Bergey's Manual of Determinative Bacteriology". 8th edn. xxvi + 1246 pp. Williams & Wilkins, Baltimore.
SKERMAN, V. B. D. 1967. "A Guide to the Identification of the Genera of Bacteria". 2nd edn. xii + 303 pp. Williams & Wilkins, Baltimore.

ACTINOMYCETES
CROSS, T. & GOODFELLOW, M. 1973. Taxonomy and classification of the Actinomycetes. In "Actinomycetales: Characteristics and practical importance" (G. Sykes and F. A. Skinner, eds), pp. 11–12. Academic Press, London & New York.
HÜTTER, R. 1967. "Systematik der Streptomyceten". 382 pp. Karger, Basel & New York.
WAKSMAN, S. A. 1967. "The Actinomycetes. A Summary of Current Knowledge". vi + 280 pp. Roland Press, New York.

MEDICALLY IMPORTANT BACTERIA
COWAN, S. T. & STEEL, K. J. 1965. "Manual for the Identification of Medical Bacteria". x + 217 pp. Cambridge University Press, London.

PLANT PATHOGENIC BACTERIA
BRADBURY, J. F. 1970. Isolation and preliminary study of bacteria from plants. *Rev. Pl. Path.* **49**: 213–218.
DESCRIPTIONS OF PATHOGENIC FUNGI AND BACTERIA 1964 on. Commonwealth Mycological Institute, Kew. (Sets 2, 5, 13, 24 and 38.)

ELLIOTT, C. 1951. "Manual of Bacterial Plant Pathogens". 186 pp. Chronica Botanica, Waltham, Mass.
STAPP, C. 1961. "Bacterial Plant Pathogens". 292 pp. Oxford University Press.

VIRUSES

BURNET, F. M. & STANLEY, W. M., eds. 1959. "The Viruses. Biochemical, Biological and Biophysical 'Properties'". 2 vols. Academic Press, New York & London.
FRANKEL-CONRAT, H. 1974. "Descriptive Catalogue of Viruses". Comprehensive Virology Vol. 1. x + 191 pp. Plenum Press, New York.
WILDY, P. 1971. "Classification and Nomenclature of Viruses". Monographs in Virology No. 5. 81 pp. Karger, Basel.

ANIMAL VIRUSES

ANDREWS, C. H. & PEREIRA, H. G. 1972. "Viruses of Vertebrates". 3rd edn. 451 pp. Bailliere Tindall, London.

PLANT VIRUSES

BAWDEN, F. C. 1964. "Plant Viruses and Virus Diseases". 4th edn. vii + 361 pp. Ronald Press, New York.
DESCRIPTIONS OF PLANT VIRUSES 1970 on. Commonwealth Mycological Institute and Association of Applied Biologists, Kew.
MARTYN, E. B., ed. 1968. Plant virus names. *Phytopath. Papers* 9: i–ix + 1–204 and *Suppl.* 1: 1–41 (1971).
MATTHEWS, R. E. F. 1970. "Plant Virology". xv + 778 pp. Academic Press, New York & London.
NOORDAM, D. 1973. "Identification of Plant Viruses". 207 pp. Centre for Agricultural Publishing and Documentation, Wageningen.
SMITH, K. M. 1972. "A Textbook of Plant Virus Diseases". 3rd edn. x + 684 pp. Longman, London.
  Information on most viruses recorded to 1972.
SMITH, K. M. 1977. "Plant Viruses". 6th edn. ix + 241 pp. Chapman and Hall, London.
  A general introduction.

The Systematics Association Publications

2. THE SPECIES CONCEPT IN PALAEONTOLOGY (1956)
   Edited by P. C. SYLVESTER-BRADLEY
3. FUNCTION AND TAXONOMIC IMPORTANCE (1959)
   Edited by A. J. CAIN
4. TAXONOMY AND GEOGRAPHY (1962)
   Edited by D. NICHOLS
5. SPECIATION IN THE SEA (1963)
   Edited by J. P. HARDING and N. TEBBLE
6. PHENETIC AND PHYLOGENETIC CLASSIFICATION (1964)
   Edited by V. H. HEYWOOD and J. MCNEILL
7. ASPECTS OF TETHYAN BIOGEOGRAPHY (1967)
   Edited by C. G. ADAMS and D. V. AGER
8. THE SOIL ECOSYSTEM (1969)
   Edited by J. SHEALS
9. ORGANISMS AND CONTINENTS THROUGH TIME (1973)†
   Edited by N. F. HUGHES

LONDON. Published by the Association

Systematics Association Special Volumes

1. THE NEW SYSTEMATICS (1940: reprinted 1971)
   Edited by JULIAN HUXLEY
2. CHEMOTAXONOMY AND SEROTAXONOMY (1968)*
   Edited by J. G. HAWKES
3. DATA PROCESSING IN BIOLOGY AND GEOLOGY (1971)*
   Edited by J. L. CUTBILL
4. SCANNING ELECTRON MICROSCOPY (1971)*
   Edited by V. H. HEYWOOD
5. TAXONOMY AND ECOLOGY (1973)*
   Edited by V. H. HEYWOOD
6. THE CHANGING FLORA AND FAUNA OF BRITAIN (1974)*
   Edited by D. L. HAWKSWORTH
7. BIOLOGICAL IDENTIFICATION WITH COMPUTERS (1975)*
   Edited by R. J. PANKHURST
8. LICHENOLOGY: PROGRESS AND PROBLEMS (1976)*
   Edited by D. H. BROWN, D. L. HAWKSWORTH and R. H. BAILEY
9. KEY WORKS (1978)*
   Edited by G. J. KERRICH, D. L. HAWKSWORTH and R. W. SIMS
10. MODERN APPROACHES TO THE TAXONOMY OF RED AND BROWN ALGAE (1978)*
    Edited by D. G. IRVINE and J. H. PRICE

*Published by Academic Press for the Systematics Association
†Published by the Palaeontological Association in conjunction with the Systematics Association